UNIVERSITY OF ST. THOMAS LIBRARIES

MAKING SUSTAINABLE COMMITMENTS

An Environment Strategy for the World Bank

The World Bank
Washington, D.C.

Contents

FIGURES

MAPS

Regional

Environmental

Preface

This Environment Strategy outlines how the World Bank will work with client countries to address their environmental challenges and ensure that Bank projects and programs integrate principles of environmental sustainability. The Strategy sets a vision, objectives, and a course of action for the longer term and suggests specific actions, targets, and institutional measures for the next five years, as described in Tables 1 and 2 of the Executive Summary. Table 1 links proposed measures with key development objectives, while Table 2 sets targets and monitorable indicators.

The Strategy is the product of a multiyear effort, including an extensive evaluation of the Bank's past performance by the Bank's independent Operations Evaluation Department (OED) and numerous workshops and consultations with client governments, civil society, academia, multilateral and bilateral development agencies, and representatives of the private sector (see annex J for details). These consultations have played an important role in shaping the final document. We are profoundly grateful to all those who have taken the time and trouble to contribute to the process.

Within a strategic framework, we recognize that one size does not fit all. The countries served by the World Bank differ enormously in their stage of development and in the nature of their economic, social, and environmental concerns. It would be both presumptuous and futile to define a small set of specific problems that we would tackle in all or most of our client countries. A central theme of the Strategy, therefore, is the importance of working in collaboration with our clients and partners to identify the critical environmental issues that should be addressed in specific circumstances. Detailed country environmental diagnostic analysis based on National Environmental Action Plans (NEAPs) and other strategies and assessments, along with other country-specific assessments, is part of the input for the Bank's Country Assistance Strategies (CASs).

This Strategy does not attempt to provide a detailed assessment of the state of the environment, natural resources, and ecosystems in our client countries or in the world. It draws on work undertaken by client countries, the World Bank, and many others. This work includes NEAPs, strategies and assessments, the World Resources Institute's *World Resources* series, the Worldwatch Institute's *State of the World* series, the United Nations Environment Programme's *Global Environmental Outlook 2000*, and the Bank's *World Development Indicators* series. It also builds on a rich storehouse of analytical work that spells out a broader vision of development and its environmental linkages and maps out options for broadening the benefits of economic development while reducing its adverse environmental effects. The results of such assessments—including assessments prepared for the Intergovernmental Panel on Climate Change (IPCC), the Organisation for Economic Co-operation and Development (OECD), the United Nations, and the U.K. Department for International Development (DFID)—are widely available.

The 2003 *World Development Report* (WDR), subtitled *Sustainable Development with a Dynamic Economy*, will provide an opportunity to take a comprehensive look at the various dimensions of sustainable development. This Environment Strategy provides one of the building blocks for the WDR. The Strategy is an operational document that guides the Bank's actions in the environment area and that recognizes that environment is part of the sustainable development challenge; points to close linkages with other areas of development; and emphasizes the need to integrate environmental issues into sectoral and macroeconomic policies, strategies, and actions, taking into account evolving institutional conditions and capacity constraints in client countries.

The Environment Strategy works in a complementary fashion with other Bank strategies and action plans. For example, in 1999 the Bank's Board of Directors discussed *Fuel for Thought*, an environmental strategy for the energy sector. The Environment Strategy builds on the analysis undertaken for *Fuel for Thought* and incorporates that strategy's objectives and actions. The Bank is also preparing or planning to prepare strategies for its activities in a number of other fields, including forestry, water resources, rural development, and social development. These strategies have implications for issues that are important concerns for the Environment Strategy, in particular, in natural resource management. The concerns, approaches, and conclusions of these strategies are reflected here, though they are not discussed in detail.

The World Bank Group (WBG) includes four closely associated but distinct institutions that support development in low- and middle-income client countries. The International Bank for Reconstruction and Development (IBRD) and the International Development Association (IDA) have a mandate to lend to sovereign governments. Together, they are often referred to as the World Bank (WB). The WB, through its ongoing dialogue with client governments on a wide range of issues and its financial support to the public sector, is in a position to influence government policy directly. The International Finance Corporation (IFC) promotes sustainable private sector investment as a way of enhancing economic growth and improving peoples' lives. It operates principally through direct or indirect support of private sector projects. The Multilateral Investment Guarantee Agency (MIGA) provides guarantees against certain noncommercial risks (primarily political risk insurance) to foreign investors for qualifying investments in developing countries.

The four WBG institutions are aligned with the core mission of poverty reduction—and, therefore, the overall vision, strategic framework, and objectives of this Strategy, as described in Chapters 1 and 3, are shared by the entire WBG. Members of the WBG, however, are legally and financially independent and have different sets of owners and clients, structures and mandates, staffs and toolkits. Accordingly, specific operational and institutional implications differ and need to be spelled out separately. The lessons learned and the operational and institutional details described in Chapters 2, 3, and 4 of this document apply specifically to the WB (IBRD/IDA). References are made throughout the Strategy to linkages among members of the WBG, and annexes G and H provide detailed information on the approach to supporting sustainable development taken by the IFC and MIGA.

Strategy making does not end with the publication of the document. Continuous communication and collaboration with clients, partners, and World Bank staff in diverse sector and country units, as well as systematic monitoring and assessment of the Strategy's effectiveness, are essential to its updating, improvement, and successful implementation.

Acknowledgments

T he preparation of the Environment Strategy was overseen by the Environment Sector Board, chaired by Environment Director Kristalina Georgieva, and co-chaired by Robert Watson, Chief Scientist and Director of the Environmentally and Socially Sustainable Development Network (ESSD). Kristalina Georgieva guided the Strategy preparation process.

All members of the Environment Sector Board played an active role in the strategy preparation process: Richard Ackermann (South Asia Region), Sherif Arif (Middle East and North Africa Region), Glen Armstrong (International Finance Corporation), Charlotte Bingham (Africa Region), Zafer Ecevit (East Asia Pacific Region), David Freestone (Legal Department), Jane Holt (Europe and Central Asia Region), Anupam Khanna (Development Economics Vice Presidency), Michele de Nevers (World Bank Institute), Maria Teresa Serra (Latin America and Caribbean), Martyn Riddle (International Finance Corporation), and David Wheeler (Development Economics Vice Presidency).

Magda Lovei (ENV) managed the preparation of the Environment Strategy. The core Strategy drafting group also included Julia Bucknall (ECSSD), Gordon Hughes (Consultant), Stefano Pagiola (ENV), and Lars Vidaeus (ENV). Anjali Acharya (ENV), Kulsum Ahmed (LCSES), Sherif Arif (MNSRE), Aziz Bouzaher (SASEN), Gonzalo Castro (ENV), Kirk Hamilton (ENV), David Hanrahan (ENV), Martin Fodor (ENV), Hans-Olav Ibrekk (ENV), Todd Johnson (ENV), Agi Kiss (AFTES), Stephen Lintner (ENV), Kseniya Lvovsky (SASEN), Ajay Mathur (ENV), Jean-Roger Mercier (ENV), Judith Moore (ENV), and Mahesh Sharma (ENV) all participated in the Strategy working group. Many others contributed or provided advice and comments, including Gayatri Acharya (WBIEN), Motoko Aizawa (CTEED), Jo Albert (ENV), Mohammed Bekhechi (LEGOP), Rob Crooks (EASES), John Dixon (ENV), Giovanna Dore (EASES), Yoko Eguchi (ESDVP), Indumathie Hewawasam (AFTERS), Christiane Kraus (WBIEN), Ken Newcombe (ENV), and Nightingale Rukuba-Ngaiza (LEGOP). Alethea Abuyuan (ENV) assisted the team with research and data.

General guidance was provided by the Operations Policy Committee, which is chaired by Shengman Zhang, and the ESSD Council, which is chaired by ESSD Vice President Ian Johnson. The preparation of the six Regional Environment Strategies was overseen by Regional Sector Directors and Managers: Richard Ackermann (South Asia), Hans Binswanger and Roger Sullivan (Africa), Kevin Cleaver and Jane Holt (Europe and Central Asia), Zafer Ecevit (East Asia and Pacific), Doris Koehn and Salah Dargouth (Middle East and North Africa), and John Redwood and Teresa Serra (Latin America and the Caribbean).

The main authors of Regional Environment Strategies were Teresa Serra and Kulsum Ahmed (Latin America and Caribbean Region), Aziz Bouzaher (South Asia Region), Todd Johnson (East Asia and Pacific Region), Agi Kiss (Africa Region), Sherif Arif and Maria Sarraf (Middle East and North Africa Region), and Jane Holt and Konrad von Ritter (Europe and Central Asia Region). Many others contributed, including Angela Armstrong, Gabriela Boyer, Sergio Margulis, Kirsten Oleson, Rocio Sarmiento, and Laura Tlaiye (Latin America and Caribbean Region); Carter Brandon, Kseniya Lvovsky, and Bekir Onursal (South Asia Region); Carter Brandon, Rob Crooks, and Giovanna Dore (East Asia and Pacific Region); Anita Gordon and Marie-Claude Verlaeten (Africa Region); Hocine Chalal, John Bryant Collier, Nicole Glineur, Roger Gorham, Samuel O'Brien-Kumi, Allan Rotman, Kanthan Shankar, Shobha Shetty, Manuel Shiffler, and Shatory Ueda (Middle East and North Africa Region); and Marjory-Anne Bromhead, Julia Bucknall, Amy Evans, and Vesselina Hekimova (Europe and Central Asia Region).

The Strategy draws on several background papers and notes prepared by working groups on the fol-lowing topics: *Capacity Building for Environmental Institutions,* led by Ina-Marlene Ruthenberg (LCSEN) and Mohammed Bekhechi (LEGOP); *Climate Change,* led by Ajay Mathur, Todd Johnson, and Mahesh Sharma; *Country Assistance Strategies and Environment,* led by Kirk Hamilton (ENV); *Donor Survey on Environmental Aid Effectiveness,* led by Hans-Olav Ibrekk (ENV); *Environment and Natural Resources* chapter in *Poverty Reduction Strategy Paper Sourcebook,* led by Julia Bucknall (ECSSD), Kirk Hamilton (ENV), Nalin Kishor (WBIEN), and Poonam Pillai (WBIEN); *Health and Environment,* led by Kseniya Lvovsky (SASEN) and Maureen Cropper (DECRG); *Natural Resource Management,* led by Jan Bojo (AFTE1) and Stefano Pagiola (ENV); *Outcomes and Indicators,* led by Aziz Bouzaher (SASEN); *Partnerships,* led by Ken Newcombe (ENV) and Nalin Kishor (WBIEN); *Poverty and Environment,* led by Julia Bucknall (ECSSD) and Poonam Pillai (WBIEN); *Reducing Vulnerability to Environmental Variability,* led by Mahesh Sharma (ENV); *Safeguards,* led by Stephen Lintner, Jean-Roger Mercier (ENV), and Glen Morgan (EASES); *Strategic Environmental Assessments* led by Olav Kjorven (Consultant) and David Hanrahan (ENV); *Urban Air Quality Management,* led by Masami Kojima (COCPO) and Magda Lovei (ENV); *Urban Environmental Priorities,* led by Carl Bartone (INFUD) and David Hanrahan (ENV); *Environmental and Water Resources Management,* led by Rafik Hirji and Hans-Olav Ibrekk (ENV); and *World Bank and the Global Environment,* led by Lars Vidaeus and Gonzalo Castro (ENV). Several of these background papers are summarized in the annexes.

Judith Moore (ENV) organized external consultations in collaboration with regional coordinators: Gabriela Boyer (LCSES), Giovanna Dore (EASES), Elena Heitman (Consultant), Vandana

Sareen (ECSSD), Maria Sarraf (MNSRE), and Marie-Claude Verlaeten (AFTE1), as well as Anita Gordon (Consultant) and Elke Nickel (Consultant), who worked on the North American and Western European consultations. Martin Fodor (ENV) managed the electronic web consultation and coordination.

The Strategy team is grateful for the guidance and comments from Marisela Montoliu Munoz (Operations Policy and Country Services). Many others provided valuable comments, advice, and input to the Strategy: John Briscoe, Csaba Csaki, Jim Douglas, Odin Knudsen, Robin Mearns, and Robert Thomson, (Rural Development); Steen Jorgensen (Social Development); Nemat Talaat Shafik (Private Sector and Infrastructure); Jamal Saghir and Lee Travers (Infrastructure, Water and Sanitation); John Flora and Ken Gwilliam (Urban Transport); Carl Bartone (Urban Development); Chas Feinstein and Richard Spencer (Energy); Mariam Claeson and Christopher Lovelace (Health); Michael Klein and Syed A. Mahmood (Private Sector Development); Kiran Pandey, Jo Ritzen, Zuarak Shalizi, and David Wheeler (Development Economics); Giovanna Prennushi (Poverty); John Todd (Corporate Strategy Group); Nicolette Dewitt (Legal); Manuel Penalvar-Quesada (South Asia Region), Kathleen Stephenson (Resource Mobilization); Richard Caines, Gavin Murray, Andreas Raczynski, Bernard Sheahan, and Peter Woicke (International Finance Corporation); and Harvey Van Veldhuizen and Gerald West (Multilateral Investment Guarantee Agency).

The Strategy has also benefited from a review of the Bank's environmental performance undertaken by the Operations Evaluation Department (OED). This review included an analysis of the Bank's environmental policies, procedures, and activities and their impacts; regional consultation meetings with a range of stakeholders; and two electronic discussion forums. The Strategy team received valuable comments from the following in OED: Robert Picciotto, Greg Ingram, Alain Barbu, Andres Liebenthal, and Jed Shilling. Annex L summarizes the OED's recommendations and the Bank responses and actions outlined in the Strategy.

The Strategy team is grateful for the constructive discussions and comments provided by the Committee for Development Effectiveness and the Board of Directors.

Editorial support was provided by Bob Livernash (Consultant). Additional editorial advice was provided by Nancy Levine, Daniel Litvin, and Jenepher Moseley (Consultants). Jim Cantrell (ENV) managed desktop publishing, design, and production. Administrative and logistical support were provided by Isabel Alegre, Sriyani Cumine, Nenuca Munoz Robles, Vessela Radeva Stamboliyska, and Jason Steele (ENV).

Many organizations and individuals outside the Bank provided constructive oral or written comments. These comments have been valuable inputs in shaping the Strategy. We are indebted to the hundreds of people who participated in the meetings and who provided thoughtful comments in person, by mail, or by e-mail. Because of space constraints, we can only acknowledge a few of the organizations that helped organize meetings; however, we thank all the individuals and organizations that participated. Their contribution was invaluable.

We thank the governments of Japan, Norway, Sweden, and Switzerland for their financial support, which made the consultations possible. We thank

Monitor International (Annapolis, USA) for their advice, convening and facilitation skills, and their independent reports of a number of the meetings. We thank the members of the GEF-NGO network, for their participation in most of the meetings, helping to identify and convene participants, and contributing to reports on findings. We also thank Stratos, Inc. (Ottawa, Canada) for their advice and facilitation of the final joint OED/ENV workshop held in Washington, DC.

We are indebted to all of the government agencies, expert organizations, and individuals who generously shared their time and knowledge with us. In each region some organizations assumed special roles in the process. In Africa, meetings were organized by the Environmental Liaison Centre International (ELCI, Nairobi, Kenya); the World Conservation Union (IUCN) Country Office in Pretoria, South Africa; and the IUCN Country Office in Ouagadougou, Burkina Faso. EnerWise International submitted an independent report of the meeting held in South Africa.

In Asia, the Japanese Foundation for Advanced Studies on International Development (FASID) supported a regional meeting in Bangkok, Thailand; the Foundation for the Philippine Environment and Monitor International prepared reports of the meeting. In Japan, meetings were organized by Keidanren (Japan Federation of Economic Organizations), the Environment Assistance Study Group of the Japan International Cooperation Agency, the Japan Bank for International Cooperation, the Economic Cooperation Bureau of the Ministry of Foreign Affairs, the International Bureau of the Ministry of Finance, the Ministry of the Environment, and FASID.

In the Europe and Central Asia Region, the Regional Environment Center (Budapest, Hungary), the Bank's office in Moscow, and the Ministry of Environment of Georgia organized regional meetings. CEEWEB and the Georgian Center for the Conservation of Wildlife provided independent reports on the meetings held in Hungary and Georgia.

In the Middle East and North Africa, IUCN provided assistance with the first consultation in Amman, Jordan; for the second meeting, the Ministries of Planning and Environment in Jordan provided assistance.

We would like to acknowledge the following organizations in Latin America and the Caribbean: Central American Commission for Environment and Development (CCAD, El Salvador), the Fundación Futuro Latinoamericano (Quito, Ecuador), the Fundación Vida (Cartagena, Colombia), Nouveau Promoções e Marketing Direto (Rio de Janeiro, Brazil), and CEGESTI, a nonprofit organization that specializes in clean production and environmental management (San Jose, Costa Rica), as well as the United Nations Environment Programme (UNEP) for its active involvement in each of the sessions. The Caribbean Conservation Association and Fundacion Ecologica Universal provided independent reports on the meetings in Costa Rica and Brazil.

For assistance in Western Europe, we thank to Euronatur (European Natural Heritage Fund), the German Federal Ministry for Economic Co-Operation and Development (BMZ), the Swiss State Secretariat for Economic Affairs (SECO), and U.K. Department for International Development (DFID).

In North America, we would like to acknowledge the Bank Information Center (Washington DC, USA), Canadian International Development Agency (CIDA), the North-South Institute (Ottawa, Canada), and the World Affairs Council (San Francisco, USA).

Executive Summary

Economic development has led to dramatic improvements in the quality of life in developing countries, producing striking gains unparalleled in human history. But the picture is far from entirely positive. Gains have been unevenly distributed, and a large part of the world's population remains desperately poor. At the same time, environmental factors such as indoor and outdoor air pollution, waterborne diseases, and exposure to toxic chemicals threaten the health of millions of people, and natural resources—land, water, and forests—are being degraded at alarming rates in many countries. Simultaneously, far-reaching trends—globalization, the increased role of the private sector and of civil society, and rapid technological advances—have been reshaping the world, causing development and environmental challenges to be ever more intertwined.

As a development institution, the World Bank has been involved in addressing environmental issues for many years. This Environment Strategy draws on lessons learned on the basis of the Operations Evaluation Department's (OED's) environmental review (OED 2001); adjusts to a changing global context; and reaffirms the Bank's commitment to environmental sustainability. It sets a direction for the World Bank's future actions in the environment area for the longer term, as well as specific actions for the next five years. It emphasizes the need to tailor our assistance according to differences in institutional development and environmental management capacity in client countries. It is based on an understanding that sustainable development, built on a balance of economic growth, social cohesion, and environmental protection, is fundamental to the Bank's core objective of lasting poverty alleviation—a link that has been recognized by international environmental conventions and in the International Development Goals (IDGs) set forth in the United Nations Millennium Declaration in 2000.

ENVIRONMENT AS INTEGRAL PART OF THE DEVELOPMENT CHALLENGE

Many view concern over environmental issues as a rich-country luxury. It is not. Natural and man-made environmental resources from agro- to freshwater, forest, and marine ecosystems represent an important element of countries' wealth, and provide a foundation for economic growth and livelihoods.

People in most developing countries are increasingly concerned about their environment. They are particularly worried about the impacts of pollution and natural resource degradation on their health and on prospects for sustainable growth. While industrial countries have successfully addressed many of the environmental problems that directly affect people's livelihoods, environmental factors continue to impose considerable human, economic, and social costs in many developing countries, threatening the foundation for sustainable development. The economic costs of environmental degradation have been estimated at 4 to 8 percent of gross domestic product (GDP) annually in many developing countries.

Distorted policies, governance structures, institutional frameworks, incentives, and pressures to export natural resources may favor a short-term focus, making programs with a long-term horizon difficult to implement. The "grow now, clean up later" approach to development, however, imposes very high costs—costs that could be avoided by adopting policies and programs that prevent serious environmental damage.

Although there are many "win-win" opportunities to simultaneously achieve economic, environmental, and social objectives, balancing these aspects of development through everyday decisions inevitably involves value judgments and societal choices, which often require difficult tradeoffs. These tradeoffs—among generations, social groups, and countries—influence what different people see as sustainable development. These tradeoffs may only be *apparent*—that is, when the time dimension is added and the full social cost of the economic ac-

tivity is considered, they may disappear. Overfishing, for example, may temporarily improve people's income, making conservation seem costly. But these costs will pay off if they help avoid the collapse of fisheries, which deprives people of both nutrition and income in the longer term. Similarly, the considerable social costs of pollution can justify the costs of measures that prevent and mitigate it.

While countries and societies may differ in their choices about environmental priorities and other aspects of sustainable development, these choices have to be informed by good analysis and the participation of the key stakeholders affected by them. The challenge for the World Bank and other institutions concerned with development assistance is to work with clients to develop and implement policies, programs, and investments that not only support continued economic development but also:

- Distribute the gains of development in a more equitable manner, with a particular focus on reducing poverty
- Avoid sacrificing the interests of future generations to meet the needs of the current generation
- Build on the emerging global consensus that natural resources and other valuable environmental assets must be managed sustainably.

This Strategy discusses how we will support our clients and partners as they face these challenges.

OUR RECORD SO FAR

During the past decades, the World Bank has developed safeguard policies, procedures, and examples of good practice for addressing the environmental and social aspects of our projects, and these have become internationally accepted references and models. We have helped client countries develop National Environmental Action Plans (NEAPs) and strengthen their systems of environmental regulation through institutional development projects. We have built up a portfolio of investments devoted to environmental issues and have made considerable progress in "mainstreaming" environmental objectives into our sectoral lending programs. As an implementing agency for the financing mechanisms of international environmental conventions and their protocols, specifically the Global Environment Facility (GEF) and the Multilateral Fund for the Montreal Protocol (MFMP), we have taken on a key role in dealing with threats to the global environmental commons, such as climate change, desertification, biodiversity loss, the depletion of the ozone layer, and the degradation of international waters.

Our clients, often with our help, have made significant progress. They have introduced environmental policies, regulations, and institutions; implemented projects and programs to improve environmental conditions; and heightened the public awareness of environmental issues. Environment is now clearly a significant concern on peoples' minds, and it is on the political agenda in many of our client countries. Nevertheless, as was pointed out in the OED's environment review, the Bank has been only partially successful in supporting environmental sustainability in client countries. Our achievements overall have fallen short of our own high expectations and those of others, even bearing in mind that by itself, the Bank can never stem the tide of global environmental change. Several broad factors have constrained the Bank's effectiveness in promoting sustainable development:

- Our commitments have sometimes outpaced our and our clients' capacity to deliver. We have been overoptimistic in setting environmental objec-

tives, designing complex interventions, and targeting tight deadlines, without giving sufficient attention to the complexity and practicalities of implementation and the competing pressures in our client countries.

- The environment has yet to be fully mainstreamed into the Bank's operations. Although Bank professionals in general are aware of the importance of environmental issues, they often see them as a self-standing agenda and not as an element of their core task of supporting development and poverty reduction. Environmental professionals have an ongoing challenge to make the "business case" for sustainable development.

- Similarly, awareness of the importance of environmental issues is still evolving in many of our client countries. While they increasingly recognize that environmental concerns are important for making development sustainable, our clients face difficult choices in allocating scarce resources among pressing development needs, and environment often has a hard time competing with other goals.

We have learned many lessons about complying with safeguard policies, preparing and implementing environmental projects, and undertaking policy dialogue. We have learned that in order to be effective, we have to demonstrate the benefits of environmental improvements and the links between environmental and development objectives; listen to people and respond to our clients' aspirations and concerns; and assist with building awareness, commitment, and capacity to help clients face their development and environmental challenges. Our Strategy applies these lessons to our future efforts.

Our Strategy also responds to a changing global context—globalization, rapid technological progress, the changing roles of private and public sectors, and civil society—and to evolving new approaches to development assistance—programmatic, as well as bottom-up community-based instruments. The Bank has reaffirmed its commitment to poverty reduction and the IDGs and has adopted the Comprehensive Development Framework (CDF), which emphasizes a long-term, holistic, client-focused, and participatory approach to development assistance. To respond to these changes, we have been adjusting our lending and nonlending instruments including those that support community-driven development, poverty reduction strategies and long-term development programs. Our work on the environment must adapt to these changing conditions.

THE STRATEGIC FRAMEWORK

The Bank's mission of lasting poverty reduction requires that development be sustainable. This means that proper attention has to be paid to the social and environmental aspects of development challenges, as stated in our mission statement: "*To fight poverty with passion and professionalism for lasting results. To help people help themselves and their environment by providing resources, sharing knowledge, building capacity, and forging partnerships in the public and private sectors… .*"

The goal of the Environment Strategy, therefore, is to promote environmental improvements as a fundamental element of development and poverty reduction strategies and actions. The Bank will do this by helping our client countries set and address their environmental priorities and challenges, including those of a regional or global nature; and by supporting sustainability through its operations.

This Environment Strategy outlines the priority actions the World Bank plans to take to help its clients address the environmental challenges of development. In keeping with the World Bank's mission of reducing poverty within a framework of economic development, the Environment Strategy gives priority to issues where the links between poverty and the environment are particularly strong. Therefore, the Strategy puts the environmental challenge into a local perspective, focusing on people in client countries and on the way environmental conditions and resources affect them. The Strategy's overall framework, its objectives, and the necessary adjustments in Bank instruments and actions are outlined in matrix form in table 1 at the end of this summary.

Our objectives

In support of our goal, the Strategy sets three interrelated objectives: improving people's quality of life, improving the prospects for and the quality of growth, and protecting the quality of the regional and global environmental commons.

Improving the quality of life. We will focus on three broad areas where environment, quality of life, and poverty reduction are strongly interlinked:

- *Enhancing livelihoods.* Because poor people often depend heavily on the productivity and environmental services of ecosystems and natural resources, the World Bank will help improve the sustainable management and protection of these resources. This includes helping communities sustainably manage natural resources such as land, water, and forests; helping clarify and establish property rights; strengthening or reforming incentive systems that influence how resources are used; and building the analytical base and institutional capacity to improve natural resource management.

■ *Preventing and reducing environmental health risks.* Environmental factors, such as unsafe water and air pollution, are major contributors to the total burden of disease and impose significant economic costs, particularly for poor people. Our interventions will focus on cost-effective measures to prevent and reduce environmental health risks through reducing people's exposure to indoor and urban air pollution, waterborne diseases, and toxic chemicals. Measures include improved access to cleaner commercial fuels by households, the phaseout of leaded gasoline and the introduction of cleaner transport fuels, and improved design and coverage of safe water and sanitation services to increase health benefits.

■ *Reducing people's vulnerability to environmental hazards.* Millions of poor people are vulnerable to natural disasters and environmental hazards, a threat that is expected to increase as a result of climate change. Our interventions will aim to reduce this vulnerability and the cost of natural disasters by supporting upland resource management and payments for environmental services; assessing the impacts of natural disasters; improving weather forecasting and the dissemination of weather-related information; providing information to communities about the risks they face; and stabilizing hillsides and coastal zones.

Improving the quality of growth. It is not enough to improve the quality of people's lives today; we have to ensure that short-term gains do not come at the expense of constrained opportunities for future development. Sustainable environmental management, therefore, is an essential condition for long-term economic growth and lasting improvements in people's well-being. There is also increasing evidence that attention to the environmental and social aspects of business development increases the international competitiveness of our client countries. Recognizing the important changes in the respective roles of the public and private sectors, our interventions will focus on promoting better policy, regulatory, and institutional frameworks for sustainable environmental management, on the one hand, and harnessing the role of the private sector to become an engine for sustainable development, on the other:

■ *Supporting policy, regulatory, and institutional frameworks for sustainable environmental management.* In cooperation with client countries and development partners, we will help client countries (a) strengthen their environmental policy, regulatory, and institutional frameworks with a special focus on local environmental institutions; (b) strengthen environmental assessment systems and practices; (c) reinforce the positive role of markets and the environmental benefits of sectoral and macroeconomic reforms; and (d) support good governance, institutions for collective action, increased transparency, access to environmental information, and public participation in decisionmaking.

■ *Supporting sustainable private sector development.* We will assist in harnessing the role of markets and the private sector in promoting sustainable development by helping clients introduce environmental regulations that allow flexible market mechanisms to achieve environmental objectives and by helping to create markets for environmental goods and services. As part of the World Bank Group, IFC and MIGA will promote, through their investments and guarantees, respectively, environmental and social responsibility and good environmental management in the private sector. We will facilitate partnerships between the public and private sectors and civil society to resolve environmentally sensitive issues and to agree on benchmarks for good environmental management.

Protecting the quality of the regional and global commons. The search for solutions to sustainability needs to go beyond individual countries. The deteriorating quality of the regional and global commons—climate change; the degradation of land, forests, water resources, and biodiversity—threatens many developing countries. They face potential conflicts over shared resources, such as scarce water resources and fertile land. They are also expected to suffer most of the worst effects of climate change despite the fact that over 75 percent of the cumulative greenhouse gas (GHG) emissions have been emitted by industrialized countries over the past 150 years, and per capita GHG emissions today are still five times less in developing than in industrialized countries.

A poverty-focused environmental agenda will require an increased emphasis on the local aspects of global environmental challenges, on reducing the impacts of the degradation of the global environmental commons on developing countries, and on interventions that are carefully targeted to benefit developing countries and local communities. Therefore, in addressing global challenges, we will apply the following key principles:

■ Focus on the positive linkages between poverty reduction and environmental protection

■ Focus first on local environmental benefits, and build on overlaps with regional and global benefits

■ Address the vulnerability and adaptation needs of developing countries

■ Facilitate transfer of financial resources to client countries to help them meet the costs of generating global and environmental benefits not matched by national benefits

■ Stimulate markets for global environmental public goods.

As implementing agency of the GEF and MFMP, we remain fully committed to our mandate to help client countries address the objectives of international environmental conventions and associated protocols including the conventions on climate change, ozone, and biodiversity. We will engage in these and other partnerships that help facilitate technical assistance, the transfer of financial resources and environmentally friendly technologies, and the development of markets for environmental goods and services.

Our toolkit

Environment is not a sector or an add-on. It has been long recognized that environmental considerations have to be reflected from the early stages of decisionmaking processes. The Environment Strategy emphasizes the importance of continuing our efforts to work with clients to integrate, or mainstream, environment into investments, programs, sector strategies, and policy dialogue mindful of the institutional requirements and capacity constraints. This translates into actions throughout the Bank. The Strategy stresses improvements in three key areas:

1. *Strengthening analytical and advisory activities*—the foundation for defining strategic environmental priorities and informing policy dialogue and decisions on projects and programs. A systematic approach is needed to ensure that environmental considerations enter the development planning process at an early stage by taking a multisectoral and long-term view of development.

   ■ *Country-level environmental analysis* will build on NEAPs and other country-led environmental work, as well as analyses undertaken by the Bank and development partners to assess environmental trends and priorities, policies, and institutional capacity in managing environmental resources and risks. Country-level environmental analysis work will become part of our diagnostic tools that inform country dialogue, poverty reduction strategies, and country assistance strategies (CASs).

■ *Strategic—sectoral, regional, and policy-focused—environmental assessments* (SEAs) will be used more systematically as analytical tools through a structured learning program involving clients and partners for addressing complex cross-sectoral environmental issues and for integrating environment at early stages in sectoral decisionmaking and planning process.

■ In our *advisory activities,* we will respond to client demand, priorities, and capabilities and build on the Bank's comparative advantage in working across sectors and throughout the world to transfer good practices in policy and technical issues. We will help clients set and address their own environmental priorities and improve their environmental management capacity. We will pay particular attention to poverty-environment linkages, the economic valuation of environmental resources and of their degradation, and environmental policy analysis.

2. *Addressing environmental priorities through project and program design.* Addressing environmental priorities that affect the long-term sustainability of development requires a proactive approach. Some environmental problems are best addressed by dedicated projects, others by integrating environmental activities into sectoral projects and programs. Depending on client demand and circumstances, we will work on both fronts with attention to the following areas:

■ *Improving the design and performance of environmental projects and components.* Our experience has shown that environmental projects or project components work best when they are based on a good understanding of the causes of the problem, are expected to have a major impact, and have the commitment and capacity of local stakeholders, so that project outcomes are sustainable after the project is over. We will continue to ensure that the lessons from our growing experience in environmental projects are disseminated and applied to new projects.

■ *Coordinating investments and policy reforms.* Some investment projects are unlikely to bring lasting results in a distorted policy environment. At the same time, individual investment projects may lead to a dialogue on policy reform. We will consider carefully the proper sequencing of policy reform efforts and specific investments in each case.

■ *Applying a location-specific focus.* Because the linkages between natural resource management and poverty are complex and location-specific and because implementation capacity varies, efforts to integrate environmental considerations into investment projects, adjustment lending, and programs will clearly vary from country to country. We will rely on enhanced analytical work and dialogue with clients to assess the best location-specific interventions in priority countries.

■ *Supporting capacity development.* Capacity-building efforts will be targeted, based on client demand, and tailored to existing environmental regulatory and institutional framework. We will collaborate with other development partners involved in environmental capacity development to improve overall development effectiveness. In a few cases where strong commitment exists in the country to undertake environmental institutional reform, we will apply a programmatic approach.

■ *Enhancing the environmental outcome of adjustment lending.* Considering the importance of the policy framework to environmental sustainability, we will pay special attention to reinforcing the positive and minimizing potentially negative environmental outcomes. Strengthened analytical work will inform policy dialogue, help identify environmental trends and resources at threat, assess country institutional capacity to manage resources sustainably, and prepare guidelines for good practice. Systematic upstream reviews and monitoring will help to ensure that environmental concerns are appropriately integrated into the changing lending profile. These issues will be further elaborated during the update and conversion of the Operational Directive on adjustment lending.

3. *Improving the safeguard system.* The Bank's safeguard system is an essential tool for integrating environmental and social concerns into development policies, programs, and projects by providing minimum requirements that all Bank-supported operations must meet. We will continue improving the quality and consistency of the application of our safeguard policies with increased attention to results on the ground, where many issues are intertwined. Improving the safeguard system is a dynamic process that involves both the Bank and its clients in a series of actions designed to create better linkages between policies and their application in projects and programs. We will follow a two-pronged approach:

■ *Addressing short-term priorities.* Our immediate priority is to strengthen compliance with the safeguard policies, establish an integrated safeguard system, and improve results on the ground. To this end, we will (a) continue to strengthen the Bank's internal review, monitoring, and tracking system to improve corporate consistency and compliance in applying the policies; (b) integrate environmental, social, and legal policies into an integrated safeguard compliance system including the use of the Integrated Safeguard Data Sheet (ISDS); and (c) help improve in-country capacity for safeguard implementation through enhanced training and technical assistance.

■ *Reforming the safeguard system.* In parallel, we will (a) respond to new challenges posed by a greater variety of lending instruments including programmatic lending and projects implemented at the grassroot levels; (b) help move safeguard considerations earlier into the decisionmaking process; (c) work with clients and partners to coordinate and harmonize good practice; and (d) focus increasingly on client ownership, capacity and safeguard systems. We will prepare a medium-term plan for reforming the safeguard system to adapt to a changing lending profile, direct more attention to clients' own capacity for good environmental management, and develop a risk management system that takes into account not only the risk characteristics of projects but also the capacity of countries to comply with safeguards. Over the long term, the Bank seeks to develop a single unified safeguard policy to provide a consistent approach.

Our ultimate objective is to help clients introduce and implement their own safeguards to manage their environmental resources sustainably. To this end, we and our partners need to increase our emphasis on capacity development at the national and sub-national levels. We need to search for ways of assessing and helping develop in-country capacity to adopt and internalize the principles of sustainable development, and create incentives and rewards for good performance by delegating responsibilities to borrowers with demonstrated capacity to manage the environmental aspects in their own programs.

The need for selectivity

The action agenda described above is diverse and challenging. In order to be effective, we will have to be selective to guide implementation at three levels:

1. *At the corporate level*, the Strategy defines corporate environmental priorities in detail, and guides their integration into Regional Strategies and country-level programming.

2. *At the regional level*, Regional Strategies (summarized in annex A) show the linkages between the corporate strategic framework and the regional context, reflecting regional and sub-regional differences.

3. *At the country level*, the Strategy provides a framework for setting priorities for environmental assistance. Using the corporate strategic framework, selectivity for environmental assistance at the country level will be based on a diagnosis of environmental priorities and management capacity, country demand, and consistency with the CAS. At the same time, the Bank is committed to ensure the implementation of its safeguard policies to all Bank operations in all countries.

INSTITUTIONAL REALIGNMENT

Sustainable development is a long-term goal. Its achievement requires a concerted pursuit of economic prosperity, environmental quality, and social equity and calls for behavioral changes by individuals and organizations. Throughout the world, this change is occurring.

Within the Bank, too, implementing the Strategy requires institutional change. We need to align our incentives, resource allocation, and skills mix to accelerate the shift from viewing the environment as a separate, freestanding concern to considering it an integral part of our development assistance. We then need to put this understanding into practice in our analytical work, policy dialogue, and project design.

In order to strengthen Bank staff's ability to manage this shift, those working on environmental issues have to be articulate advisors on the many linkages between poverty alleviation and environment and play an active, supportive role in the formulation of country and sector programs. Table 2, at the end of this summary, outlines indicators and actions of an institutional nature that would accompany the implementation of the Strategy.

Accountability and incentives. The Bank is reviewing its accountability framework to establish clear lines of responsibility and incentives throughout the institution. This framework has to be client-centered, acknowledging that our core responsibility is to support the sustainable development of our clients. Regional environment strategies and the annual business plans will help operationalize the Strategy. Consistent with its mandate, the Environment Board will be responsible for guiding and overseeing the implementation of the Strategy and will report regularly to senior management and, on request, to the Board (the specific responsibilities are described in table 4.1).

Training and skills mix. The increasing focus on cross-sectoral work and the shift in emphasis from project-level safeguards toward integrated portfolio-level risk assessment and quality enhancement will require a gradual shift in staff skills. Environmental staff will be trained to enhance their ability to influence sector and country programs and will be assessed on their effectiveness in this area. In the assessment of the performance of environmental staff, particular attention will be paid to addressing complex environmental challenges and implementing the safeguard policies. At the same time, a shift toward improved environmental skills among nonenvironmental specialist staff will take place through more systematic training in safeguard policies, poverty-environment linkages, and cross-sectoral issues. Tracking of training delivery will be improved to better target and customize both mandatory safeguards training and training on cutting-edge environmental issues. "Green Awards" will create positive incentives for nonenvironmental staff to mainstream environment into their operations and programs.

Budget. Better integration of environmental concerns into the Bank's work program is expected to yield strong benefits in relation to all three objectives of this Strategy, anchored as they are in the Bank's mission of poverty alleviation. Achieving these objectives, however, will require that resources be dedicated to the task. Such resource allocations are premised on the principle of exercising selectivity at all levels and on the need to guide a transition toward new ways of delivering development assistance, including programmatic lending. Wher-

ever possible, existing resources will be realigned within existing work programs. For the Bank to meaningfully address the objectives of the proposed Strategy, Bank budget funding would need to increase over the next five years. Key elements of this incremental Bank budget would be for:

- Improving the safeguards and compliance system, including the strengthening of compliance with policies and a comprehensive review of the safeguards policy framework to fit the needs of a changing Bank
- Mainstreaming support, with special emphasis on environmental mainstreaming in IDA countries in accordance with IDA requirements; linking corporate environmental priorities and global public goods with country programs, with an emphasis on upfront work on preparation of Poverty Reduction Strategy Papers (PRSPs) and CASs; facilitating cross-sectoral and cross-institutional approaches and work programs to address environmental issues; and addressing subregional and regional environmental challenges.

The Bank will work with interested partners to bring about the successful implementation of the Strategy and will avail itself of trust funds from bilateral partners and others. Nevertheless, the comprehensive actions needed to address the environmental challenges of economic development in client countries, as described in the Strategy, justify adequate deployment of Bank resources.

Partnerships. Partnerships with other development institutions, civil society, and the private sector can contribute to our objectives and can effectively leverage scarce Bank resources. Applying the principles of the Comprehensive Development Framework, partnerships at the country level are aimed at increasing development effectiveness and reducing transaction costs through coordination led by the countries and through the harmonization of operational policies and practices of development partners. At the regional and global levels, we will engage in partnerships where strong international consensus exist for global action with the aim of contributing to global public goods, where close links can be established with country assistance programs, and where significant resources can be catalyzed. We will continue our constructive partnerships in the framework of the GEF, the Multilateral Fund for the Montreal Protocol, and the Prototype Carbon Fund (PCF) to help implement major international conventions. We are currently engaged in numerous other partnerships in a range of areas. The Strategy provides a set of criteria for managing and evaluating partnerships, and we will apply these to systematically review and align our partnerships with the Strategy.

Monitoring progress. To ensure accountability and the capacity to learn from experience, we will introduce a performance monitoring and reporting framework that will track the Bank's performance on the environment, monitor implementation of the Strategy, and report regularly on progress. We will use the Internet and other means of communication with key stakeholders to make available reports and information about the Bank's environmental performance, discuss issues, and receive feedback. The core categories of periodical institutional reporting to senior management and the Board will include (a) environmental projects and programs, (b) mainstreaming and policy integration, (c) safeguard compliance, and (d) training. (See box 1 for some of the key benchmarks for monitoring Bank performance in implementation.)

BOX 1

Key benchmarks for monitoring Bank performance in Strategy implementation

- Country diagnostic studies carried out to assess environmental priorities and management capacity to inform CASs and PRSPs in 5–15 priority countries annually. Level of environmental mainstreaming in CASs improved.
- Targeted environmental input (analytical work and training) in 5–15 priority PRSP countries annually.
- Structured learning on SEAs based on 10–20 SEAs carried out annually to inform sector projects and programs. Level of mainstreaming in key sectors improved.
- Systematic client training delivering 20,000–25,000 "participant training days" annually.
- Improved safeguard compliance indicators.
- Ninety percent of all operational Bank staff and managers trained in environmental safeguards.

CONCLUSION

Real progress toward poverty reduction and sustainable development requires changes in a challenging array of policies, tools, and institutional priorities. Figure 1 presents the key adjustments in the World Bank's approaches that are envisioned by the Environment Strategy and that are vital if the Strategy is to achieve its goals.

The Strategy builds on and internalizes lessons learned in the past decade from our own efforts to support sustainable development, and from those of our clients and others, and it proposes to adjust our tools and institutional priorities to a changing global context and to changing Bank priorities. It places strong emphasis on development-environment links and on the environmental conditions that affect people's livelihoods, health, and vulnerability.

Figure 1
What's new in the Environment Strategy

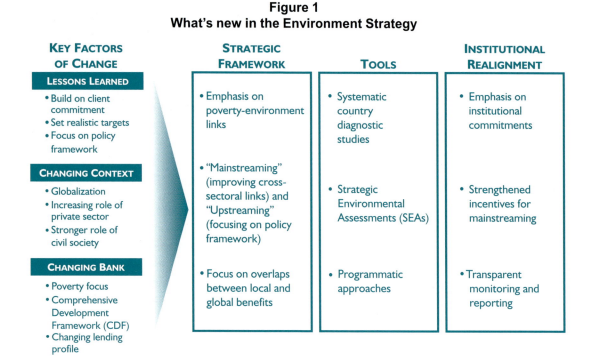

KEY FACTORS OF CHANGE	STRATEGIC FRAMEWORK	TOOLS	INSTITUTIONAL REALIGNMENT
LESSONS LEARNED • Build on client commitment • Set realistic targets • Focus on policy framework	• Emphasis on poverty-environment links	• Systematic country diagnostic studies	• Emphasis on institutional commitments
CHANGING CONTEXT • Globalization • Increasing role of private sector • Stronger role of civil society	• "Mainstreaming" (improving cross-sectoral links) and "Upstreaming" (focusing on policy framework)	• Strategic Environmental Assessments (SEAs)	• Strengthened incentives for mainstreaming
CHANGING BANK • Poverty focus • Comprehensive Development Framework (CDF) • Changing lending profile	• Focus on overlaps between local and global benefits	• Programmatic approaches	• Transparent monitoring and reporting

In implementing the Strategy, we will give priority to certain aspects that are particularly urgent, such as integrating environmental considerations into the PRSPs. Other elements of the Strategy, such as work toward systematic application of country environmental analysis and the Strategic Environmental Assessments, will be undertaken gradually focusing first on refining methodologies, coordinating with clients and partners, piloting, and learning.

Our environmental assistance (including non-lending and lending services) to client countries will be tailored to country need and capacity based on demand, on a diagnosis of environmental priorities and environmental management capacity undertaken by client countries, development partners, and the Bank; and on consistency with Country Assistance Strategies. We will ensure that country assessments and programs consider and reflect regional and global situations and priorities with a view to harmonizing local, regional, and global ben-

efits, facilitating resource transfers for global action, and helping client countries benefit from global public goods generated by international action.

To date, environmental issues have too often been the concern of a small, specialized group. This is clearly insufficient. To make a substantial and lasting difference, we must ensure that environmental concerns are fully internalized—"mainstreamed"—into all Bank activities. Internally we can strengthen our institutional commitment to the Strategy's objectives, and we can play a leadership role in more precisely measuring the impact of environmental interventions.

The success of the Strategy, however, depends on more than the Bank's actions. The Bank can help develop capacity in addressing environmental issues in client countries, and it can become a role model in supporting environmental sustainability in its operations. But in the end, the commitment of countries is needed if they are to take the necessary measures toward making their development sustainable. This is a gradual process that requires time, perseverance, a concerted effort by different parts of societies, and the support of the development community.

The Environment Strategy is clearly, and deliberately, for the long term. After all, its ultimate goals—sustainable development and lasting poverty reduction—stretch into the future. Short-term gains, as has been experienced too often, can be overwhelmed by larger adverse changes. We are looking to long-lasting achievements. That does not imply a lack of action in the meantime. We are not beginning from a standing start; we have the advantage of a well-established work program and an ever-expanding body of experience in environmental issues. Building on this foundation, we will work with our clients, together with development partners, to move forward toward creating a better and more sustainable world for all.

Table 1 Strategic framework matrix

Strategic focus		Adjustments in Bank instruments and actions		
Development objectives	Intermediate goals	Analytical and advisory activities	Policy integration	Project design and lending
Improve the quality of life				
Enhance livelihoods of the poor through improved natural resources management. • Increase incomes • Enhance long-term productivity • Improve poor people's access to natural resources	• Reduce land degradation, combat desertification, and restore degraded landscapes • Promote sustainable forest management • Reduce rates of biodiversity loss (genes, species, and ecosystems) • Improve land tenure systems and property rights • Support communal natural resource management • Establish pilot systems of payments for environmental services	• Provide training on sustainability and resource management issues in client countries • Develop and apply practical tools for measuring the value of environmental services • Undertake studies on access and use of natural resources as impacted by macro policy and political frameworks • Undertake studies on resource degradation and productivity and their linkages to poverty • Help assess the state of ecosystems and their links to livelihoods in client countries • Develop good practice in integrating economic and social factors into ecosystem management	• Enhance analytical work and cross-sectoral dialogue and training on poverty-environment issues in priority PRSP countries and CASs • Integrate environment-related indicators into PRSPs • Help establish incentive frameworks that promote sustainable NRM, including (a) removing policy-induced distortions that undermine sound NRM; and (b) using economic instruments to address externality problems • Promote institutional reform focused on user organizations and cost recovery	• Reflect economic, social, and ecological benefits in project design • Adopt a long-term perspective on NRM by using long-term lending instruments, e.g. APLs • Integrate sustainable ecosystem management objectives into infrastructure and rural development projects • Support participatory tenure and property right reform projects
Protect people's health from environmental risks and pollution to reduce the disease burden. Reduce: • Child mortality • Respiratory diseases • Blood lead levels • Deaths due to malaria • Exposure to toxic substances	• Improve air quality (particularly concentrations of fine particulates and lead) in cities • Increase the share of cleaner commercial fuels and improved cooking/heating systems in households to reduce indoor air pollution • Phase out leaded gasoline • Increase the coverage of water supply and sanitation and facilitate hygiene and behavioral change • Improve drainage in irrigation projects • Reduce the generation and impacts of industrial wastes and toxic materials	• Undertake cross-sectoral assessments of the key sources of environmental health problems • Identify cost-effective measures to reduce environmental health risks in sectors, e.g. water, energy, transport, agriculture • Undertake studies of policies and options to reduce the health impacts of indoor air pollution • Support lead phaseout initiatives and actions, clean fuel studies, Clean Air Initiatives and programs, and information dissemination and learning programs	• Integrate environmental health issues into PRSP dialogue, training, and indicators • Promote market-based solutions to environmental health problems relevant for poverty reduction and growth • Integrate health and environmental linkages into the implementation of PRSPs and CASs • Facilitate dialogue on policy reforms and investments programs that lead to least cost solutions to air quality problems including the coordination of transport, environment and energy policies • Raise awareness among various stakeholders of environmental health issues	• Design projects based on integrated air quality assessment in the urban, transport, and energy sectors • Support the switch to cleaner fuels (e.g. biomass to LPG conversion in rural households, coal-to-gas in urban households) • Support water supply and sanitation, energy, and irrigation projects that have specific environmental health outcomes based on integrated water resource management

Reduce people's vulnerability to environmental risks, including moderate and extreme natural events. Minimize: • Loss of life and livelihood • Injuries and disabilities • Temporary and permanent dislocation • Destruction of social, physical, and natural capital	• Raise awareness of the potentially high economic and social returns that investments in vulnerability reduction can yield • Strengthen regional institutions to improve weather forecasting, dissemination, and verifications systems • Enable adoption and encourage enforcement of building codes and land use policies • Promote resilience through better management and protection of the natural resource base	• Study the social and economic impacts of natural disasters and assess the vulnerability in countries/sub-regions with a history of natural disasters • Develop a framework for vulnerability assessments, disaster preparedness, and early warning systems • Support the preparation of building codes, siting, and land use guidelines • Develop learning programs on planning, predicting, and adapting to climate change	• Include disaster prevention and management in policy dialogue • Promote the integration of vulnerability reduction measures in sectoral planning and regulatory reforms • Support the integration of disaster management into regional, national, and local land use and development plans and water resources management policies, strategies, and planning	• Support community-based ecosystem service initiatives to reduce the impacts of flooding (reforestation, conservation, and restoration of wetlands) • Build and strengthen early warning systems, including community-based systems for effective dissemination of information • Support vulnerability reduction investments, including investments for adaptation to climate change
Improve the quality of growth Promote policy, regulatory and institutional frameworks for environmentally sustainable growth. • Improve the effectiveness of environmental regulatory frameworks in client countries • Enhance the integration of environmental concerns in sectors that affect the environment, e.g. energy, agriculture, transport • Promote sustainable financing of environmental services • Promote good environmental practices in private sector development • Encourage the private sector's participation in markets for environmental goods and services	• Promote the introduction and enforcement of efficient environmental and NRM institutions, policies, and regulations • Increase national and local capacity to adopt and implement environmental regulations and EA systems • Help integrate environmental concerns in projects and programs • Promote the adoption of independently verifiable good environmental management and natural resource use practices in the private sector • Increase the flow of private sector investments to environmental projects	• Strengthen client capacity through training, advisory services, and technical assistance in environmental assessment, policy, management and enforcement • Enhance analytical work to strengthen the application of safeguards in client countries • Undertake regional initiatives to strengthen and develop EA capacity • Transfer good practices and relevant lessons learned in environmental policy, management, and technical issues across Regions and countries • Identify good practices and promote environmentally and socially sound private sector development • Develop and apply benchmarks and good practices in environmental management for key areas of Bank operations	• Strengthen the integration of environmental aspects into CDFs, PRSPs, and CASs • Emphasize the linkages between public expenditure, poverty reduction, and environmental quality • Emphasize sectoral reform projects that promote environmentally appropriate policies and instruments (e.g. water and energy sectors) • Promote policies that support private sector participation and sustainable natural resource management in service provision (e.g. energy, transport, and water) consistent with sound regulatory frameworks for managing the resource • Address environmental issues systematically in privatization and private sector development programs	• Increase support to priority countries, identified in Regional Environment Strategies and business plans, to help strengthen environmental management framework • Use policy-based lending to address key environmental and NRM issues • Promote environmental responsibility and good environmental management practices in the private sector through IFC investments and MIGA guarantees • Support the establishment of markets for ecosystem services and the adoption of independent certification of sustainable natural resource use

Table 1 Strategic framework matrix (*continued*)

Strategic focus		Adjustments in Bank instruments and actions		
Development objectives	Intermediate goals	Analytical and advisory activities	Policy integration	Project design and lending
Protect the quality of regional and global commons				
Address transboundary, regional and global environmental problems. • Reduce the impacts of transboundary and regional environmental problems • Promote equitable solutions to global environmental problems • Improve countries' capacity to adapt to changing global environments.	• Help client countries benefit from global public goods • Help countries to address local, national, and regional environmental priorities in a manner that also results in global benefits • Enhance countries' capacity to participate in global environmental conventions • Enhance capacity in countries to reduce vulnerability to natural disasters and impacts of climate change. • Help client countries to access markets for global public goods (e.g. trade in greenhouse gas emissions)	• Build capacity among client country institutions to consider the regional and global dimensions of national sustainable development strategies • Support the assessment of the vulnerability of client countries' agriculture, forest, water resources, coastal zones, and urban infrastructure to climate change as part of a broader poverty reduction strategy • Support efforts by riparians and littoral communities to diagnose, analyze, and plan actions to address the degradation of shared ecosystems • Support client capabilities to address Persistent Organic Pollutants (POPs) and other toxic pollutants • Support client learning programs on understanding the implications and responsibilities under global environmental conventions	• Help understand linkages between global public goods and national development strategies • Mobilize external resources to help integrate global environmental concerns into sectoral strategies for forestry, water, energy and rural development • Link local and global environmental issues to development and poverty reduction strategies • Link conservation and sustainable use of biodiversity with NRM and poverty dialogue • Mainstream energy efficiency, renewable energy, vulnerability–reduction, and climate adaptation activities in relevant sectors • Facilitate the phaseout of the consumption and production of ODS and POPs through national programs and use of market-based instruments	• Focus interventions on improving local environmental quality and management that also provide regional and global benefits • Promote lending for biodiversity through NRM projects that address sustainable use of ecosystems and their services • Support efforts to build capacity and invest in international waters, and pilot river basin approaches to water resources management • Use GEF funds strategically to better blend with and catalyze Bank and other funding to help enhance the livelihood of the poor and reduce vulnerability • Support clients' participation in and benefit from trade in environmental goods and services through the Prototype Carbon Fund and to better prepare for the CDM.

xxxii

Table 2 Strategy implementation and monitoring matrix

Objectives	Medium-term target (5-year)	Fiscal 2002 target: Realignment with the Strategy
Strengthen analytical and advisory activities		
Strengthen country-level environmental analysis and advisory activities to inform country dialogue	• Complete about 5-15 country diagnostic studies annually in connection with CAS processes • Improve environmental sustainability indicators and mainstream them into country indicators • Refine methodologies and mainstream economic assessment into project analysis including the assessment of climate change impacts • Develop and disseminate good practice case studies and guidance notes on environmental policy and regulatory issues • Strengthen client training and capacity development activities in environmental management	• Review good practice and refine methodology for preparing country diagnostic studies in coordination with client countries and development partners • Prepare country diagnostic studies in connection with CASs preparation • Prepare good practice and guidance notes for a number of key issues • Develop and start implementing a client training and capacity development program
Strengthen analytical work on poverty-environment linkages and inputs to PRSPs	• Provide analytical and capacity development support on demand to about 5-15 PRSP processes annually in addressing environmental sustainability • Improve the understanding of poverty-health-vulnerability linkages and improve assessment methodologies in countries where household survey data are available • Systematically share knowledge with decisionmakers in PRSP countries on poverty-environment issues and effective interventions to address them	• Continue analytical work and development of methodology, including enhanced use of household survey data and develop a typology of country-environment links • Develop training programs and a system to share knowledge with decisionmakers in PRSP countries on poverty-environment issues and effective interventions to address them • Support upstream environmental analytical work in at least 5 countries preparing PRSPs • Undertake an ex-post review of environmental aspects of PRSPs
Use Strategic Environmental Assessments (SEAs) more systematically to address environmental concerns early in sectoral decisionmaking and planning processes	• Undertake a structured learning program on SEAs including the development and dissemination of good practice based on about 10-20 SEAs annually • Use SEAs regularly as a tool for upstreaming environment into policy dialogue and improvement in the quality of sector operations • Integrate the findings of Energy-Environment Reviews into project and program design	• Develop and disseminate methodologies, procedures, and guidance for SEA application • Commence a series of priority SEA studies • Undertake Energy-Environment Reviews as part of implementing *Fuel for Thought*
Improve project and program design		
Mainstream environment into CASs	• Achieve satisfactory coverage of environmental issues in CASs where environmental issues are strongly linked to country priorities	• Establish a process for identifying priority CASs and supporting CAS preparation • Undertake in collaboration with OPCS an assessment of environmental coverage in CASs
Improve the performance and development effectiveness of environment projects and programs	• Achieve satisfactory or better QAG ratings for quality at entry and supervision for at least 90 percent of the environment portfolio • Improve corporate environmental portfolio tracking, quality assessment, and enhancement system • Reduce the number of environment projects at risk • Review and improve the alignment of the environment portfolio with strategic priorities • Review the development effectiveness of environment projects and programs	• Maintain QAG quality at entry and supervision performance ratings for environmental projects and programs • Establish a portfolio quality enhancement mechanism

Table 2 Strategy implementation and monitoring matrix (*continued*)

Objectives	Medium-term target (5-year)	Fiscal 2002 target: Realignment with the Strategy
Mainstream environment into sector programs and portfolios	• Increase the extent of measurable mainstreaming over current levels in selected sectors • Improve the integration of GEF resources into project and program lending • Review environmental activities in other sectors and their alignment with the Strategy • Implement joint work-programs with other sectors and networks to address priority environmental objectives	• Establish cross-sectoral work programs • Establish scorecards and a mechanism for monitoring, review, and feedback on environment mainstreaming in key sectors
Improve the safeguard system		
Strengthen the implementation of safeguard policies, including the use of a tracking system for safeguard compliance by policy	• Establish an integrated risk management framework • Strengthen corporate consistency and oversight • Integrate safeguard tracking and reports on safeguard policy compliance into project management system • Adopt and use compliance indicators on a routine basis for the entire portfolio • Establish and meet targets for safeguard performance during quality at entry and supervision in QAG reviews	• Establish and implement an integrated safeguard system and operationalize the Integrated Safeguard Data Sheet (ISDS) • Establish and operationalize a corporate safeguard compliance tracking and monitoring system • Strengthen corporate oversight • Achieve target ratings for the environmental aspects of quality at entry and supervision for the Bank's portfolio • Review all projects at risk and take measures to reduce risk • Establish systematic staff safeguard training program
Review the current safeguard policies and evaluate their application to new lending instruments and changing approaches to development assistance	• Develop the medium-term workplan for reforming the safeguard system • Address safeguard policy issues in a consistent manner by undertaking regular reviews to identify lessons	• Develop a medium-term workplan for reforming the safeguards system • Identify good practice and guidance for addressing safeguard policy issues in sector adjustment lending and new lending instruments such as CDD projects
Work with clients and other development institutions to review and strengthen client safeguard capacity, and harmonize safeguard procedures	• Engage with at least 10 countries in discussions on in-depth EA capacity assessment and strengthening • Implement a comprehensive client safeguard training plan	• Agree on a methodology for client capacity assessment • Engage with at least two countries in discussions on in-depth EA capacity assessment and strengthening • Prepare and pilot a comprehensive client safeguard training plan
Support institutional realignment		
Improve incentives for work on cross-sectoral activities and policy issues.	• Establish a comprehensive performance evaluation, incentive and reward system for cross-sectoral work	• Give specific attention to cross-sectoral work in annual results agreements for all environmental staff • Launch Green awards

Achieve a shift in skill mix through training, strategic hiring and joint appointments	• Implement strategic human resource development • Undertake targeted staff training on cross-sectoral issues • Provide safeguard training to all managers of A and B rated projects and to others on demand • Train 90 percent of all operational staff, including managers, in safeguards policies • Provide environmental training for staff in other sectors on demand on development-environment issues	• Define the needs in cross-sectoral skills and a plan for strategic human resource development • Develop targeted pilot staff training programs for environmental mainstreaming in selected sectors • Continue to refine safeguard policies training program and launch safeguard policy training for managers • Provide training on demand
Improve the funding mechanism for environmental activities in the Bank	• Operationalize the Mainstreaming Fund with regular reporting and feedback • Undertake an evaluation of the Mainstreaming Fund to assess its effectiveness • Align the use of trust funds with strategic priorities	• Set up Mainstreaming Fund and develop procedures • Review the use of trust funds and their alignment with the Strategy
Leverage the role of institutional engagements and partnerships to support the implementation of the Strategy	• Realign partnerships with strategic objectives • Improve governance, management, and reporting on partnerships	• Update and evaluate the partnership portfolio • Set guidelines for improving governance, management, and reporting on partnerships
Undertake systematic monitoring and reporting on performance	• Establish and operationalize an environmental management system	• Develop a systematic performance monitoring and reporting framework • Establish a performance monitoring and reporting unit in ENV • Start regular reporting on the implementation of the Strategy

Abbreviations and Acronyms

AAA	Analytical and Advisory Activities
ADB	Asian Development Bank
AEAP	Annual Environmental Action Plan
AfDB	African Development Bank
APL	Adaptable Program Loan
ARES	Africa Region Environment Strategy
ARI	Acute Respiratory Infection
AusAID	Australian Agency for International Development
BMZ	Federal Ministry for Economic Co-Operation and Development, Germany
BNPP	Bank-Netherlands Partnership Program
CAO	Compliance Advisor/Ombudsman
CAS	Country Assistance Strategy
CASE	Country Assistance Strategies and the Environment
CBD	Convention on Biological Diversity
CCAD	Central American Commission for Environment and Development
CCD	Convention to Combat Desertification
CDC	Centers for Disease Control
CDD	Community-Driven Development
CDF	Comprehensive Development Framework
CDM	Clean Development Mechanism
CDR	Country Development Review
CDS	City Development Strategy
CEDARE	Center for Environment and Development for the Arab Region and Europe
CEE	Central and Eastern European Countries
CEPF	Critical Ecosystem Partnership Fund
CESP	Country Environment Strategy Paper

CGIAR	Consultative Group on International Agricultural Research
CI	Conservation International
CIDA	Canadian International Development Agency
CMU	Country Management Unit
CODE	Committee on Development Effectiveness
COPD	Chronic Obstructive Pulmonary Disease
CPF	Collaborative Partnership on Forests
DALYs	Disability-adjusted Life Years
DANIDA	Danish International Development Assistance
DBSA	Development Bank of South Africa
DECVP	Development Economics Vice Presidency
DFID	Department for International Development (UK)
DGF	Development Grant Facility
EA	Environmental Assessment
EAP	East Asia and Pacific Region
EB	Environment Board
EC	European Commission
ECA	Europe and Central Asia Region
ECLAC	Economic Commission for Latin America and the Caribbean
EER	Energy Environment Review
EIA	Environmental Impact Assessment
EIB	European Investment Bank
ELCI	Environment Liaison Centre International
ENV	Environment Department
EPSAL	Environmental and Privatization Support Adjustment Loan
EPU	Environmental Projects Unit
ESB	Environment Sector Board
ESCO	Energy Service Component
ESDVP	Environmentally and Socially Sustainable Development Vice Presidency
ESMAP	Energy Sector Management Assistance Programme
ESMRS	Environment Strategy Monitoring and Reporting System
ESP	Environmental Support Program
ESRP	Environmental and Social Review Procedure
ESSD	Environmentally and Socially Sustainable Development
ESW	Economic and Sector Work
EU	European Union
Euronatur	European Natural Heritage Fund
FAO	Food and Agriculture Organization of the United Nations
FASID	Foundation for Advanced Studies on International Development
FFT	Fuel for Thought
FMTI	Forest Market Transformation Initiative

FUG	Forest User Group
GDP	Gross Domestic Product
GEF	Global Environment Facility
GHGs	Greenhouse Gases
GRI	Global Reporting Initiative
GTZ	Gesellschaft für Technische Zusammenarbeit (Germany)
HD	Human Development
IBRD	International Bank for Reconstruction and Development
ID	Institutional Development
IDA	International Development Association
IDB	Inter-American Development Bank
IEM	Integrated Ecosystem Management
IFAD	International Fund for Agricultural Development
IFC	International Finance Corporation
IFI	International Financial Institution
ILWMAP	Integrated Land Water Management Action Program for Africa
IPCC	Intergovernmental Panel on Climate Change
IPRSP	Interim Poverty Reduction Strategy Paper
ISDS	Integrated Safeguard Data Sheet
IUCN	World Conservation Union
JEP	Joint Environment Program
JBIC	Japan Bank for International Cooperation
JI	Joint Implementation projects
JICA	Japan International Cooperation Agency
JSA	Joint Staff Assessment
KfW	Kreditanstalt für Wiederaufbau
LAC	Latin America and the Caribbean
LCR	Latin America and the Caribbean Region
LEGVP	Legal Vice Presidency
LIL	Learning and Innovation Loan
LPCD	Liters Per Capita Per Day
LPG	Liquid Propane Gas
MAP	Mediterranean Action Plan
MBC	Mesoamerican Biological Corridor
M&E	Monitoring and Evaluation
MEA	Millennium Ecosystem Assessment
MEF	Middle East and North Africa Environmental Fund
MEIP	Metropolitan Environmental Improvement Program
MELISSA	Managing the Environment Locally in Sub-Saharan Africa
METAP	Mediterranean Environmental Technical Assistance Program
MFMP	Multilateral Fund for the Montreal Protocol

MIGA	Multilateral Investment Guarantee Agency
MNA	Middle East and North Africa Region
NEAP	National Environmental Action Plan
NEP II	Brazil Second National Environment Project
NGO	Nongovernmental Organization
NIS	Newly Independent States
NORAD	Norwegian Agency for Development Cooperation
NRM	Natural Resources Management
NSS	National Strategy Studies
OAS	Organization of American States
OD	Operational Directive
ODA	Official Development Assistance
ODS	Ozone-Depleting Substances
OECD	Organisation for Economic Co-operation and Development
OED	Operations Evaluation Department
PAGE	Pilot Analysis of Global Ecosystems
PAHO	Pan American Health Organization
PAL	Programmatic Adjustment Loans
PCF	Prototype Carbon Fund
POP	Persistent Organic Pollutants
PPAH	Pollution Prevention and Abatement Handbook
PREM	Poverty Reduction and Economic Management
PRGF	Poverty Reduction and Growth Facility
PROFOR	UNDP Programme on Forests
PROPER	Program for Pollution Control, Evaluation, and Rating
PRS	Poverty Reduction Strategy
PRSC	Poverty Reduction Strategy Credit
PRSP	Poverty Reduction Strategy Paper
PSAC	Programmatic Structural Adjustment Credit
PSAL	Programmatic Structural Adjustment Loan
PSI	Private Sector and Infrastructure
PV	Photovoltaic
QACU	Quality Assurance and Compliance Unit
QAG	Quality Assurance Group
QPM	Quality Project Management
RED	Regional Environment Department
REEF	Renewable Energy and Energy Efficiency Fund
RHA	Respiratory Hospital Admissions
RMT	Regional Management Team
RVP	Regional Vice President
SAL	Structural Adjustment Loan

SDP   Strategic Directions Paper
SDC   Swiss Agency for Development and Cooperation
SDG   Solar Development Group
SEA   Strategic Environmental Assessment
SECAL   Sectoral Adjustment Loan
SECO   State Secretariat for Economic Cooperation of Switzerland
SFP   Strategic Framework Paper
SIDA   Swedish International Development Cooperation Agency
SLRM   Sustainable Land Resources Management
SME   Small and Medium-Size Enterprise
SRI   Socially Responsible Investing
TACIS   Technical Assistance for the Commonwealth of Independent States
TF   Trust Fund
UNCCD   United Nations Convention to Combat Desertification
UNCED   United Nations Conference on Environment and Development
UNCHS   United Nations Centre for Human Settlements (Habitat)
UNDP   United Nations Development Programme
UNECE   United Nations Economic Commission for Europe
UNEP   United Nations Environment Programme
UNESCO   United Nations Educational, Scientific, and Cultural Organization
UNFCC   United Nations Framework Convention on Climate Change
UNFPA   United Nations Population Fund
UNIDO   United Nations Industrial Development Organization
UMP   Urban Management Program
URBAIR   Urban Air Quality Management Strategy
USAID   US Agency for International Development
VAF   Vulnerability and Adaptation Facility
VDC   Village Development Committees
WB   World Bank
WBG   World Bank Group
WBI   World Bank Institute
WCD   World Commission on Dams
WCED   World Commission on Environment and Development
WDR   World Development Report
WHO   World Health Organization
WMO   World Meteorological Organization
WPA   Work Program Agreement
WRI   World Resources Institute
WSS   Water Supply and Sanitation
WWF   World Wide Fund for Nature

Introduction

Economic development has led to dramatic improvements in the quality of life in developing countries. Higher incomes, better infrastructure, access to cleaner fuels, and improved access to health services have significantly reduced the toll on infant mortality and adult disease linked to exposure to indoor air pollution, contaminated water, human waste, and vector-borne diseases. Education, improvements in human skills and technical knowledge, and capital investments have permitted farmers and other rural communities to obtain much greater incomes from their land, water, and other natural resources.

The striking gains in development in the past decades have been unparalleled in human history. But the picture is far from entirely positive. Gains have been unevenly distributed, and an unacceptably large portion of the world's population remains desperately poor. Approximately 1.2 billion people live on less than a dollar a day, and the gap between the richest and poorest countries has doubled in the past 40 years (World Bank 2000a). Growth has also been accompanied by an alarming rate of environmental degradation, which has reduced its benefits and in some cases threatens the very foundations of economic activity.

Environmental problems are complex, interlinked, and daunting. They are a fundamental part of the development challenge.

THE ROLE OF THE ENVIRONMENT STRATEGY

This Environment Strategy discusses how we will work with our clients and partners to help them address environmental problems as an integral part of their sustainable development strategies. The close relationships among poverty, environment, and development are increasingly understood. The links between poverty and environment are particularly close when poverty is viewed as a multidimensional phenomenon rather than simply a matter of income. This is reflected in the UN Millennium Declaration's International

Development Goals for 2015, which closely associate the goals of poverty reduction, health improvements, and environmental protection.

The world's environmental problems are vast. We at the World Bank can best contribute to their solution by focusing on those areas where we can achieve the greatest results. The Strategy is intended to be realistic about what has to be done; about our strengths and weaknesses; about how to utilize the resources available to improve our performance; and about the potential for our assistance to have positive development outcomes. To help achieve its goals, the Strategy adopts a threefold approach:

- *Learning and applying lessons.* The Strategy builds on the achievements and lessons of both our own past efforts and those of others. It does not seek to change the direction set at the Earth Summit in 1992 and articulated in the 1992 *World Development Report,* but to internalize lessons learned in the last decade, bolster commitments, and accelerate progress toward integrating environment and development.

- *Adapting to a changing world.* A number of trends—often referred to under the common label of "globalization"—have been reshaping the world. In response to these trends and to continued learning from our past efforts, the Bank has also been changing. It has reaffirmed its commitment to poverty reduction and committed to a bottom-up, client-focused development, and it is moving toward new lending approaches. Our work on the environment must also adapt to these changing conditions.

- *Deepening our commitment.* To date, the environment has been the concern of a small, specialized group. This is clearly insufficient. To make a substantial and lasting difference, we must ensure that environmental concerns are fully internalized throughout the Bank.

If we are to help improve people's lives, development opportunities, and prospects for a sustainable future, it is critical for the Bank to steer this course successfully. The Environment Strategy emphasizes the importance of integrating—or "mainstreaming"—environment into country development programs, sector strategies, and investments.

ORGANIZATION OF THIS REPORT

Chapter 1 begins by tracing the connections between development, poverty, and the environment. A clear understanding of the problems being faced and of their causes is essential to any effort to address them. Chapter 2 then reviews the Bank's record to date in helping its client countries address environmental problems. The last decade has seen some notable achievements, but there are also areas in which we have fallen short of our own expectations and those of others. It is important to carefully examine these past efforts, and to incorporate the lessons from them into our future activities. On this basis, chapter 3 sets out the Bank's Environment Strategy. Of course, given the enormous diversity of conditions and priorities among our client countries, country-specific strategies will differ substantially. Several common themes emerge, however. Chapter 4 discusses the measures we plan to take within the World Bank to ensure that this strategy is implemented and how we plan to monitor our progress.

Chapter 1

Development, Poverty, and the Environment — Tracing the Connections

Helping our client countries face the environmental challenges of development requires a clear understanding of the links between development, poverty, and the environment. This chapter reviews our understanding of these connections.

THE EVOLUTION OF THINKING ABOUT SUSTAINABLE DEVELOPMENT

The 1980s witnessed a growing recognition that a growth-based development model, by itself, was not sufficient to ensure long-term sustainability and an equitable sharing of economic progress. *Our Common Future*, the 1987 report of the World Commission on Environment and Development chaired by Gro Harlem Brundtland, then prime minister of Norway, suggested that sound development required concerted efforts to protect the environment. Sustainable development, the Commission noted, "is development that meets the needs of the present without compromising the ability of future generations to meet their own needs" (WCED 1987).

The 1992 United Nations Conference on Environment and Development (UNCED) took *Our Common Future* several steps further by formally endorsing the concept of sustainable development through the Rio Declaration on Environment and Development. According to the definition in Principle 3 of the Declaration, sustainable development would "equitably meet development and environmental needs of present and future generations." The sustainable development concept clearly calls for a more comprehensive, integrated, systemic approach that takes a long-term view of development and balances its different dimensions—economic growth, social equity, and long-term environmental sustainability. Stating the goal is easy; putting it into practice is not. Reaching it often implies difficult choices among competing development paths. A critical challenge for the world is to find an appropriate mix of policies, institutions, and technologies that will make these multiple dimensions of development compatible.

Significant progress has been made since the UNCED Conference. In September 2000, key themes of the sustainability challenge were reiterated at the United Nations Millennium Summit. The Millennium Declaration adopted at the summit by 150 heads of state or government included a series of concrete international development goals to be achieved by 2015 (see box 1.1). These goals have been widely accepted as key indicators of sustainable development. They are interdependent, and together they represent a formidable challenge for countries and the development community. Achieving them requires a concerted effort by governments, civil society, and a diverse range of development partners. The World Bank is developing its corporate strategy around these international development goals as a frame of reference for its mission of fighting poverty with lasting results.

TRADEOFFS, CHOICES, AND PRIORITIES

Sustainability is a long-term concept, but one that is directly affected by short-term financial and political considerations. Arriving at a definition of sustainability and indicators for measuring it has been a serious challenge (see box 1.2). Distorted policies, governance structures, institutional frameworks, and incentives, along with pressures to export natural resources, may favor a short-term focus, making programs with a long-term horizon difficult to implement. The "grow now, clean up later" approach to development has imposed very high costs—costs that could be avoided by adopting policies and programs that prevent serious environmental damage.

It may be rational to draw down stocks of natural resources in order to finance investments in education, skills, infrastructure, and other productive assets. That, however, is different from mining stocks of natural resources to support consumption without regard to long-term productivity—a practice that cannot be sustained. Moreover, resource extraction is often undertaken in ways that yield

BOX 1.1
Goals for international development

The major international development institutions—including the United Nations (UN), Organisation for Economic Co-operation and Development (OECD), International Monetary Fund (IMF), and the Bank—are working to develop a common set of international development goals. The discussions, which are in progress, are focusing on integrating the International Development Goals agreed to by the OECD, UN, IMF, and the Bank with goals set forth in the UN's Millennium Declaration.

The goals focus on key aspects of human well-being: poverty reduction, education, gender equality, health, and sustainable development. For each goal, indicators are specified to track progress toward the goal.

There are seven broadly agreed goals:

- Eradicate poverty and hunger
- Achieve universal primary education
- Reach gender equality and empower women
- Reduce child mortality
- Improve maternal health
- Combat HIV/AIDS, malaria, and other diseases
- Ensure environmental sustainability

To monitor progress toward the environmental sustainability goal, there are three indicator targets: integrating the principles of sustainable development into country policies and programs and reversing the loss of environmental resources; halving, by 2015, the proportion of people without sustainable access to safe drinking water; and, by 2020, achieving a significant improvement in the lives of at least 100 million slum dwellers.

significantly lower benefits than are possible; indeed, at times the benefits are lower than the costs of extraction. In these cases, it is essential to increase the productivity of natural resource stocks by better management, since incomes cannot be in-

BOX 1.2
Indicators of sustainable development

In order to pursue sustainability, it is important to measure it. A few examples of indicators proposed or used by countries, international and other organizations are listed here:

■ *Genuine Savings* (World Bank). Change in total wealth, accounting for resource depletion and environmental damage.

■ *Genuine Progress Indicator* (Redefining Progress, a nonprofit public policy organization), and *Index of Sustainable Economic Welfare* (United Kingdom and other countries). An adjusted GDP figure, reflecting welfare losses from environmental and social factors.

■ *Living Planet Index* (WWF). An assessment of the populations of animal species in forest, freshwater, and marine environments.

■ *Environmental Sustainability Index* (World Economic Forum). An aggregate index spanning 22 major factors that contribute to environmental sustainability.

■ *Ecological Footprint* (Redefining Progress, WWF, and others). A measure of the land area required to produce, in renewable form, the energy consumed by individual countries.

■ *Resource Flows* (World Resources Institute). Total material flows underpinning economic processes.

■ *Environmental Pressure Indices* (Netherlands, EU). A set of aggregate indices for specific environmental pressures such as acidification or emissions of greenhouse gases.

■ *UN System of Environmental and Economic Accounts*. A framework for environmental accounting.

■ *UN Commission for Sustainable Development.* Prototype sustainable development indicator sets for individual countries.

creased or even maintained by current patterns of use. Especially for the rural poor, achieving the international development goal of halving extreme poverty by 2015 will depend heavily on improving resource management.

There are many "win-win" opportunities to simultaneously achieve economic and environmental objectives. At times, however, there can be tradeoffs between sustainable resource use and environmental protection. Conserving natural habitats, for example, may constrain their present use, which may deprive resource-dependent people of their livelihoods. In a long-term perspective, this apparent tradeoff sometimes disappears. Overfishing, for example, may temporarily improve people's income, making conservation seem costly. But if overfishing causes the collapse of fisheries, as has happened time and again, these same people will soon be deprived of both nutrition and income.

Balancing the various objectives and tradeoffs requires value judgments. The relative weights given to the various forms of wealth through everyday decisions are political, social, and cultural choices, but they have to be informed choices, made with the participation of affected stakeholders.

Regardless of the specific environmental issue, three broad factors underlie many decisions and strategies concerning environmental problems. All three relate to equity and fairness in the use of environmental resources over space and time.

■ *The tradeoff between present and future generations.* Exactly what and how much the present generation leaves for the future are important questions underlying many decisions about resource use and consumption.

■ *The issue of equitable access* to resources and the impacts of resource use and the differing impacts of degradation between rich and poor, both within a country and among countries.

- *The perceived lack of overlap* between actions that address local and global environmental concerns.

These three issues have created tensions in the environmental analysis and management arena and in the minds of decisionmakers. They influence what different people see as sustainable development, and they have shaped key concepts about environmental protection and conservation (see box 1.3). The challenge facing the World Bank and other institutions concerned with economic development is to work with their clients to develop and

---

BOX 1.3
From protectionism to sustainable ecosystem management

Conservation approaches have slowly evolved from a focus on species and strict protection to a focus on the sustainable use of biological resources and sustainable ecosystem management.

According to the Convention on Biological Diversity, "ecosystem management seeks to meet human requirements to use natural resources, whilst maintaining the biological richness and ecological processes necessary to sustain the composition, structure, and function of the habitats or ecosystems concerned."

Ecosystem management is the ecological pillar of sustainability, but its application in practical terms requires management approaches with varying degrees of intensity. Modern conservation approaches include protected areas, which themselves have been categorized by the World Conservation Union (IUCN) along a continuum from strict protection to intensive sustainable use; biological corridors; agrobiodiversity and pastoral systems; and heavily modified landscapes, as long as their configuration and impact are compatible with broader ecosystem management goals.

---

implement policies and investment programs that not only support continued economic development, but also:

- Distribute the gains of development in a more equitable manner, with a particular focus on reducing poverty
- Avoid sacrificing the interests of future generations to meet the needs of the current generation
- Build on the emerging global consensus that natural resources and other valuable environmental assets must be managed sustainably.

Many of the easiest gains from introducing better water management, providing clean water and sanitation, encouraging the use of cleaner fuels, and reducing the impact of floods and droughts have already been captured. Yet millions of children still die each year, and many families lose their assets and sources of income, as a result of diseases and disasters that are linked to the quality of their environment. There are indications that progress in the 1990s was much slower than in previous decades. In some countries, the situation is clearly getting worse, particularly in Sub-Saharan Africa, where the effects of the AIDS epidemic and civil wars are undermining past progress in reducing the burden of disease and promoting better management of natural resources.

THREE LINKS BETWEEN ENVIRONMENT AND DEVELOPMENT

The key environmental concerns are associated with three broad but interrelated aspects of development:

- *Quality of life—especially with respect to the livelihoods, health, and vulnerability of the poor*
- *Quality of growth*
- *Quality of the regional and global commons.*

The quality of life

Falling rates of infant mortality and increasing life expectancy are important indicators of the substantial progress made over the past four decades in reducing the burden of disease associated with poor environmental conditions. Even so, environmental factors have major effects on people, often falling disproportionately on the poor (see annex B for more detail about poverty-environment linkages). The effects of environmental conditions on poor people can be grouped into three categories: livelihoods, health, and vulnerability.

Threats to livelihoods. Nearly a billion rural households rely directly on the services of natural capital stocks and intricately interdependent ecosystems—water resources, land and soils, forests, and fisheries—for their daily livelihood (see annex D for more detail on management of natural resources). As the availability of these resources decline and their quality deteriorates, these livelihoods are threatened (see box 1.4). Collapsing ecosystems can undermine the social fabric of societies and pose threats to security. The major threats to the livelihoods of rural households, especially poor households that often

depend on natural resource services for as much as 30 to 50 percent of their total income, are posed by:

- *Overuse, mismanagement, and contamination of freshwater resources.* Almost one third of the world's population faces water scarcity or water stress, especially in Africa, the Middle East, Latin America and the Caribbean, and large parts of South Asia. Rapid degradation of wetlands and coastal zones is a major environmental management problem in many regions, in part exacerbated by over-abstraction of water and by pollution.

- *Degradation of soil,* caused by erosion, the buildup of salts, and compaction brought about by poor irrigation and cultivation practices or overgrazing, especially in areas with highly variable rainfall. Erosion, salinization, compaction, and other forms of degradation affect 30 percent of the world's irrigated lands, 40 percent of rainfed agricultural lands, and 70 percent of rangelands.

- *Rapid depletion of forests, fisheries, and biodiversity,* often as a consequence of unclear property rights and perverse economic incentives and poor gov-

---

BOX 1.4
Environmental degradation and economic productivity

The *Pilot Analysis of Global Ecosystems (PAGE): Agro-ecosystems* is the first comprehensive assessment of the ability of the world's agriculture to provide sufficient food, goods, and services, which are vital for sustaining human life. The report notes that soil degradation, including nutrient depletion, erosion, and salinization, is widespread and has dramatically reduced crop productivity, with severe consequences likely for poor, heavily populated countries. Irrigation is draining more water than is being replenished, causing water tables to fall and threatening future water availability for irrigation and other uses. Moreover, many water sources are being polluted by excessive use of agrochemicals.

The PAGE report sets the stage for the Millennium Ecosystem Assessment (MEA), launched by the World Resources Institute (WRI), the United Nations Environment Programme (UNEP), the World Bank, and the Global Environment Facility.

Source: IFPRI, CGIAR, WRI 2000.

ernance. About 70 percent of the world's fisheries are either depleted, overexploited, or fully exploited. Global rates of forest loss have reached alarmingly high levels, especially in the upland forests of the Andes, Central America, East and Central Africa, and Southeast Asia . More than one fifth of the world's tropical forests have been cleared since 1960.

Threats to health. Environmental degradation is an important contributing factor to the burden of disease, influencing the quality of life and economic opportunities for many people (see annex C for more detail on environmental health issues). Premature death and illness caused by environmental factors account for one fifth of the total burden of disease in developing countries, which is comparable to the toll from malnutrition (15 percent). Millions of children and adults die every year from diseases that could be avoided by improving environmental quality. The primary environmental hazards of concern in developing countries are:

- *Water-related diseases,* caused by lack of access to clean water and adequate sanitation, which claim an estimated 3 million lives each year—mostly children under 5 years of age—and exacerbate exposure to vector-borne diseases.
- *Exposure to indoor air pollution,* caused by burning dirty fuels in inefficient stoves without proper ventilation, which results in nearly 2 million deaths of women and children annually, including about 500,000 deaths in India and about 300,000 in China.
- *Exposure to urban air pollution,* primarily due to fine particles emitted by households that burn coal and other dirty fuels for heating and by two-stroke motorcycles and poorly maintained diesel vehicles. Air pollution causes close to a million premature deaths and severe respiratory problems.

- *Exposure to agricultural and industrial chemicals and waste* is a modern environmental health risk that exacerbates the impacts of traditional environmental health risks in many developing countries.

The burden of disease associated with limited access to clean water and sanitation and with indoor air pollution falls disproportionately on the poorest 20 to 40 percent of households. In both rural and urban areas, the poor are less likely to be served by water and sanitation infrastructure and are more likely to rely on dirty fuels for cooking. Urban air pollution affects all urban inhabitants, but the poor tend to suffer more severely because its effects are worse for those in poor health and because poor people have limited opportunities to protect themselves or to move to less polluted areas. Preventing and reducing these environmental hazards would make a major contribution toward meeting the International Development Goal of reducing infant and child mortality by two thirds and maternal mortality rates by three quarters by 2015.

Vulnerability. In 1992, Hurricane Andrew hit the southeastern coast of the United States and caused 32 deaths. In the same year, a cyclone of similar intensity hit Bangladesh and caused 100,000 deaths. Poor people are particularly vulnerable to both natural disasters and changes in environmental conditions. Changing patterns of resource use have often undermined traditional arrangements for managing and sharing such natural risks as droughts, floods, fires, and earthquakes. Pressures on resource stocks have prompted many poor households to live and work in vulnerable zones such as floodplains, drought-prone areas, or earthquake faults. Vulnerability is increased by specialization in the use of particular natural resources, so that households have few alternatives when disaster strikes. Furthermore, the poor have less capacity to cope when disasters occur. Access to credit is more difficult than for better-off households, and the poor have fewer assets to sell or consume in times of hardship. Natural disasters, therefore, often have catastrophic effects on the poor.

The quality of growth

Economic growth is essential if poverty is to be reduced and welfare is to be improved. But it is a mistake to imagine that there is a simple dichotomy between "growth" and "no growth." Growth can take a variety of forms, and, as several recent studies have shown, the *quality of growth* matters (World Bank 2000b). A focus on maximizing growth—narrowly defined in GDP terms to the exclusion of all other considerations—often imposes substantial costs and proves unsustainable.

Improving the quality of growth is far from simple. In the case of environmental issues, improving incentives for the sustainable use of environmental and natural resources is a key issue. When markets work well, economic theory and experience both tell us that resource use will be "efficient." But in practice, markets do not always work well. This is particularly true in the case of environmental goods and services, which have special characteristics (see box 1.5). Environmental problems are usually caused by market failures, policy failures, or both.

■ *Market failures.* Markets for many environmental services often function poorly or not at all. As a result, the observed "prices" for environmental goods or services often do not reflect their value to society. In many cases, there is no observed price at all, making these goods and services appear to be either free, so that they tend to be overconsumed, or worthless, so that they tend to be underprovided. Environmental regulations that correct such failures—for example, by making pollution costly—are necessary. Often, market failures are due to incomplete *property rights*, where resources are not assigned to an identified owner. Examples include the fisheries in international waters; nonexclusive property rights, where many owners have rights to

---

BOX 1.5
What makes environmental problems different?

Environmental problems have several unique characteristics:

■ *Delayed impacts.* Many potential environmental changes have significantly delayed impacts. This argues for long lead times in implementing appropriate prevention or mitigation actions.

■ *Spatial impacts.* Sources and environmental impacts are often separated in space (for example upstream/downstream or hills/valleys), making it necessary to have a framework that can address diverse stakeholder interests.

■ *Cumulative impacts.* Individual actions often have little effect on the environment, but the cumulative effect of many such actions can be substantial.

■ *Irreversible damages.* A significant number of environmental outcomes are fundamentally irreversible, and the implications of such changes are hard to predict.

■ *Need for government intervention.* Environmental problems are often a consequence of market failures. Without government intervention to introduce regulations and create markets where they do not exist, the private sector alone cannot achieve optimal environmental outcomes.

■ *Multisectoral links.* Environmental problems reverberate across a range of sectors through many pathways, calling for coordinated policies and concerted efforts.

■ *Regional and global implications.* Many environmental impacts have broad cross-boundary and global effects that require international frameworks and agreements to deal with them.

---

the same resource, such as communal grazing lands; unenforced property rights, where, if resources are stolen or damaged, there are no consequences; and nontransferable property rights, which cannot be sold or leased, as is common for land.

- *Policy failures.* An important reason that prices of environmental goods and services may fail to reflect their value to society is that government interventions often distort these prices. Subsidized prices, for example, often encourage the inefficient and excessive use of resources. Such subsidies are common for energy or irrigation water. In many countries, especially in Africa, government regulations such as export quotas, overvalued exchange rates, and artificially low prices set for agricultural products by state marketing boards have created strong disincentives for long-term investment in the productivity of resources; when the value of an output is low, the value of natural resources used as inputs to its production remains also low.

Addressing these market and policy failures is important for improving the quality of growth. If such failures persist, environmental goods and services will continue to be overconsumed and underprovided, imposing costs on those who depend on such goods, now and in the future. But the effects will also extend much further: infrastructure investments will be different when water and energy uses are subsidized, for example, and the decisions made on such investments will have long-lasting effects on patterns of development. Distorted prices will also direct research efforts to focus on certain crops and agricultural practices and neglect others, limiting the technical options available to future decisionmakers.

Improving incentives in the use of environmental goods and services will have different implications in different cases. In particular, there is an impor-

tant distinction between cases dominated by on-site effects and those dominated by off-site effects:

- In the case of *on-site effects,* resource users already have powerful incentives to address any resulting problems, since they are affected directly. Farmers, for example, tend to have strong incentives to manage the soil of their farms sustainably, as the condition of the soil affects their current and future harvests and hence their livelihoods. The main need in this case is to remove obstacles to the proper functioning of existing incentives. This often involves the introduction of exclusive-use rights.

- Conversely, in the case of *off-site effects,* decisionmakers usually have little or no incentive to address environmental problems, since the consequences do not affect them. Farmers, for example, have no incentive to help protect hydrological flows because others, often far downstream, will enjoy the benefits in improved water availability. In such situations, appropriate incentives need to be created to (a) remove policy-induced distortions that undermine sound resource use; (b) complement market signals with taxes/fees that reflect social opportunity costs, or payments that reflect social benefits; and (c) selectively regulate the remaining externalities.

Establishing an appropriate incentive and regulatory framework requires good governance structures. At least three barriers stand in the way. First, difficult tradeoffs have to be evaluated and choices made. In the high-income market economies, it has taken nearly five decades to agree on and implement policies that dramatically improved local environmental conditions. Even now, many environmental issues remain highly contentious. Second, achieving a more efficient use of environmental goods and services will inevitably impose costs on some members of society. Often, politically influential groups stand to benefit heavily from inefficient use of resources, and they are likely to strongly resist moves to improve efficiency. Powerful elites can manipulate resource use to their own advantage and exclude the powerless and voiceless parts of society from its benefits. Third, "efficiency" is not the only objective. There are many other important social objectives—for example, social equity—and cultural and religious values that may influence the way decisions and choices are made by societies.

Markets can become an essential part of an effective environmental regulatory framework. Market-based instruments that allow flexibility in achieving environmental objectives (such as environmental charges and taxes, pollution offsets, tradable fishing quotas and pollution permits), and mechanisms that harness private initiatives in improving compliance with environmental regulations (such as voluntary compliance measures), have been increasingly important elements of environmental policy implementation around the world.

One of the ingredients in good governance is increased public awareness. People are frequently unaware of the value and importance of healthy and sustainable ecosystems, or of the causes and consequences of environmental damage, including the impacts of pollution on their health. Information about the impacts of unsustainable natural resource use is often in the hands of central agencies, not of the users themselves. Building on indigenous knowledge and empowering local communities to use such knowledge are invaluable in promoting good resource management practices. Women, for example, play an important role in resource management but have little voice or access to information. Thus, meeting the International Development Goal of empowering women is also likely to help improve natural resource management.

Contrary to common belief, it is not necessary to sacrifice the interests of future generations in order to improve the incomes and welfare of those living today. Avoiding such conflicts should be the primary objective of the work to devise and implement better policies and more effective regulatory arrangements. Much has already been achieved, especially in middle-income countries, and progress can be accelerated in all countries as people become more concerned about their environment (see box 1.6). Our efforts must be focused on issues and in places where it is possible to play a catalytic role in supporting positive change.

BOX 1.6
Industrial and developing countries have different perspectives on environmental challenges

The fourth annual *International Monitor* published by Environics International, Ltd. outlines the results of the largest environmental public opinion survey ever conducted, including interviews with some 35,000 people in 34 countries. The survey found that the environmental divide is widening in the world. In industrial countries, most people rate the quality of their local environment as good; in poorer countries, most people rate it as poor.

As this and previous surveys indicate, in wealthier countries people tend to take a longer-term global view of environmental problems, while in poorer countries environmental concerns are more focused on local issues. In half the countries surveyed, particularly in the poorer ones, the majority of people believe that environmental problems affect their personal health a great deal. People are most concerned about the quality of their water and air, and there is growing concern globally about the depletion of natural resources. Majorities of people in nearly all countries, however, think that environmental protection laws, as currently applied, are inadequate.

Source: Environics International, Ltd. 2000.

The quality of the regional and global commons

Many environmental services are global public goods, and their degradation affects people across the world (see box 1.7). Ecosystems and the environmental impacts of development do not respect administrative boundaries. Many pollutants travel long distances and affect people's health and the environment in neighboring countries and regions. The successful pursuit by individual countries of environmentally sustainable development, including poverty alleviation, will ultimately depend on the protection of the global commons, such as climate, the diversity of life, and shared water resources. These commons are being degraded at disturbing rates in many places, indicated by the rapid deterioration of regional and global ecosystems (see WRI 2000).

The management of the world's shared river basins, groundwater aquifers, and large marine ecosystems poses a challenge for riparian and littoral states. The major threats to the health, productivity, and biodiversity of these shared resources come from human activities on land. Some 80 percent of the pollution in the oceans originates from land-based activities. To combat pollution and arrest degradation it is essential for countries to find effective ways of cooperating in the management of these shared resources.

The poorest countries are often the ones that are most threatened by the degradation of the regional and global environmental commons. Climate change is projected to cause significant increases in famine and hunger in many of the world's poorest areas, in part because of decreasing precipitation in many arid and semi-arid areas, especially in Sub-Saharan Africa. It could also displace millions of people from small island states such as the Maldives, and from low-lying delta areas of Bangladesh, China, and Egypt; increase the incidence of vector-borne diseases such as malaria and dengue; and lead to rapid shifts in the distribution and productivity of terrestrial and aquatic ecosystems, resulting in loss of biodiversity and livelihoods.

Loss of biodiversity also poses serious threats for developing countries. Genetic varieties, species, and plant and animal communities have critical uses as food, sources of new crop varieties, commodities, medicines, pollinators, soil formers, attractions for

---

BOX 1.7
Global environmental issues

Global environmental issues fall into one of two categories:

1. *Global commons issues,* which are directly related to the maintenance of major components of Earth's systems, include:

- *Climate change*
- *Ozone depletion*
- *Accumulation of persistent organic pollutants (POPs)*
- *Loss of certain biodiversity elements,* such as migratory species that cross national borders and globally important genetic resources.

To address these issues effectively, all countries need to take coordinated action.

2. *Natural resource degradation at the global scale,* including:

- Most *biodiversity* issues not listed above
- *Degradation of international waters and marine ecosystems*
- *Land degradation and desertification*
- *Degradation and loss of forest resources.*

Although these issues are largely national or regional in nature, the severity of the problem often requires coordinated international action.

tourists, and moderators of climate and hydrology. Loss of biodiversity can thus undermine agricultural productivity both now and in the future, reduce water quantity and quality, and compromise economic benefits from recreation opportunities. In addition, many people consider biodiversity as having intrinsic value, for moral, religious, or cultural reasons. These various values have been recognized in the Convention on Biological Diversity, as well as the more targeted Ramsar Convention on Wetlands. Despite these commitments, the planet is losing species at a rate higher than at any time in its history—an extinction spasm that undermines future options.

These outcomes occur because—in the absence of enforceable international regulatory and incentive systems—individual countries are unable to capture the economic value of conservation and environmental protection measures that generate regional or global benefits. While the benefits of measures to reduce carbon dioxide (CO_2) emissions and protect genetic resources accrue to mankind, the costs of these measures have to be borne locally. Similarly, riparian or littoral countries linked to transboundary aquatic and terrestrial ecosystems are unable to capture the full value of national measures to address resource degradation.

Arresting global and regional environmental degradation therefore depends squarely on international cooperation. Following the UNCED Conference in Rio, now almost 10 years ago, several international conventions were created to promote such collaboration. These agreements cover climate change, loss of biodiversity, desertification, and, most recently, persistent organic pollutants. With the notable exception of the convention to phase out ozone-depleting substances (ODSs), progress in the implementation of these conventions and their resource protocols has been slow. The political, scientific, and technical complexities of the challenge are at the root of this failure.

The great majority of the Bank's client countries, being parties to the global conventions, have committed themselves to addressing the degradation of the global commons. They believe they will suffer, along with others, if insidious trends in global environmental deterioration continue. They face, however, difficult decisions in defining the appropriate level of effort they should devote to global environmental management. In particular, developing countries perceive real and critical tradeoffs (a) between meeting short-term needs for food, water supply, and sanitation services for the poor and investing in environmental management for the medium and long term; and (b) in deciding between allocating expenditures for local and regional pollution abatement or for taking action on global environmental change and its local impacts. Action is also impeded by a lack of adequate institutional, policy, and management capacity to address either short- or long-term environmental concerns. Last, but not least, there is a realization that the impacts of global environmental problems will have a disproportionately adverse effect on developing countries. For example, developing countries are most vulnerable to climate change despite the fact that their contribution to the problem has been small compared to that of the industrialized world. More than 75 percent of the cumulative greenhouse gas (GHG) emissions have been emitted by industrialized countries over the past 150 years, and per capita GHG emissions today are still five times less in developing than in industrialized countries.

Involving developing countries in solutions to global problems is critical. The Bank needs to be ready to assist client countries in their preparations for effective participation in the global conventions and implementation of national programs in support of the conventions' objectives. Bank support for national sustainable development can generate important complementary regional and global benefits. Beyond that, special resource transfer mechanisms have been established in connection with international conventions to help developing countries finance the costs of generating global environmental benefits that are not matched by domestic benefits. The World Bank Group is one of the implementing agencies for two such global financing mechanisms: since 1989, the Multilateral Fund for the Montreal Protocol for the Phaseout of Ozone Depleting Substances (MFMP), and, since 1991, the Global Environment Facility (GEF).

CHANGING GLOBAL CONTEXT

Our strategy is tailored to reflect a rapidly changing global context. Trade and private capital flows have increased dramatically, bringing substantial gains but also making countries vulnerable to events far beyond their shores. The cross-boundary and international character of many environmental issues further accentuates the growing interlinkages between countries. Decisions about such natural resource management matters as forestry, water resources, and the use of nonrenewable energy resources in a single country have far-reaching medium- and long-term implications for whole regions and for the world. These trends pose new environmental challenges but also open new opportunities for environmental stewardship.

Increased private sector role

The relative roles of the public and private sectors are changing, with the private sector taking over many functions that were previously the domain of the public sector. The private sector is becoming a decisive factor in influencing environmental performance and long-term environmental sustainability (see box 1.8). External flows of private resources to developing countries, which have significantly surpassed official development assistance (ODA) during the 1990s, have contributed to this process—especially in the middle-income countries, where these flows have been concentrated.

Partnerships between public and private sectors, particularly for large infrastructure projects, are likely to increase in many client countries, given the availability of private capital and governments' need to reduce their expenditures. As a result of these trends, the investment climate has become a crucial dimension of development. In turn, accountable and effective public sector governance is critical to establishing a favorable investment climate.

Political changes

Decentralization of political and economic decisionmaking to subnational levels opens opportunities for broader institutional change, increased democratization, and participation and a greater voice for civil society. Its desired effects, however, may be constrained by lack of capacity to cope with an increasing set of responsibilities and the existence of unequal power structures at local levels. The spread of democratization, the increasing role of civil society, and increased access to information in the developing world provide channels and mechanisms whereby environmental issues can more easily reach decisionmakers and influence economic and sectoral policies.

Technological change

Rapid progress in science and technology has created opportunities for more efficient and cleaner

BOX 1.8
Corporate responsibility: The triple bottom line

Many corporate leaders now recognize that social development, environment, and growth are not always in conflict. For a variety of reasons—reducing costs, creating new market development opportunities, protecting and gaining consumers, and managing risks—companies are adopting sustainable development as a management framework to build long-term value in line with shareholders' and society's expectations. Commitment to corporate social responsibility moves companies to a triple bottom line of financial excellence, social justice, and environmental superiority. Public information and comparative benchmarking influence consumers, investors, public interest groups, and governments to put pressure on company performance to meet environmental and social standards.

■ *Socially Responsible Investing (SRI)*. Institutional and individual investors are increasingly selecting investments that meet minimum standards for environmental and social criteria. In the United States alone, assets in SRI funds have grown to about $3 trillion. In Europe, enabling legislation, such as the UK requirement that pension funds disclose the social and environmental performance of their bond portfolios, provides a fruitful ground for SRI. As a group, Socially Responsible Investors are active and vocal, frequently organizing internet-based public information campaigns to encourage investors to boycott companies whose actions or investments conflict with the principles advocated by the particular SRI group.

■ *The Global Reporting Initiative (GRI)*, sponsored by the Coalition for Environmentally Responsible Economies and UNEP, seeks to make sustainability reporting as routine and credible as financial reporting in terms of comparability, rigor, and verifiability. Specifically, the GRI's goals are to (a) elevate sustainability reporting practices worldwide to a level equivalent to financial reporting; (b) design, disseminate, and promote standardized reporting practices, core measurements, and customized, sector-specific measurements; and (c) ensure a permanent and effective institutional host to support such reporting practices worldwide.

■ *Product certification*. Product certification efforts aim to create standards and use public information to harness consumer awareness and preferences in support of products produced in accordance with environmental and social standards. Certification standards are now under development or dissemination for forest products, shade-grown coffee, marine fisheries, tropical aquarium fish, and dolphin free tuna, among others.

Source: WBCSD 2000.

production, safer and healthier products and processes, the exploration of new resources, and easier access to information. Advances in information technology have created unparalleled opportunities for a global knowledge network. A challenge for developing countries is to build the human, policy, and institutional capacity to use these opportunities for harnessing their development efforts.

Population growth and demographic changes

In parallel with these relatively new trends are others of long duration. Global population continues to grow rapidly, despite recent reductions in fertility, and is expected to reach 7 billion in 2013, 8 billion in 2028, and 9 billion in 2054. The bulk of this growth will occur in developing countries. Africa alone will grow from 0.8 billion currently to 1.8 billion in 2050, and Asia from 3.6 billion to 5.3 billion. This growth will inevitably increase the pressures on, and the demand for, environmental resources (see box 1.9).

The challenge this growth poses is enormous: agricultural production will need to nearly double in

15

BOX 1.9
Poverty, population, and environment links

Population growth rates are often highest in the world's most sensitive ecosystems, including drylands and tropical forests. The complex linkages between poverty, population, and environmental degradation tend to be most pronounced in regions with the following characteristics:

- High dependence on natural resources for subsistence
- Scarcity of renewable resources such as water
- Vulnerability of soils to rapid degradation
- Inadequate human and social development
- Inequitable access to natural resources
- Limited role of women in social and economic decisionmaking.

Understanding these linkages has to be part of poverty reduction strategies.

Source: UNFPA, UNEP, and IUCN 1998.

the next 30 years, while land is becoming increasingly scarce, and new land taken into cultivation is often marginal compared with that removed by urbanization or due to degradation. Water use grew at more than twice the rate of population increase during the twentieth century, and already many regions are chronically short of water. About one third of the world's population lives in countries experiencing moderate to high water stress, partly resulting from increasing demands from a growing population and human activities. By 2025, as much as two thirds of the world's population is expected to be under water stress.

In terms of economic and environmental sustainability, recent analysis emphasizes the challenge posed by high population growth (Hamilton 2000). It is estimated that in some 50 countries, the rate of growth of total wealth is less than the growth rate of population—a clear indication of unsustainable development.

Population, poverty, and environmental degradation are inextricably linked. A significant proportion of high infant and child mortality (especially under-5 mortality) is caused by environmental factors. High infant and child mortality are linked to higher fertility because mothers bear more children to ensure that at least some will survive. With many children, however, poor families have difficulty investing in education and proper nutrition. In developing countries that have implemented effective family planning programs and have increased their child survival rates and educational levels, fertility rates have declined. Lower fertility rates and smaller families, in turn, can free women to take part in other activities.

Besides population growth, there are important demographic changes that shape environmental and development agendas. One of these is rapid urbanization, particularly in the poorest regions of the world. Major cities are home to more than 50 percent of the world's population today, compared with only 14 percent in 1900. Urban areas have become the engines of economic growth, but have created growing environmental concerns. Environmental services, institutions, and policies have been often failing to keep pace with rapid urbanization. As a result, many cities in the developing world are characterized by inadequate and deteriorating infrastructure, high levels of air and water pollution, slums, and poor waste management. These issues pose considerable health damage and economic costs, which often outweigh the costs of prevention or mitigation.

GREATER SCOPE FOR MARKETS WITH EFFECTIVE PUBLIC REGULATION AND OVERSIGHT

In today's world, so strongly characterized by globalization and the widening reach of the private sector, the rationale for public action is stronger than ever. The public sector has traditionally played an important role as a steward of the environment and natural resources. This role is closely linked with the special properties of environmental issues, especially the existence of extensive market failures arising from the public goods nature of many environmental benefits and services, from externalities such as pollution, and from the cross-sectoral, cross-boundary, and global nature of many environmental issues.

Traditionally, the public sector has controlled the exploitation of natural resources—forestlands, subsoil minerals, and oceanic resources in coastal areas—as the owner of such resources and has provided environmental infrastructure services through state-owned utilities. Recognizing the opportunities for improved efficiency and financial sustainability through the private provision of environmental services and private management of resources, governments recently have been moving away from a role as owner and provider to one of regulator and enabler.

The role of governments, however, remains especially important in establishing a policy, regulatory, and institutional framework for sustainable resource management and environmental performance. Governments play a key role in introducing mechanisms for addressing environmental externalities and cross-sectoral and cross-boundary environmental issues. They can regulate the management of open-access resources such as fisheries by, for example, issuing individually tradable quotas. The protection of downstream users through better upstream management of a watershed involves large transaction costs and can be managed best by public authorities. For example, public authorities could develop systems of payments for environmental

services to compensate upstream users for providing these services. Governments can also facilitate public access to environmental information and participation in decisions affecting the environment. An emerging area for public authorities involves creating markets for environmental services through regulation and the development of new mechanisms, such as carbon sink funds, green certification, and ecotourism.

In parallel with the changing relative roles of the public and private sectors, the ongoing decentralization of regulatory functions from central to local government levels worldwide has increased the need for local government involvement in many areas of environmental regulation, and enhanced the role of civil society in influencing decisionmaking. The new challenges created by decentralization for effective environmental regulation and management at the local levels deserve special attention in capacity building efforts.

Traditional command-and-control regulations and enforcement are often expensive and institutionally unfeasible. Therefore, a wider range of policy tools is needed to complement traditional regulatory instruments; examples include methods that encourage self-regulation and greater environmental responsibility in the private sector, such as increased disclosure requirements and assurance-based compliance programs. Market mechanisms often encourage the private sector to achieve the same goals as under regulation, but often cheaper and in a shorter time. Environmental regulation, therefore, must harness the role of markets and the private sector to support sustainability.

Even with improved incentive structures, there will always be a need for regulation and enforcement. The private sector typically responds fastest to regulatory measures that threaten its license to operate. Empty threats in the form of regulations that cannot be adequately enforced send a counterproductive message. Enforcement has to be consistent to create a level playing field; it has to promote good operating practice; and it has to provide a predictable environment for investment. The so-called "80:20 rule of environmental regulation" holds true even in the best-governed countries. This rule suggests that if it is possible to get 80 percent volun-

tary compliance with environmental laws and standards, then an effective regulatory agency can take action against the 20 percent who do not comply. An active civil society and a changing culture of corporate responsibility in the private sector have been important in improving compliance and contributing to positive environmental change. The Bank's Environment Strategy will reinforce these positive developments.

Chapter 2

Lessons from World Bank Experience

The World Bank's environmental agenda has evolved gradually. The main focus in the 1970s and 1980s was on safeguards—on mitigating the potential environmental damage associated with projects, especially those that financed physical investments in infrastructure, energy, and agriculture. Gradually, a more comprehensive and positive agenda has developed. The Bank's views on environmental sustainability were comprehensively expressed in the 1992 *World Development Report*, which highlighted key environmental challenges and provided a framework for the integration of environment and economic development. Our environmental agenda has also been influenced by our mandate of helping to implement global environmental agreements and special financing mechanisms. This chapter describes our experience in these three key areas—safeguards, the integration of environment into development assistance, and global environmental issues. It then summarizes lessons learned building on the review of the Operations Evaluation Department (OED), and outlines how we can best assist countries in meeting their environmental goals (OED 2001).

SAFEGUARD POLICIES AND PROCEDURES

The Bank has 10 key safeguard policies, and the entire project pipeline is subject to systematic screening as a standard requirement of the project preparation and approval process.[1] The overarching objective of the safeguard system is to support the development efforts of our client countries in a manner that is environmentally and socially sustainable. The World Bank's environmental and social safeguard policies and procedures provide guidelines for staff in identifying and preparing programs and projects. They serve as an important tool for integrating environmental and social concerns into the design and implementation of Bank-supported activities and promoting sustainable development objectives. Nine out of the 10 safeguard policies also apply to IFC and MIGA. Because of the private sector orientation of these institutions, OP/BP 7.60 on Projects in Disputed Areas does not apply to them. IFC and MIGA policies also include a Policy Statement (dated March 1998) on Child and Forced Labor. Environmental assessment in IFC and

MIGA is guided by their respective Environmental and Social Review Procedures, which turn the principles of OP/BP 4.01 into specific requirements. For further details on IFC and MIGA, see annexes G and H.

Our safeguard policies reflect the principles of international and regional environmental agreements signed by client countries. The policies complement national and local laws, and procedures concerning environmental and social issues, as well as national requirements for environmental assessment. The safeguard policies were not developed as an integrated set of procedures however, and this can present a challenge for interpretation and application. Nevertheless, they share complementary objectives, and their underlying principles provide a sound basis for supporting development activities. They have become internationally recognized references and are often used as benchmarks for the development of national environmental assessment systems in developing countries. In addition, many other development organizations and client countries make use of the Bank's *Environmental Assessment Sourcebook* and the *Pollution Prevention and Abatement Handbook 1998* (World Bank, 1999b) as key references in undertaking their environmental work.

Progress made in applying environmental assessment

Environmental Assessment (EA) has been a key instrument in helping the Bank and our clients to incorporate environmental and social aspects of proposed investments into the decisionmaking process. EA provides a mechanism for evaluating the overall environmental and social soundness of proposed projects, assisting in the evaluation of alternatives to the proposed project, and setting out mitigation and monitoring actions to ensure project

sustainability. The Operational Directive on Environmental Assessment (OD 4.01), issued in October 1989, mandated a systematic screening of all proposed projects and preparation of an environmental assessment for projects that might have significant negative impacts on the environment.[2] Subsequently, Operational Directives were updated and converted into Operational Policy/Bank Procedures (OP/BP) format, and a number of additional policies were added to further protect specific aspects of the environment, potentially vulnerable populations, and physical cultural property. These new policies reflect the continually broadening scope of the safeguard approach, from an evaluation of potential physical, biological, and socioeconomic impacts using the environmental assessment process, to inclusion of complementary instruments such as resettlement plans, indigenous peoples' development plans, and pest management plans.

With the exception of occasional project-specific problems, the scope of coverage and the quality of application of the safeguard policies at the project level have gradually improved over the past two decades. Between 1990 and 2000, 210 projects required full environmental assessment (category A), and another 1,006 required less comprehensive environmental reviews (category B). The share of category A projects varied between 4 and 24 percent of the total annual lending volume, and that of category B projects, between 26 and 43 percent (see figure 2.1). More than 80 percent of lending commitments in six sectors—oil and gas; electric power and energy; transport; water supply and sanitation; mining; and urban development—required environmental assessment or analysis.

Recent evaluations have concluded that Bank projects are usually well designed to avoid envi-

Figure 2.1
IBRD/IDA commitments by EA category,
fiscal 1990–2000

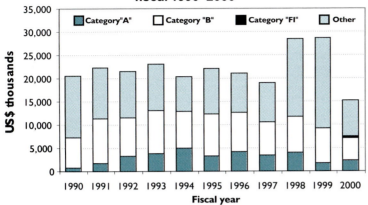

Note: A—lending subject to full environmental assessment; B—lending subject to environmental analysis; FI—lending subject to environmental screening and assessments by financial intermediaries. Other—lending not subject to environmental assessment or analysis.

ronmental damage and have good environmental management action plans (see for example, Goodland and Mercier 1999; World Bank 1997b). According to the quality-at-entry assessment in calendar year 1999 by the Quality Assurance Group (QAG), the EA process for investment lending is now largely mainstreamed, and 90 percent of projects receive satisfactory quality ratings. In many cases, EAs have led to better project design, and environmental management plans have introduced improvements in project implementation, resulting in greater attention to environmental issues in Bank-financed projects. For example, before 1989, 60 percent of Bank-financed urban water supply projects did not consider how the increased use would affect water resources. Today, water supply projects routinely consider sanitation and water pollution problems and look for innovative ways to address them (World Bank 1997a).

In part, improved performance reflects the increased skill of our clients and staff in identifying—through the use of EA and related safeguard-mandated studies—investments that might have significant adverse environmental and social impacts, in advance of project approval and implementation. Equally important, our clients, staff, and partners have acquired experience in using EA as a tool for considering alternatives, consulting with affected stakeholders, and modifying the design of projects to avoid or mitigate harmful environmental effects. In this respect, the experience of working on Bank projects has contributed to strengthening local capacity to carry out EAs and to implement environmental management plans in many countries.

The public consultation and disclosure mechanisms of the EA process have become useful tools for enabling societies to discuss alternative development options and impacts from proposed programs and for helping communities and individuals benefit more fully from development activities. The Bank's performance in following its disclosure requirements has improved significantly over time.

EA is only one element of a larger environmental management system used by the Bank and its borrowers to both "do no harm" and promote good environmental management. The implementation of safeguard policies depends on the regulatory, institutional, and incentive frameworks established by environmental legislation in countries where projects are planned, implemented, and operated. In this respect, the Bank has assisted many countries over the past decade in introducing environmental policies and procedures, including the introduction and strengthening of national EA capacity. In the framework of the Environmental Management Capacity Building Project in India, for example, we are working with the Ministry of Environment and Forests to strengthen implementation of India's Environmental Impact Assessment (EIA) policies. Similar actions are under way in the Mediterranean region as part of the Mediterranean Environmental Technical Assistance Program (METAP), which is jointly funded by the World Bank, the European Commission (EC), the European Investment Bank (EIB), and the United Nations Development Programme (UNDP). (See box 3.3 in chapter 3.)

Notwithstanding improved capacity building, the increasing costs of adhering to these safeguard policies during project preparation and implementation have become a concern for both the Bank and our clients. Some are concerned about the chilling effect safeguard policies could have on complex development projects, particularly in currently sensitive sectors and areas. There is a perceived rigidity in policy application despite the flexibility built into policy guidelines. There is room for enhancing the benefits and development effectiveness of safeguard policies and reducing the costs by helping strengthen countries' own safeguard systems and implementation capacity beyond individual projects financed by the Bank.

Experience also indicates that the costs and the time required for the preparation of EAs and other related safeguard studies can be reduced by identifying these issues at the earliest phase of program or project development and fully integrating the studies into the overall planning, review, and decisionmaking process. This approach also reduces implementation costs for compliance, since concerns are directly factored into the decisionmaking and design process rather than being added on. The

main challenge in this area is to introduce at the earliest possible stage of the project the safeguard policies and related national requirements used both by the Bank and cooperating countries. Measures to support more cost-effective and more timely preparation of safeguard-policy-related studies and their implementation within projects is an area that should continue to be a focus of attention for the Bank and our clients.

Areas for further improvement

Early attention to environmental issues. EAs are now routinely used at the project level by the Bank, its clients, and its partners. It has been much more difficult to address environmental and social concerns when strategic decisions are being made at the sectoral and program levels. EA is often narrowly viewed as something to be carried out only after a development option has been selected and a project is under preparation. A 1996 OED review found that many of the EAs prepared for Category A projects did not adequately consider alternative designs and technologies and that the EA process was often started too late to have sufficient influence on the decisionmaking process (see figure 2.2 for a description of the way upstream environmental input and safeguard issues are integrated into the Bank's decisionmaking and project cycle). This problem is not unique to the Bank or its clients. The recognition that better environmental outcomes can be achieved at lower cost by integrating such concerns at the planning and design stages has spread slowly throughout the world. This recognition has led to an increased use of EAs at the strategic level (strategy, program, region, and sector, for example), complemented by project-specific EAs or related types of environmental planning and management actions, so that decisionmakers can evaluate development options and alternatives in a

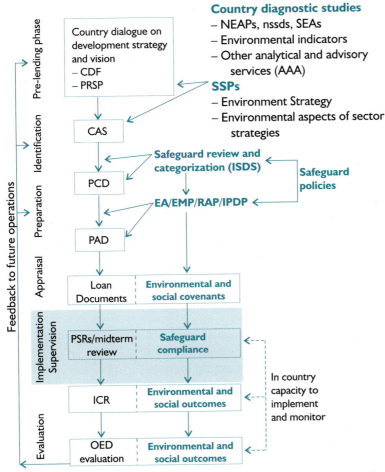

**Figure 2.2
Environmental and safeguard input into the Bank's decisionmaking and project cycle**

Note: EA: Environmental Assessment, EMP: Environment Management Plan, ICR: Implementation Completion Report, IPDP: Indigenous Peoples Development Plan, ISDS: Integrated Safeguard Data Sheet, PAD: Project Appraisal Document, PCD: Project Concept Document, PRSP: Poverty Reduction Strategy Paper, PSR: Project Supervision Report, RAP: Resettlement Action Plan, SEA: Strategic Environmental Assessment, SSP: Sector Strategy Paper.

during supervision is generally weaker than compliance during preparation. In fiscal 1999-2000, 86 percent of projects received at least a satisfactory rating for supervision, compared with 90 percent for preparation. Problems during project implementation are usually due to inadequate performance in undertaking agreed mitigation, monitoring, and institution-strengthening actions. Problems also arise when project designs are adjusted in the course of implementation and safeguard policy issues are not adequately reexamined. The relative weaknesses in implementation of environmental action plans and delays in addressing the environmental and social aspects of project implementation have been attributed to weak borrower commitment and capacity, and to inadequate allocation of resources for su-

more comprehensive manner. A recent review revealed that during fiscal 1997-2001, more than 20 Strategic Environmental Assessments (SEAs) or strategic analyses have been completed in connection with Bank projects in the transport, water, urban, and energy sectors (Kjorven and Lindhjem 2001). The application of SEAs in client countries is also evolving, with encouraging examples, as in South Africa and Central Europe.

Increased emphasis on supervision during project implementation. Implementation of safeguard policies

pervision. Addressing this problem also requires careful evaluation of client countries' commitment, access to resources, and skills needed to undertake the agreed environmental and social actions during the project implementation process.

Consistency in the application of safeguard policies. Assessments by the Quality Assurance Group have highlighted weaknesses in the systematic application of the safeguard policies. Problems in the implementation of policies have also been linked to perceptions, by staff and management, of ambiguities in the scope, intent, and requirements of the policies (World Bank 2000f). Management is addressing these issues through a number of mechanisms, including the conversion and clarification of policies, as well as management accountabilities. A major implication of new lending instruments will be an expanded need to increase country capacity and to develop new types of monitoring approaches for Bank supervision of the application of safeguard policies.

Emerging challenges

Developing an integrated safeguard system. Within the Bank, the application of the various environmental, social, and legal safeguard policies as an integrated suite of measures for promoting project

quality and ensuring compliance is still evolving. The challenge of developing an integrated safeguard system has been recognized by the Bank and its clients. Staff from the Bank's Environment, Rural, and Social Development Networks and its Legal Department are working together in the Quality Assurance and Compliance Unit (QACU) of ESSD to provide critically needed bridges between their respective types of safeguard expertise.

Responding to a changing lending profile. The ongoing shift in the Bank's lending operations to include an increased emphasis on policy and programmatic lending, use of innovative instruments, and the expansion of Community Driven Development (CDD) poses new challenges and opportunities for safeguard policies (see box 2.1). It shifts attention from safeguard application in the context of indi-

BOX 2.1
Community Driven Development: The challenges of acting locally

The World Bank has increasingly been working with communities, empowering them and assisting them to steer their own course of development by defining their own priorities and managing their own resources. This Community Driven Development (CDD) approach creates new challenges and opportunities for mainstreaming the environment. It provides the opportunity for those most affected by environmental degradation to take charge of reversing it for their own benefit.

Given that most resource management decisions are ultimately made at the local level, CDD is likely to play an important role. Working at this level poses many challenges, however, including the complexities of establishing or assisting local institutions. Capacity building is important but must take different forms than in the more traditional case of strengthening institutions such as ministries.

CDD is most likely to play a useful role in addressing environmental issues when both their causes and their effects are found within the communities involved, as may be the case, for example, with management of communal forests or pastures. CDD is less likely to be useful where the consequences of degradation are felt elsewhere—for example, land use change within the community that affects waterflows downstream—although the institutions created for CDD could help in broader efforts to address these problems.

CDD should not be seen as a panacea. An important question is how safeguard principles are to be applied under this approach. Under CDD, environmental issues must compete directly with the many urgent short-term needs and priorities identified by communities. Thus, we need to develop an approach that builds on the positive linkages between empowering communities to manage their resources and practicing due diligence in protecting the environment from undue harm.

vidual projects to entire sectors and sub-sectors. It requires a stronger focus on assessing and strengthening country capacity to systematically implement proper safeguards.

Expanding coordination with partners on safeguard policies. Use of EA and other safeguard policies and instruments can be enhanced by expanding coordination and cooperation with our development partners from other international financial institutions, donor organizations, export credit agencies, and the private sector. The IFC is coordinating an effort to map the environmental and social safeguard procedures and practices of international finance institutions, and the Bank continues to be engaged in regular meetings of multilateral development banks with the aim of better harmonizing their environmental assessment practices. Measures that support the use of common approaches to EA and other types of studies enhance their utility in decisionmaking, improve their quality, increase the efficiency of consultants and other specialists, and reduce the cost and time of studies. Development of coordinated approaches to safeguard policies at the institutional and/or project level avoids conflicts over the nature and extent of analysis, proposed mitigation measures, procedures for consultation, and disclosure of information.

INTEGRATION OF ENVIRONMENTAL CONCERNS AND ECONOMIC DEVELOPMENT

Beginning in the late 1980s, the Bank saw the need for a more proactive approach to addressing the pressing environmental challenges of development. Such an approach required a focus on identifying key environment-development linkages and environmental priorities; building capacity in client countries to develop strategies, policies, institutions,

and a regulatory framework for environmental management; and providing assistance to improve environmental conditions and management practices in a range of areas.

Setting environmental priorities

Analytical work: Making it timely and relevant. Country-specific, thematic, and regional environmental studies and strategies have been prepared in many areas (see the bibliography for a selected list) and have been essential in shaping the Bank's portfolio and policy dialogue. A recent management review of analytical work, however, notes an overall decline of such work in the Bank and points to particularly disturbing statistics in the environment area. According to the report, environment is one of the two areas in which analytical work is most outdated. During 1995–99, analytical work less than five years old was available for only 14 percent of countries (World Bank 2000b).

Focus-group discussions with environmental experts reviewing past experience indicate that analytical work can have a significant impact on client countries' policies and investment decisions particularly when:

- Environmental issues are part of a major national priority and the costs of inaction are recognized, as was the case with projects to reduce salinization in irrigation schemes in Central Asia and to improve water resource management in China, the Middle East, and North Africa
- Environmental issues are a key part of a larger Bank intervention with strong country interest, as was the case with environmental issues in the EU accession countries
- The Bank team and key counterparts in the country have a shared view of and interest in the objectives of the study

25

■ Local counterparts collaborate in the study, have a high capacity to absorb, internalize, and disseminate its findings, and are able to influence public awareness and policymaking.

Experience has also shown that analytical work funded by external sources, such as trust funds, has a serious impact only if sufficient Bank resources are allocated for managing, discussing, and vetting the work and linking the results with policy dialogue and lending operations.

National Environmental Action Plans: The need for local participation and ownership. The Bank has supported the preparation of environmental strategies and National Environmental Action Plans (NEAPs) to identify countries' major environmental concerns and the principal causes of problems and to formulate policies and actions to deal with the problems. The preparation and implementation of NEAPs also included a variety of technical assistance programs to strengthen human and institutional capacity for policy reform in support of sustainable development.

NEAPs have been successful in raising general environmental awareness among important stakeholders and in creating a framework for discussing the environmental aspects of economic development. In some instances, NEAPs have guided the allocation of domestic and donor financing for environmental purposes. The impact of NEAPs on environmental management capacity, however, has been uneven (see, for example, box A.8 in annex A). The later generation of NEAPs has often benefited from a broad participatory approach. Lessons from The Gambia, Ghana, Madagascar, Mauritius, and other countries suggest that environmental strategies have a better chance for suc-

cessful implementation when a range of stakeholders participates in their preparation.

According to the OED, however, NEAPs have often been supply-driven, without substantial local ownership (OED 1997), and they did not succeed in stimulating the integration of environmental considerations into economic and social decisionmaking and policy reforms (OED 1996). Many governments initiated NEAPs primarily to comply with the requirements of the IDA and of donor countries. NEAPs have generally been considered a product rather than a process that needs to be nurtured and integrated into development strategies. Pressure to accelerate the preparation of NEAPs often reduced local participation and ownership, and the lack of systematic attention to follow-up and implementation constrained their role. A remaining challenge is to build on the experience and achievements of the NEAPs in strengthening mechanisms and capacity in client countries to support sustainability in their development.

Country Assistance Strategies: Integration of environment into the process. To date, the recognition of environmental aspects has been uneven in Country Assistance Strategies (CASs), which form the central instrument for the Bank's development assistance dialogue. The environmental component of a typical CAS is often isolated from the rest of the document, and little attempt has been made to link environmental concerns to the core issues being discussed in the CAS. Many CASs treat environment as a distinct sector—with separate funding, objectives, activities, and so on—rather than as a cross-sectoral theme. Data and indicators relating to the environment and natural resources are generally lacking, as is any analysis of environment and natural resource issues and their linkage to the development process. Reviews of how CASs treated the environment in 1997 and 1999 reveal that there has been little improvement over this period. There are several good examples, however (see, for example, box 2.2).

BOX 2.2
The FY99 Lesotho Country Assistance Strategy

The Lesotho CAS recognizes that rural poverty is linked to the serious environmental problems confronting Lesotho. The CAS makes a clear distinction between the impacts of environmental degradation on the urban and rural poor. Urban problems are linked to health problems, while rural environmental degradation is linked to a decline in income levels. Urban environmental degradation is managed through government programs that upgrade the basic infrastructure of the poor: potable water supply, and sewerage and solid waste disposal.

Rural environmental degradation is viewed as a formidable challenge to poverty reduction in Lesotho and is manifested in severe soil erosion, resulting in diminished soil fertility and crop yields, deforestation, and rangeland overgrazing. The government, with support from the Bank, the EU, and other donors, is developing a comprehensive agricultural sector investment program to address these issues.

Source: Hamilton 2000.

A pilot program on Country Assistance Strategies and the Environment (CASE) has produced several lessons on dealing with the environment and natural resources in the CAS:

- Integrating the environment into the CAS is most successful when there is a strong connection to economic outcomes.
- Environmental indicators are effective in raising the profile of environmental issues with both country teams and national officials.
- In selecting environmental priorities, it is essential to identify linkages between environment

and natural resource issues and other sectors—such as agriculture, infrastructure, and tourism, as well as macro issues such as trade.

An inherent limitation of the CAS is that it is a medium-term document, setting priorities for Bank development assistance for the subsequent three years in individual countries. More recently, the Comprehensive Development Framework (CDF) has provided an opportunity to expand the time horizon of the Bank's and clients' strategy work in coordination with the broader development community.

Lending for environmental activities

Since the late 1980s, the Bank has complemented the application of safeguard policies by supporting projects dedicated to improving environmental conditions and management. The primary focus of these environmental projects has been institutional capacity development, sustainable natural resource management, and pollution management. In addition, as described in greater detail in the next section, the World Bank Group acts as implementing agency for the majority of projects funded by the GEF and the Montreal Protocol (see annexes D, E, F, and I for a more detailed discussion of natural resource management, urban environmental priorities, climate change issues, and links with the GEF program). In mid-2000, the core environment portfolio (excluding GEF and MFMP projects) consisted of 97 active projects with combined lending of nearly $5.2 billion. This constituted 3.4 percent of the Bank's active projects and 2.1 percent of total Bank lending.

Evaluating the quality of lending. OED ratings of the performance of completed projects indicate that the outcome, sustainability, and institutional impact of environmental projects have improved over time. During 1995-98, 58 percent of closed projects had "satisfactory" outcomes; 50 percent were judged "likely" to be sustainable, or better; and 25 percent had "substantial" institutional development impact. These ratings were lower than the Bankwide average ratings for the period, which were 71, 48, and 34 percent, respectively. By 1999-2000, the OED ratings had improved substantially. Seventy-five percent of closed projects received "satisfactory" ratings on outcome (compared with 73 percent Bankwide); 50 percent were rated "likely" or better on sustainability (compared with 57 percent Bankwide); and 50 percent had a "substantial" or better institutional development impact (compared with 43 percent Bankwide).

The Quality Assurance Group has completed three assessments of the quality-at-entry of active Bank projects. The second assessment (QAE2) evaluated nine environment projects, while the third (QAE3) assessed five projects. In these reviews, the quality-at-entry rating for environment projects was 94 percent, second only after the urban sector. Three rapid supervision assessments, however, indicated that supervision quality was lower than the Bank average, with a declining trend.

The core environment portfolio, however, represents only part of Bank lending with environmental objectives. Because environment is not a traditional sector, most "environmental projects" are implemented in a sectoral context (rural and urban development, water and sanitation, transport, energy, and so forth). Since 1992, lending through self-standing environmental projects has gradually shifted toward environmental lending as a component of

sectoral projects. Environmental components are increasing in many sectors, such as agriculture, energy, urban development, and water and sanitation (see figure 2.3).

Responding to the changing role of the private sector. In the past decade, our portfolio has gradually shifted away from sectors where the role of the private sector has increased. This has had important implications for our approach to environmental issues. For example, in the 1970s and 1980s we supported several industrial pollution control projects, often implemented by public enterprises. As our involvement in the industrial sector declined, our approach to industrial pollution abatement has changed from financing investments to facilitating good industrial practices and helping establish the regulatory framework and incentives for improved environmental performance of the private sector. The Bulgaria Environmental and Privatization Support Adjustment Loan, for example, supports the government's efforts to integrate environmental issues into the large-scale privatization of enterprises (see box 2.3).

Involving stakeholders and local communities. Involving key stakeholders in setting priorities and imple-

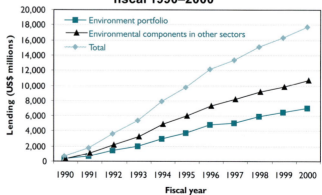

**Figure 2.3
World Bank environmental lending,
fiscal 1990–2000**

Note: Excluding GEF and MFMP lending, shown in figure 2.4. Environment components in other sectors include environmental components in the agriculture, energy, urban development, and water and sanitation sectors.

BOX 2.3
Environmental adjustment lending

The Bulgaria Environmental and Privatization Support Adjustment Loan (EPSAL), approved by the World Bank Board in 2000, is one of the few Bank loans for environmental adjustment lending. The loan provides budgetary support to the government to cover the costs of integrating environmental issues into the large-scale privatization of enterprises (supported by a parallel financial sector adjustment loan). Specifically, EPSAL supports the introduction of an environmental policy, regulatory, and institutional framework; strengthens mechanisms for ensuring that privatized industries will comply with environmental regulations; and introduces a framework for integrating environmental concerns into privatization contracts. It also addresses environmental liabilities, including remediation for past damages.

The EPSAL is a good example of mainstreaming environmental issues, optimizing the environmental benefits of privatization, and harnessing the role of the private sector in pursuing sustainable development.

menting projects has been time-consuming but rewarding in terms of strengthened local ownership and commitment to project objectives. In the natural resource management area, local communities are increasingly involved in the design and implementation of projects (see box 2.4). In Egypt, the Matruh Natural Resources Project helped tribes improve the management of water resources. In Colombia, the Natural Resources Management Program assisted indigenous and Afro-Colombian communities on the Pacific Coast to prepare natural resource management plans and financed the collective titling of over 3 million hectares of land (nearly a third of the land area of the Pacific Coast).

BOX 2.4
Improving livelihoods by better natural resource management in Nepal

Rural livelihood systems in Nepal depend heavily on forest resources for fodder, fuelwood, food, building materials, medicinal plants, and fertilizers. Non-timber forest products also provide a direct source of income and account for up to 50 percent of rural household income in certain areas. Improving the management of forest resources is thus critical for rural welfare.

The *Hill Community Forestry Project* aimed to establish community-based forest management systems to conserve and expand forest resources. It is one of the most successful community forestry efforts in the world. The strategy involved turning over responsibility for management of forest resources to local communities through a program of transfer of rights and benefit sharing, supported by a sound policy and legal framework. The program has already established almost 9,000 forest user groups (FUGs), representing over 40 percent of rural households in the hills of Nepal. To date, usufruct rights over 400,000 hectares of forest have been transferred in perpetuity to local communities, and are now sustainably managed by the Nepali rural poor. Forest regeneration and community investments have improved, and have generated significant income increases through higher production of non-timber forest products, fuelwood, fodder, and timber. The program has also helped improve agricultural production by reducing soil erosion, improving water availability, improving access to credit through user group revolving funds, and micro-enterprise development. The synergies with environmental conservation are also evident: large areas of formally degraded forests have been regenerated, with forest cover increasing by as much as 11 percent in some districts.

The participation and vast cultural knowledge of these local communities made possible the protection of the region's fragile riverine ecosystems and biodiversity. Consensus-building efforts have also been successful in setting urban environmental strategies and action plans; examples include the Metropolitan Environmental Improvement Program (MEIP) and the URBAIR programs. The Mauritania Rainfed Natural Resource Management Project, for example, is financing the first 5 years of a 20-year program to activate a process of natural regeneration of land fertility, rangeland vegetation, and livestock and forest production by encouraging sustainable approaches to resource use (see box D.1 in annex D). This lesson is also supported by work on the water and sanitation sector, which now often includes hygiene education and community involvement.

Supporting capacity development. The lack of effective institutions for environmental management is often an important constraint on achieving better environmental outcomes. In addition to analytical and advisory assistance, support for the development of environmental institutions has therefore been a key area in environmental assistance. Environmental institutional development (ID) projects have been implemented in nearly 30 countries. Successes have been recorded in, for example, the Poland Environment Management Project and the Chile Environmental Institutions Development Project. In many projects, however, practical improvements in the functioning of the institutions concerned have been elusive. The reasons may be traced to familiar weaknesses with technical assistance activities in many sectors. One lesson is that ID projects often lacked a clear focus and encompassed disparate components implemented by a variety of agencies without a common goal and effective coordination. ID projects have traditionally approached capacity development as organizational engineering, focusing on improvements in formal organization and physical improvements. All too often, such projects have sought to build capacity without commitment and to do too much too quickly. As a result, projects may have not been implemented adequately, or gains made during the project may have been rapidly reversed once the project ended.

In recent years, our focus on capacity development has shifted from self-standing technical assistance projects to government agencies toward fostering a constructive relationship between the public and private sectors and civil society, as well as improved collaboration among the members of the development community. We have supported projects aimed at establishing an incentive framework to improve the environmental performance of private companies. In Guadalajara, Mexico, for example, a pilot project tested how large private companies can help their suppliers improve their environmental performance. In the framework of the Chief Executive Officer's Initiative, enterprises holding timber concession over several million hectares in the Congo Basin have set up a structured framework for collaboration with governments and international NGOs to adopt a code of conduct that would hold them accountable for environmental performance. It is likely that this effort will lead to placing over 10 million hectares of the Congo Basin's production forests under independent certifiable sustainable logging within the coming five years. We have supported innovative environmental policy and regulatory approaches in several countries (see, for example, box 2.5).

Through our research and technical assistance activities, we have helped promote the establishment and dissemination of environmental information

BOX 2.5
Assistance to support payments for environmental services

Many of the themes and actions discussed in the Environment Strategy come together in specific work plans, such as that on payments for environmental services. The services provided by many ecosystems, such as the regulation of waterflows provided by forests, are a key dimension of the link between environment and the livelihoods, health, and vulnerability to natural disasters of the poor. Because of market failures, these valuable services are often lost. The World Bank is working with several clients to develop systems of payments for environmental services that would help substitute for these missing markets. A system is already in place in Costa Rica, and work is under way in El Salvador.

This effort is a good example of the complexity of addressing many environmental problems and of the Bank's comparative advantage in helping address them. Establishing a system of payments for environmental services requires both analytical work (to identify and quantify services such as regulation of hydrological flows) and investment projects (to assist client countries in establishing the system of payments). The work is cross-sectoral, touching especially on land management and water issues. It requires close attention to economic incentives and to local social and institutional dynamics, and close participation with a wide range of stakeholders, ranging from large municipalities to small farmers eking out a subsistence living on the steep slopes of upper watersheds. It involves a mix of site-specific characteristics and lessons that are applicable in a range of countries.

disclosure programs such as PROPER—Program for Pollution Control, Evaluation, and Rating—in Indonesia. Based on the positive results in Indonesia, a PROPER-type program (ECOWATCH) was established in the Philippines in 1997, and additional programs are under development in China and Vietnam, also with World Bank support. The Ghana Environmental Resource Management Project developed a strategy for increasing public awareness of environmental issues with the help of government and NGOs, including the Green Forum for Development, the Wildlife Clubs of Ghana, and the Ghana Wildlife Society. The Madagascar Environment Project supported the training of environmental specialists and the promotion of environmental awareness and education at all levels of Malagasy society. We have also been working on making information on environmental conditions easily accessible. The annual *World Development Indicators* report includes a large number of environmental indicators, which are also available separately in the *Little Green Data Book*. In

Thailand and the Philippines, we have produced *Environment Monitors*, which summarize trends in local environmental conditions and make them available to civil society.

Lessons from environmental lending

The lessons from environmental lending, whether in the form of self-standing projects or components in sector projects and programs, are broadly consistent with the lessons of aid effectiveness (see box 2.6 for a summary of OED's environmental assessment, and annex L for recommendations and the Bank's responses in the Strategy).

The importance of ownership and commitment. Lack of government commitment and "ownership" is often cited as the greatest obstacle to improving environmental management and achieving sustainable natural resource use. While the Bank and other donors often advocate environmentally related reforms and have sometimes linked major budget support operations to them, experience shows that

BOX 2.6
Evaluation of the Bank's past environmental performance

In 1999-2001, the World Bank's independent Operations Evaluation Department (OED) carried out a comprehensive assessment of the Bank's past environmental performance. The assessment concluded that the Bank had made significant progress in safeguarding investments financed by the Bank and in helping developing countries address their environmental challenges. It pointed out, however, that significant challenges remain on both fronts. The report recommended emphasis on three key areas:

- Demonstrating the critical role of environment in sustainable development and poverty reduction, and incorporating environmental objectives into its core strategy and operations.
- Improving the Bank's environmental safeguard policies and their implementation
- Making a shift in the approach to global issues by focusing on local-global overlaps.

Source: OED 2001.

external forces rarely have a real and lasting impact at the policy level. The infusion of external funds may lead countries to follow institutional models that are neither realistically sustainable nor particularly efficient, may cause difficult decisions to be deferred, and may undermine rather than strengthen government ownership and accountability. National environmental institutions become dependent on erratic donor financing rather than sustained public expenditure in support of national policy objectives. Transforming public concern about the environment into political action has been most successful when it has been part of a larger reform, as, for example, in two particularly successful cases of environmental management projects, in Chile and Poland.

Focus on the policy framework. Weak environmental management is often a symptom of poor incentives. Efforts to tackle the symptom will be rapidly undermined if little is done to alter the underlying constraints. Thus, for example, projects to introduce improved water management practices in irrigation may not be successful if the policy framework tends to reinforce the wasteful use of water. Careful thought must be given to how best to sequence policy reforms and investments. A recurring temptation has been to incorporate policy reform efforts into investment projects, but experience has shown that investment projects often make poor vehicles for policy reform. Projects that have focused on either policy reform or specific investments have tended to do better than projects that attempted to do both. On the other hand, environmental projects often lead to policy dialogue and changes in the policy and institutional framework affecting environmental outcomes. Through lending for sanitation in China, for example, dialogue with the central government helped establish nationwide tariffs for wastewater collection and treatment. The example of the Bank's call and support for the phaseout of leaded gasoline demonstrated that positive environmental outcomes can sometimes be achieved without Bank financing by changing policies and building a consensus among stakeholders (see box E.1 in annex E).

The importance of linking environment and development objectives. Environmental interventions that are closely linked with development objectives and local concerns tend to be more successful than those that attempt to pursue pure conservation objectives. A recent OED review showed, for example, that Bank-financed forest projects contributed to poverty reduction and sustainable development in several countries, including Cambodia, China, and India. The same review noted that the conservation-oriented 1991 Forest Strategy was only partially implemented because the Bank was unable to maintain its presence in the forest sectors in countries such as Brazil and Indonesia. The review called on the Bank to integrate forests more closely into its overall mission of reducing poverty and to bring forest strategies into rural development programs.

The benefits of fostering integrated, cross-sectoral analysis and coordination. Environmental interventions have been more successful when they were guided by a cross-sectoral strategic assessment of the most critical environmental problems, their key causes, and cost-effective remedies. Our role in fostering cross-sectoral coordination and involving environmental regulatory agencies in macroeconomic and sectoral policy dialogue is often more effective than self-standing technical assistance loans designed to strengthen environmental management capacity. Lending operations in infrastructure, rural development, forest management, transport, and other sectors have included capacity development components as part of Environmental Management Plans. Because these project components are closely linked with project performance, they generally have more specific performance measures than generic capacity development projects.

Environmental aspects of adjustment lending

The environmental implications of adjustment lending have received increasing attention since the late 1980s. Measures aimed at restoring macroeconomic stability and implementing structural reforms, such as the removal of price distortions and the promotion of market incentives, often produce simultaneous economic, social, and environmental gains. Adverse effects may occur, however, when such reforms fail to take into account market or institutional failures. Trade liberalization, for example, encourages timber exports in forest-rich economies, but unsustainable deforestation may be an undesirable outcome where policy failures leave forested lands as effectively open-access resources.

Policy reforms may have additional—and often unpredictable—long-term environmental effects through changes in employment and income distribution. Adjustment-induced changes often generate new economic opportunities, thereby alleviating poverty and reducing pressures on the environment caused by overexploitation of fragile resources by communities living on marginal lands. However, while growth is an essential element of sustainable development, without an effective environmental regulatory and institutional framework it may intensify pressures on environmental resources. As structural changes take place, a mechanism to assess and strengthen the environmental regulatory and management capacity of client countries is essential.

Conditionality in adjustment lending. Since the mid-1980s, environmental components have been explicitly included in adjustment lending operations, particularly in the energy, forestry, infrastructure and industrial sectors. According to a recent review, the share of structural adjustment operations with environmental conditionality averaged 23 percent in the 1990s. Adjustment operations in the energy, forestry, and water sectors had the highest share of conditions with environmental focus (World Bank 2001a). In the particular case of the forestry sector, a review by the World Resources Institute (WRI) of selected adjustment operations incorporating forest sector reforms indicates that in a few cases—for example, in the forest sector in Papua New

Guinea—the Bank successfully influenced resource management practices. The review concludes, however, that environmental conditionality in that sector often resulted in easily reversible measures, and it has rarely succeeded in addressing the institutional challenges that constrain the implementation of systemic reform (Seymour and Dubash 2000).

A 1999 review of quality-at-entry by the Quality Assurance Group (QAG) showed an increase in the coverage of environmental dimensions, with the share of operations rated "satisfactory" rising in that aspect from 50 percent in 1998 to 77 percent in 1999. Only a small share of adjustment loans, however, included environmental indicators as integral components of their monitoring and evaluation systems. In a few cases, sector adjustment loans were able to draw on previous environmental analytical work to define specific conditionality aimed at improving the environmental performance of the sector. In the case of the Russia and Poland Coal Sector Adjustment Loans, for example, extensive sectoral environmental assessments and parallel technical assistance activities addressed environmental issues. In Indonesia, previous analytical work on environmental issues in the water sector informed the Water Sector Adjustment Loan.

New trends in adjustment lending. Adjustment lending support has broadened over the last two decades from an exclusive focus on short-term macro issues and economic distortions in the 1980s to a wider development approach in the 1990s. This approach includes a complex institutional reform agenda that requires a longer time horizon, greater adaptability, and support for programs owned by the countries. Programmatic structural adjustment loans and credits, introduced in 1998, apply a more comprehensive approach to adjustment operations,

including support to a sustained medium-term program of parallel advisory work, capacity building, institutional reform, and integrated Bank and donor support of a single government program. On the one hand, this trend presents opportunities for environmental improvement by strengthening the linkages between public expenditure, poverty reduction, and environmental quality and by focusing on environmental policy and institutional improvements. It also provides a longer time horizon and greater focus on institutional aspects. On the other hand, good practice suggests a systematic assessment of the environmental aspects of adjustment operations and an increased focus on environmental institutional capacity and interagency coordination.

In 1999, when the Operational Directive on environmental assessment was revised and converted into OP/BP 4.01, sector adjustment loans became subject to its requirements. OP/BP 4.01 requires environmental screening followed by an environmental assessment, as appropriate. The policy applies to all sector adjustment operations for which a Public Information Document was first issued after March 1, 1999. The existing Operational Directive on adjustment lending, OD8.60, will also be updated and converted into an OP/BP format during fiscal 2002.

ADDRESSING REGIONAL AND GLOBAL ENVIRONMENTAL CHALLENGES

Ten years ago, at a time of rising worldwide concern over the state of the environment, we began to help our client countries address regional and global environmental objectives. Our initial role was to act as an implementing agency for two global financing mechanisms: the Multilateral Fund for the Montreal Protocol (MFMP) and the Global

Environment Facility (GEF). Since then, we have multiplied and diversified our initiatives, partnerships, projects, and funding sources in an effort to better help our client countries meet the objectives of the global conventions. Moreover, there has been a slow but growing realization that global environmental concerns, such as long-term climate change and loss of biodiversity, should be addressed as an extension of the local, national, and regional environmental issues that underpin sustainable development. The Environment Strategy offers the opportunity to implement this goal.

Projects and programs for the global environment

A sizable portfolio that directly addresses global environmental concerns has emerged over the last 10 years. It supports efforts by our client countries to contribute to global action to arrest the deterioration of the global commons, such as climate change and ozone-layer depletion, as well as the degradation or loss of biodiversity, forests, water, and land resources, which is proceeding on a scale that gives rise to global concern (World Bank 2000g).

Since 1991, the Bank has committed more than $1.5 billion dollars in combined GEF and MFMP funding, with associated funding of $5.0 billion for climate change mitigation, biodiversity conservation, the phaseout of ozone-depleting substances (ODS), and protection of international waters (see figure 2.4).

The Bank's MFMP program has contributed to the phaseout of more than 70 percent of the total amount of ODS targeted by the MFMP. Success is attributable to the narrow program fo-

cus, the well-defined technical solutions, innovative financing mechanisms, and the streamlining of internal Bank approvals. The GEF program has catalyzed funding for local action in support of global environmental objectives, effectively engaged NGOs and other elements of civil society in the country dialogue on environmental management, and piloted innovative approaches to financing biodiversity conservation and renewable energy development (see annex I for more detail). With access to GEF resources, we have also been able to help riparian countries and stakeholders agree and act on regional environmental priorities, supporting the development and implementation of regional conventions or agreements for the management of a number of international river basins, shared lakes, regional seas, and shared groundwater aquifers. GEF resources have also been successful in catalyzing private sector financing for environmental improvements (see box 2.7).

Because of its focus, the MFMP program has been relatively independent from Bank operations. There are, however, untapped opportunities for GEF to be mainstreamed with Bank operations in the rural (forestry and agriculture), energy, transport, and water sectors. The Bank and the GEF are making

Figure 2.4
GEF and MFMP commitments, fiscal 1992–2000

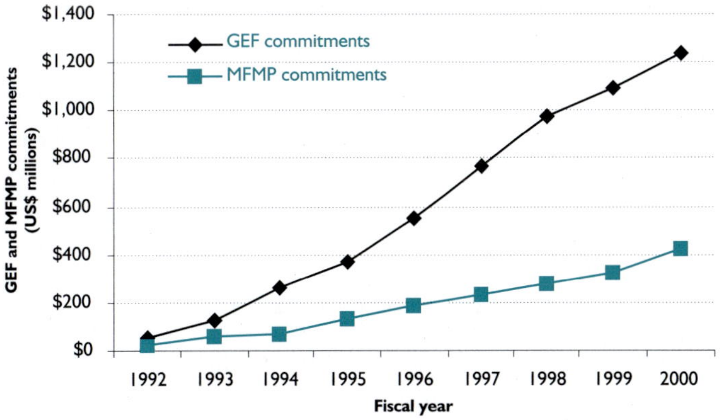

Note: Commitment amounts are based on World Bank management approvals.

35

BOX 2.7
IFC–GEF cooperation

The IFC, with support from the GEF in some cases, has helped create a series of innovative investment funds that support various environmental objectives, including

- The Terra Capital Fund, which invests in private ventures that can sustainably utilize or conserve biodiversity
- The global Renewable Energy and Energy Efficiency Fund (REEF), which is designed to mobilize equity and debt as well as to support smaller and riskier projects
- The Solar Development Group (SDG), which builds on important lessons learned from IFC's SME investment and project development facilities as well as Bank/IFC experiences in solar PV business finance

With access to GEF and other donor resources, IFC has also been able to stimulate additional private sector activity and/or NGO partnerships in such areas as energy efficient lighting, advanced renewable energy technologies or applications, ESCO financing, sustainable forestry, ecotourism, organic agriculture, and carbon finance.

Source: GEF and IFC documents.

progress in integrating GEF resources with Bank lending. The proportion of Bank-GEF projects with directly associated IDA or IBRD funding rose steadily from 23 percent in fiscal 1995 to 65 percent in fiscal 2000. The quality of association, or blending of GEF resources with Bank funding, needs to be improved to better harmonize global objectives with local environmental and developmental objectives (see annex I for a more detailed discussion).

The Bank has been working with GEF (through the International Waters Program), the Global Programme of Action, and other partners to actively support the development and implementation of regional conventions for the management of international river basins, shared lakes, regional seas and, recently, shared groundwater aquifers. It has also undertaken national projects to support the implementation of regional conventions through the control of non-point source pollution from agriculture, coastal zone management, and the conservation of wetlands.

The GEF and MFMP programs complement a significantly larger share of Bank lending targeted toward the conservation and sustainable use of biodiversity, the sustainable use of forests, the management of fresh and marine water resources, and the halting of land degradation. The broader country and sector dialogue and consequent lending indirectly support such concerns. For example, lending for energy pricing reform creates incentives for adoption of climate-friendly technologies. Assistance for agricultural intensification or rural nonfarm employment often serves to reduce pressures on natural habitats and biodiversity. Capacity building for management of local environmental issues will help overcome barriers to addressing global concerns. These impacts need to be better understood and evaluated.

Mainstreaming the global environment in the country dialogue

Continued progress in incorporating global environmental objectives at the project level depends on how well the environment and its global dimension are mainstreamed in the country dialogue. Progress on this front has been mixed. The analysis of CASs completed in fiscal 1999 showed that a limited number addressed local environmental issues of global concern and that GEF activities, although mostly identified, were only in part linked strategically to the CAS objectives. With a few notable exceptions, CASs did not acknowledge a role for the Bank in helping countries address their responsibilities under global environmental conventions.

Although operational policies and sectoral strategies are largely responsive to global environmental objectives, the analytical tools and skills for measuring global externalities and understanding their links to national sustainable development and poverty are not sufficiently available. Improved country sector work focused on the global environment and linkages with local priorities is needed to inform the country dialogue.

Partnerships

The Bank has entered into numerous formal and informal partnerships, which aim to address issues of regional and global importance that cannot be addressed at the country level. These partnerships have provided an important adjunct to the traditional Bank-government relationship by building on the emergence of a vocal civil society and the increasing importance of private sector investments.

In a number of these partnerships, we have played the role of a facilitator to forge consensus between stakeholders on standards of good practice designed to improve the environmental performance of the private sector. Through the CEO Forum on Forests, we have sought to apply the process of inde-

pendent, transparent multistakeholder verification of compliance with forestry management standards that protect the livelihoods of the poor. Under the IUCN/World Bank-sponsored World Commission on Dams (WCD), government, NGO, and industry representatives have laid out key considerations governing the development of dams (see box 2.8). We have also helped catalyze new market mechanisms, as in the case of the Prototype Carbon Fund (PCF), which demonstrates the feasibility of trading greenhouse gas emission reductions under the emerging regulatory framework of the Kyoto Protocol's Clean Development Mechanism (CDM). The World Bank/WWF Forest Alliance was formed in 1998 as a result of both organizations' deep concern about the continuing depletion of forests around the world and the effect of this depletion on many of the world's poorest people. The goal of the alliance is to significantly reduce the rate of loss and degradation of forests of all types. Other partnerships have engaged civil society in implementing projects with significant global environmental benefits. The Critical Ecosystem Partnership Fund, for example, provides small grants to NGOs to manage ecosystem hot spots around the world (see annex K for a list of selected partnerships).

Factors critical to successful partnering include selectivity based on alignment with sectoral strategies; support for the Bank's country programs; realistic expectations of success; and the complementarity of capacity, skills, knowledge, and competencies of partners. In addition, partnering arrangements need to be based on a time-bound commitment (including a budgetary one), evaluation, and an exit strategy. Finally, mainstreaming calls for transparency, communications, and feedback mechanisms to country programs.

BOX 2.8
World Commission on Dams

The Report of the World Commission on Dams (WCD), issued as *Dams and Development: A New Framework for Decision-Making* (November 2000), was the product of an effort to bring governments, the private sector, and civil society together to break the impasse in the dams debate—to review the development effectiveness of large dams and develop a framework for options assessment, criteria, and guidelines to advise future decisionmaking. The Commission concluded that dams had contributed significantly to power and water supply, food production, and flood protection, but that shortfalls in technical, financial, and economic performance had occurred. These had been compounded by significant social and environmental impacts, the costs of which were disproportionately borne by poor people, indigenous peoples, and vulnerable groups—costs that could have been avoided, mitigated, or compensated through better decisionmaking and benefit sharing.

The Commission's proposed framework for decisionmaking is based on five core values—equity, efficiency, participation, sustainability, and accountability. It proposes:

■ A rights and risks approach for identifying stakeholders in negotiating development choices and agreements.
■ Seven strategy priorities for water and energy resources development: (1) gaining public acceptance; (2) comprehensive options assessment; (3) addressing existing dams; (4) sustaining rivers and livelihoods; (5) recognizing entitlements and sharing benefits; (6) ensuring compliance and sharing rivers for peace; and (7) development and security.
■ A set of 26 guidelines for review and approval of projects at five stages of decisionmaking.

The Report provides invaluable reference material. It is an important reference document that the Bank can use to assess dams and discuss these issues with governments and other stakeholders. The Bank is developing and implementing an action program, in response, to promote good practices and support innovations that includes actions in the following areas: (a) work with borrowers in moving upstream, (b) support for institutional reform for more efficient use of water and energy, (c) effective implementation of the Bank's safeguard policies, (d) support for borrowers in improving the performance of existing dams, (e) adoption of a more proactive and development-oriented approach to international waters, and (f) support for innovative approaches for dealing with complex water resources and energy management.

Source: WCD 2000.

THE CHANGING BANK CONTEXT

A changing global context has shaped the Bank and its approach to development. Globalization and the growing roles of the private sector and civil society have altered the role of our traditional main interlocutors—national governments in client countries—but have brought new approaches and new vitality. This shift has been evident during the past decade, in our changing lending profile, instruments for delivering development assistance, and our increased involvement in partnerships with the private sector and civil society.

New strategic approaches

The renewed efforts to fight poverty, the need to respond to a rapidly changing global context, and emerging lessons on development aid effectiveness call for a reinforced effort to focus on the needs and aspirations of client countries by supporting broad-based growth, bottom-up initiatives, openness, and partnerships with stakeholders affected by development decisions. These principles are expressed in the Comprehensive Development Framework (CDF)—a new approach to development assistance outlined by the World Bank and endorsed by the development community (see box 2.9).

BOX 2.9
The Comprehensive Development Framework

The CDF favors a holistic approach to development. It seeks a better balance in policymaking and implementation by highlighting the interdependence of all elements of development—social, structural, human, governance, environmental, macroeconomic, and financial. This approach requires a transition from donor-led development assistance strategies to the development of a country strategy led by a country itself, with vigorous participation by civil society and the private sector and with the support of multilateral and bilateral organizations. The key principles of the CDF are:

- A long-term comprehensive vision
- Ownership by the country
- Partnership with internal and external actors
- A focus on development outcomes.

The CDF is meant to provide a compass—not a blueprint. How the principles are put into practice will vary from country to country, depending on economic and social needs and the priorities of the stakeholders involved.

The CDF builds on lessons concerning development-aid effectiveness such as the need for social inclusion, better governance, and understanding of the cooperative roles of civil institutions, the private sector, and donors. It offers an opportunity to approach environmental challenges holistically, by catalyzing local initiatives, taking a long-term perspective on development, and focusing on coordinated strategies among development partners. These principles require new ways of delivering development assistance. Traditional investment projects remain important, but they are supplemented by new initiatives that can support long-term programmatic approaches, such as Adaptable Program Loans (APLs), Programmatic Adjustment Loans (PALs), and Poverty Reduction Strategy Credits (PRSCs), which support the implementation of Poverty Reduction Strategies Papers.

The Bank's Strategic Framework Paper (SFP) identifies two main pillars of our assistance to clients in fighting poverty: (1) building a climate for investment, jobs, and sustainable growth, and (2) empowering poor people to participate in development. These pillars together embody key elements of sustainable development. The SFP also calls for selectivity (a) *within countries* based on the CDF principles; (b) *across countries,* guided by income, poverty, and performance—focusing on countries where the overall policy environment favors aid effectiveness; and (c) *at the global level,* based on clear linkages to our core institutional objective, our leveraging and catalytic effect, and a balancing of resources and risks.

Finally, this Strategy must reflect important changes in the character of the World Bank Group's activities. It is likely that programmatic and adjustment loans and/or credits and a more comprehensive cross-sectoral approach to development will account for a larger share of Bank lending in some client countries. The boundaries between the activities of the Bank and the IFC in promoting private sector development and financing investments in infrastructure are changing, as Bank projects focus more on supporting structural reforms while the IFC plays a larger role in financing specific investments. These shifts have important consequences for the nature and balance of the activities of the environment community within the World Bank Group.

These changes in the context and the way in which we work must be recognized and incorporated into our Environment Strategy. Improving the environmental dimensions of investment projects—traditionally, the Bank's most important tool—is only part of the solution. We have to improve our analytical work to provide the knowledge base for moving environmental considerations upstream in country and sector programs. New approaches also mean that we need to adjust our tools to ensure that they continue to fulfill their functions. And these approaches must take advantage of the new opportunities created by the active participation of a much broader range of actors.

The need for selectivity

The Bank's environmental activities have to compete for staff and budget with sectors such as health, education, social welfare, and rural development, which more directly address issues of poverty. The expectations of clients, external groups, management, and operational staff are often at odds and greatly exceed what can reasonably be achieved by the Bank in assisting client countries in this area. The response has too often been to adopt overly ambitious plans, programs, and policies and to raise expectations, leading to disappointment with the outcome on all sides.

What external assistance can and cannot do. Part of the gap between expectations and actual performance arises from different assessments of what the Bank can realistically achieve. Much of the external and internal dissatisfaction reflects a belief that the Bank should help developing countries avoid what are now perceived as mistakes made by rich countries and the consequent environmental damage. This belief is reinforced by current knowledge and modern technologies that seem to offer the opportunity for a much less damaging path of development—the "leapfrogging" discussed with such enthusiasm in the literature. It is a mistake, however, to interpret what is happening in our client

countries as a mere rerun of what has happened elsewhere in the past. Each country has to find its own balance between its many development goals and the constraints on development. The Bank and other development agencies may be able to help by providing advice and finance, but the role of outside agencies will always be small in relation to domestic concerns and the broad incentives provided by the external economic environment.

These considerations are important when designing interventions in any sector. Lessons on the development effectiveness of aid have shown that development interventions tend to be successful in circumstances where the client country has a reasonably good policy and institutional environment (Dollar and Pritchett 1998). These general lessons have been confirmed by the experience of development agencies in the area of environment (Ibrekk 2000).

The environment is a relatively new concern for many developing countries and is often seen as a particular concern of rich countries. Environmental institutions within developing country governments are usually new and weak, and their weakness is compounded by the fact that they do not control significant financial resources. Environmental concerns sometimes seem to conflict with the goals of short-term economic growth, partly because the benefits of environmental protection often appear only over the long term and help groups that are different from those who bear the costs. Our lending and nonlending services have to take into account these differences in client capacity and priorities.

Setting priorities for the World Bank. The situation outlined above highlights the hard choices faced by the Bank in allocating its limited budgetary resources. If we get involved in too many issues or prepare too many projects in order to help as many clients as possible, resources become too thinly spread, to the detriment of advice and projects. Environmental projects and programs have to be selective. Although it is important to adhere to the safeguard policies in implementing development projects and programs supported by the Bank, environmental objectives and programs, apart from safeguards, cannot be an important element of every country assistance strategy. They have to depend on an assessment of environmental priorities and capacity, county commitment and interest in addressing them, and the Bank's comparative advantage vis-à-vis other development partners in supporting them.

Our primary commitment is, rightly, to our clients. In the case of Bank loans, clients are government agencies who are ultimately responsible for either repaying or guaranteeing repayment of project funds. In the case of IFC financing and MIGA guarantees, clients are private sector entities. We can achieve our objectives only with our clients' active participation in designing projects and their commitment to implementing them in an effective manner. Our priorities and the focus of our assistance must therefore reflect our clients' concerns and capacity, as well as our understanding of the issues and of effective measures for addressing them.

IDA credits and programs are executed with donor funds. IDA Deputies have consistently emphasized the importance of environmental action, and successive replenishments have seen a growing focus on environmental issues, including the institutionalization of the EA process, the undertaking of NEAPs (initiated in IDA9), and follow-up activities to implement selected NEAP priorities. In the IDA12 replenishment, the Deputies emphasized the importance of greater mainstreaming of environmental sustainability and recognized the challenges of integrating the outcomes of NEAPs and other participatory environmental planning exercises into country dialogue and CASs, and ultimately into lending operations. They recognized the need for continued capacity development over a sustained period of time in many poor IDA countries—through nonlending activities as well as lending operations, where possible—in order to build support for environmental measures and the institutional and regulatory infrastructure to ensure their implementation over time. Capacity development has been important to ensure that resources are effectively used for projects and programs that elicit the commitment of those who will ultimately be responsible for implementing them.

The Bank's comparative advantage as a basis for selectivity

The World Bank Group plays an important role in global development. It is active in policy dialogue, provides lending and nonlending services to its clients, and extends private sector financing and guarantees through the IFC and MIGA. Through its convening power and its capacity to mobilize support and resources from a variety of sources, it can work with many development partners and organizations toward common objectives.

The Bank's comparative advantage in the environment area lies in our ability to leverage policy dialogue, our comprehensive sectoral coverage, our extensive project development skills, and our convening power and global presence. We should use these strengths to:

■ Encourage countries to adopt policies that create appropriate incentives for the proper management and efficient use of environmental and natural resources—for example, by reducing energy subsidies or adjusting taxes that encourage the use of dirty fuels, or by pricing water to reflect its scarcity

- Work across sectors to enhance the environmental benefits of projects and programs that provide access to infrastructure and basic services or promote rural development—for example, by combining good management of water resources with the development of irrigation schemes, or adjusting the design of water and sanitation projects to increase their health benefits
- Help countries develop and implement projects that focus on critical environmental problems that can be substantially improved or resolved through specific investments and policy reforms—for example, by promoting the use of clean fuels for heating to improve urban air quality, or helping to establish schemes that give local populations both the incentive and the means to protect wildlife
- Bring together groups of countries and stakeholders to facilitate the transfer of good practices and knowledge and to tackle common problems and issues of global importance in a coordinated manner that draws on worldwide lessons of experience.

This approach is consistent with the view that we should focus increasingly on the broad goal of sustainable development. It emphasizes, however, a somewhat different perspective. Our strength lies in mobilizing expertise, financial resources, and government commitment to implement specific programs that are designed to achieve clear short- and medium-term goals—for example, improvements in urban air quality. Delivering concrete improvements that matter to local populations can provide a basis for developing a longer-term policy

framework for sustainable development. This approach builds on the skills and role of the World Bank and draws lessons from the evolution of environmental policies in countries that industrialized earlier.

From the point of view of maximizing the impact of our involvement, we should link the level of our efforts to our clients' overall commitment to tackling environmental problems, and specifically to the effectiveness of the counterparts with whom we work. Applying these criteria would result in more Bank involvement in middle-income countries, where analytical and advisory work have established the basis for projects that reflect local priorities and capacity and where there is a strong commitment to address environmental issues as part of the development agenda.

To increase the impact of our activities, we must find ways of working effectively in countries where commitment and capacity are limited or almost nonexistent. In a few cases, this may be achieved by concentrating on very specific environmental concerns that can be addressed in stand-alone projects. Otherwise, the best approach is to work through interventions in other sectors—mainly rural development, infrastructure, urban development, and health—so that environmental concerns are addressed as an integral part of programs to reduce poverty and improve the quality of life.

The need for a cross-sectoral approach

Our experience suggests that confining our approach to environmental issues within a traditional sectoral framework can hinder the adoption of effective solutions to many environmental problems. Projects and advisory services that focus exclusively on environmental institutions and policies will usually have only a minor impact on the key environmental concerns in most countries. Such activities can sometimes be very productive when dealing with narrowly defined concerns—for example, large point sources of pollution or threats to specific natural resources or habitats. But the causes of and solutions to the poor quality of the environment or the degradation of natural resources lie in a combination of incentives, policies, and institutions that arise out of broad economic and social factors. These can only be addressed by working across sectoral boundaries to focus on specific outcomes or goals. For example, improving water management requires an integrated approach, including pricing policies that reflect the social value and scarcity of water; coordination among the competing users of water (including agricultural, industrial, municipal, and recreational users); recognition of the value of the ecological functions of water that support livelihoods and long-term development; and mechanisms for stakeholder participation in decisions affecting the availability and quality of water. This has to be based on a clear set of criteria for environmental sustainability for the water sector, coordination among agencies that deal with urban and rural water supply and, when appropriate, public health interventions.

The difficulty of pursuing a cross-sectoral approach to environmental issues is compounded by the fact that our client countries are organized along traditional sectoral lines, and an integrated environmental management approach presents serious institutional challenges for them and for the Bank as well. Overcoming these difficulties is a long-term challenge.

The need for institutional realignment

There is an ambiguity as to whether environment should be treated as a sector or a theme. The re-

organization in 1996 positioned environment in the Bank as a sector, and introduced country-based programming and budgeting. This organizational framework has provided few incentives for working across sectors and toward outcomes that are influenced by a multitude of interventions in a range of areas. As a result, environment units often pursue their own projects rather than influencing other sectors, and there are few incentives for task managers in other sectors to integrate environmental objectives into sectoral projects beyond the minimum safeguard requirements.

The current allocation of resources is largely determined by the size of new projects rather than by the complexity of issues and risks. This leads to risk aversion and to disincentives to prepare complex but small projects that may have significant environmental benefits. Country-based budgeting provides little opportunity to address complex transboundary environmental challenges in a systematic manner. In the next chapters, we describe how the Environment Strategy proposes to overcome these disincentives and problems.

NOTES

1. The 10 safeguard policies are Environmental Assessment (Operational Policy/Bank Procedures (OP/BP) 4.01), Natural Habitats (OP/BP 4.04), Forestry (OP/BP 4.36), Pest Management (OP/BP 4.09), Involuntary Resettlement (OD 4.30), Indigenous Peoples (Operational Directive (OD) 4.20), Cultural Property (OP/BP 11.03), Safety of Dams (OP/BP 4.37), Projects in International Waterways (OP/BP 7.50), and Projects in Disputed Areas (OP/BP 7.60). These policies are complemented by OP/BP 17.50, on Disclosure of Operational Information.
2. Several safeguard policies, however, existed even earlier: Operational Manual Statement (OMS)

2.32 on Projects on International Waterways (1977); OMS 2.33 on Social Issues Associated with Involuntary Resettlement in Bank-Financed Projects (1980); OMS 2.34 on Tribal People in Bank-Financed Projects (1982); OMS 2.35 on Projects in Disputed Areas (1983); and OMS 2.36 on Environmental Aspects of Bank Work (1984).

Chapter 3

The Strategic Framework

The Bank's mission of lasting poverty reduction requires that development be sustainable. This means that proper attention has to be paid to the social and environmental aspects of development challenges, as set forth in our mission statement: "*To fight poverty with passion and professionalism for lasting results. To help people help themselves and their environment by providing resources, sharing knowledge, building capacity, and forging partnerships in the public and private sectors... .*"

The goal of the Environment Strategy, therefore, is to promote environmental improvements as a fundamental element of development and poverty reduction strategies and actions. The Bank will do this by working with our client countries to set and address their environmental priorities, including those of a regional or global nature, and by supporting sustainability through our operations.

This Environment Strategy outlines the priority actions the World Bank plans to take to work with its clients address the environmental challenges of development. In keeping with the World Bank's mission of reducing poverty within a framework of economic development, the Environment Strategy gives priority to issues where the links between poverty and the environment are particularly strong. Therefore, the Strategy puts the environmental challenge into a local perspective, focusing on people in client countries and the way environmental conditions and resources affect them.

What is required is an approach that focuses on the ways the environment affects people's lives; that takes a long-term view of development and of the environmental factors that affect sustainability; and that considers the cross-sectoral and spatial dimensions of environmental challenges. Our approach builds on:

- *Learning and applying lessons.* The broad goals of sustainable development are well established. This Strategy is not about setting new directions but about improving our effectiveness in making the journey. It builds on the achievements and lessons of our past efforts and those of others, and on feedback from our clients and development partners. It seeks to internalize these lessons, strengthen commitments, and accelerate progress toward integrating environment and development. Given the magnitude of the world's environmental problems, the Strategy focuses on areas where the greatest results can be realized. It is intended to be realistic about what has to be done; about our strengths and weaknesses; about how to utilize available resources to improve our performance; and about the potential for our assistance to have positive development outcomes.

■ *Adapting to a changing world.* Globalization and other trends have been reshaping the world. The Bank has also been changing in response to these trends and learning from our past efforts. It has reaffirmed its commitment to poverty reduction and support for a holistic, client-driven Comprehensive Development Framework (CDF). These same principles must be applied to the Environment Strategy. We should also be prepared to respond to and utilize more programmatic lending approaches and a changing Bank lending profile to promote environmental sustainability. The Strategy has to guide this transition.

■ *Deepening our commitment.* To fight poverty through long-term sustainable development, we have to promote a strategic shift from viewing environment as a constraint on development, or as a separate sector, toward viewing it as an integral part of development. Environment can no longer be only the concern of a small, specialized group. To make a substantial and lasting difference, we must ensure that environmental concerns are fully internalized throughout the Bank.

This chapter focuses on the substantive actions we plan to take; Chapter 4 discusses the institutional realignment necessary to implement these actions.

There is an enormous diversity among the environmental challenges faced by the countries assisted by the World Bank. The specific actions required to assist each country will vary substantially because they will be tailored to national and local needs and priorities. Some of this diversity can be seen in annex A, which outlines the priorities for action in each region. Within this diversity, however, several common themes emerge. This chapter describes these common themes.

OUR OBJECTIVES

The Strategy sets three interrelated objectives: improving people's quality of life; improving the prospects for and the quality of growth; and protecting the quality of the regional and global environmental commons. As described in this section, our main objective is to improve the quality of people's lives—their livelihoods, health, and security—through better environmental conditions. But it is not enough to improve the quality of people's lives today. It is also important to ensure that the use of natural resources today does not undermine the long-term prospects for development and improved welfare in the future. This requires attention to policies, economic incentives, institutions, and social structure—the quality of growth. Finally, the search for solutions needs to go beyond individual countries because deterioration in the quality of the regional and global commons—including shared natural resources and climate change—threatens many developing countries and global ecological balances.

Improving the quality of life

Environmental quality is inextricably linked with the quality of people's lives. It plays a particularly important role in the lives of the poor. It is the poor whose health is most endangered by air and water pollution, whose livelihoods are most affected by the loss of forests and fisheries or by soil erosion, and who are most likely to be at risk from droughts, floods, and environmental catastrophes. Efforts to achieve concrete environmental improvements that make a difference to people's lives must be an integral part of economic development and poverty reduction programs. Our first goal, therefore, is to improve the quality of life by focusing on environmental improvements that affect livelihoods, health, and vulnerability, especially of the poor:

■ *Enhance livelihoods by protecting the long-term productivity and resilience of natural resources and ecosystems.* Because poor people often depend heavily on the productivity and environmental services of natural resources such as land, water, and forests, we will help improve the management of these resources. This means, for example, helping communities form local organizations to manage watersheds and forests; assisting farmers to invest in their land or in commonly held areas; and granting or clarifying property rights. Community Driven Development (CDD) projects and programs provide a framework for supporting such local initiatives. We will encourage and assist the reform of incentive systems that influence how resources are used. This means help in strengthening or establishing property rights, removing government-induced distortions, and piloting new mechanisms, such as systems of payments for environmental services, to deal with market failures. Where our understanding of the linkages between resource degradation and livelihoods is inadequate, we will build the analytical base and institutional capacity to improve natural resource management, and we will help governments design appropriate policies and identify opportu-

nities for interventions to stem degradation in particular areas (see box 3.1 and annexes B and D for more details).

■ *Prevent and reduce environmental health risks.* Environmental factors such as unsafe water and pollution are key contributors to the total bur-

---

BOX 3.1
Improving livelihoods through sound management of micro-watersheds

In Nigeria, a project under development (the Micro-watershed and Environmental Management Project) would support community-managed investments in micro-watersheds in six states within three macro-watersheds: the Niger Trough, the Upper Benue Trough, and the Anambra/Imo Trough. The project would support direct investments at the community level, giving decisionmaking authority to community associations. The investments may include activities to mitigate gully erosion, promote reforestation, or provide basic water supply and sanitation and environmental education.

The project, which is a partnership with a Bank-financed Community Driven Development project, would also provide support to the federal, state, and local levels of government to (a) develop an enabling environment; (b) reduce the potential for conflict among the stakeholders; (c) provide incentives for long-term investments; and (d) develop capacity at all levels for environmental assessments. The project would promote partnerships and collaborative arrangements in wildlife and biodiversity management, including incentives for promoting sustainable use of biodiversity. Direct program benefits are expected to include (a) decreased land degradation in upland areas; (b) reduction of downstream flooding; (c) increased production of fodder, fuelwood, and grasses; (d) increased agricultural productivity on arable lands; and (e) improved management and use of biodiversity and natural habitats. The project places special emphasis on improving the economic and social conditions of women and vulnerable groups.

den of disease and impose significant economic costs, particularly for the poor. Our interventions will focus on cost-effective measures to prevent and reduce environmental health risks. Specifically, we will concentrate on work with clients on reducing people's exposure to indoor and urban air pollution, waterborne diseases, and toxic chemicals (see box 3.2 and box B.2 in annex B). Our activities will include a cross-sectoral assessment of the key sources of environmental health problems; identification of cost-effective solutions in a range of sectors, including water and sanitation, energy, transport, health, and agriculture; and projects and programs designed to achieve specific health outcomes. While mea-

BOX 3.2
The South Asia Urban Air Quality Management Initiative

South Asia remains the only region in the world where extremely high levels of urban air pollution show no sign of stabilization or improvement. Regionwide, urban air pollution is estimated to cause over 250,000 deaths and billions of cases of respiratory illnesses every year. The urban poor are especially vulnerable to the health impacts of urban air pollution.

The majority of policy interventions to date have focused on controlling emissions from road traffic, but the actual contribution from road traffic is not known with any degree of certainty. The South Asia Urban Air Quality Management Initiative is aimed at addressing these issues. Environment, energy, and infrastructure staff in the Bank are developing the strategy, in partnership with client countries and other donors. The strategy is aimed at supporting the regionwide process of developing and adopting cost-effective and realistic policies and efficient enforcement mechanisms to reverse the deteriorating trend in urban air quality in South Asian countries, and particularly to reduce the ambient concentrations of fine particles (the most serious threat to public health in the region).

suring the health outcome of individual interventions is often not feasible, it is important to establish the pathways of impacts and use proxies to measure progress. Because our main objective is to improve health outcomes, we will establish baselines and monitor trends in environmental health indicators when feasible. In addition to avoiding much human suffering, these measures will also reduce the high costs borne by many countries for expensive curative measures (see annex C for more details).

■ *Reduce people's vulnerability to environmental hazards.* Millions of poor people are vulnerable to natural disasters and environmental hazards. Climate change, which is predicted to increase the frequency and severity of such events, may further increase the vulnerability of many poor countries and areas (see annex F for more detail). Our environmental interventions will aim to reduce this vulnerability by assessing the impacts of natural disasters, supporting upland resource management and payments for environmental services, improving weather forecasting and the dissemination of weather-related information, providing information to the poor about the risks they face, and stabilizing hillsides and coastal zones. As in the case of environmental health risks, these measures will also help lessen the vast burden imposed on developing countries to repair the damage caused by natural disasters.

Improving the quality of growth

The sustainable management of man-made environments and natural resources—forests, land, and water—is an essential condition for long-term economic growth and lasting improvements in people's well-being. Sustainable economic growth depends on the effectiveness of government policies, regulations, and institutional frameworks. The importance of an appropriate policy environment that creates a climate conducive to investment has become even greater as the role of the private sector has expanded.

Recognizing the important changes in the respective roles of the public and private sectors, our interventions will focus on the environmental policy, regulatory, and institutional framework on the one hand, and on the role of the markets and the private sector in supporting sustainable development on the other. We will:

■ *Help improve the policy, regulatory, and institutional frameworks for sustainable environmental management.* Our interventions in this category will (a) assist client countries improve their environmental policy, regulatory, and institutional frameworks at the national and sub-national levels to ensure that their natural resources are effectively managed and that people's health is protected from environmental factors; (b) support client countries in strengthening their environmental assessment (EA) systems and practices including analytical and technical support for moving environmental assessments to earlier stages of decisionmaking (see box 3.3); (c) reinforce the positive role of markets and the environmental benefits of sectoral and macro-economic reforms, such as those affecting energy or water prices, property rights, fiscal and trade reforms, and resource management; and (d) support better governance, increased transparency and access to environmental information, public participation in decisionmaking, and environmental education in client countries. The Bank has a strong comparative advantage in this area because of its long-term dialogue with client countries and involvement in investment

BOX 3.3
Strengthening national EA capacity:
The METAP experience

To improve the business climate while achieving sustainable economic development, clear and transparent environmental rules, regulations, and legal liabilities are needed. In 1998, METAP initiated an Environmental Assessment (EA) Institutional Strengthening project, through the World Bank's Development Grant Facility (DGF), to assist Mediterranean basin countries in acquiring the necessary technical and policy tools to establish credible and operational EA systems. EA systems in Albania, Croatia, Egypt, Jordan, Tunisia, Turkey, and the West Bank and Gaza were assessed, and the results were used to define specific action plans to improve national EA systems and to increase their coherence with international norms and World Bank and EC environmental guidelines. A second phase, initiated in 2000, established an EA Center in Tunisia; extended the assessment of EA systems to Algeria, Morocco, Lebanon, Syria, and Yemen; undertook collaborative workshops; and established a network of EA directors. A third phase of the project is now envisaged to test the feasibility of establishing full compliance with World Bank EA procedures so that responsibility for overseeing the EA process can be shared with national governments in selected countries. This third phase would also build capacity to carry out strategic impact assessments and to assess the implications of international trade for the environment.

programs and projects; its ability to transfer experience from other developing countries; and its work with development partners.

■ *Support environmentally and socially sustainable private sector development.* The private sector is becoming a major player in many areas previously controlled by the public sector, including environmental issues. The Bank will play a key role in helping our clients improve the investment climate, so as to enhance investor confidence and stimulate private investment. As part of this effort, we will work to support incentives and programs that encourage the private sector to become a driving force in sustainable development. Increasingly, it is recognized that environmental sustainability improves competitiveness. As part of the World Bank Group, the IFC and MIGA will promote, through their investments and guarantees, environmental and social responsibility and good environmental management practices in the private sector. IFC will also invest in environmentally friendly private sector operations (see annex G for more details). The World Bank will take a strategic approach toward addressing the environmental aspects of programs supporting private sector development, such as environmental issues in privatization programs. We will facilitate partnerships between the public and private sectors and civil society to resolve environmentally sensitive issues and agree on benchmarks for good environmental management. A critical part of this agenda is to identify those areas in which a strong public sector role—for example, through regulation—remains indispensable.

Protecting the quality of the regional and global commons

The degradation of regional and global environmental resources can constrain economic development. It often disproportionately affects developing countries and poor people. Addressing such issues requires international policy dialogue and action to resolve conflicting views and interests.

As noted in the preceding chapters, the Bank has accepted the mandate to help client countries address the objectives of the international environmental conventions and their associated protocols, including the conventions on climate change, ozone, and biodiversity. It provides this assistance in its role as implementing agency for the financing mechanisms of these conventions, including the

Global Environment Facility (GEF) and the Multilateral Fund for the Montreal Protocol (MFMP). In moving the Environment Strategy into implementation, we remain fully committed to these obligations. Similarly, through our continued work under the Prototype Carbon Fund (PCF) and other ongoing programs, we will be able to help client countries prepare for their effective participation in the Climate Change Convention and in proposed carbon markets through instruments such as the Kyoto Protocol's Clean Development Mechanism and Joint Implementation Initiative.

Recognizing the potential synergy between local, regional, and global environmental management, we will seek ways to improve the quality of the regional and global commons, principally through interventions that simultaneously bring local benefits to developing countries (see box 3.4). Together with WRI, UNEP, and the GEF, the Bank is supporting the Millennium Ecosystem Assessment to improve our understanding of the state of global ecosystems and links with development. (Box 3.5 provides background on the Millennium Ecosystem Assessment and the related activities of the Intergovernmental Panel on Climate Change.)

Our experience has shown that interventions with regional or global environmental objectives can only be effective if such programs take into account the development needs, local priorities, and constraints of countries and communities. Going beyond the complementarity between national and global benefits will require compensation from the global community and its financing mechanisms, such as GEF and MFMP. Accordingly, our global environmental interventions will build on the following five principles:

- *Focus on the positive linkages between poverty reduction and environmental protection.* Many in-

BOX 3.4
Linking local and global benefits: Energy efficiency projects in China

Local environmental benefits are a primary motivating factor for China in pursuing global climate change mitigation activities such as energy conservation, fuel switching, and renewable energy development. Industrial boilers, not including electric power boilers, account for some 30 percent of total coal consumption in China and together with small furnaces are responsible for some 45 to 50 percent of local air pollution impacts. The *WB-GEF Fuel Efficiency Boilers Project* is transferring advanced, efficient, and cleaner international industrial boiler technology to China, which will dramatically lower the energy requirements of China's coal-fired boiler industry. For instance, the project is supporting "fluidized-bed combustion" boiler technology, which improves fuel efficiency and can lower sulfur emissions by 75 to 95 percent. The project also supported the transfer of advanced particulate control technologies to reduce particulate emissions and improve local air quality. Overall, the project is providing financial benefits by lowering the energy requirements of boilers, improving local air quality by reducing sulfur and particulate emissions, and lowering global CO_2 emissions in a cost-effective way.

terventions designed to reduce poverty by improving local environmental quality and sustainable natural resource management will also provide regional and global benefits. Our Strategy focuses on these areas of overlap. For example, community-based forest management projects can support sustainable livelihoods while reducing forest loss and preserving biodiversity and carbon sinks.

- *Focus first on local environmental benefits, and build on overlaps with regional and global benefits.* There are many areas of potential overlap between local and global environmental benefits. For example, replacing low-quality biomass fuels with modern and renewable energy sources in rural and peri-urban households reduces indoor air pollution, mitigates respiratory diseases, and reduces greenhouse gas emissions. Similarly, switching from coal to gas heating for urban households yields both local and global benefits. Our Strategy focuses on these areas of overlap.

- *Address the vulnerability and adaptation needs of developing countries.* Poor countries suffer disproportionately from the degradation of the global commons and from its consequences, such

as climate change. The Bank will help assess the long-term impacts of climate change on the vulnerability of people in client countries. These assessments will contribute to broader poverty reduction strategies.

- *Facilitate transfer of financial resources to client countries to help them meet the costs of generating global environmental benefits not matched by national benefits.* In cases where actions designed to address regional and global concerns are not in the short- and medium-term interest of developing countries, the Bank will seek to engage the GEF (see annex I for details), the MFMP, or other special financing mechanisms to compensate countries for the incremental costs they incur to protect the global commons. In this regard, assistance with the phaseout of persistent organic pollutants (POPs) will be an important new area in which we can put the lessons learned under the MFMP program to work. We will also facilitate the establishment of cooperative mechanisms for the joint management and development of shared natural resources such as water.

- *Stimulate markets for global environmental public goods.* We will help our client countries develop

BOX 3.5

Providing decisionmakers with scientific information: The Millennium Ecosystem Assessment and the Intergovernmental Panel on Climate Change

Significant international environmental conventions have been agreed on in recent years—among them, the UN Framework Convention on Climate Change (UNFCCC), the Convention on Biodiversity (CBD), the Convention to Combat Desertification (CCD), and the Wetlands Convention (Ramsar). To assist policy decisions under these agreements, governments and the public need timely and trustworthy scientific, technical, and economic information. Two international bodies are charged with meeting this need.

- *The Millennium Ecosystem Assessment* is a four-year international scientific assessment of the past, present, and future condition of Earth's ecosystems; the potential impacts of changes in ecosystems on their ability to meet human needs; and policies, technologies, and tools for improving ecosystem management. The MA will provide information not just on the biological aspects of managed and unmanaged ecosystems but also on the economic values of the goods and services produced by ecosystems and the potential economic and health impacts of ecosystem changes. Assessments will be conducted at the global and subglobal (regional, national, and local community) levels.

- *The Intergovernmental Panel on Climate Change* (IPCC) assesses past, present, and future changes in the Earth's climate; the impact of climate change on human health; ecological systems, and socioeconomic sectors; and technologies, practices, and policies for adapting to or mitigating climate change, with attention to estimates of the economic costs. The assessments emphasize the regional aspects of climate change and cross-cutting issues such as development, equity, and sustainability.

To carry out these activities, more than a thousand natural and social scientists and technologists, drawn from academia, governments, and the private sector worldwide, are involved in information preparation and in peer-review.

The MA and the IPCC will assist the implementation of the World Bank's environment, forestry, water, and rural strategies. For example, the IPCC's vulnerability assessments identify ways of incorporating climate variability and climate change considerations into sector (water resource management, agriculture, forestry, and health) planning. The indicators developed through the MA will expand policy-relevant information on ecosystem goods and services available to clients, and strengthen clients' capacity to undertake critical assessments of ecosystem goods and services.

and benefit from trade in environmentally credible goods and services, such as greenhouse gas emission reductions through the PCF, and from independently verified, sustainably harvested, natural resources.

OUR TOOLKIT

Environment is not a sector or add-on. It has been long recognized that environmental considerations have to be reflected at early stages of decisionmaking processes. The Environment Strategy emphasizes the importance of continuing our efforts to integrate, or "mainstream," the environment into development programs, sector strategies, and policy dialogue, mindful of the institutional requirements and capacity constraints in our client countries. This emphasis will translate into actions throughout the Bank. A number of instruments—our "toolkit"—are available to the Bank in working toward its environmental objectives and mainstreaming environmental considerations into programs and projects.

This section outlines the main elements of an action plan for using this toolkit in implementing the Strategy. We begin with our analytical and advisory activities, which help identify and prioritize environmental problems and feed into the formulation of countries' development strategies and our own assistance strategy. Once identified, key environmental priorities can be addressed in a number of ways. The main tools are investment projects (stand-alone environmental projects, environmental components in sector projects, or improved project design), technical assistance, and policy-based lending. Finally, in addition to addressing environmental challenges through projects and programs, proper safeguards and good environmental management practices must be applied in all our lending in order to avoid or mitigate significant adverse environmental and social impacts. Improving the safeguard policies and their application, therefore, is another important pillar of the Strategy.

The actions described here are a mixture of short-term and long-term measures. Taken as a whole, the Environment Strategy is clearly—and deliberately—a long-term strategy that will require adjustments in our programs, tools, and institutional incentives. It will take some time before all its elements are fully in place. This does not imply a lack of action in the meantime. We are not beginning from a standing start; rather, we are building on a well-established work program. The Strategy provides a framework for refocusing our efforts and realigning our programs, tools, and institutional incentives to become more effective.

In implementing the Strategy, we will give priority to certain areas that are particularly urgent. For example, integrating environmental considerations into the new Poverty Reduction Strategy Papers (PRSPs) is an urgent task. Work on this is currently being piloted, giving us an opportunity to ensure that environmental issues are fully integrated from the beginning (see box B.3 in annex B). The pilot program, which started in November 2000, entails (a) a systematic review of all interim and full PRSPs from an environmental perspective to rate the degree of mainstreaming (see box B.3 in annex B); (b) workshops on mainstreaming for PRSP teams in client countries; (c) training for World Bank staff; (d) development of the Environment Chapter in the PRSP Sourcebook; and (e) analytical work on poverty-environment links. This program is actively pursuing partnerships with other interested donors.

Other elements of the Strategy, such as the work toward systematic application of country environmental diagnostic analysis and the structured learning on applying Strategic Environmental Assessments (SEAs), will be undertaken gradually. During the first year of implementing the Strategy, we will focus on refining methodologies, coordinating with clients and partners, piloting, and learning. Table 2 in the Executive Summary provides details about targets for implementing the Strategy in the short and medium term.

Strengthening analytical and advisory activities

Analytical work is the foundation for defining strategic priorities and integrating environmental concerns into projects and programs. A systematic approach is needed to ensure that environmental considerations enter the development planning process at an early stage by taking a multisectoral and long-term view of development. The country policy dialogue, as well as the quality of lending and policy related interventions, depends on a spectrum of information to influence decisionmaking. Some of the critical questions in the policy dialogue concern setting priorities for environmental interventions, managing the assets (including natural assets) on which development depends, and building up country capacity to implement, monitor, and enforce environmental legislation and regulations.

Country-level environmental analysis. A good overview of conditions in a country is an indispensable first step toward designing an appropriate strategy to address the challenges it faces. The Bank regularly monitors and reports on many aspects of conditions in its client countries—through poverty assessments and public expenditure reviews, for example. Diagnostic work on environmental issues, by contrast, has tended to be sporadic. There is a need to make it more systematic by building on and complementing NEAPs and other country-led environmental work, as well as assessments by the Bank and development partners to inform and deepen the Bank's country dialogue, particularly in connection with the preparation of PRPSs and CASs. Country diagnostic work, including an assessment of environmental policy, regulatory, and institutional capacity, will be also essential in connection with the enhanced role of programmatic lending in some countries. Monitoring environmental trends has to be an important part of country environmental diagnostic work. The Bank has developed macroeconomic sustainability indicators such as genuine savings (saving rates adjusted by changes in natural capital and by damage caused by pollution), which are useful tools for monitoring trends in the way economies use their resources. We will make targeted efforts to ensure that key national environmental and sustainability indicators become an integral part of the core country indicator set (the "Country at a Glance" tables that appear in loan documents and other key publica-

tions) and that they are used routinely in CASs. We will work to improve the coverage of the genuine savings indicator to include the impacts of air and water pollution, soil degradation, and depletion of subsoil water. We will continue to publish a range of macro environmental indicators (for example, access to safe water and sanitation, rates of deforestation, emissions of CO_2) for all client countries, as part of the *World Development Indicators* series. We will work with clients and development partners to coordinate assistance in preparing and making available the results of country-level environmental analyses.

Strategic Environmental Assessments (SEAs). SEAs—sectoral, regional, and policy-focused—will be applied as an analytical tool to address complex cross-sectoral environmental issues; and to help integrate environmental aspects at an early stages in the decisionmaking process of sector strategies, programs, and projects (see box 3.6). We will develop a structured learning program on SEAs. We will build on our experience with SEAs in energy-environment linkages (Energy-Environment Reviews), urban air quality management, and river basin management and will gradually expand their application to other areas (see box F.1 in annex F). The Bank will play a catalytic role in building and strengthening SEA capacity in client countries. Over time, a more systematic application of SEAs will reduce the costs of project-level safeguards, improve compliance, and help integrate environment into upstream policy dialogue and programmatic lending programs.

Advisory activities. Our advisory activities are essential in helping client countries assess their environmental challenges, set priorities, apply effective policies and regulatory instruments, and build en-

BOX 3.6
Strategic environmental assessments

Environmental Assessment (EA) has proved to be a powerful tool for minimizing the possible adverse environmental impacts of specific projects. It is limited, however, by its narrow scope—by the time an EA is conducted, fundamental policy decisions have generally been made, often involving far more significant environmental tradeoffs than the specific investment itself. In addition, EA is essentially reactive, ignoring environmental problems that are not associated with planned projects.

Strategic Environmental Assessments (SEAs) can complement project-specific EA, providing a tool for proactively examining and prioritizing environmental problems at the national, regional, subregional, or sectoral level. They make possible an integrated approach to identifying the causes of environmental problems, applying an ecosystem approach, and suggesting areas in need of interventions—whether projects or policy changes (or targeted, in-depth analytical work).

By examining a broad range of environmental issues, SEAs can help in prioritizing, both among environmental problems and across sectors. And by moving environmental assessment upstream in the policymaking process, SEAs can ease the task of shifting from remedial to preventive approaches in dealing with environmental problems. SEAs can also enable the assessment of broad policies and programs that fall outside the scope of traditional project-level EA.

Unlike the formalized approach of project-level EAs, SEAs consist of sets of guiding principles and menus of analytical and consultative approaches that are applied flexibly and that are carefully tailored to the specific context of the country, including its political, socioeconomic, and cultural setting. By their nature, SEAs are intended to be consultative processes, involving stakeholders both at central policy levels (government ministries, national assemblies) and in civil society.

vironmental management capacity. In addition to assistance with systematic assessments, these activities will include issue- and country-specific analytical and advisory work to support the policy dialogue with countries. It will focus on areas with the greatest likelihood of having a significant impact on country policies or programs, and on countries where our counterparts are committed and able to apply the results. The aim will be to build on indigenous knowledge and in-country capacity and on work undertaken by others. This requires better collaboration with clients and development partners and a mechanism for capturing and disseminating information and knowledge. We will use a variety of mechanisms to provide advisory services including formal training, technical assistance, and an enhanced use of the electronic media and distance learning opportunities. Priorities for analytical and advisory assistance include areas where the Bank has an advantage compared with clients and development partners. The key themes to be covered include:

- *Poverty-environment linkages.* The linkages between environmental degradation and poverty are often location-specific. A better understanding of these linkages is essential for influencing poverty reduction strategies. Environmental issues need to be integrated into the analysis undertaken for PRSPs. Several environmental indicators are expected to be standard parts of PRSPs, such as lack of access to clean water and adequate sanitation, and reliance on dirty fuels that cause indoor air pollution in many poor countries—both major contributors to excess mortality and disease among the poor. Integrating environmental issues, particularly those related to natural resource management, into poverty reduction strategies and policy lending will require analysis of household data and the introduction into household surveys of new questions on the use of environmental resources. We will support pilot studies and programs to integrate environmental questions into household surveys and will strengthen local capacity to understand poverty-environment linkages and design effective interventions. We will also support the analysis of environmental health linkages for poor households.

■ *Economic evaluation of environmental resources and environmental degradation.* The costs of environmental degradation are considerable, but they need to be better quantified to be of use to economic decisionmakers. The Bank has developed methodologies and macroeconomic sustainability indicators, such as genuine saving rates, and methods for the economic valuation of health damages and environmental services. Further work is needed to refine methodologies, to share them with clients, to extend the scope of assessments—including methodologies for assessing climate change aspects—and to mainstream their use into Bank project assessment and client practice. Considerable efforts have also been devoted to capacity building in this area, in collaboration with the World Bank Institute and other organizations such as IUCN, OECD, and CEPAL.

■ *Cross-country transfer of good practices in environmental policy and management.* The World Bank is in a good position to capture and apply relevant lessons among countries and regions in environmental policy, management, and technical issues and to identify and transfer experience and good practices among developing countries. We have developed a strong knowledge base and will build on it in our capacity development efforts. We will also continue preparing and disseminating good practice notes, guidelines, and papers in key areas of environmental

assessment, management, and policy, and will support this activity with appropriate training programs both for our clients and for our staff (see box 3.7 for an example).

Addressing environmental priorities through projects and programs

Addressing environmental priorities that affect the long-term sustainability of development requires a proactive approach to find and implement cost-effective solutions though investment projects and addressing key policy issues through projects and programs (see box 3.8 for the principles guiding our involvement).

Investment projects have traditionally been the Bank's main tool and remain an important vehicle for pursuing development objectives and achieving results on the ground. All investment projects have to consider environmental aspects and adopt good

---

BOX 3.7
Promoting good practice in environmental management

The Bank Group's *Pollution Prevention and Abatement Handbook 1998* (1999b) provides a comprehensive set of policy- and industry-specific guidelines for international good practice in pollution management. It emphasizes pollution prevention rather than control and underlines the role of good management rather than sole reliance on technical solutions.

The *Handbook* was prepared jointly by the Bank and the IFC, drawing on technical expertise and inputs from the UNEP and the UNDP. WHO, bilateral governments, industry specialists, private sector organizations, and civil society provided extensive comments.

The Bank Group is making a special effort to disseminate the lessons and guidelines summarized in the *Handbook* and to continue preparing, discussing, and disseminating policy and sector-specific guidance notes on emerging issues.

BOX 3.8
How we will work

In preparing and implementing our environmental assistance, the World Bank will aim to adhere to the following guiding principles:

- We will be selective and will work on the highest-priority problems.
- We will promote cost-effective solutions.
- We will promote market-based solutions to environmental problems.
- We will consider the long term to promote environmental sustainability.
- We will take an ecosystem-focused and cross-sectoral approach.
- We will set realistic targets.
- We will listen to and work with people in our client countries and incorporate their views into our activities.

environmental management principles according to the safeguard policies. In addition, priority environmental problems can also be addressed by dedicated projects or by including environmental activities in sector projects. Depending on country conditions and demand, we will work on both fronts but will focus particularly on ensuring that sectoral investment projects take full advantage of opportunities to incorporate environmental considerations into their objectives and design. We will apply programmatic lending instruments to environmental issues, for example, in support of long-term environmental policy change (see, for example, box 3.9).

Improving the design and performance of environmental projects and components. Our investment projects are most effective when they address specific aspects of a problem; when the problem can usefully be addressed by financing investments; when clients have capacity to implement; and when the project can be expected to have a major impact on the problem. Thus, while analysis should be

multisectoral, investments should be relatively simple and commensurate with the institutional capacity of clients, and the outcomes should be sustainable after the project is over. Environmental investments also perform best where the lack of finance is a clear barrier to improving environmental conditions. In addition, environmental projects or project components have been most successful when local political and economic stakeholders are committed to improved environmental management and when local officials are exceptionally capable of implementing the project. In designing environmental interventions, it is therefore important to measure them against four clear criteria (in addi-

BOX 3.9
Adaptable Program Loan for improving environmental management in Brazil

The Brazil Second National Environmental Project (NEP II), approved in December 1999, allows eligible states to receive grants from the Ministry of Environment for the protection or sustainable use of high-priority environmental resources. Typically, grants are made available to *stakeholder coalitions* consisting of municipalities, state and/or federal government agencies, private sector corporations, and NGOs. To be eligible for grants, states must demonstrate that they have carried out environmental management policy reforms. As states attain higher levels of fulfillment, the grants are increased.

The NEP II is designed as an Adaptable Program Loan (APL) with three phases. A scoring system measures the aggregate level of fulfillment of policy reforms by all the states. When the aggregate score of all states participating in the system is reached, the next phase is triggered, and new loan funding can be released. States may apply for more than one grant, but only by progressing to a higher level on the reform matrix. The Ministry of Environment provides technical assistance to help states undertake the selected policy reforms.

tion to the criteria the Bank normally applies to any investments):

■ Do we have a good understanding of the causes of the environmental problem? Is the analysis multisectoral? Does it take a long-term view?

■ Have we identified implementable interventions that tackle the most important part of the problem?

■ Is lack of finance a major reason the problem persists? Are we sure that money will make a difference? Is financing sustainable?

■ Is the solution sustainable? Can we ensure that the problem will not return or that the situation will not revert once the project is over?

These criteria will help project designers to assess what they are trying to achieve and how they should go about it. Exceptions will always be possible, but using these criteria would put the onus on the team proposing the investment to show why the particular activity should be carried out. In addition, we will apply the criteria set out under "Protecting the quality of the regional and global commons" in this chapter to build on overlaps between local, regional, and global environmental benefits and to use grant financing through the GEF, MFMP, and other mechanisms to support interventions with global benefits.

Improving the use of project-level indicators. As mandated by BP 10.00, outcome indicators are intended to influence the design and implementation of projects. Guidelines for project indicators are currently available in a second-edition note on *Performance Indicators for Environmental Projects* (Segnestam 1999). Methods for indicator design following the input-output-outcome-impact model are now well developed as part of the Logical Framework process. Making better use of project-level indicators and extending them to instruments

such as CDD will be a challenge in future work. Improving the design of these activities requires work on several fronts.

Coordinating investments and policy reforms. Experience shows that investment projects should be considered not in isolation but in the context of a broader strategy. In particular, investment projects are unlikely to bring lasting results in a distorted policy environment. At the same time, experience also indicates that individual investment projects are often poor vehicles for policy reform—interventions tend to be most effective when they either attempt to change specific local environmental conditions in one geographic area or attempt to make broad policy or macro-level changes. Interventions that try to do both—that mix specific investments with broad policy changes—tend to be less successful. This Strategy, therefore, promotes interventions that are clearly in one category or another. The actions under each category are specific and are oriented, as much as feasible, toward concrete, measurable objectives. In each case, careful thought needs to be given to the proper sequencing of policy reform efforts and specific investments.

Applying a location-specific focus. Because the linkages between natural resource management and poverty are complex and location-specific, and because implementation capacity varies, the details of efforts to integrate environmental considerations into investment projects, adjustment lending, and programs will clearly vary from country to country. In some cases, the links between environment, poverty reduction, and economic growth are already reasonably well understood, thanks to data availability and prior analysis. Such countries will provide opportunities for early interventions, and the lessons could then be applied elsewhere. In some cases, the lack of adequate data and analysis may mean that we can only raise questions and outline what would be necessary to provide reasonable answers. Nonetheless, it is important to recognize the limits of our knowledge and understanding.

Supporting capacity development. Improving country capacity to address environmental issues is a key challenge. Capacity development requires commitment to reform and positive change and long-term involvement in policy dialogue and institutional reform. It cannot be effectively addressed by traditional short-term projects. The Bank's comparative advantage lies in linking environmental capacity development with its ongoing sectoral operations and policy dialogue, rather than in self-standing technical assistance projects for general institutional development. In a few cases where strong commitment exists in the country to undertake environmental institutional reform, we will apply a programmatic approach and seek long-term involvement to support the process and monitor its results. The Bank will collaborate at the country level with other development partners involved in environmental assistance to improve overall development effectiveness (see box 3.10).

Enhancing the environmental outcome of adjustment lending. The basic structure of incentives in an economy should promote the sustainable use of natural resources and encourage activities that mitigate pollution and other forms of environmental damage. The natural framework for pursuing this goal is by contributing to policy development through integrating environmental considerations into adjustment operations where possible and appropriate. In some countries, adjustment lending will be the most important lending instrument for the Bank. In low-income countries, Poverty Re-

BOX 3.10
Capacity development activities by other international organizations

- *United Nations Environment Programme (UNEP).* Capacity building is an integral part of UNEP's programs. Recently, UNEP and UNCTAD established a Task Force on Trade, Environment and Development to assist developing countries in better integrating their policies in these areas.
- *United Nations Development Programme (UNDP).* UNDP's flagship activity is the Capacity 21 Program, launched at the 1992 UNCED Conference, which supports capacity-building programs and public-private partnerships in developing countries.
- *Organisation for Economic Co-operation and Development (OECD).* A Task Force established following the 1992 UNCED Conference has published guidelines on Capacity Development in Environment.
- *Asian Development Bank (ADB).* The ADB has substantially increased its capacity-building portfolio in environment in the last five years. Priority is given to environmental management and institutional strengthening.
- *Inter-American Development Bank (IDB).* The IDB has a substantial portfolio of operations in strengthening national environmental management. Under the auspices of the Forum of Environment Ministers of Latin America and the Caribbean, the World Bank and the IDB have been engaged in promoting a south-south dialogue on experience with institutional development projects.

duction Support Credits (PRSCs), which are based on PRSPs, are emerging as key lending instruments. We will help enhance the positive environmental outcome of programs supported by these loans.

We are beginning the process of updating and converting the Operational Directive on adjustment lending (OD8.60) into an Operational Policy/Bank Procedure (OP/BP) format. The broad issues to be addressed during the conversion include both positive actions with regard to the environment in adjustment loans, and the mitigation of negative consequences. Initial considerations for good practice and, possibly, operational policy, include:

- *Upstream reviews.* One issue for consideration is how Regional environment units may carry out upstream reviews of adjustment loans in order to improve the design of any environmentally sensitive components.
- *Country diagnostic studies and assessments.* Strengthening analytical work on country diagnostic analysis and SEAs may be particularly important and useful in countries undergoing significant structural change; they can assist in identifying resources at risk, defining strategic environmental priorities, and assessing environmental management capacity.
- *Monitoring.* It is being proposed that resources identified as being at risk be monitored during structural adjustment programs.

Improving the safeguard system

The Bank's safeguard system is an essential tool for integrating environmental and social concerns into development policies, programs, and projects. It has to reflect evolving international good practice in environmental assessments and management, respond to changing development contexts, and adapt to new lending approaches. Improving the safeguard system is a dynamic and incremental process that involves both the Bank and its clients in a series of actions designed to create better linkages between policies and their application to projects and programs. We will follow a two-pronged approach:

1. *Addressing short-term priorities.* In the short term, our priority is to focus on improving compliance with the safeguard policies, establishing an integrated compliance system, and improving results on the ground, as follows:

- *Strengthening compliance with safeguard policies.* We are placing increased emphasis on the implementation of safeguard policies, primarily through greater attention to the consistency of application across the Bank, stronger central oversight, and greater transparency in monitoring and reporting. We will improve supervision, particularly the implementation of environmental management plans and other commitments related to project-level safeguards. We will enhance systematic training of operational staff and management on safeguard policies and implementation (see chapter 4 for more detail).
- *Building an integrated safeguard compliance system.* We will complete the process of integrating the implementation of the safeguard policies at both Regional and central levels. A major focus of ongoing work by the Quality Assurance and Compliance Unit (QACU) and the Regional Environment Units has been the elaboration of an enhanced compliance system that includes the use of a new instrument, the Integrated Safeguard Data Sheet (ISDS), as part of the project identification, preparation, and appraisal process. The ISDS will provide for the comprehensive review of the application of all 10 safeguard policies and will better capture potential cumulative impacts. This approach will allow the safeguard policies to be viewed in relationship to each other, reduce the risk of individual policies being overlooked in the project process, and provide for more effective disclosure of information. Following the adoption of the ISDS, priority will be given to improving coordination between environmental and social analysis of project impacts and risks.

■ *Improving results on the ground.* Our objective is to improve project performance on the ground. Fuller integration of safeguard principles within project design, and especially in project implementation, ultimately requires greater reliance on national-level safeguard systems. Thus, the Bank will strive to support in-country improvement in safeguard capacity, effective implementation, and transparency in processes. To this end, we will strengthen our capacity building efforts through training and technical assistance, and encourage the participation of local communities and independent organizations in monitoring activities. A comprehensive set of environmental indicators, which has been developed by the Bank over the years, will be incorporated into operational work.

2. *Responding to new challenges.* Over the long term, the Bank seeks to develop an integrated policy framework to replace the current 10 free-standing safeguard policies. Development of a single unified safeguard policy would strengthen performance, provide for a consistent broad-based approach, allow greater flexibility in application, and permit harmonization of requirements and processes with client countries. This integrated framework would improve the Bank's performance in internalizing the environmental objectives and principles embedded in safeguard policies. We would systematically apply them in the program and project design, implementation, and evaluation processes. Specifically, an integrated framework would respond to a series of challenges:

■ *Adapting to a changing lending profile.* There is a gradual shift in Bank lending toward using programmatic lending instruments, such as Poverty Reduction Support Credits (PRSCs), Adaptable Program Lending (APL), Learning and Inno-

vation Loans (LILs), and Programmatic Structural Adjustment Loans and Credits (PSALs/ PSACs). Programmatic lending instruments may involve lending for a series of projects (for example, APLs), support for policy reforms (for example, PSALs/PSACs), or approaches for low-income countries (for example, PRSCs) (see World Bank 2000c for a description of lending instruments). While most Bank projects and programs are carried out by government entities, CDD projects are implemented at the grassroots level. These new types of lending operations and instruments provide important opportunities and challenges for the innovative application of the principles of the safeguard policies in cooperation with clients and partners. In this context, the Bank will develop and apply a systematic review system, enhanced analytical and diagnostic tools, guidelines for good practice, and indicators to ensure that the environmental implications of the changing lending profile are properly considered. The use of new instruments and the application of safeguard policies to these activities will require a targeted training program for Bank and client staff involved in these activities and evaluation of experiences to develop good practices and to internalize the lessons learned.

■ *Moving safeguard policies upstream in the decisionmaking process* by integrating them into the strategic planning processes used at the national, regional, program, and sectoral levels. This can be accomplished by improving the analytical underpinning as a routine part of Bank and client development planning processes. Increased attention will be given to early identification of issues, evaluation of alternatives, and assessment of risks at the country and sector levels. Strengthened analytical work such as SEAs will help evaluate complex short-, medium-, and long-term environmental issues in critical sectors. This approach will support integration of safeguard policy issues during early planning stages and allow for cross-sectoral and ecosystem-based analysis. In the next five years, a structured learning program for SEAs will be introduced to gradually increase SEA application, identify good practices, and disseminate lessons learned.

■ *Working with partners on coordination, dissemination, and harmonization.* The Bank Group will continue to take an active role in working with other international financial institutions to better coordinate efforts on the development and application of safeguard policies, dissemination of good practice, and specific measures to facilitate harmonization of policies and processes. The primary mechanism for this process is a Working Group on the Environment of International Financial Institutions (IFIs), which has an ongoing work program that includes a comparative review of policies and procedures and identification of key elements of environmental management systems. The Bank is actively cooperating to transfer experience between institutions in addressing environmental aspects of operations that use financial intermediaries. Comparable steps to improve coordination on safeguard policies with the private sector will be undertaken in cooperation with the IFC, MIGA, and the IFI Working Group.

■ *Focusing on client ownership, capacity, and safeguard system.* In the longer run, environmental assessments and safeguards, in general, will have the greatest impacts if they are internalized by borrowers in their own development programs. Our ultimate objective is to help client countries introduce and implement their own environmental safeguards to manage their environ-

mental resources sustainably. Successful medium- and long-term environmental and social performance of clients, in both the public and private sectors, mandates mainstreaming of the principles of safeguard policies, effective use of EA and other instruments, and client ownership of the consultation and disclosure processes. The Bank, therefore, will need to search increasingly for ways of making safeguards more uniform and accessible across donor programs, assessing capacity to adopt and internalize the principles of sustainable development and meet international good practice, supporting capacity development, and creating incentives and rewards for good performance by delegating responsibility increasingly to borrowers with demonstrated capacity to manage environmental aspects in their own programs. To achieve this, the Bank and its partners will need to increase their emphasis on capacity development at national and sub-national levels in governments, academic and applied research organizations, private sector and consulting firms, and NGOs. These capacity-building measures should recognize the importance of national policies, laws, and procedures and seek to adapt the application of safeguard policies to local conditions. Gaps between borrower and Bank requirements will be narrowed through initiatives focused on achieving greater levels of harmonization between Bank and client procedures. We will assess the EA capacity and systems of our client countries and consider such capacity in the review, clearance, and monitoring process of Bank-funded projects.

SELECTIVITY IN IMPLEMENTATION

The action agenda for the Strategy described in this chapter is diverse and challenging on numerous fronts. In order to be effective, we will have to apply the principle of selectivity to guide implementation. The Bank's Strategic Framework Paper (SFP) and Strategic Directions Paper (SDP) provide a framework for selectivity at three levels:

1. *At the corporate level*, priority is given to programs supporting global public goods that convey shared benefits worldwide and to corporate advocacy in priority areas that enable the Bank to fulfill its poverty reduction mandate. Specifically, these corporate priorities include the protection of global environmental commons (climate, water, forests, biodiversity, and ozone depletion) and corporate priorities for advocacy in a range of areas with strong environmental linkages including environmental health, governance, empowerment, and conditions for good investment climate. The Strategy defines corporate environmental priorities in detail, and guides their integration into regional strategies and country-level programming.

2. *At the regional level*, Regional Strategies (summarized in annex A) have set regional and subregional priorities reflecting critical assessments of environmental constraints on poverty reduction and growth; outlined the Bank's comparative advantage in supporting actions on agreed priorities; and selected cost-effective ways to deliver our support. Regional Strategies are essential to show the linkages between corporate objectives and the regional context, reflecting regional differences and synthesizing corporate priorities with country-focused programming. Annual business plans will further specify actions to be undertaken in accordance with the Strategy.

3. *At the country level*, priorities and the mixture of Bank assistance instruments will be determined by many factors, including progress in policy reform, the size of the economy, and access to external finance and markets. The Strategy provides a framework for setting priorities for environmental assistance at the country level. Using the corporate strategic framework, selectivity for environmental assistance at the country level will be based on a diagnosis of environmental priorities and management capacity, country demand, and consistency with the CAS. At the same time, the Bank is committed to ensure the implementation of its safeguard policies in all countries. Country capacity will be an important consideration in the allocation of Bank resources and attention to safeguard compliance.

This means that we will not work on all fronts of the Strategy in all countries. Also, while new means for delivering our services to client countries are introduced, our engagement in other areas will diminish, taking the lessons on effectiveness to heart. On the lending side, this may well reduce our involvement in supporting large-scale end-of-pipe pollution control projects and traditional freestanding environmental institution-building projects. On the nonlending side, there will likely be an increased emphasis on Bank assistance in support of a policy dialogue on poverty-environment linkages and environment-growth linkages and a reduced involvement in highly specialized technical studies.

Due to the great diversity among the Bank's client countries in their environmental challenges, environmental policy and management frameworks, and other country conditions, no simple guidelines can be set for matching country types with priority Bank assistance. During the implementation of the Strategy, enhanced country diagnostic work, the annual business planning process, and its alignment with the corporate Strategy framework will enable us to improve the environmental input to country programming and priorities.

The success of the Strategy depends on more than the Bank's actions. The Bank can help develop capacity in addressing environmental issues in client countries, and it can support environmental sustainability in its operations. But in the end, countries themselves have to become committed to take the necessary measures toward making their development sustainable. This is a gradual process; it takes time, perseverance, a concerted effort of different parts of societies, and support of the development community.

Internally we have to strengthen our institutional commitment to the Strategy's objectives, play a leadership role in measuring the impact of our environmental interventions, and become a role model in corporate responsibility. These issues are discussed in further detail in the next chapter.

Chapter 4

Institutional Realignment

Sustainable development is a long-term goal. Achieving it requires a concerted pursuit of economic prosperity, environmental quality, and social equity. It calls for behavioral changes by individuals and organizations. Throughout the world, this change is occurring. By virtue of our long-term development focus, World Bank management and staff are naturally expected to take the lead in making a commitment to corporate environmental responsibility and to ensure that this commitment is increasingly reflected at all levels of our organization. We understand that social and environmental issues are integral parts of development and prosperity and that overcoming associated costs and constraints requires true corporate commitment. Since it also requires institutional realignment, it would not be a sudden move but a gradual process.

The global context in which we operate is rapidly changing. New directions of development assistance emphasize holistic, client-driven, and programmatic approaches to delivering lending and nonlending services and build on new alliances with a broad range of stakeholders. This means that, while we have to learn from past lessons to improve our performance in traditional lines of business, we also need to prepare for a transition to changing development assistance.

This chapter defines how the above requirements translate into an institutional realignment that includes actions to (a) strengthen accountability and incentives, (b) coordinate work across sectors in the Bank, (c) adjust the skill mix, and (d) align resources with strategic objectives. It also calls for striving for partnerships with others—members of the UN family, conservation organizations, bilateral donor agencies, private sector companies, and civil society groups—to ensure more efficient use of scarce development resources. Finally, it defines a transparent system for measuring and monitoring progress in implementing the strategy.

STRENGTHENING ACCOUNTABILITY AND INCENTIVES

The Bank's Environment Strategy calls, first, for an accountability framework that is client-centered, acknowledging that our core responsibility is to support sustainable development in our client countries. This framework has to distinguish between actions depending on client demand and those for which Bank staff are responsible, so that we can ensure that the proper incentives are in place and that our staff performance can be measured accurately. Within the Bank, the Strategy underscores the importance of maintaining clear lines of responsibility and a strong and consistent set of incentives applied throughout the institution. (Table 4.1, at the end of this chapter, summarizes key responsibilities in a matrix form).

As with other strategies, implementation of the Environment Strategy will be closely monitored by senior management, and progress reports will be submitted to the Board periodically. To ensure that feedback is properly channeled to operational managers, implementation reports will be disseminated to regional management and network teams.

Given the Bank's organizational structure, implementing the Environment Strategy will require the collaboration of two overlapping groups within the Bank: (1) the operational departments, including the country management units that are responsible for formulating the Bank's assistance strategy in each country and assigning budgetary resources, and the regional non-environmental sector units that support them, and (2) the Bank's environment professionals in regional sector departments, field offices, the central Environment Department (ENV), and other parts of the Bank (see description of the environment family below). So far, the burden of responsibility for the Bank's environmental activities has been on the Bank's environment professionals alone. While the role of the latter remains critical, properly addressing environmental problems requires that environmental awareness be fully integrated into the work of the operational departments.

The organizational structure varies significantly among Regions, including the place of environmental units, mechanism of cross-sectoral coordination, and the level of decentralization to field offices. These differences—together with the large variation among Regions in number of countries, development and environmental challenges, and ongoing programs—make it impossible to have a one-size-fits-all model. There are many common issues, however. This section describes the respective roles of operational and environment groups in implementing the Strategy and how incentives will be aligned with these roles.

Operational departments

Regional Vice Presidents (RVP) and Regional Management Teams (RMTs). Regional Vice Presidents are responsible for resource allocation to the implementation of the Regional Environment Strategies and for aligning accountability for mainstreaming environment. RVPs also share with the ESSD Vice President (ESDVP), responsibility for compliance with Bank safeguard policies, monitored and overseen by safeguard compliance teams in each Region, and the Quality Assurance and Compliance Unit (QACU) in ESSD. RVPs are accountable for overall compliance with safeguards in their regional portfolio and pipeline, for ensuring adequate funding levels for compliance, and for carrying out bi-annual safeguard risk assessments that identify spe-

cial-risk projects to be monitored at the corporate level. RVPs are jointly accountable with ESDVP for corporate signoff for special-risk operations. In addition to safeguard compliance, achieving better development outcomes requires that key environmental priorities are identified at the regional, sector, and country levels and that RMTs have a meaningful process in place to promote appropriate programmatic responses and support cross-sectoral collaboration, as needed.

Regional sector departments. Regional sector departments are responsible for undertaking the work programs of their respective sectors based on country-focused programming and budgeting. Environment is one of the regional sector departments (see discussion below). Any effort to integrate environmental considerations into other sectors' activities will, therefore, require close collaboration with staff from these units. As mentioned above, however, efforts will be needed to improve institutional incentives to work cross-sectorally. Working with regional sector units also raises issues of training, as discussed below.

Country Management Units (CMUs). The strategy calls for increased attention to mainstreaming environment into country and sector programs, for which country teams and other sectors are responsible. CMUs play a particularly important role, in that they have the primary responsibility for country and sector policy dialogue, designing lending and nonlending services, prioritizing interventions, coordinating with sector units (see below), and allocating Bank resources to different activities. Understanding the constraints that country teams face in properly integrating environmental considerations into their work is critical to improving the Bank's role in addressing environmental problems.

■ *Understanding the role of the environment.* For the environment to be fully integrated into Bank activities, constraints facing CMUs in incorporating environmental concerns into their programs need to be fully understood. Because of their day-to-day interaction with clients and awareness of their problems, CMUs are aware that good environmental planning and management are integral parts of good development, not simply a bureaucratic requirement. Few country managers would disagree with the notion that environmental problems can play an important role, but this understanding is not always accompanied by a clear sense of how environmental problems affect development issues in the countries they work on, what tools are at their disposal to address these problems, and what institutional support they can draw on to develop realistic options to address them. There remains, therefore, an important place for advocacy and *specialist support*—although this support must be demand-driven, specific, targeted, and appropriately integrated into country-team work, rather than generic or supply-driven—and for *training* that fully takes into consideration country conditions and constraints. The efforts discussed in the previous chapter to improve our *knowledge* of environmental problems through enhanced analytical work and indicators will play a critical role in this regard.

■ *Prioritizing interventions.* The primary task of CMUs is to respond to clients' poverty reduction agendas. In doing so, they face many demands on their scarce resources and must decide how to allocate them across activities in their client countries. With so many pressing concerns to address, it is inevitable that some worthy activities will have to be cut. Here too, attention to environmental issues beyond the proper

implementation of safeguards cannot be decreed. CMUs, with their detailed knowledge of country conditions and priorities, are best placed to prioritize interventions. This is a heavy responsibility, and the temptation to micro-manage should be resisted. But CMUs will be unable to properly assess the importance of environmental issues without adequate information on their extent and severity, so here, too, the analytical activities described in the previous chapter will play a key role. The farther upstream in the decisionmaking process this information is available, the more useful it is—hence the emphasis on country-level analysis, SEAs, and similar analytical tools.

■ *Responding to institutional incentives.* The incentive system—budgets, reporting, and performance evaluation—as it currently exists, does not provide enough support to working on environmental issues, particularly when they require cross-sectoral work. Thus, operational staff members need to be provided with enhanced incentives and rewards for giving proper consideration to environmental issues. In order to recognize good performance, the environment family of the Bank will institutionalize high-profile "green" awards for staff and managers in other sectors and areas of the Bank for their collaboration in safeguards and for mainstreaming environment into analytical work and operations. Emphasis will be given to recognizing contributions to addressing priority environmental challenges and effective supervision of projects with complex environmental and safeguard issues. The system of quality assessments and rewards will be reviewed and revised to focus on best practice, due diligence, and results on the ground.

The environment family

Within the Environmentally and Socially Sustainable Development Network (ESSD), the Bank Group's environment professionals are organized as a family, with members from Regional Environment Departments, the central Environment Department, environment staff in the Legal and Development Economics Vice Presidencies, the World Bank Institute (WBI), and IFC. It is led by the Environment Board (EB), which consists of directors and managers of these units (see figure 4.1). A fundamental principle of this Strategy is to align the role of the environment family with common practice. Its core functions ought to be to regulate, advise, and facilitate the activities of the rest of the Bank to promote environmental sustainability.

Regional Environment Departments (REDs). The REDs have three major roles: they (1) are responsible for overseeing and providing technical guidance to implement environmental safeguard policies; (2) undertake analytical and advisory activities; and (3) help prepare and supervise lending activities. The organizational structure of departments, and the relative importance they assign to these roles, varies across Regions. The Strategy is being translated into detailed annual business plans, to be approved and monitored by RVPs. The lead responsibility for facilitating the preparation of the regional business plans rests with the environment sector directors/managers. In these plans, particular attention would be paid to integrating environment into the Bank's poverty agenda; moving environment upstream in country strategy processes, including CAS preparation; working with clients preparing PRSPs; and conducting early environmental review of programmatic and policy-based lending. As part of implementing the Strategy, Regional environment directors /managers are ac-

Figure 4.1
Environment in the ESSD network

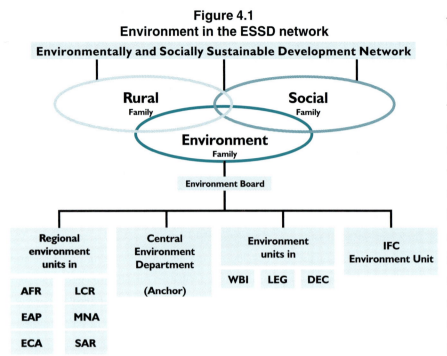

Environmentally and Socially Sustainable Development Network

Rural Family

Social Family

Environment Family

Environment Board

| Regional environment units in | Central Environment Department | Environment units in | IFC Environment Unit |

AFR   LCR

EAP   MNA

ECA   SAR

(Anchor)

WBI   LEG   DEC

Note: AFR – Sub-Saharan Africa; EAP – East Asia and Pacific; ECA – Europe and Central Asia; DEC – Development Economics; IFC – International Finance Corporation; LCR – Latin America and the Caribbean Region; LEG – Legal, MNA – Middle East and North Africa; SAR – South Asia Region; WBI – World Bank Institute.

countable for their efforts to stimulate cross-sectoral coordination and for providing technical guidance for integrating environmental considerations into the CAS and sector policy dialogue.

The annual business planning and reporting process is expected to overcome the weaknesses of the current incentive structure, which favors project management and is not well suited for encouraging advisory services and cross-sectoral coordination. It is expected to enhance communication with other sectors, heighten management attention, strengthen accountability, and ensure consistency with corporate priorities.

Recent changes in the safeguard system have addressed other weaknesses of the current system—the conflict between clearance and advisory functions, and inadequate corporate consistency and oversight. They have also raised the profile of staff performance in this area. Staff members who pro-

vide technical guidance on policy application are better recognized, and more weight is given in performance evaluation to due-diligence service. In addition, more attention is being paid to corporate accountability aspects in performance evaluation of staff and managers in other sectors. Likewise, greater weight needs to be given in evaluations to cross-sectoral work. For environment staff, annual results agreements and performance evaluations will be routinely used by environmental managers to assess staff performance and reward staff for their effectiveness in influencing sector and country programs.

Central Environment Department (ENV). ENV, like other central departments of the Bank, has several key functions. It (a) coordinates the Strategy preparation and the monitoring of its implementation; (b) provides operational support to turn innovations into reality and to help identify and transfer good practices in environmental management and project design across Regions (*knowledge management*); (c) facilitates *quality enhancement* of lending and non-lending activities; and (d) provides the public face of the World Bank on environmental matters and coordinates *corporate programs and partnerships.* Three aspects, however, make ENV different from other central departments: (1) its role

69

in ensuring the implementation of safeguard policies; (2) the need to coordinate with other sectors; and (3) its role in fulfilling the Bank's global environmental mandate. Some of these special functions have only recently been explicitly recognized. ENV will continue to fulfill these roles, focusing on efforts to support the Bank's transition to fully integrating environmental concerns across all its activities, and particularly on poverty alleviation efforts; assisting CMUs in dealing realistically with specific constraints that they face in addressing environmental programs; and adapting work on the environment to changing conditions. This transition will not happen overnight; ENV will support it through advocacy and technical support, by monitoring progress and by working with other parts of the Bank to adjust the Strategy in light of results.

The *Legal Vice-Presidency* (LEGVP) works closely with the environment family on implementation of the safeguard policies. LEG has primary responsibility for 2 of the 10 safeguard policies (OP/BP 7.50, Projects in International Waterways; and OP/BP 7.60, Projects in Disputed Areas). In particular, the environmental law specialists in ESSD and the International Law Group in the LEGVP provide expertise to assist client countries in introducing environmental and natural resource policy and regulatory frameworks, including land tenure and property rights regimes; in strengthening environmental compliance programs; and in the implementation of international conventions.

The *Vice Presidency of Development Economics (DECVP)* carries out research and collaborative work with operations in a number of key areas, including ongoing work on the role of market and nonmarket instruments in addressing local and national environmental externalities and on protect-

ing the global environmental commons. In alignment with the Strategy, future work is planned on poverty, growth, and environmental linkages; environmental performance indicators; and environmental health issues. Additionally, the DECVP, in collaboration with ESSD, will undertake major research on sustainability issues in preparation for the 2003 *World Development Report—Sustainable Development with a Dynamic Economy*.

The World Bank Institute (WBI) is responsible for developing and delivering learning programs and promoting knowledge networks for clients and staff on a broad range of sustainable development issues. Most WBI programs target poverty-environment linkages; social issues, such as conflicts over natural resource management; governance aspects of environmental policy, such as environmental enforcement and compliance, international environmental rulemaking, the international conventions; and safeguards. In recognition of the continuing challenges of mainstreaming, WBI is increasingly targeting non-environmental audiences, such as economic policymakers and macroeconomists, to highlight the linkages between environment and other issues central to poverty reduction and broader economic development. Learning activities in Africa in support of the Poverty Reduction Strategy (PRS) process focus on the interface of poverty-natural resource management-environment issues. In the next year, in support of the 2002 Earth Summit, learning programs will focus on linking the PRS process and target of implementing national sustainable development strategies expressed in the International Development Goals.

Environment Board (EB). While responsibility for the implementation of Bank strategies rests with senior Bank management, the EB plays a critical

role in leading and overseeing the Environment Strategy implementation process. The EB will review the annual regional business plans to support corporate consistency in regional strategic planning and to facilitate the sharing of experience across Regions. At the corporate level, the EB, supported by ENV, plays a key role in establishing and coordinating a systematic strategy implementation monitoring and reporting system. Its consolidated findings are the basis for reporting to senior management. The EB also oversees the strategic development and deployment of human resources, the mobilization and allocation of resources in support of the Strategy, and the consistency and quality of environmental work throughout the Bank.

Senior management

Certainly, the success of the Environment Strategy will build on the continued commitment of senior Bank management. As mentioned earlier, implementation of the environment strategy will be closely monitored at the Managing Director level, for a number of reasons. First, the cross-sectoral nature of environmental issues requires senior oversight to ensure coordination among a variety of actors. Second, success in integrating environmental considerations into Bank operations more systematically increases the sustainability of Bank-supported projects and programs. Third, improved environmental performance reduces corporate risk and improves the Bank's credibility in undertaking its development mandate. Past experience with mainstreaming environment in the Bank clearly indicates that the greatest progress can be made if senior management support is sustained, visible, based on a candid view of what can be attained at the country level, and supported by adequate resources within institutional resource constraints.

COORDINATING ACROSS SECTORS AND NETWORKS IN THE BANK

Environmental problems are inherently cross-sectoral. The need to integrate work on environmental problems closely with sectoral work is a key theme of this Strategy. The degree of overlap obviously varies from case to case, but the widespread recognition of the importance of environmental dimensions in other sector strategies, such as rural and urban development, energy, transport, and water, is an encouraging indication that environment is slowly becoming part of mainstream thinking.

Cross-sectoral coordination must, of course, go beyond implementing safeguards and recognizing the importance of environmental issues in sector strategies. There is also a need to coordinate analytical and operational work. Cooperation between the environment and other sectors and networks occurs at the project level, and it is often focused on country- or region-specific issues. At the corporate level, coordination and joint work with other networks is already under way in several areas (see also figure 4.2).

Environmentally and Socially Sustainable Development (ESSD). Within ESSD, environment and rural development families have joint programs undertaken by teams comprising specialists from the environment and rural development families on land, forest, and water resources management issues. Biodiversity specialists from the environment family, with support from the GEF, are also integrated into joint teams. In land management, the rural development family is taking the lead in addressing on-site productivity issues, while the environment family is taking the lead in addressing off-site externality issues. Because, in practice, land degradation problems always involve both issues to

Figure 4.2
Environmental interface with other networks and families

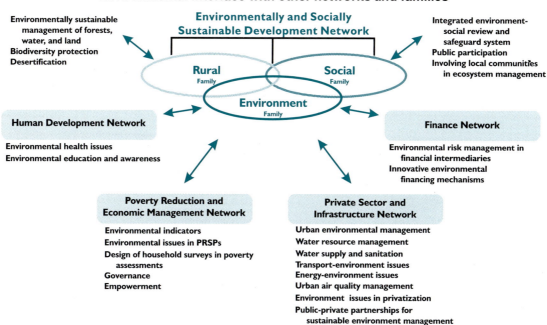

varying degrees, close cooperation is necessary. The practical outcome of this deepening cooperation is increasingly reflected in the rural portfolio. There is close collaboration between the social development family on developing an integrated social and environmental review and risk management system, on promoting social and environmental responsibility in operational programs, and on approaches to enhancing the role of local communities in ecosystem management.

Private Sector and Infrastructure (PSI). The environment family is collaborating with the PSI network in several areas. The environment and energy families jointly prepared *Fuel for Thought*, an environment strategy for the energy sector, and they are working closely on its implementation, including the preparation of Energy and Environment Reviews; support for the preparation of projects with environmental objectives; and integration of climate-friendly approaches to energy development (see box 4.1 and box F.1 in annex F). The environ-

ment family's work on the economic costs of fuels has contributed to setting priorities in the energy sector. There is longstanding coordination between the environment family and the water and sanitation and urban families on such issues as urban environmental priorities, priority-setting in water resource management, and cost-effective measures to address environmental health priorities (see annexes C, D, and E for more detail on environmental health, water resource management, and urban priorities). Urban air quality management has been an area for collaboration between the energy, urban transport, and environment families (see annex E for more detail). There is an emerging need to collaborate more closely on private sector development and disaster management.

Human Development (HD). Collaboration between the environment and HD on environmental health issues has begun, but relatively little formal collaboration has been established at the corporate level. In South Asia, a joint work program is addressing

BOX 4.1
Collaborating with the energy sector: *Fuel for Thought*

Fuel for Thought (FFT): An Environment Strategy for the Energy Sector is the product of collaboration between the environment and energy sectors of the Bank Group to outline the strategic environmental priorities in the energy sector and to move from "do no harm" to a more proactive stance considering environment as an integral part of energy development. Accordingly, the work included an examination of ways in which the Bank could switch from mitigation of local and global impacts of energy use to actively seeking opportunities for integrating environmental considerations into sector planning and development.

A joint team of energy and environment staff was formed to do the work. One of the most important findings of the stocktaking and analytical work undertaken in support of the Strategy was that, to be effective at the energy-environment nexus, cross-sectoral interventions were required. As a result, the Strategy makes operating in cross-sector teams a priority—an approach that is strongly evident in the implementation of FFT.

Though the bulk of the interventions and collaborations are with staff from energy and environment operational units, people from transport, urban, health, and human development sectors also participate in the implementation as needed (for example, to work on the critical issue of indoor air pollution and its linkages with child and female health). Evaluation, training, and other activities now routinely involve both energy and environment staff.

indoor air pollution, a key environmental health issue. The link between sanitation and health is a subject of discussions with the health and sanitation sectors, with the aim of trying to target interventions to improve health outcomes. A broader effort is under way to better understand the full range of environment and health linkages, which

are estimated to result in over 20 percent of the health burden of many countries. This work is also building increased collaboration with external health agencies such as WHO and the U.S. Centers for Disease Control and Prevention (CDC). There are obvious opportunities for increasing such collaboration in both the health and education areas.

Poverty Reduction and Economic Management (PREM). PREM and ENV are working together on environmental indicators and, increasingly, on poverty-environment links as part of an effort to integrate environmental considerations into PRSPs. There is clearly scope for much greater collaboration on poverty-environment linkages, specifically on integrating environmental considerations into household data analysis, updating guidelines for the PRSP Sourcebook, and assisting countries to prepare and implement PRSPs. Future collaboration is also expected to improve in other areas, including environmental aspects of public sector management, public expenditure reviews, and governance issues.

Finance. Linkages with the Finance network have been established on a case-by-case basis, particularly in connections with financial intermediary lending. More systematic collaboration in this area, as well as in relation to innovative environmental financing mechanisms, will be needed in the future.

In each case, the environment family needs to be more proactive in seeking out areas of possible collaboration and in converting them into meaningful operational programs.

IMPROVING SKILLS

Staff skills surveys indicate that the Bank has a relatively robust environmental skills base, especially in natural resource management and biodiversity; environmental policy and planning; environmental engineering; and water resource management. The Bank's environment professionals include some of the leading experts in their respective fields. As a result of targeted training and experience, more than one third of the current 253 environmental staff members have developed expertise in environmental assessment. Figure 4.3 provides information on cross-sectoral experience among environmental staff based on a self-assessment survey. The figure indicates relatively low levels of cross-sectoral affiliation in macroeconomics, poverty, health, and finance.

Continuing to realign the skill mix

The change in the lending profile of the Bank, the need to respond to new ways of delivering development assistance, and a changing emphasis from project-level safeguards toward integrated portfolio-level risk assessment and quality enhancement,

client outreach, and development effectiveness will require a gradual realignment of environmental staff skills. An enhanced role for programmatic lending instruments poses both a challenge and an opportunity to integrate environmental considerations into macroeconomic and sectoral planning. Environmental staff, therefore, must be able to make a stronger contribution to the upstream policy dialogue. Such dialogue should be based on solid analytical work and effective communication with country teams and other sectors, as well as an ability to work with clients and development partners and to provide high-quality inputs to the design of programs and projects.

Improving integration and cross-sectoral skills. While technical expertise will remain important, the capacity to integrate across a wide range of development issues will become critical. Environmental staff, therefore, should enhance skills and knowledge in other areas—such as economics, health, rural development, or urban management—in or-

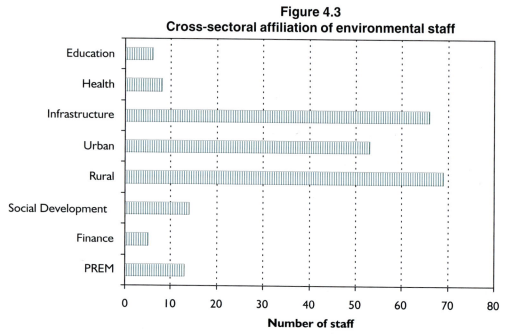

Figure 4.3
Cross-sectoral affiliation of environmental staff

Note: Environment staff is collaborating with a range of sectors and themes. This figure does not reflect all aspects and details of such cross-sectoral affiliation.

der to work as core members of teams in these areas. In particular, more policy, economic, institutional, and process management knowledge will be needed to contribute to macroeconomic work and decentralized activities such as community-based development programs. Emphasis should be given to the ability to communicate effectively, not just to manage self-standing tasks.

As work programs increasingly call for cross-sectoral expertise, the need for staff with both environmental and sector-specific knowledge and skills will increase, as noted above. At the same time, a gradual shift toward improved environmental skills in non-environmental specialist staff is expected to take place through operational experience in using new approaches, formal training in integration of environmental issues into programs and project design, and new hiring of experienced professionals. Since sector boards play an important role in human resource issues, there will be a need to coordinate these functions across sector boards—for example, to facilitate joint appointments or the rotation of staff.

Joint appointments, secondment, and training

The integration of environmental objectives into country and sectoral programs and projects, and a shifting accountability for environmental performance beyond the environment sector, assume a cultural and institutional change. This shift will be encouraged through joint appointments, staff rotation, and secondments with other sectors (rural and urban development, energy, water), thematic areas (macroeconomic policy, poverty, public sector management, and private sector development), and, where feasible, partner organizations, private sector companies, and consulting firms. Priority will

be given in external secondments to placing Bank staff in developing country settings.

Staff and client training programs will be aligned with the Environment Strategy to maximize understanding of the key themes of the Strategy. Target audiences will include both environment staff in the Bank and officials from environment and related ministries in client countries, as well as key economic policymakers in the World Bank and in client countries. To the extent possible, staff and client training will be integrated to encourage joint learning, foster closer teamwork between staff and clients, and create a shared vocabulary and knowledge base.

Safeguard policies are a key area of emphasis in our training program for staff and clients. In order to improve the Bank's performance in implementing environmental safeguards, we propose to deliver a systematic and mandatory training program for all relevant Bank staff over a five-year period. Training for clients on Bank safeguard policies is in the initial stages and will be increased over the next few years.

To support the integration of environment into sector and adjustment programs, training will focus on three conceptual pillars of the Strategy: improving the quality of life, the quality of growth, and the quality of the regional and global commons. A core course on sustainable development will be built around poverty-environment themes and will support the integration of environmental issues into Poverty Reduction Strategies. Modules will include linkages between poverty and health, between poverty and natural resources, and between vulnerability to natural disasters and management of natural resources, as well as the political economy of land use changes—for example, conversion of forests to agriculture—and the effects of these changes on food security. The course will also include modules on methodologies and analytical tools to enable environmental specialists to assess poverty impacts and linkages. Staff training will focus, in particular, on integrating environmental aspects into poverty assessment tools.

REALIGNING BUDGETS

Increasing the integration of environmental concerns into the Bank's work plan promises to bring strong returns by improving livelihoods, reducing health risks and vulnerability, improving the prospects for and the quality of growth, and improving the quality of the regional and global commons—all objectives that are at the core of the Bank's mission of poverty alleviation. But there is no free lunch. Achieving these objectives will require that resources be dedicated to the task. This is all the more important because the relative newness of environmental activities, their cross-sectoral complexity, and global public policy aspects mean that they tend to be more costly than traditional single-sector operations.

This section presents the budgetary implications of implementing the Environment Strategy. It is based on projected levels of key activities over the next five years that would begin to have a meaningful effect on the objectives and could realistically be delivered during this period, assuming availability of the required resources. Underpinning the budget realignment are two fundamental considerations: (1) the need to guide a transition toward adapting to new ways of delivering development assistance, including programmatic lending, and (2) the need to exercise selectivity in our programs and realign current budget allocations according to strategic priorities.

Managing the transition while exercising selectivity

The cost of implementing the Strategy is inevitably increased by the fact that the strategy will support an adjustment of the Bank's environmental policies and programs to meet the requirements of a Bank in transition. Key themes of the transition are a greater focus on poverty, enhanced responsiveness to client needs, and a shift toward more programmatic lending in many countries. This transition, however, has to be carefully managed to make sure that we honor current corporate commitments and that we ensure environmentally responsible Bank performance in the application of current Bank assistance instruments and policies. At the same time, we need to move forward on revisiting policies and developing instruments to respond to new approaches to development assistance, while helping our developing country partners build the capacity to manage such concerns through more effective implementation of their own enhanced regulatory frameworks.

Effectively addressing the diverse environmental challenges in client countries requires selectivity at the corporate, Regional, and country levels. The Strategy sets an overall framework for setting priorities that are further refined in the Regional Environment Strategies and the corresponding annual business plans. As discussed in chapter 3, the Bank's engagement is likely to diminish in some areas. At the same time, the Bank is facing emerging challenges. This will be increasingly reflected in the Bank's external relations and partnerships (see below).

Realigning our programs, tools, and partnerships with the priorities described in the Strategy will be a gradual process. Several activities in the first year of the Strategy (fiscal 2002) will focus on preparing for this transition, starting to redeploy resources to the new uses emphasized by the Strategy, refining and disseminating methodologies, launching pilot exercises, and developing better tools and mechanisms to influence the PRSP and CAS process (see table 2 in the executive summary).

Budget requirements

Defining the Bank budget allocated for environmental work precisely is not straightforward. Environmental costs are an integral part of project preparation and supervision, while environmental input is often integrated into analytical work prepared by other sectors. With these caveats, the Bank's current annual administrative budget for environmental is in the order of $25 million, covering work on the environmental components of projects, self-standing environment projects, analytical work and advisory services to clients, as well as safeguard compliance tracking and monitoring for the entire Bank portfolio. Additionally, GEF and MFMP resources in the amount of approximately $28 million fund the administrative budget of staff working on these programs and projects, while bilateral trust funds may be available to supplement Bank budget for analytical work and non-lending services based on criteria established for the trust fund.

Some of the requirements of this Strategy can be met by realigning budget allocations in response to changes in work program priorities and by delivering on such priorities more efficiently. Others have to be met by allocating new and additional resources or in combination with realignment gains. For the Bank to meaningfully address the objectives of the proposed Strategy, an annual incremental Bank budget of $5 million to $7 million over the next five years would be needed through Regional and

ESSD budget allocations. The two key components of this incremental funding are:

1. *Safeguards and compliance.* In addition to long-overdue measures to improve the implementation of the compliance system, the incremental activities under the Strategy over the next five years include completing environmental management capacity assessments in our client countries and associated support for country capacity building; introducing and expanding the use of SEAs to upstream environmental consideration in decisionmaking; and conducting a comprehensive review of the safeguards policy framework to fit the needs of a changing Bank—all to facilitate the transition to an environmental compliance system better suited to a changing Bank lending profile.

2. *Mainstreaming support.* Additional resources will be required to supplement current Regional operational budgets for environment if we are to bring about effective mainstreaming of the environment in the country assistance dialogue and programs. A proposed new instrument, the Mainstreaming Fund for Environment, would focus on mainstreaming environmental issues, with special emphasis on IDA countries in accordance with IDA requirements; linking corporate environmental priorities and global public goods with country programs, with an emphasis on upfront work on CAS preparation; facilitating cross-sectoral and cross-institutional approaches and work programs to address environmental issues, particularly with respect to the environment, health, and poverty interface; and addressing subregional and regional environmental activities.

In addition, if we are to successfully move toward full compliance on safeguards and effective mainstreaming, we need to invest in enhanced skills for our staff and, through training and capacity building, to raise awareness of the role of environmental sustainability in addressing poverty reduction and sound economic growth. The incremental costs of these activities will be reflected in the Bank's overall training program.

Systematic assessment of progress made, feedback, and adjustment are essential parts of Strategy implementation and enhanced corporate environmental responsibility. In the first year, we will plan for phase-in of a significantly enhanced comprehensive and transparent monitoring and reporting framework. Establishing such a framework will take time, cultural change, and adequate resources.

The Bank will work with interested partners in bringing about the successful implementation of the Strategy. This means that, wherever possible, the Bank will rely on work produced by partners that may have a comparative advantage in certain areas and, in a strategic and cost-effective fashion, avail itself of trust funds from bilateral partners and others. On the other hand, the comprehensive actions needed to address the environmental challenges of economic development in client countries described in the Strategy (including the prudential management of trust fund resources and coordination of analytical contributions from development partners) will require adequate deployment of Bank resources.

EXTERNAL RELATIONS AND PARTNERSHIPS

In an increasingly complex international and global arena, no single public agency has the legitimacy, credibility, and financial and organizational capacity to influence decisively all major development issues alone. The coordination of activities across development agencies in the environment area is particularly important because many environmental issues have strong global public aspects.

The Bank, according to its Articles of Agreement, deals primarily with governments. However, in response to a changing development framework in which civil society and the private sector are playing an increasingly significant role in many areas, including environment, the Bank has expanded its dialogue and involvement in partnerships with civil society organizations and the private sector. These notions are expressed in the CDF, which underlines the importance of participation of key stakeholders in the decisionmaking process and encourages partnerships to enhance development effectiveness.

Partnerships are collaborative relationships based on a common vision and objectives, consideration of the comparative advantages and roles of the various parties, and a division of responsibilities and activities (see World Bank 1998). In many areas of environmental assistance, the Bank has limited comparative advantage and reasons for direct involvement. Through its convening power and informal or formal partnerships, however, it can play a catalytic role.

Our engagement has been substantial in international policy dialogue and through a wide variety of collaborative arrangements and partnerships in the environment area. These have ranged from project-level to regional- and corporate-level relationships. Partnerships also differ by level of engagement, accountability, and allocation of financial resources. A recent review in the ESSD Network has identified the key types of partnerships (see box 4.2).

Realigning with corporate priorities

We recognize that partnerships can yield major benefits by harnessing the Bank's development effectiveness. We also recognize, however, that they require careful management attention, staff time, and a mechanism for linking partnerships with core country programs and operations in order to be effective.

BOX 4.2
Partnerships review in the ESSD network

A recent review has identified three types of partnerships in the ESSD network:

1. *Institutional engagements* provide a framework for dialogue and coordination of activities between the Bank and development partners, but do not involve structured programs and specific commitments. Examples include collaboration with UNEP, WHO, OECD, IUCN, WBCSD, and many others.

2. *Collaborative arrangements* are formal agreements among partner organizations to address a certain issue or implement a time-bound program. Typically, participating organizations allocate resources to achieve specific goals. Examples include the UNDP-World Bank International Waters Partnership, the WWF-World Bank Forest Alliance, and the Mesoamerican Biological Corridor.

3. *Corporate partnerships* are entities legally established to address specific high-priority issues of global and corporate importance. They have their own governance structure, and involve high levels of institutional commitment. They can generate strong benefits but may also present high operational risks. They may address commitments to implement international agreements (such as the GEF activities*)*, new mechanisms for targeting specific global issues, or new approaches to creating global public goods (such as the Prototype Carbon Fund).

The rapid rise in the number of partnerships in recent years has raised management concerns about spreading the Bank's resources and attention among too many partnerships instead of focusing on only those partnerships in which we can most effectively catalyze action and achieve results. Given the visibility and sensitivity of some of the issues addressed by partnerships, they may also raise unreasonable expectations about what the Bank can achieve or contribute and expose the Bank to high reputational risk.

Choosing which partnerships to invest in when deciding how to allocate scarce staff, management time, and budget resources is critical. The Bank's draft Strategic Framework Paper (SFP) and draft Strategic Directions Paper (SDP) for fiscal 2002–04 have outlined broad corporate priorities and criteria for selectivity. The preliminary framework for corporate priorities distinguishes between corporate advocacy and global public goods priorities, including work toward solutions to environmental challenges. Corporate advocacy priorities are important enablers of poverty reduction that the Bank is particularly well qualified to champion by sharing knowledge, building awareness with clients, development partners, and other stakeholders.

The SFP and SDP emphasize the importance of supporting the Bank's global mandate and its capacity to implement global programs at the country level. They also call, however, for a stronger linkage between corporate priorities and country activities. A paper on *Partnership Selectivity and Oversight* (World Bank 2000d), which was discussed by the Board in April 2000, listed common criteria to be applied to assessing all potential partnerships. The criteria are:

■ Clear linkage to core institutional objectives and country operational work

- A strong case for Bank participation in terms of comparative advantage
- Potential risks to the Bank, assessed at the outset
- Thorough analysis of the expected level of Bank resources needed
- Guidelines for implementation and management of new commitments, time frame, and exit strategy
- A plan for communicating with and involving key stakeholders and for informing and consulting with EDs.

These selection criteria and the priorities of the Environment Strategy provide a comprehensive organizing framework for realigning the Bank's environmental partnerships. As part of the implementation of the Strategy, we will apply this framework rigorously to review and realign our current partnerships in the various categories (see figure 4.4). Some areas where the Bank has a strong comparative advantage to support corporate environmental priorities include:

- Working toward multi-stakeholder agreements on good, socially acceptable environmental man-

agement practices in key sectors where the Bank has significant involvement

- Working with multinational development banks in harmonizing EA procedures
- Convening key stakeholders and development partners to address regional and global environmental problems
- Building knowledge-sharing mechanisms.

A key focus for the Bank's external institutional dialogue and collaborative arrangements in the coming year will be to collaborate with clients, other UN agencies, NGOs, and private sector leaders in preparing for the next Earth Summit, to take place in Johannesburg in September, 2002.

Stocktaking and realignment

The current portfolio of partnerships has evolved over the past decade (see annex K for a list of selected external partnerships). To enhance its effectiveness, we need to strengthen its consistency with corporate criteria and strategic priorities by taking action in the following areas:

- *Portfolio update and evaluation.* During fiscal 2002, the environment family will finalize the

**Figure 4.4
Realigning partnerships**

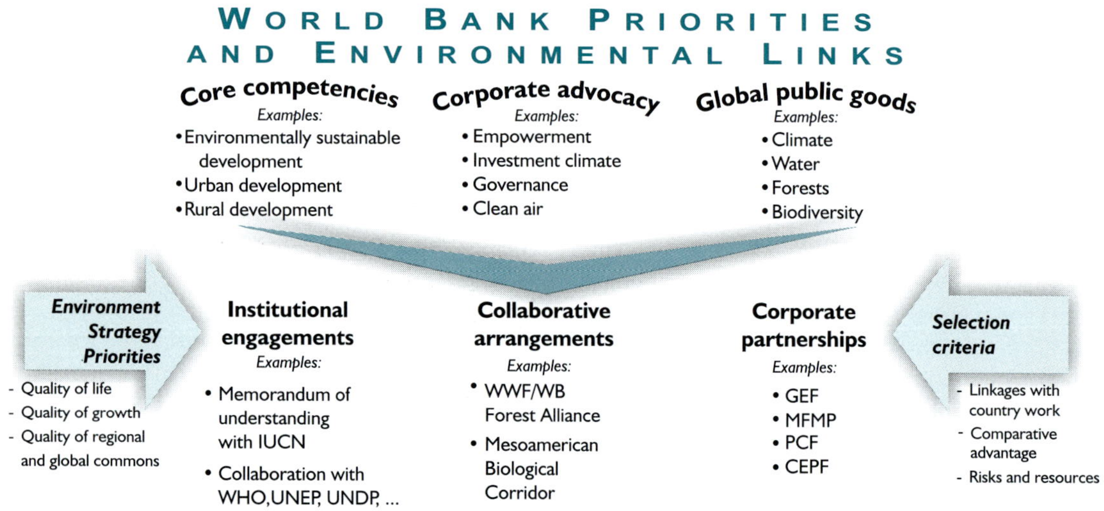

partnership portfolio review, evaluate it in relation to priorities outlined in the Strategy, and assess its effectiveness. Applying the partnership typology established in the ESSD Partnership review to clarify oversight, the EB will define more precisely monitoring, quality enhancement, and reporting responsibilities.

- *Realignment.* The EB will apply the corporate priorities and directions of the Strategy to plan for a gradual realignment of the partnership portfolio. It will review the exit strategies for existing partnerships to ensure effective transition, if necessary, and will avoid extending continuous support simply because a partnership already exists. At the same time, the EB will be open to creativity and innovation in identifying and catalyzing new partnerships that may contribute powerfully to the Strategy's implementation. The EB will coordinate with the Partnership Council to ensure that the transaction costs imposed by new partnerships on operational staff are agreed upon and affordable.

- *Governance, management, and reporting.* The EB will set guidelines for improving the governance, management, and reporting of partnerships, including donor communication, resource management, risk management, and accountability. Additionally, the Partnership Council of the Bank is in the process of identifying a corporate framework for managing corporate partnerships, which will be monitored and reviewed at the corporate level. With the EB's oversight, accurate records will be kept on partnerships, their budgetary implications, and their performance. The EB will initiate periodic reviews of the performance of our current partnerships, their links with country programs, and their alignment with our strategic priorities.

PERFORMANCE MONITORING AND REPORTING

Both internal and external consultations on the Environment Strategy have emphasized a focus on implementation and accountability for results. To ensure accountability and the capacity to learn from experience, we will introduce a performance monitoring and reporting framework that will track the Bank's performance on the environment, monitor implementation of the Strategy, and support regular reporting on progress, constraints, and steps taken to overcome the constraints. It will use the Internet and other means of communication with key stakeholders to make available reports and information about the Bank's environmental performance.

Performance monitoring and reporting will be based on joint reporting responsibilities of the ENV, RMTs, and REDs, overseen by the EB. A small performance monitoring and reporting unit will be set up in ENV, with the objectives of (a) collecting, in collaboration with the Regions, relevant data on key environment performance indicators; (b) preparing quarterly Strategy implementation reviews for the EB and senior management; (c) supporting knowledge sharing and dissemination of good practices; (d) in collaboration with the Staff Association, collecting data and reporting on our institutional footprint; and (e) publishing Environment Performance Reports in *Environment Matters,* the Environment Department's Annual Review.

The first tasks of the unit will be to examine the menu of institutional performance indicators and to assess the applicability, costs, and benefits of reporting and the sustainability of data collection in order to ensure the efficiency and utility of the system. The core categories of institutional reporting will include:

■ *Safeguard compliance.* Safeguard compliance will be carried out jointly with QACU. A unified monitoring and tracking system is being introduced to track projects and trigger safeguard policies. Biannual risk assessments will be undertaken by all Regions. Additionally, the review of safeguard-related issues by the Quality Assurance Group (QAG) will be strengthened in the areas of quality-at-entry and supervision. QAG ratings will be monitored and targets set for satisfactory ratings in the next fiscal year. Compliance reporting will also include a GHG emissions review, to be carried out by the Climate Change Team, in response to Bank policy requirements to estimate and report GHG emissions from Bank-funded projects.

■ *Mainstreaming and policy integration.* ENV, in collaboration with the Regions, will undertake regular reviews of CASs, PRSPs, adjustment loans, and the environmental aspects of key sector strategies and programs to assess how environmental issues have been addressed. The results will be shared and discussed with RVPs and RMTs and reported to senior management as part of annual Environment Strategy implementation reports. The environmental review of CASs will be coordinated with Bankwide CAS retrospective reviews prepared every 18 months for review by the Bank's Board of Directors. PRSP-environment reviews will be carried on a regular basis.

■ *Environmental projects and programs, including analytical and advisory activities.* The environment portfolio, including analytical and advisory activities, is monitored by REDs, which are responsible for their performance and quality. ENV will provide the EB with cross-Regional assessments of portfolio quality. Additionally, ENV will set up a corporate portfolio monitor-

ing system to track and monitor the environmental components of key sector portfolios. These data will be shared and discussed with the relevant Sector Boards and Regional sector units and reported as part of the annual Environment Strategy implementation reports.

■ *Training.* ENV and WBI will report on progress in delivering management, staff, and client-training programs. Tracking of training delivery will be improved to better target and customize both mandatory safeguards training and training on cutting-edge issues of sustainability, environmental policy, and poverty and environment.

CONCLUSION

As the Strategy suggests, making real progress toward poverty reduction and sustainable development requires changes in a challenging array of policies, tools, and institutional priorities.

It means looking back at the past and ahead to the future. Based on past experience, we know that we need to build on our clients' commitment, set realistic targets, and focus on the policy framework. Looking ahead to the future, we need to understand the implications of globalization and of rapid changes in science and technology, increase the role of the private sector, and strengthen the role of civil society.

It means sharpening our strategic framework by increasing the emphasis on poverty-environment links; raising environmental issues at the earliest possible stage of new development projects; more effectively merging the environment and development mindsets; and seizing every opportunity to link local action with global benefits and enhance global public goods.

It means adjusting our tools to respond to changing approaches to development assistance—through a greater use of strategic assessments; a more systematic review of adjustment lending; and more programmatic approaches.

It means institutional changes, including a greater emphasis on institutional commitments; strengthened incentives to incorporate environmental issues into development; and a more transparent monitoring and reporting system.

Most fundamentally, it means a serious commitment to the role of environmental issues in poverty reduction and development, and a wholehearted institutional commitment to see that the future of development and the effort to end poverty in this century will not be undone by environmental degradation.

Table 4.1 Institutional accountabilities for promoting environmental sustainability

Position	Responsibilities
President	• Provides overall leadership on sustainable development
Senior Management	• Oversee the implementation of the Environment Strategy through regular implementation Reviews • Hold RVPs accountable for implementation, including compliance with safeguard policies And mainstreaming • Ensure that, when justified in light of competing corporate priorities, Corporate Incentive Funding be available to help leverage resources needed to implement the Strategy. Monitor that budget management in ESSD and the Regions takes into account the costs of implementing the strategy.
Regional Vice Presidents	• Oversee the implementation of the corporate strategy through Regional Environment Strategies and annual business plans including compliance with safeguard policies and Mainstreaming • Ensure that Regional budget allocations are adequate for implementing the Strategy • Hold CDs accountable for timely completion or update of environmental diagnostic work in preparation for PRSPs and CASs, adequate mechanisms for involving environmental stakeholders in CAS consultations • Hold SDs/SMs accountable for integrating environmental issues into sectoral programs and Projects
Country Directors	• Ensure the timely completion or update of environmental diagnostic work in preparation for PRSPs and CASs including the use of environmental indicators to monitor trends • Ensure that priority environmental issues are addressed • Involve environmental stakeholders in CAS consultations and country programming
Regional Environment Departments	• Support CDs' environmental mainstreaming efforts and ensure that lessons and guidance from SSP work are transferred in a timely fashion to CASs and other task teams. • Undertake analytical and advisory activities and ensure that priority environmental issues Are addressed through policy dialogue and sectoral operations • Review Regional portfolios and clear projects and programs for safeguard compliance • Coordinate with QACU to ensure corporate consistency in safeguard policy implementation • Help prepare and supervise lending activities • Contribute to corporate reporting on the implementation of the Strategy • Through representation in the EB, ensure corporate consistency in Strategy implementation
ESSD Vice President	• Takes responsibility—together with RVPs—for compliance with safeguard policies, and for oversight of the Quality Assurance and Compliance Unit (QACU) • Manages, through QACU, the integrated corporate safeguard system and corporate risk projects, and provides advice to the Regions to resolve disputes about safeguard issues • Monitors quality indicators of compliance with safeguard policies • Coordinates sustainability issues with other networks • Oversees corporate partnerships and ensures timely submission of partnership issues to the Partnerships council • Ensures cost-effectiveness of resource allocation within ESSD and timely deliverables.
Central Environment Department	• Coordinates, monitors, and reports on strategy implementation • Provides operational support to the Regions to help mainstream environmental issues—including global issues—into operations • Oversees quality assessment of environmental lending and nonlending services • Liaises with partners and coordinates corporate partnerships

(continued)

Table 4.1 Institutional accountabilities for promoting environmental sustainability (continued)

Position	Responsibilities
Environment Board	• Reviews annual environmental business plans and strategy implementation reports • Oversees strategic deployment of resources including human resource management • Oversees the quality of the environment portfolio, and the compliance of the Bank portfolio with safeguard policies • Oversees environmental mainstreaming and coordinates with other Sector Boards
Legal Vice Presidency	• Responsible for the implementation of 2 of the 10 safeguard policies • Assists in client capacity building and institutional development projects and activities
Development Economics Vice Presidency	• Carries out research in environmental and sustainability issues • Prepares the 2003 WDR: Sustainable Development with a Dynamic Economy
World Bank Institute Vice Presidency	• Allocates staff and budget to support training on environmental safeguards and mainstreaming • Ensures that effective environmental training is delivered to staff and clients
Other Sector Boards	• Integrate environmental objectives into sector strategies • Oversee the implementation of environmental aspects of sector strategies • Coordinate with the EB on priority environmental issues in the sector
Quality Assurance Group	• Refines methodology and carries out regular assessments of the safeguard compliance at quality at entry and supervision of selected projects • Carries out regular quality at entry and quality of supervision assessments of the environment portfolio, and quality assessment of environmental ESW
Operations Evaluation Department	• Evaluates and provides independent advice to the Board on the effectiveness (outcome, sustainability, and institutional impact) of Bank projects and processes. The evaluation considers environmental aspects and compliance with relevant safeguard policies.

Regional Strategies

The countries and geographic regions assisted by the World Bank face a wide range of environmental challenges. The specific actions called for in each country will thus also vary substantially. The Bank's primary contact with clients is through the Bank's six Regions—East Asia and the Pacific, Europe and Central Asia, Latin America and the Caribbean, the Middle East and North Africa, South Asia, and Sub-Saharan Africa. As part of the Strategy preparation process, each Region prepared its own strategy applying the corporate strategic framework and reflecting the specific needs and priorities of its client countries. This annex summarizes these regional environmental strategies. Complete documents are available at <http://www.worldbank.org/environment/>.

East Asia and the Pacific

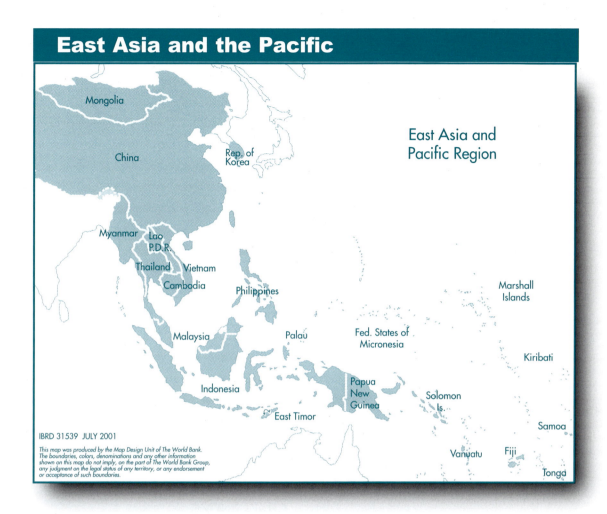

Mongolia

China

Rep. of Korea

East Asia and Pacific Region

Myanmar

Lao P.D.R.

Thailand Vietnam

Cambodia

Philippines

Marshall Islands

Malaysia

Palau

Fed. States of Micronesia

Kiribati

Indonesia

Papua New Guinea

Solomon Is.

East Timor

Samoa

Vanuatu Fiji

Tonga

IBRD 31539 JULY 2001

This map was produced by the Map Design Unit of The World Bank.
The boundaries, colors, denominations and any other information
shown on this map do not imply, on the part of The World Bank Group,
any judgment on the legal status of any territory, or any endorsement
or acceptance of such boundaries.

REGIONAL CONTEXT AND KEY ENVIRONMENTAL ISSUES

The countries in the East Asia and the Pacific Region (EAP) confront a wide variety of environmental problems. Two distinguishing features of the region have implications for the environment: extremely high population densities, and relatively rapid rates of economic growth. The region is home to about 1.8 billion people, and this number is expected to reach 3 billion by 2015. About 1.2 billion people—nearly two thirds of the region's total—live in rural areas, with farming or other resource-dependent occupations as their primary means of livelihood. Between 1980 and 1998, the urban population nearly doubled, from 310 million to over 600 million people, placing additional strains on the environment.

In spite of the economic crisis of the late 1990s, the EAP Region has experienced the fastest rate of economic growth in the world over the past 25 years. In some ways, this growth created the potential to benefit the environment by introducing cleaner technologies and generating new sources of revenue for addressing environmental externalities. However, rapid industrial growth and expanding urban populations have generally outpaced the ability of new technologies and pollution abatement investments to reduce overall pollution loads, resulting in deteriorating air and water quality and increased solid waste pollution in most countries of the region.

Pollution. In terms of immediate socioeconomic costs, air and water pollution stand out as the region's most serious environmental issues.

87

■ *Water pollution.* Studies show that more than 500,000 infants die each year in the region as a result of waterborne diseases linked to polluted water. Deficient rural water supplies account for about 60 percent of these deaths, and lack of sanitation in urban areas for another 30 percent. These impacts are equivalent to shortening the average life expectancy of everyone in the region by nearly two years.

■ *Air pollution.* Air pollution impacts are serious in many megacities of the region (Jakarta, Manila, and Bangkok, for example) and are extremely costly in China. In terms of human health, the most damaging air pollutants are fine particulates, produced primarily by fuel combustion. Air pollution in China is estimated to cause over 200,000 premature deaths each year, with total health damages in some cities equivalent to 20 percent of annual income.

■ *Indoor air pollution.* As long as solid fuels, such as coal, charcoal, and biomass, remain a significant part of residential energy supplies, indoor air pollution will continue to pose a large health problem, especially to women and children.

Despite high economic and social damages, pollution impacts are largely reversible, as evidenced by the vast improvements in air and water quality in the region's most developed countries, Japan, the Republic of Korea, and Singapore. Nonetheless, large economic and social gains can be achieved by addressing pollution problems earlier.

Natural resources. The growing pressure on natural resources, and irreversible damage to them as manifested in loss of ecosystems, species extinctions, and permanent damage to groundwater supplies, are long-term environmental concerns. Although these costs are more difficult to measure than pollution costs, the stakes are high, since what is involved is

the sustainability of key natural resource–based activities, such as agriculture, fishing, and forestry, and of human settlement patterns. Two issues in particular stand out:

■ *Deforestation.* In the early 1990s, deforestation rates in East Asia were the highest of any region. Indonesia alone lost about 20 million hectares of forest cover between 1985 and 1998. In the Philippines, nearly 90 percent of productive old-growth forests has been lost since the 1960s.

■ *Degradation of marine and coastal ecosystems.* In Southeast Asia and the Pacific island nations, marine and coastal ecosystems such as coral reefs and mangroves, on which many people depend, have been permanently damaged and are being progressively destroyed. Climate change will exacerbate many of these natural resource problems, and it is a major threat to small islands, coastal areas, and dryland and nonirrigated agricultural systems.

THE BANK'S RECORD AND FUTURE CHALLENGES

Pollution abatement. The Bank has been an important source of finance for environmental infrastructure in the EAP Region. In the sanitation sector, the Bank has promoted the creation of autonomous water and wastewater companies and the establishment of tariffs and pollution charges—both to reduce emissions and as a means of financing operation and maintenance to guarantee long-term sustainability. By far the largest share of the Bank's pollution abatement investments in the region has been for water pollution. This holds true for China, where damages from air pollution have been identified as exceeding those from dirty water. Future public investments for water and air pollution management will depend on solutions being found for recurrent financing issues, which in turn requires political commitment to the adoption and reform of environmental and resource policies.

Natural resource management (NRM). Despite more than a decade of attention, policymakers in the region are just beginning to recognize the importance of NRM issues for sustainable economic development. Most Country Assistance Strategies (CASs) have not been effective in highlighting the macro-economic, policy, and institutional factors that affect a country's environmentally sustainable development. Over the past 10 years, the region has prepared strategy studies on forestry, watershed management, and biodiversity. Some studies, including those for the Philippines, Indonesia, and Vietnam, have been instrumental in shaping natural resource management programs in those countries (see box A.1). While many agricultural development projects, particularly those in China, have been successful in raising farm-level incomes, they have not generally been effective in promoting sustainable NRM. The challenge is to redirect rural develop-ment initiatives away from individual agricultural production projects and toward sustainable NRM.

Institutional development. The World Bank has provided technical assistance to strengthen national environment agencies in the region as a way of enhancing the importance of environment issues. Through their role as implementing agencies for Bank-supported environment projects, many provincial and municipal agencies (environment, transport, construction, and utilities) have improved their technical, financial, and assessment capabilities in the environment field. To be effective over the longer term, Bank support for environmental capacity must emphasize strengthening local environment systems, community participation, environmental education, and the importance of institutions other than environment agencies (for example, those dealing with forestry, agriculture, and industry) in order to promote policy reform and to follow through on implementation. Institutional capacity building is a necessary component of overall

BOX A.1
Analytical work shapes natural resource management in East Asia

Several recent studies have helped shape the Bank's natural resource management (NRM) program in East Asia.

Philippines. Forestry, Fisheries, and Agricultural Resource Management. Led to investments promoting decentralization and community-based development to address problems in fragile uplands and improve protection of nature conservation areas. Examples include the Environment and Natural Resources Sectoral Adjustment Loan and the Conservation of Priority Protected Areas Project.

Indonesia. Forest, Land, and Water: Issues in Sustainable Development. Led to substantial changes in the Bank's rural development portfolio, including a variety of experimental and innovative approaches to biodiversity conservation and integrated pest management. Pilot river basin management programs are being supported under the Java Irrigation and Water Resources Management Project, while water users' associations and the introduction of irrigation service fees are being promoted under the Irrigation Subsector II Project.

Vietnam. Environment Program and Policy Priorities for a Socialist Economy in Transition. Led to projects for the protection of nature conservation areas (Forest Protection and Rural Development Project) and coastal wetlands (Coastal Wetlands Development and Protection Project).

environmental improvement and must be done in tandem with environment and policy development, environmental infrastructure investments, and awareness-raising.

STRATEGIC PRIORITIES AND ACTIONS

In three areas—quality of life, quality of growth, and quality of the regional and global commons—the Bank can promote both poverty reduction and environmentally sustainable development in the EAP Region.

Quality of life

Pollution management. Nearly all client countries in the region are experiencing severe health problems related to water pollution. The Bank will continue to support activities to improve urban drainage and sanitation, as well as rural water supply and sanitation. Health and hygiene education is one of the most cost-effective interventions for reducing health impacts. New and increased support for urban sanitation and drainage investments and for rural and periurban water supply and sanitation activities is envisaged in most countries in the region.

Many parts of the region face serious air pollution problems. In their impact on human health, the most damaging air pollutants are fine particulates, produced primarily by fuel combustion. The Bank is supporting a number of cost-effective approaches to urban air quality management in EAP through its lending and nonlending services. Among the interventions are the expansion of the use of natural gas and other clean fuels in residential, commercial, and industrial activities (China, Vietnam), improvements in space heating in northern climates (China), and reduction of transport sector expo-

sures. In the transport area, interventions promote a switch to unleaded gasoline (Indonesia, Vietnam), improvements in fuel quality (Indonesia), improved traffic management (China, the Philippines, Vietnam), introduction of cleaner vehicle technologies and improved maintenance and inspection (Thailand), and urban planning that is less traffic-intensive (the Philippines).

As long as solid fuels such as coal, charcoal, and biomass remain a significant part of residential energy supplies in the region, indoor air pollution will continue to pose a large health problem, especially to women and children. A pilot indoor air pollution project has recently begun in Mongolia to reduce health impacts associated with inefficient home heating and cooking stoves. The Bank should continue to discuss assessments and potential interventions in China, where several hundred million people still rely on solid fuels for cooking and heating.

Natural resource management (NRM). Better management of natural resources—through soil and water conservation, forest protection, coastal zone and marine management, and ecosystem and biodiversity conservation—is essential for enhancing rural livelihoods in the EAP Region. To effectively address these issues, a long-term, concerted effort is required, including integration of natural resource policy within the macroeconomic policy and agricultural development agendas of national governments. A priority for the Bank is to identify critical NRM issues in countries of the region and to ensure that policies supporting sustainable resource management are incorporated within CAS, Comprehensive Development Framework (CDF), and Poverty Reduction Strategy Paper (PRSP) processes. The Bank will also support additional investments in high-quality analytical work on natural resource issues.

The Bank is developing regional and country water strategies to address water resource management (in both river basins and aquifers), water scarcity, water pollution, and watershed management. Operations to strengthen water resource management are under way or planned in China, Indonesia, the Philippines, and Vietnam. A water strategy study for China, now being prepared, will highlight water stresses in several northern river basins and the need for effective river basin management, water pricing, and conservation options for agricultural, industrial, and residential users. The Bank is also supporting pollution control investments in several water-scarce river basins in northern China

Aside from the "5 million hectare" afforestation program in Vietnam, the Bank will primarily support smaller-scale community forestry programs, with an emphasis on conservation and sustainable forestry development. Sustainable forestry programs are under way or planned in China, Laos, Papua New Guinea, and the Solomon Islands. In Indonesia, the Bank and other donors have linked forestry (and water) policy reforms to discussions of overall economic reform. A resumption of Bank support to the forestry sector in Indonesia is dependent on progress on two issues: broadening the dialogue on forestry policy and management to nonforest agencies, and delegating management authority over degraded forests to parties outside the forestry bureaucracy, such as local communities, nongovernmental organizations (NGOs), the private sector, and other natural resource agencies.

Reducing vulnerability to natural disasters is a critical issue in the region. The Bank has provided support for relief and reconstruction following floods, volcanic eruptions, and earthquakes. Moving from curative to preventive actions, the Bank plans to become more involved in addressing long-term risk reduction and mitigation measures as part of its advisory assistance and investment operations. Examples include flood control, preparedness, and prevention initiatives in China and Vietnam and, in the Pacific, measures for risk reduction and for adaptation to climate variability and extreme weather events.

Quality of growth

The World Bank will support environmentally sustainable growth in the region by promoting macroeconomic and sector policy reforms that strike a balance between growth and environmental protection; by working with clients to build environmental assessment and regulatory capacities; by supporting efforts to increase public participation and environmental awareness; and by effectively implementing the Bank's own environmental safeguard policies.

Policy environment. In the macroeconomic and sector policy arena, the Bank will promote policy reforms that improve natural resource use and reduce pollution externalities. In addition to investment projects, the Bank can promote environmentally sound policies within the context of sectoral adjustment loans, as exemplified by the ongoing discussions in Indonesia on forest and water policy reforms.

Institutional development. Throughout the region, the Bank will continue to provide support for environmental assessment and regulatory capacities. In Thailand, for example, an environmental institutional development project will strengthen local environmental planning and regulatory capacities, support regulatory reforms to improve compliance, and improve environmental financing. Similar efforts are needed elsewhere, especially in the poorest countries. The Bank will cooperate with other donors and partners to provide such assistance.

The Bank is actively promoting new approaches in environmental regulation through both lending and nonlending policy dialogue. Public disclosure of environmental information is an indirect but promising measure for encouraging pollution prevention and abatement. Rating systems, such as PROPER in Indonesia and the EcoWatch Program in the Philippines, make public the environmental performance, both good and bad, of industrial enterprises. Even in countries with significant public ownership of industries and limited environmental regulatory capacities, this type of program has the potential to improve environmental performance at low cost. The Bank recently initiated pilot environmental information and disclosure programs in Hanoi (industrial water pollution) and in Hohhot and Zhenjiang, China. It has also collated and published environmental indicators in Thailand and the Philippines, with the aim of increasing their accessibility to civil society.

Another area of work concerns strengthening the application of safeguard policies, both within the Bank and within our client countries. This is an important precondition for expanding the role of the private sector. Recent reviews of the Bank's safeguards record indicate that increased attention needs to be paid to building local environmental management and environmental assessment capacity, improving public consultation, and integrating environmental and social assessments. The other area of concern is the need to focus on the implementation of environmental management plans. To date, safeguards measures have been biased toward preparation and appraisal of projects. Continued emphasis on thematic reviews of projects in the EAP region is needed to improve effective implementation of safeguard policies. Finally, there is a need for harmonization of safeguard policies among countries and in the donor community. The EAP Region is funding several country reviews to identify differences in World Bank and country safeguard requirements, especially in the area of social safeguards.

Quality of the regional and global environment

Regional environment issues. As a multilateral institution, the Bank can play an important role in helping address regional environment issues, such as river basin management and acid rain. Some of these issues have already gained the attention of policymakers in the region. The Global Environment Facility (GEF) recently approved support for the Mekong River Commission to establish mechanisms to promote and improve coordinated and sustainable water management, including reasonable and equitable water utilization by the countries of the Mekong basin, and to protect the basin's environment, aquatic life, and ecological balance. Since 1991, the Bank has supported research and training on acid rain issues, through the RAINS-Asia program, and it recently began a technical assistance project in China to assess direct and indirect impacts of sulfur emissions and cost-effective mitigation options.

Climate change. In the climate change area, the Bank will support mitigation efforts that yield large local economic and environmental benefits, as well as global benefits. In addition to energy sector reform, which can have the largest impact on the efficiency of energy production and use, and thus on greenhouse gas reduction, the Bank will support energy efficiency and fuel switching (including greater use of renewables) through the GEF and other concessional resources (see also box 3.4 in chapter

3). The EAP Region has considerable experience in supporting energy efficiency and renewable energy projects through the Asia Alternative Energy Program. Many of these investments also target the poor—for example, by increasing access to energy for the rural poor through development of renewable energy. New operations to support climate change mitigation are planned for Cambodia, China, Mongolia, the Philippines, Thailand, and Vietnam. Given the importance of climate change impacts to the region, the Bank also plans to support vulnerability and adaptation assessments, beginning with pilots in countries with a history of climate disasters, such as Vietnam and the Pacific island nations.

Biodiversity. In the face of serious threats to ecosystems and biodiversity in the region, the Bank will raise these issues country by country in the context of natural resource and development policies. The Bank will mainstream biodiversity concerns in both policy and investment activities, with the assistance of GEF and other grant resources. The EAP Region has an extensive portfolio of biodiversity projects, most of which take an ecosystem approach to conservation, and focus on biodiversity management, both within protected areas and beyond their boundaries into the production landscape. Increasingly, biodiversity projects in the region will be more closely related to natural resource management interventions, which in turn will emphasize community participation and improved livelihoods. Biodiversity projects in Indonesia, the Philippines, Thailand, and Vietnam will support sustainable forestry, coastal zone and marine protection, and river basin management.

ODS and POPs. Supporting the phaseout of ozone-depleting substances (ODSs) is a continuing priority in the region. The China ODS program has recently been supplemented with the chlorofluorocarbon (CFC) phaseout program to further advance China's efforts toward accomplishing the goals of the Montreal Protocol. Given the region's intensive industrialization and widespread use of agricultural chemicals, there are plans to develop a major program to address persistent organic pollutants (POPs).

IMPLEMENTATION ARRANGEMENTS

To effectively implement the strategy, both internal and external coordination is needed. Within the Bank, the strategy has the support of the country departments and will be led by the key sector units involved in environment-related projects, especially the Rural Development, Urban Development, and Energy units. Externally, the strategy framework has been broadly endorsed by client countries in the region. It is now necessary to develop a sound implementation plan with countries and with other development partners, including international and bilateral donors and the private sector (see box A.2).

Partnerships. The Bank is developing a number of formal and informal partnerships in the EAP Region to address both pollution and natural resource issues. Most of these partnerships are related to specific project interventions. A number of forestry activities in the region—including the policy discussions in Indonesia—are being undertaken as part of the World Bank/World Wide Fund for Nature (WWF) Global Forest Alliance. The Bank is also partnering with The Nature Council, Birdlife International, and other conservation NGOs on biodiversity conservation initiatives in Indonesia, Papua New Guinea, and Vietnam.

Following up on work in the region on acid rain and urban air pollution, a regional initiative to improve air quality management is getting under way.

BOX A.2
Preparing an environmental strategy for East Asia

This strategy paper reflects the results of nine months of stocktaking and consultations by EAP staff to realign its environment work so as to more directly address poverty reduction and sustainable development. It builds on a number of recent environment and sector studies; internal consultations within the World Bank among key sectoral units (rural development, urban development, energy and mining, transport, and environment); and external consultations with regional stakeholders in Tokyo (May 2000), Singapore (June 2000), Bangkok (October 2000), and Beijing (February 2001).

The key studies are:

- "Natural Resources Management: A Strategic Framework for East Asia and the Pacific" (Crooks and others 1999)
- *Clear Water, Blue Skies: China's Environment in the 21st Century* (Johnson and others 1997)
- *Can the Environment Wait? Priorities for East Asia* (World Bank 1997a)
- "Indonesia Environment and Natural Resource Management in a Time of Transition" (World Bank 2001c)
- "China: Environment Sector Strategy Update" (World Bank 2001b).

Under this Clean Air Initiative, the Bank will collaborate with multilateral and bilateral donors, the private sector, and regional governments to share lessons on effective air quality management. The Bank is also developing a cooperative program under the Knowledge Partnership with Korea to share that country's environmental experiences with other countries of Asia, specifically China and Vietnam. Bank-Korea cooperation, currently focused on industrial pollution and environmental management, could expand to cover other issues of importance to the region, such as forestry, wetland protection, and river basin management.

Next steps. To begin implementing the strategy over the next six to nine months the Bank will disseminate the framework within the Bank and to external stakeholders; refine the medium- and longer-term priorities for implementing the strategy by key sectors, countries, and Bank instruments; and assess to what extent staff and budgets need to be realigned to achieve the desired outcomes.

Europe and Central Asia

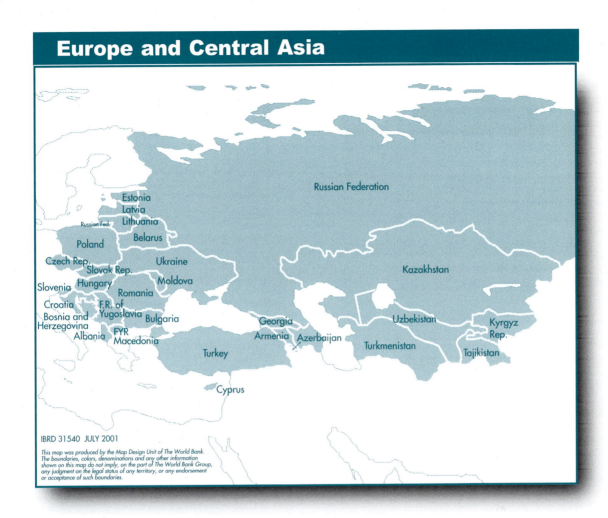

IBRD 31540 JULY 2001

This map was produced by the Map Design Unit of The World Bank.
The boundaries, colors, denominations and any other information
shown on this map do not imply, on the part of The World Bank Group,
any judgment on the legal status of any territory, or any endorsement
or acceptance of such boundaries.

REGIONAL AND ENVIRONMENTAL CONTEXT

The Europe and Central Asia (ECA) Region comprises 27 countries. All but Turkey are in various stages of transition from centrally planned economies. Some are well on the way to joining the European Union (EU), while others have a large, unfinished reform agenda that encompasses profound and far-reaching economic and social changes. Regionwide, poverty increased from 16 million in 1987 to 90 million in 1998, particularly in the newly independent states (NIS) and the Balkans, although it remains low compared with other regions. Poverty rates vary significantly, from below 10 percent in countries in Central Europe to 68 percent in Tajikistan. Civil conflicts, natural disasters, refugees, and ethnic problems are major complicating factors in Central Asia, the Balkans, and the Caucasus.

Changes in environmental performance have been closely linked with the economic reform process. Important structural reforms related to the environment sector include the introduction of incentives for efficient energy use (for example, by eliminating fuel subsidies and making the energy sector competitive); reform of municipal utilities through such measures as eliminating subsidies and raising tariffs; privatization of the consumer and industrial sectors; promotion of free trade; establishment of basic environmental protection and management systems; improvement of natural resource management; and public participation in environmental issues.

The political dynamics in the region often make it difficult to implement the necessary reforms. Governments are reluctant to eliminate energy subsidies or raise tariffs for fear that populations cannot afford the increases. Wage arrears, barter payments, lack of metering, and the relative insolvency of many municipalities complicate utility reforms. Where acceptable, privatization with effective regulation is proving more successful than attempts to reform municipal enterprises through traditional technical assistance and investment projects.

Lack of domestic energy supplies is driving a rush for new strategic alliances and generating proposals for new oil and gas pipelines that raise environmental concerns associated with construction and potential oil spills. In energy-rich countries such as Russia and Kazakhstan, the desire to maximize export earnings of oil and gas places renewed pressure on domestic users to burn dirtier fossil fuels, particularly coal. For energy-poor countries, the increasing prices of energy inputs and the absence of reforms at the distribution level have led to the collapse of district heating plants, the burning of alternative dirtier fuels, and the installation of less-efficient small boilers.

Although most ECA countries have a relatively good legal and regulatory framework for environmental management, institutional capacity to implement and enforce regulations is weak, and government officials do not always agree on the importance and urgency of environmental issues. On the positive side, expanding freedoms have led to an increasingly vocal and influential civil society, including NGOs and independent journalists, who are pressing for the laws to be upheld.

KEY ENVIRONMENTAL CHALLENGES

ECA's key environmental challenges vary significantly, depending on the stage of progress in moving to a market economy and differences in topography, geology, climate, natural resource availability, development patterns, and per capita income. In comparison with most other parts of the world, pressures on the environment and natural resources are not high, except in Central Asia. Populations are decreasing, and the general decline in economic activity has significantly reduced air pollution. Nevertheless, there are problem areas. Environmental challenges stemming from past liabilities remain an issue in highly polluting industries such as chemicals, petrochemicals, and metallurgy. In many areas, access to clean water is endangered by the deteriorating financial condition of municipal water and wastewater utilities. In Central Asia, the poor condition of irrigation infrastructure and bad agricultural practices threaten livelihoods and contribute to land degradation. Natural resource management and preservation of coastal ecosystems are important issues in some countries.

Differing situations by country group. In summarizing the key challenges, it is useful to group countries as follows:

- *The Baltics, Central and Southeastern Europe, and Turkey* includes a range of countries, from those that have implemented sustainable reforms and developed good institutional and regulatory capacities for managing environmental issues (for example, Estonia, Hungary, Poland, and Slovenia) to others where the reform process has been sharply interrupted in the past or the institutional and regulatory framework for dealing with environmental issues is still developing (for example, Albania, Bosnia and Herzegovina, Macedonia, and Romania).[1] Some countries have generally higher per capita income and strong capacity to manage the environment and can rely largely on private sector financing to fund environmental investments. Others have particularly difficult challenges related to dependence on large energy imports or emergence from conflicts. Where substantial progress in restructuring industry and realigning the roles of the public and private sectors to better fit a market-based economy has occurred, pollution intensity has been reduced as industry modernizes, incorporates proper pollution abatement techniques, or shifts to less-polluting sectors. In general, however, environmental issues include the potential collapse of water and wastewater services where reforms are weak; water contamination from agricultural or industrial pollutants; energy inefficiency; threats to natural resources; coastal, forest, and landscape management; and some residual hazardous waste hotspots, including land mines and other residues from war.

■ *The Western NIS countries* have made substantially less progress on reforms than the Central and Eastern European countries.[2] They have highly urbanized populations, localized ambient air pollution in selected cities, and water pollution from municipal and industrial waste, and they are threatened by the potential collapse of water and wastewater services. Hazardous waste contamination and other existing environmental liabilities are an issue in highly polluting industries such as chemicals, petrochemicals, and metallurgy. Large areas in Belarus and Ukraine were affected by radioactive fallout from the Chernobyl nuclear accident.

■ *Russia* shares the characteristics and environmental problems of the NIS subgroup but merits special mention because of its enormous energy resources, land mass, forest cover (22 per-

cent of the world's forests), and greenhouse gas emissions (17 percent of the OECD total). Its forest management and carbon balance are consequently of enormous relevance globally as well as nationally. Another problem particular to Russia is the deteriorated condition of many of its oil pipelines, which represent a disaster waiting to happen. Sound management of arctic and riparian ecosystems and preservation of biodiversity and unique areas such as Lake Baikal are other important challenges.

■ *Central Asia and the Caucasus* includes three of the poorest countries in ECA and some of the slowest reformers.[3] All suffer from many of the same issues as the Western NIS countries, but this region has a larger share of rural population. The Caucasus faces coastal and land degradation issues, as well, and oil-rich Azerbaijan and Kazakhstan are concerned with oil drilling, pipeline construction, degradation, and oil spill prevention and cleanups. For the Central Asian countries, water resource management is the top environmental priority. These countries are situated in an arid zone, where cultivation is impossible without irrigation. An elaborate irrigation system was built by the Soviet Union, diverting water on such a scale that the Aral Sea nearly dried up. The system depended on complex arrangements for trading crops, energy, water, and agricultural inputs, and these arrangements have collapsed. The irrigation system infrastructure is now crumbling as a result of a chronic lack of maintenance, and poor irrigation practices have led to salinization of the soils. The result is some of the worst poverty in the region. Safe drinking water is also an issue in some rural areas, as groundwater is often polluted by runoff from agriculture and mining. Better price incentives for farmers and restructuring of water user associations could partially help, but it is likely that only a fraction of the irrigation system can be made sustainable over the long term. An uneven distribution of water resources among countries exacerbates these problems and raises transboundary tensions. Efforts to sustainably link energy supplies with water releases and to agree on an overall water management system for the riparian countries have not yet succeeded.

Regional waters. The management of regional seas and rivers is an important challenge for virtually all countries in the region. In addition to the dessication of the Aral Sea, the Caspian Sea is threatened by pollution from the Volga and other rivers, pollution and accidental spills from the oil industry, and uncontrolled poaching, which threatens biodiversity, especially the sturgeon fishery. Regional agreements on management of the Caspian and Aral Seas remain difficult, making Bank-assisted programs hard to implement. The Black Sea is affected by nutrient and wastewater discharges carried by the Danube River. The experience of the Baltic Sea, where similar problems with pollution and oil spills are being reversed by regional cooperation, shows the potential for improvement.

LESSONS LEARNED

The Bank initially focused on the environmental implications of shifting from a command to a market economy, emphasizing the removal of distorted incentives and subsidies in agriculture, energy, and water and the establishment of a regulatory framework and institutional capacity for environmental management. More recently, this agenda has been broadened to include assistance with natural resource management, biodiversity conservation, global commons concerns, agricultural and irrigation practices, and access of rural populations to clean water and to sanitation facilities. The Bank has addressed environmental issues through a wide variety of instruments, including adjustment operations, investment projects, technical assistance, assistance to policy reform, and analytical work, which have both a direct and an indirect bearing on environmental issues.

Setting priorities. Considerable effort has been devoted to developing a broad consensus on environmental issues among governments, donors, NGOs, and civil society. The Bank led the preparation of an Environmental Action Program for Europe (later adopted by the Lucerne Ministerial Conference in 1993), which emphasized synergies between reform and the environment. Subsequently, the Environment for Europe ministerial conferences, in Sofia in 1995 and in Århus in 1998, took up several priority issues. The Århus Conference adopted the broad recommendations and agenda for environmental improvement laid out for the NIS. Most countries have prepared some form of National Environmental Action Plan (NEAP) or environment strategies, often with active Bank support. Many are now preparing second-generation NEAPs to correct earlier deficiencies, better prioritize investments, and develop least-cost options. Efforts to prioritize environmental issues have also been made in numerous Country Assistance Strategies (CASs) and, more recently, in PRSPs.

Sector studies and analytical work. Sector studies undertaken by the Bank include efforts to understand the links between environmental problems and health; to evaluate the links between energy and environment; to argue the case for phasing out leaded gasoline, adopting cleaner fuels, improving traffic flow, and promoting more fuel-efficient vehicles; to quantify the fiscal and environmental impacts from better natural resource management, particularly management of forests; to link increased tourism with better coastal management; and to link agricultural productivity and rural livelihoods to better agricultural practices and irrigation restructuring.

Capacity development. Capacity development has been supported throughout the region. A number of countries have received institutional development grants, GEF grants for enabling activities, and, in the cases of Russia and Poland, major technical assistance loans. However, governments are generally unwilling to borrow for technical assistance, and even grant assistance is often ineffective unless it is genuinely desired by the recipients and well integrated with local expertise.

Environmental investments. Bank investment financing has focused on industrial pollution management, reform of water and district heating utilities, energy efficiency, rehabilitation of water supply and irrigation infrastructure, water resource management, land and coastal zone management, forestry, and biodiversity (see box A.3 for an example). With GEF support, the Bank has assisted ECA countries to cease production of ozone-depleting substances. The GEF has also financed several geothermal projects, including the first one to use the Bank's Prototype Carbon Fund (PCF).

Policy adjustments. Structural Adjustment Loans (SALs) and energy policy advice, with their emphasis on ending energy subsidies and on restructuring, have helped improve energy efficiency and air quality. Ending subsidies of communal services, improving cash collection, increasing tariffs, and furthering housing privatization have improved the viability and prevented the col-

---

BOX A.3
Albania: Community-based forest management in a transition economy

Forests cover 38 percent of Albania's land area, with broad-leaved forests, mainly oak and beech, predominating. Fuelwood accounts for over 40 percent of recorded timber production. Pastureland covers 15 percent of land area, and 60 percent of the population is dependent or partially dependent on pastoralism. Forests and pastureland are owned by the state. Since 1990, Albania has moved rapidly toward market-based reforms, but there have been increasing problems relating to governance and law and order, including illegal timber harvesting.

The Community-Based Forest Management Project aimed to restore degraded state-owned forest and pasture areas and promote their sustainable use; promote conservation of natural forest ecosystems; and initiate a transition of the forestry and pasture sector to a market economy—separating commercial from regulatory functions and establishing mechanisms for self-financing of the commercial activities. In addition to assisting with improving forest management at the local level and reorganizing forest sector institutions, the project is improving trade, marketing, and pricing policies to enhance revenue; implementing, in collaboration with local governments and the Ministry of Finance Tax Inspection, an action plan to reduce illegal harvesting; and supporting community forestry by providing local communities with legal user rights for communal and forest pastures, with assistance to improve their management, and with mechanisms for reinvesting user fees in improved management and in training forest specialists in the public and private sectors.

Because of broader poverty, law and order, and governance issues, controlling illegal harvesting and improving forest management on publicly managed land has been difficult. The transfer of user rights and management to local communities has, however, worked very well; user rights have been transferred for 10 years. Local communities have been assisted with development of management plans and have invested user fees in improving the resource. This component is being expanded and may form the basis for a follow-on natural resources and environment project.

lapse of some district heating companies and water utilities.

Support for private sector activities. Recognizing that environmental investments in a market economy are made primarily by the private sector, the Bank has promoted policies that help the private sector address past and future environmental liabilities. In Bulgaria, as part of the privatization process, the Bank helped finance government costs associated with historical environmental liability (see box 2.3 in chapter 2). The Russia Forestry Guarantee Project offers political risk guarantees for private sector investors in timber companies that abide by sustainable forestry and timber processing practices. In several instances, the Bank has attempted to provide financing for pollution abatement investments through financial intermediaries, but high foreign exchange risks, the financial risks of borrowing enterprises, limited demand for environmental projects, and weaknesses in the banking sector have limited the success of these projects.

STRATEGIC PRIORITIES AND ACTIONS

ECA's Environment Strategy is shaped by the ECA Region's broader priorities of (a) facilitating EU accession for the fast-reforming countries of Central and Eastern Europe, (b) reversing poverty and reviving growth in the NIS, (c) helping to bring about peace and prosperity in the Balkans, and (d) fostering cooperation on regional and global environmental issues.

Quality of life

The Strategy aims at improving the quality of life through environmental interventions. Priority actions include:

- Improving access to safe drinking water by (a) rehabilitating or expanding urban infrastructure, in conjunction with utility reforms and privatization efforts, and (b) supporting community-developed water supply and sanitation investments in rural areas
- Mitigating health threats from toxic substances and industrial accidents by (a) assisting effective environmental management and protection systems and (b) financing cleanups, where appropriate
- Reducing health problems associated with air quality by promoting (a) conversion to less-polluting sources of heat and. in part, by increased metering and privatization of housing, (b) higher fuel standards, increased vehicle inspections, and improved traffic management, and (c) energy reforms that will reduce power plant emissions
- Improving livelihoods through sustainable NRM by (a) assisting sustainable forest management and community-based watershed management, (b) promoting an integrated water basin approach in Central Asia, and (c) promoting energy conservation and efficient use
- Improving security though prevention and mitigation of natural disasters by (a) assisting clients in mitigating the impact of natural disasters, such as earthquakes in Turkey and Armenia, droughts in Central Asia, and floods in Poland, and (b) assisting clients to improve dam safety.

Quality of growth

The strategy aims at ensuring the quality of growth through the following priority actions:
- Integrating environmental considerations into macro and sector policies and public sector management by (a) building local capacity to assess the environmental impact of policies,

(b) conducting economic valuations of environmental degradation, (c) supporting a transparent legal and regulatory framework, and (d) improving environmental regulations by strengthening environmental review capacity

- Removing environment-related impediments to investment by helping governments address environmental liability issues within the context of privatization.

Quality of the global commons

To improve the quality of the regional and global commons, the priorities for action in ECA's Environment Strategy are to:

- Assist governments to address climate change and to achieve the aims of the Kyoto Protocol. ECA countries emit about 20 percent of the world's greenhouse gases—the most of any Bank region. We will assist governments to complete and update their national strategies; we will provide technical assistance; and, if requested and if the projects are consistent with the relevant CASs, we will support projects with local and global benefits via GEF, the PCF, and Bank financing.
- Support biodiversity conservation by (a) helping to protect fragile or endangered ecosystems and involving local communities in the management of biodiversity and protected areas, and (b) identifying and supporting areas where global and local benefits overlap.
- Promote corporate management of international waters by (a) assisting regional bodies to develop regulations for use and protection of international waters and their flora and fauna, (b) helping to preserve the Caspian sturgeon, (c) working for reducing nutrient discharges into the Black Sea, and (d) help arresting the deterioration of the Aral Sea. We will support monitor-

ing and multicountry consensus building regarding the competing demands of irrigation, energy, and other uses of scarce water resources.

- Complete programs to finance the phaseout of residual production and consumption of ozone-depleting substances.

The specific priorities clearly vary across the region. The EU accession countries need Bank advice on cost-effective ways to meet the requirements of EU environmental legislation. To a limited extent, we will continue promoting air quality improvements, mainly through interventions in district heating and renewable energy with local and global benefits that are eligible for GEF financing. In Turkey, we expect to sharpen the focus on disaster prevention, water resources, and watershed and landscape management. In southeastern Europe, operations will be aligned with the Strategy for Stability and Prosperity in South Eastern Europe, developed jointly with the EU. The Danube and Black Sea Program will provide the framework for activities aimed at reducing agricultural and industrial pollution, restoring wetlands, and improving wastewater management. In Russia, we will offer support for managing urban air quality related to the transport and energy sectors, which poses an increasing threat to health. Because of the country's large GHG emissions, climate change issues are of great importance in Russia, and we will seek synergies with local air quality programs and forestry policies. In addition, we will seek to promote sounder environmental management in the oil sector. In the Western NIS and Caucasus, we are addressing issues of fisheries, tourism, wetland protection, oil transport, and oil spill prevention; supporting efforts to rationalize and rehabilitate irrigation systems, in conjunction with agricultural reforms; and working with rural communities to create sustainable community-developed rural water supply projects. In the Central Asian countries and Azerbaijan, water supply and water resource management are the overriding priorities. Through regional mechanisms such as the Aral Sea Program, we will assist the subregion in rationally allocating water resources to energy, agricultural, urban, and ecological uses. To address the related concern of soil salinization, we will offer assistance to improve irrigation and drainage management. We are supporting the development of community-driven rural water supply and sanitation projects, as well as reform of urban water supply enterprises.

IMPLEMENTATION OF THE STRATEGY

Cross-sectoral linkages. Given the many linkages between environmental issues and other sectors, implementation of this Strategy will require strong cross-sectoral alliances with colleagues working on energy, infrastructure, as well as agriculture, rural development, and forestry. Social assessments will be integrated into efforts to develop rural community-based improvement projects in water supply, irrigation, and agricultural practices. Close collaboration with our colleagues in the poverty reduction and human development groups will be required, particularly to better assess linkages between poverty, health, economic growth, structural reforms, and environment; to assess the environmental impacts of proposed structural and policy reforms; and to incorporate environmental agendas and priorities into CASs and PRSPs.

Safeguards. The region will continue to apply safeguard policies to avoid negative impacts of projects in all sectors, promote implementation of project-specific environmental management plans, and improve oversight of safeguard policy compliance during project implementation. We intend to re-

view safeguard policies implemented by financial intermediaries in client countries with credit-line projects. These efforts, along with direct assistance, will strengthen the capacity of client countries to conduct environmental assessments and protect the environment.

Project design and selectivity. Project development will use a participatory approach where appropriate, follow best practices, take into account lessons learned, and focus on results and how to measure them. To this end, result-oriented indicators will be devised and built into project design. We also intend to work with clients to cancel or restructure poorly performing projects, as warranted. We will increase our efforts to be selective and to leverage limited resources through partnerships. GEF and Post-Conflict Program (PCP) funds will be linked to Bank projects that are identified in CASs; priority for these limited funds will be given to regional projects, the NIS, and the Balkan countries. We plan to make more use of International Finance Corporation (IFC) and Multilateral Investment Guarantee Agency (MIGA) instruments in mobilizing private sector investments for environmental management, particularly to help reform urban water and solid waste services, modernize refineries, and promote energy efficiency. We envisage working with the World Bank Institute (WBI) to assist in conveying best practices and in developing avenues for clients to learn from each other—for example, through the Clean Air Initiative, which will enable selected cities to learn from best practices and from each other regarding measures for combating local air pollution.

Mainstreaming environment. Working with experts in the Bank and in core ministries in our client governments, we plan to develop broad-based indicators that will better monitor country performance on general environmental issues, including environmental management, greenhouse gas emissions, local air pollution, land degradation, carbon sequestration and conservation, and biodiversity conservation.

Leveraging resources and building partnerships. Building on established relationships, our strategy will call for avoiding duplication of other donors' efforts, simplifying collaborative mechanisms, and reducing transaction costs. In the EU accession countries, we will defer to the EU. In the Baltic countries, we will work closely with the Nordic countries and their development institutions. In the Balkans, we will continue our already substantial

coordination efforts among bilateral and multilateral donors and interested parties. In Central Asia, we will work particularly closely with the Asian Development Bank. We will strive to maximize use of mechanisms such as the Joint Environment Program (JEP) to better utilize Tacis grant needs for project preparation costs. On specific environmental issues, we will work closely with NGOs and global funds such as the GEF, the PCF, the WWF, and the Alliance for Forests. We will continue to consult with these partners as well as with our clients to ensure that our regional strategy and annual work plans are clear, complementary to the efforts of other donors, and responsive to client priorities.

Latin America and the Caribbean

The Bahamas

Mexico

Guatemala   Belize   Jamaica
El Salvador — Honduras
Nicaragua
Costa Rica
Panama

R.B. de Venezuela

Colombia   Suriname

Ecuador   Guyana

Peru

Brazil

Bolivia

Paraguay

Chile

Uruguay

Argentina

Haiti
Dominican Rep.
St. Kitts and Nevis
Antigua and Barbuda
Dominica
St. Lucia
Barbados
St. Vincent and the Grenadines
Grenada
Trinidad and Tobago

IBRD 31541 JULY 2001

This map was produced by the Map Design Unit of The World Bank.
The boundaries, colors, denominations and any other information
shown on this map do not imply, on the part of The World Bank Group,
any judgment on the legal status of any territory, or any endorsement
or acceptance of such boundaries.

Falkland Islands (Islas Malvinas)
A dispute concerning sovereignty over the islands exists
between Argentina which claims this sovereignty and
the U.K. which administers the islands.

The special features of the Latin America and Caribbean (LAC) Region include considerable heterogeneity in social and economic conditions, both within and across countries; increasing integration of economies into the world economy; the formation of regional trading blocks such as Mercosur; a high degree of urbanization, with 75 percent of the region's 500 million inhabitants living in cities and making a living in the industrial and service sectors; and a deepening of democracy, coupled with a trend toward increasing decentralization and improved governance. These factors and trends will influence environmental conditions and management policies and will shape the challenges to be faced in the coming years.

REGIONAL CONTEXT AND KEY ENVIRONMENTAL ISSUES

In the short term, governments in LAC have the formidable task of making cities more hospitable venues for economic development while improving the living conditions of the poor. Most countries in Latin America have been pursuing macroeconomic stabilization and liberalization policies. The impacts of these policies are still uncertain, but they will have both positive ramifications, such as higher environmental standards, and negative ones, such as continued or even increased reliance on the natural resource base. In the coming decade, it is likely that democracy will deepen and civil society will become more proactive. This should lead to calls for continuous integration of environmental concerns into public sector policies, notably in the fight against poverty and the creation of development opportunities.

The key environmental issues in LAC include (a) urban-industrial pollution, (b) mismanagement of natural resources in areas of existing and new settlement, and the consequent loss of terrestrial and marine biodiversity, and (c) high vulnerability of urban and rural populations to natural disasters. The causes of degradation include the poor socioeconomic condition of large segments of the region's population, the high dependence of many economies on the exploitation of natural resources, limited institutional capacity to enforce environmental regulations and policies, inappropriate pricing and subsidies and unclear property rights, weak economic incentives, limited participation by stakeholders, few partnerships with polluters, and limited data and planning methodologies.

The strong links between urban environmental degradation and poor socioeconomic conditions, coupled with high levels of urbanization, suggest that urban and industrial pollution disproportionately affects the poor (see figure B.2 in annex B). For the most part, urban populations in LAC have good access to safe water, generally in the 70 to 90 percent range. By contrast, the rural populations' access is typically 20 to 50 percent. Urban populations also generally have much better access to sanitation—70 to 80 percent in most LAC countries—but the United Nations Environment Programme (UNEP) estimates that only about 2 percent of wastewater is adequately treated. Access to clean water, sewage collection, solid waste collection, and air pollution control in large cities are at the top of the environmental agenda, especially because they more intensely affect the poor segments of society.

The region is also particularly rich in natural resources and biodiversity, and mismanagement of natural resources and threats to terrestrial and ma-

rine biodiversity rank high on the environmental agenda. According to UNEP's recent *State of the Environment* report (UNEP 2000), 6 million hectares of natural forest cover were cleared or went up in smoke per year between 1990 and 1995; 822 vertebrate species are currently in danger of extinction; and over 300 million hectares of land has been degraded, mainly due to soil erosion caused by deforestation, overgrazing or poor agricultural practices. Forest loss seems to have stabilized in much of South America but has increased significantly in Jamaica and slightly in Central America.

Vulnerability to natural disasters is at the forefront of environmental problems in the region. Such risks include droughts in northeast Brazil and upland areas in Mexico, floods and volcanic eruptions in Central America, and floods and associated landslides in slums of most metropolitan and periurban areas throughout LAC. Natural disasters closely associated with climate variability have increased in frequency and intensity over the past decades, and economic losses attributable to these events are estimated to have increased eightfold between 1961-70 and 1986-95. In both urban and rural areas, the poor are far more vulnerable to natural disasters than are higher-income groups.

THE BANK'S RECORD AND FUTURE CHALLENGES

The Bank's Latin America and Caribbean Regional Office (LCR) has not had an explicit environmental strategy in the past. The implicit strategy has been to respond to emerging country demands, needs, and priorities. There are 81 active projects, totaling $ 2.35 billion, in which environment is a primary objective. The main areas of environmental activity in the current portfolio are institutional development, biodiversity, natural resource management (NRM), water resource management, pollution management, and disaster management. In addition, there are a number of nonlending activities, including policy and strategic dialogue such as the Mexico Policy Notes and the Mesoamerican Biological Corridor Strategic Framework Paper; analytical work such as the Ecuador Land Administration Study; and initiatives such as the Clean Air Initiative (see box A.4).

In recent years, Bank assistance to the region has been characterized by (a) diversification of the environmental agenda from green to brown issues and from sectoral to integrated approaches through use of the CDF and regional (landscape-based) initiatives; (b) better integration of social concerns into environmental management through promotion of community-based initiatives, greater focus on indigenous communities and increasing attention to resettlement and other social impacts of development projects; (c) greater emphasis on participa-

---

BOX A.4
The Clean Air Initiative in Latin American cities

The Clean Air Initiative in Latin American Cities is seen as a complement to conventional lending operations in urban transport and air quality management. Its objective is to help raise awareness and increase capacity to manage air quality problems in urban areas. The initiative is a partnership between the World Bank, city governments, private and public institutions, development banks and agencies, and NGOs interested in collaborating to improve the understanding of these problems and provide city leaders with tools for making the difficult choices involved in addressing air pollution and mitigating its health impact. The World Bank acts as Technical Secretariat and provides overall management of the initiative. Management will eventually be transferred to institutions in the region.

---

tion and consultation; (d) increased use of strategic (sectoral or regional) environmental assessments; and (e) increased recognition of linkages between local and global environmental issues, entailing, among other things, assistance to countries to meet their commitments under various international and global conventions.

Mainstreaming environmental concerns across sectors is a key tenet of the corporate and regional strategies. Some examples of areas where sector-environment linkages are being explored in Bank-financed activities are (a) in the energy sector, renewable energy and energy efficiency, (b) in the urban sector, solid waste management and slum upgrading, (c) in the transport sector, air quality management through monitoring networks, technical assistance, and better traffic management, (d) in the water and sanitation sector, wastewater management and water quality standards, and (e) in the mining sector, cleanup of contaminated sites, development of regulations, and institution building. Within the Bank, a better economic case needs to be made for environmental management and for strengthening the linkages between natural resource management and poverty alleviation. Other priorities are to strengthen the linkages between the health and environment agendas and to include environment as an integral subject in early education programs.

STRATEGIC PRIORITIES AND ACTIONS

Key strategic priorities are linked to the quality of life, the long-term sustainability of growth, and the quality of the regional and global commons.

Quality of life

There are three particularly critical areas in which the Bank can help improve the quality of life: improving livelihoods through the sustainable man-

107

agement of natural resources; reducing the impact of environmental degradation on human health; and reducing vulnerability to natural disasters.

In the livelihoods area, priorities include:

■ Developing a better understanding of environment–poverty–economic growth linkages and tradeoffs, including the long-term and short-term implications of natural resource use, and incorporating environmental issues into the policy dialogue and into CASs, poverty assessments, and PRSPs

■ Promoting sustainable integrated natural resource management of land, freshwater, and marine ecosystems (for example, forestry and fisheries), with a focus on highly degraded or threatened ecosystems and disaster-prone areas, and ensuring the generation of benefits for indigenous and poor communities, preferably through community-based approaches, using strategic implementation tools such as property rights, appropriate technology, and tradable development rights.

In the health area, priorities include:

■ Developing a better understanding of environment-health linkages through analytical work and implementation of health surveillance projects to improve project design and policy dialogue, resulting in more strategically focused projects

■ Improving access in the near term to safe water; improving collection and disposal of sewage and primary treatment of wastewater, in conjunction with a plan for future wastewater treatment; and improving solid and hazardous waste management (avoiding exposure of the poor, who often live physically on and economically off poorly managed solid waste landfills)

■ Financing wastewater treatment for highly polluted or sensitive water bodies, particularly those that affect the health of downstream inhabitants and the quality of water used for agricultural, recreational, or municipal water supply purposes

■ Financing air quality improvement in critical urban areas, industrial corridors, and areas of agricultural burnoff

■ Reducing exposure to toxic substances, particularly in industry, agriculture, and mining.

Toward the goal of reducing vulnerability, priorities include assisting clients to better prepare for and respond to natural and human-induced disasters and accidents—for example, by developing early warning systems; analyzing potential hazards; identifying suitable prevention and contingency planning techniques; preparing disaster response and disaster mitigation plans; developing risk management services such as insurance schemes; financing critical infrastructure; and using urban environmental land use planning as a preventive tool.

Quality of growth

With the private sector playing an increasingly large economic role in the region, the Bank can help ensure that private sector growth is sustainable and contributes to poverty alleviation. In addition, we can play an important role in helping our clients incorporate environmental concerns into macroeconomic and sector policies. Priority actions in LCR include:

■ Developing environmentally appropriate macroeconomic policies and instruments, including growth, trade, and regional integration strategies; fiscal incentives for sound environmental management (for example, full-cost pricing that reflects environmental externalities, and reevaluation of subsidies to ensure meaningful targeting); and natural resource and expenditure accounting frameworks (see box 3.8 in chapter 3)

■ Supporting targeted institution building, including regulatory and enforcement frameworks and decision support; promoting comprehensive approaches to environmental management, including watershed management and urban development/land use planning; promoting sectoral mainstreaming and gradual decentralization, with a focus on targeted assistance for highly polluting sectors or critically polluted cities and industrial corridors; and promoting sustainable financing of environmental initiatives through the use of fiscal instruments, appropriate pricing of natural resources and of environmental services, and positive and negative subsidies (see box 2.5 in chapter 2)

■ Strengthening awareness and building environmental constituencies through education and training

■ Developing mechanisms for effective participation, negotiation, and conflict resolution, including greater stakeholder involvement in the Environmental Impact Assessment (EIA) process (for example, through public hearings); appropriate consultation on policy and program design; and use of market-based instruments, information disclosure schemes, and voluntary compliance schemes, in addition to traditional command-and-control approaches

■ Promoting clean industrial production, including environmental management systems in small and medium-size enterprises.

Quality of the regional and global commons

The LAC Region is particularly important as regards the quality of the regional and global commons. In this area, the priorities include:

■ Promoting biodiversity conservation in critically threatened ecosystems, with a focus on comprehensive approaches such as systems of protected areas, hotspots within a subregion, and biological corridors, on promotion of current or near-term financially sustainable national biodiversity strategies, and on generation of positive impacts on local livelihoods (see box A.5)

■ Assisting client countries to prepare for and respond to climate change, through mitigating greenhouse gas emissions, ensuring and protecting carbon sequestration functions of forests and rangelands, promoting renewable energy and energy efficiency options, and facilitating LAC countries' participation in international carbon markets (for example, through national strategy studies on greenhouse gas offset potential and through preparation of PCF projects)

■ Phasing out ozone-depleting substances

■ Protecting and restoring international waters.

BOX A.5

A regional approach: The Mesoamerican Biological Corridor

The Mesoamerican Biological Corridor (MBC) is a continuous ecosystem band extending from southeast Mexico to the northern departments of Colombia. The Atlantic coastal areas of this zone include the second largest barrier reef system in the world. The MBC was recently identified by the international scientific community as one of 25 critical biodiversity areas of the planet—one of the global biodiversity hotspots. For the past few years, the World Bank has worked with the GEF, national governments, regional organizations, civil society, bilateral and multilateral donors, and technical cooperation agencies in supporting the MBC initiative as a unique ecosystem approach for the conservation and sustainable use of biodiversity and forest resources in Central America and as a platform for the sustainable development of the region.

Subregional priorities

Environmental problems vary across the region, and priorities should vary accordingly. LCR sees itself as having a comparative advantage in the following areas: wastewater treatment of highly polluted or sensitive water bodies, which is important in Mexico and the Caribbean; air quality improvements in critical urban industrial corridors and areas of agricultural burnoff in Brazil, Mexico, and the Southern Cone; disaster preparedness in Mexico, Central America, and the Caribbean; promotion of clean industrial production in the Andean countries; strengthening of awareness and management capacity through environmental education and vocational training in the Andean countries; assistance to countries' preparation for and response to climate change in the Caribbean and Central America; and targeted institution building in the Andean countries, Mexico, and the Southern Cone.

At the same time, there are numerous regionwide priorities: developing a better understanding of environment-health linkages and environment–poverty–economic growth linkages and tradeoffs; promotion of environmentally appropriate macroeconomic and sectoral policies and instruments; provision of access to safe water, collection and disposal of sewage, and solid waste management; sustainable natural resource management with a focus on threatened ecosystems, on disaster-prone areas, and on indigenous and poor communities; targeted institution building; biodiversity conservation focused on comprehensive approaches to the generation of positive impacts on local livelihoods, and sustainable financing and strengthened mechanisms for effective participation, negotiation, and conflict resolution.

It should be noted that these priorities, which are based on extensive and internal consultation at the subregional level, indicate potential future areas of work for the Bank provided that they are supported by the individual country dialogues and the corresponding CASs.

IMPLEMENTATION OF THE STRATEGY

Goals. LCR's proposed near-term goals are to avoid negative impacts of projects; to mainstream environment in other sectors as well as generate critical mass in selective environmental operations; to work more effectively with our client and donor countries; and to become increasingly results-oriented. Specifically, we will:

- *Avoid negative impacts of projects* by improving screening and facilitating upstream guidance with respect to safeguard policies in operations; ensuring environmental due diligence in operations as required under Bank policies for environmental assessment and adjustment lending; emphasizing thematic supervision; and increasing the use of strategic environmental assessments

- *Mainstream and generate critical mass* by improving understanding of poverty, growth, and environment linkages; preparing background papers as input to CASs with critical environment problems; providing operational support for monitoring implementation of PRSPs, including environment in sectoral strategies; developing GEF, Montreal Protocol, and Climate Change strategies in countries and the region; emphasizing a programmatic approach; promoting mainstreaming by developing cross-sectoral products (for example, environment/infrastructure, environment/health); and improving selectivity in new environmental projects

- *Work more effectively with clients and donors* by making a case for environmental management that is convincing for finance ministers and legislators; by promoting greater collaboration within the public sector and between the public sector, the private sector, and civil society; and by seeking complementarity with respect to other donors' programs, given the Bank's comparative advantage (for example, using CDF as a tool)

- *Become increasingly results-oriented* by developing and incorporating impact indicators in project design and implementation, improving the results of operations under implementation, and being at the forefront of best practices.

Operational implications. In implementing this strategy, LCR proposes to work across different sectors in the Region. In particular, we envisage close collaboration between the Environment Group, the Poverty Reduction and Economic Management Group, and the Human Development Group, particularly given the emphasis on better understanding the linkages and tradeoffs between poverty, economic growth, and environment and between health and environment. We envisage continued close collaboration between the Environment Group and the Finance, Private Sector, and Infrastructure Group to build on the work that has already been undertaken. Within the Environment Group, we propose greater selectivity with respect to self-standing environmental projects.

Working with partners. We will continue to collaborate with our external development partners, including the Economic Commission for Latin America and the Caribbean (ECLAC), the Food and Agriculture Organization of the United Nations (FAO), the Inter-American Development Bank (IDB), the Organization of American States (OAS), the United Nations Development Programme (UNDP), the UNEP, and bilateral agencies, to en-

sure complementarity with our mutual work programs and a flow of information between parties. With respect to the GEF, our main thrust in coming years will be to help our clients integrate global environmental concerns into their national development strategies. Finally, in addition to our country clients, we expect the private sector and NGOs to play an essential role in realizing the strategy (see box A.6).

BOX A.6
Public consultation during preparation of the LAC Environment Strategy

A draft of the LAC Environment Strategy was posted on the Web in early August 2000, and an e-mail campaign promoted its widespread dissemination. Throughout the fall of 2000, participants could read the Strategy, answer a short questionnaire online, and engage in a forum for comments and questions. Three subregional consultations were held in the fall of 2000: in Cartagena, for Andean countries; in Rio de Janeiro, for the MERCOSUR countries; and in San José, Costa Rica, for Mexico and the Central American and Caribbean countries. Comments from more than 200 external participants have been received via the various consultations. More than 2,000 people from the public and private sectors, NGOs, civil society, and academia have logged on to read the Strategy. Feedback was heaviest from the more than 100 NGOs contacted and from the private sector. The dialogue was very constructive, and input from all participants helped fine-tune the environmental priorities, criteria for decisionmaking, and lessons learned. The Strategy was also presented in Mexico City in October 2000 at the Intersessional Committee of the Forum of Environment Ministers. Shortly thereafter, numerous development partners, including the FAO/CP, the IDB, the OAS, the Pan American Health Organization (PAHO), the UNDP, and the World Health Organization (WHO) attended a similar presentation and affirmed their interest in collaborating in the implementation of the strategy.

Safeguards. We propose to enhance the effectiveness of the regional Quality Assurance Team (QAT) by emphasizing a collaborative, problem-solving approach in the safeguard review process. This implies upstreaming the dialogue on safeguards to early stages of project preparation and to sectoral discussions, issuing technical guidelines, and disseminating best practices to sectoral project proponents and client countries; increasing the use of strategic environmental assessments; putting greater emphasis on compliance during implementation (for example, through thematic supervision and periodic reviews for specific safeguard policies); and carrying out due diligence in adjustment and financial intermediary lending (in addition to standard investment operations), as required under Bank policies for environmental assessment.

Challenges and risks of implementation. The challenges of implementing this first LCR Environment Strategy include (a) agreeing on realistic goals and targets with the regional management team; (b) working out the implications for a gradual shift in the assistance strategy, with its effects on budgets, strategic staffing, and partnerships; (c) establishing the proper incentive structure to support implementation of the strategy, especially mainstreaming (for example, joint products and increased cross-support); (d) ensuring compatibility with other sector strategies, including Fuel for Thought and the forestry, water, rural, and urban transport strategies; (e) incorporating this program into CASs; and (f) developing instruments and funding mechanisms for regional initiatives and nonlending services, such as the Mesoamerican Biological Corridor, the Clean Air Initiative, and the Regional NGO and Ministerial Dialogue. We propose to adopt annual work plans as a mechanism for implementation of the strategy, allowing flexibility for the Region to best respond to evolving client demand and complementary activities on the part of other development partners.

Middle East and North Africa

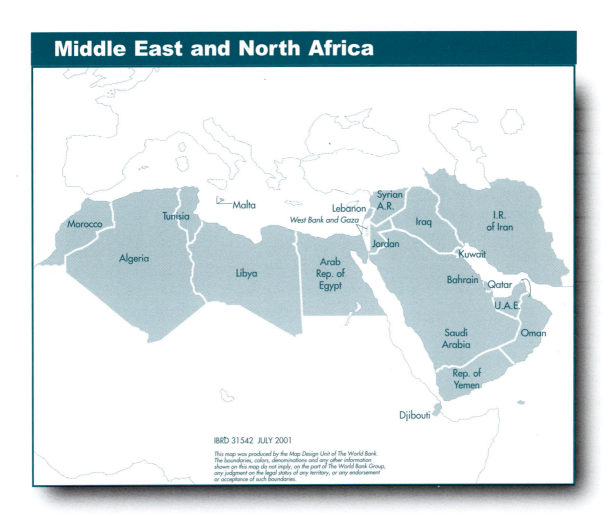

IBRD 31542 JULY 2001

This map was produced by the Map Design Unit of The World Bank.
The boundaries, colors, denominations and any other information
shown on this map do not imply, on the part of The World Bank Group,
any judgment on the legal status of any territory, or any endorsement
or acceptance of such boundaries.

In 1995, the Middle East and North Africa (MNA) Region completed its first regional environment strategy, *Towards Sustainable Development: An Environmental Strategy for the Middle East and North Africa Region*. The strategy outlined in this paper updates the 1995 strategy, the objectives of which remain valid today.

REGIONAL CONTEXT AND KEY ENVIRONMENTAL ISSUES

The MNA Region includes 20 World Bank client countries with a combined population in 1997 of 279 million. The substantial investments made since the 1960s in health, education, basic infrastructure services, and, more recently, family planning have begun to show positive results. Between 1980 and 1997, the region made impressive progress, lowering population growth from 3.2 to 2.1 percent per year, reducing infant mortality from 95 to 49 deaths per 1,000 live births, increasing life expectancy from 59 to 67 years, and increasing secondary school enrollment from 42 to 64 percent. Declining population growth, accompanied by increasing gross national product (GNP), contributed to a reduction in poverty. Between 1987 and 1998, the population living on less than $2 per day fell from 30 to 20 percent. However, the region still faces large income gaps. On average, the richest 20 percent accounts for more than 45 percent of total income, compared with less than 7 percent for the poorest 20 percent.

MNA's endowment of natural resources is uneven: the region is the world's richest in oil and gas re-

113

serves, and the poorest in renewable water and arable land. It continues to rely excessively on natural resources as a development strategy, and water and oil are being used at unsustainable levels. MNA countries have the following long-standing environmental issues, which differ among countries only in magnitude and severity:

- *Water scarcity and quality.* Annual renewable water resources per capita are expected to fall from 1,045 cubic meters per year in 1997 to 740 cubic meters per year by 2015. Water allocation is a major concern for governments. In part because of policies designed to increase food self-sufficiency, 88 percent of MNA's water resources is allocated to the agricultural sector, as against 7 percent for domestic use. The degradation of water quality is aggravating the water scarcity problem.

- *Land degradation and desertification.* Arable and permanent cropland in the region currently represents less than 6 percent of total land area and is shrinking as a result of serious land degradation and recurrent droughts. Unsustainable agricultural practices on rainfed lands, combined with natural factors such as wind and floods and with excessive fuelwood removal, have contributed to a substantial loss of productive land and to desertification.

- *Coastal degradation.* Major coastal cities in MNA are attracting local population and tourists faster than inland areas. Lack of integrated coastal zone management is exacerbating the increased competition over the allocation of land and marine resources.

- *Urban and industrial pollution.* Urban and industrial pollution causes significant public health problems in the region. The transport, industry, and energy sectors have substantial impacts on human health through the use of leaded gaso-

line and high-sulfur fuel oil, a strong reliance on polluting fuels in power generation, and particulate and sulfur oxide emissions from various industries. Solid waste collection systems are generally well developed, but proper disposal is largely lacking, especially in rural areas. Industrial hazardous waste is rarely treated adequately. Major cities bear the brunt of MNA's pollution problems.

- *Weak institutional and legal frameworks.* Environmental problems are aggravated by weak regulatory and enforcement mechanisms. Although the region has made progress by establishing ministries of the environment, preparing or enacting environmental legislation, and preparing NEAPs, the institutions are understaffed and underfunded and generally lack credibility and political power. Cross-sectoral linkages between ministries and public institutions are weak. The legal framework is based on a command-and-control approach with weak monitoring and enforcement regimes. The role of civil society in environmental management remains limited, in part because existing NGOs are small, young, local in nature, and often dependent on the government and international donors for budgetary support.

These environmental issues result in a heavy drain on the region's economies. NEAPs estimate that the annual cost of environmental damage varies from 4 to 9 percent of gross domestic product (GDP)—higher than the 5 percent estimated for Eastern Europe, and substantially higher than the estimated 2–3 percent in member countries of the Organisation for Economic Co-operation and Development (OECD). The cumulative impact of land degradation is estimated to have reached a cost of about $1.15 billion a year in lost agricultural productivity. The environmental health burden is estimated at about 14 percent of the region's total health burden. Of this total, about 8 percent is attributable to inadequate water supply and sanitation and about 3 percent to urban air pollution. The rural and urban poor suffer the most, since low-income housing is often plagued by unreliable drinking water supplies, inadequate sewerage, poor solid waste management services, and location on lands subject to floods and other natural hazards.

Emerging issues. As MNA countries struggle with their long-standing environmental problems, they must also confront the environmental dimensions of their own economic liberalization, as most are committed to market-based economic reforms, free trade agreements with the European Union, and globalization. Improving economic growth while maintaining a sustainable natural resource base and remaining competitive in international and domestic markets is a fundamental challenge for the region. As countries move forward with trade liberalization, private sector development, and privatization, the challenge is to assist them in these transitions while ensuring a sustainable use of their natural resources.

THE BANK'S RECORD AND FUTURE CHALLENGES

MNA's 1995 environment strategy marked a major milestone in guiding MNA countries, the donor community, and the Bank toward promoting sustainable development in the region. It emphasized three key strategic objectives: improving natural resource management; arresting emerging pollution problems; and strengthening environmental institutions and increasing public participation.

Lending activities. During the first five years of the strategy's implementation, investments in environment-related projects totaled $3.4 billion, includ-

ing $2.3 billion allocated to water-related projects. MNA also increased its emphasis on poverty through social funds, community development programs, rural development, natural resource management, and basic health projects, which together totaled $650 million. Notable progress was made in protecting natural resources in Algeria, Egypt, Morocco, and Tunisia. Efforts to control industrial pollution are continuing in Algeria and Egypt, and initiatives to reduce urban pollution are being implemented in Lebanon, Tunisia, and Yemen. In Algeria, Egypt, and Morocco, projects are under way that would strengthen environmental institutions and encourage greater public participation. The GEF has financed nine projects in the region.

Nonlending activities. The Mediterranean Environmental Technical Assistance Program (METAP), sponsored by the World Bank, the EC, the European Investment Bank, and the UNDP, played a major role in evaluating national environmental strategies and helped establish environmental impact assessment units in various countries (see box 3.3 in chapter 3). Regional training helped strengthen the capacity of environmental institutions. The NGO small grant program and other regional initiatives sought dialogue and participation with NGOs in the design and implementation of environmental activities. Efforts to promote regional collaboration included the water, desertification, and trade and environment initiatives.

LESSONS LEARNED

Progress has been slower than anticipated. The objectives of the 1995 strategy were too broad and were overly optimistic. Important substantive lessons have been learned:
■ Be realistic about what countries can achieve over the next five year period, especially given that most countries are now facing the impact of glo-

balization, in addition to long-term environmental and social issues. This strategy update will focus on a few high-priority actions, accompanied by outcome indicators that can be identified and monitored by the countries themselves.

■ Mainstream environmental issues in the Bank and in client countries to a greater extent. Efforts have been made to mainstream environmental issues in the Bank's core work. For example, the environment has been integrated into the latest CAS for Tunisia, the CDF for West Bank–Gaza, and the Country Development Review (CDR) for Yemen. Additional efforts are needed in the coming years to move away from stand-alone environmental projects toward inclusion of strong environmental components in other sectors, such as transport, energy, education, urban development, and rural development.

The World Bank is not alone in offering assistance to MNA countries. Since 1990, the region has witnessed a rapid surge of international and regional activities. Multilateral and bilateral donors increased their assistance in areas identified in the 1995 MNA environment strategy and in the NEAPs, drawing clients away from Bank lending. Clients prefer to borrow from the EIB because of the availability of a 3 percent EU subsidy on environment-related projects. In addition, the EU, Germany, Japan, and the United States have increased their grants and concessionary lending to the region. This change in the regional context has severely affected Bank financing of environment-related projects. Bank financing, which totaled $3.4 billion during the 1995–2000 period, is expected to decline in the coming years.

STRATEGIC PRIORITIES AND ACTIONS

Strategic priorities and actions are grouped by three interrelated aspects of development: quality of life,

quality of growth, and quality of the regional and global commons. The actions proposed in this Environment Strategy update are not intended to be add-ons or isolated actions in sectors already being addressed. Rather, they are intended to reinforce the mainstreaming effort currently under way by focusing on specific actions that are essential for ensuring sustainable development.

Quality of life

In the MNA region, action in three critical areas can help improve the quality of life: improving water resource management, controlling land and coastal zone degradation, and reducing urban pollution.

Improving water resource management. Water scarcity and water quality stand out as particularly challenging issues in this mainly arid region. The proposed actions are to:

■ Focus on integrated water resource management, emphasize demand-side management and water conservation, and facilitate the introduction of technologies that improve efficiency of water-use

■ Finance wastewater treatment plants and develop guidelines for water reuse, especially in agriculture

■ Finance cost-effective sanitation measures and hygiene education activities, especially in poor rural areas

■ Integrate monitoring and enforcement components for water quality into all water- and wastewater-related projects, strengthen the involvement of local communities in this monitoring process, and ensure widespread sharing of information on water quality.

Controlling land and coastal zone degradation. Proposed actions include the following:

- Establish reliable baseline data for water and soil contamination stemming from agricultural runoff and develop effective methods of controlling agricultural pollution; improve land management and mitigate the impacts of urban encroachment into agricultural areas; work with Bankwide natural resource management networks to pursue a unified program on land management; and provide a framework for real participation by local communities and stakeholders in the management of the natural resource base
- Develop coastal zone management strategies and programs that emphasize coordinated and preventive measures to combat coastal zone degradation.

Reducing urban pollution. To improve the quality of life in urban areas, the Bank proposes to focus on the following areas and actions:

- *Air pollution.* Conduct energy-environment reviews; develop environmental guidelines for the energy sector; develop proper legal and institutional frameworks to address market failures in the energy sector; encourage the phaseout of leaded gasoline; implement public awareness campaigns on the health impact of leaded gasoline; and introduce inspection and maintenance programs for vehicles
- *Waste management.* Develop the institutional and legal frameworks necessary to support integrated waste management; introduce affordable financing mechanisms for the collection, treatment, and disposal of waste; and increase awareness of and participation of communities in all aspects of solid and hospital waste management.

Quality of growth

The World Bank will support environmentally sustainable growth in the region in two areas: capacity building, and strengthening the private sector.

Capacity building. Proposed actions include strengthening national legal frameworks to include environment and social safeguards and improve self-monitoring and enforcement mechanisms; harmonizing national environmental assessment (EA) regulations with international requirements; assisting countries to shift from project-specific EA to sector EAs whenever appropriate; working with the public and private sectors to promote clean technologies; increasing public consultation and information dissemination through such means as an environmental awareness component and by strengthening the role of governance in appropriate projects; involving NGOs, civil society, and community leaders in the design and implementation of projects; encouraging women's participation; and building the capacity of institutions to develop early warning systems and preparedness plans for floods and droughts.

Strengthening the private sector. The manufacturing and service sectors are expected to be the primary engines of economic growth in MNA. The private sector must therefore assume an expanding role in environmental management, assisted by an effective public policy regime. Activities to improve the environmental capacity of the private sector would be designed through METAP or the Development Grant Facility (DGF). Such activities would include (a) assisting domestic banks in managing new risks and exposures to environmental regulations, and formulating reasonable and transparent environmental regulations that support both environmental objectives and private sector development, and (b) continuing the work on environment and trade begun under METAP. The latter work would include rapid country assessments to identify the sectors most sensitive to changes in environmental regulations; case studies and training to assist policymakers in understanding the implications of environmental standards for trade; assistance to countries in adapting to a new domestic regulatory environment and to international business practices; promotion of reasonable and transparent environmental regulations and standards; development of guidelines to incorporate environmental considerations into privatization transactions; and formulation of clear environmental performance objectives to deal with past environmental liabilities.

Quality of the regional and global environment

To promote the quality of the regional and global environment, the Bank will continue to support its regional initiatives in the MNA region and will integrate global environmental issues into its operations.

Regional initiatives. The Bank's involvement in three regional programs—METAP, the Desertification Initiative, and the MNA Regional Water Initiative—will continue. METAP will remain the main instrument for providing technical assistance to strengthen the Bank's environmental work. Specific programs for water quality improvement, municipal and hazardous waste management, environmental safeguards, trade and finance, knowledge management, and development of local capacity will be presented to potential donors for financing. The Bank will also continue to strengthen partnerships with regional and international agencies in designing and implementing its regional initiatives.

Global environmental issues. The pipeline includes six projects that address greenhouse gas reduction, three projects on biodiversity conservation, and two on coastal zone management. New GEF operational programs in transport and integrated ecosystem management offer new opportunities to use

GEF resources in transport, urban planning, and integrated rural development projects. A more systematic approach is needed to mainstream global environment issues into lending and nonlending activities and to assist countries in meeting their commitments under international treaties and conventions. An analysis of the lending program, matched with country priorities, should be conducted to estimate the potential for GEF projects, establish priorities in every country, and develop an action plan.

IMPLEMENTATION ARRANGEMENTS

Given the diversity among the countries in the region, actions to implement this strategy update must be specified at a country level. Bilateral grant financing will be instrumental in accelerating the implementation of these actions.

Mainstreaming the environment. The following four methods will be used to mainstream environment into the development agenda:

1. Enhance the quality and effectiveness of countries' environmental and social assessments by (a) strengthening national project approval systems, (b) introducing strategic environmental assessment of macroeconomic and microeconomic policies and sector environmental assessments, (c) training client countries to use these assessments, and (d) exchanging lessons learned about the implementation of these assessments

2. Demonstrate the economic importance of a clean environment by (a) undertaking studies to assess the cost of environmental degradation in MNA countries, (b) conducting analytical work to identify linkages between environment and trade, and (c) mainstreaming the environment into PRSPs. This analytical work will be used to identify priority environmental intervention

in the CAS. Within the scope of this strategy, the countries targeted for mainstreaming the environment into the CAS are Algeria, Egypt, and Lebanon.

3. Integrate environmental components into targeted sectoral projects in water resources management, wastewater management, solid waste management, the transport and energy sectors, and the health and education sectors. Efforts to integrate global environment issues into the Bank's operations will involve activities for the protection of biodiversity in natural resource management, community development projects, and the reduction of greenhouse gases in transport, energy, and waste projects

4. Develop a monitoring and evaluation (M&E) system, as well as indicators to measure progress at the project, program, strategy, and policy levels. To support the M&E systems, environmental profiles for each MNA country will be developed. Subject to availability of funds, a regional consultation meeting of all stakeholders will be convened every two years to monitor progress in achieving the strategic actions. In addition, the environment cluster will submit to the MNA Regional Management Team and to the Environment Sector Board an annual report on the Region's environmental performance.

Partnerships. The implementation of the proposed strategic actions would require important leadership, collaboration, and coordination activities involving various stakeholders, including NGOs, bilateral and multilateral donors, and international financial institutions. Partnerships will become an important cornerstone for the Bank's environmental assistance in the MNA Region. At the country level, the Bank would be prepared to participate or

convene a donor-country coordination group on environment to achieve greater integration of efforts and reduce overlaps. The CAS and the CDF will be the instruments for highlighting government and bilateral donor policies in undertaking the appropriate strategic actions. The Bank would continue to seek cofinancing and to mobilize grant and concessionary lending resources with bilateral and multilateral donors such as the EU, Japan, and the U.S. Agency for International Development (USAID) and with international and regional financial institutions such as the EIB, the German KfW, and the Islamic Development Bank. At the regional level, the Bank would seek collaboration between METAP activities and other regional organizations such as the Mediterranean Action Plan (MAP), the Centre for Environment and Development for the Arab Region and Europe (CEDARE), various NGO networks, and the Environment-Development and Actions of Maghreb.

Selectivity. The Bank will refocus some of its activities by:

- Gradually shifting from stand-alone environmental technical assistance projects to integration of environmental technical assistance components into sector operations with well-defined outputs
- Discontinuing the preparation of additional environment sector notes or NEAP updates
- Refocusing the functions and responsibilities of the Region's environment staff toward providing upstream technical and policy support, ensuring compliance with the Bank's environment and social safeguard policies, and improving the implementation of environmental components in various projects.

South Asia

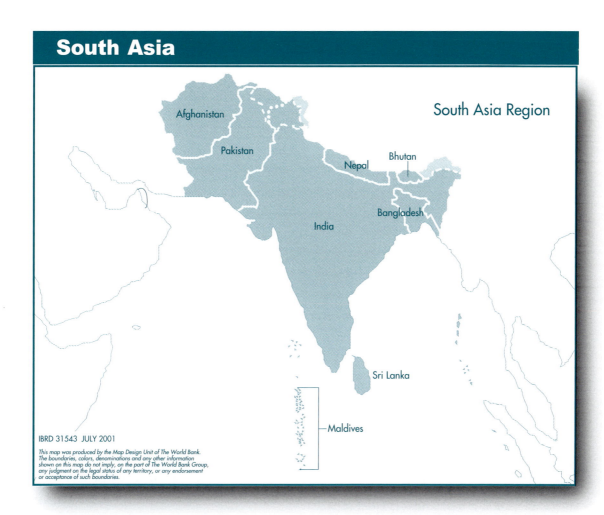

South Asia Region

Afghanistan

Pakistan

Nepal

Bhutan

Bangladesh

India

Sri Lanka

Maldives

IBRD 31543 JULY 2001

This map was produced by the Map Design Unit of The World Bank.
The boundaries, colors, denominations and any other information
shown on this map do not imply, on the part of The World Bank Group,
any judgment on the legal status of any territory, or any endorsement
or acceptance of such boundaries.

REGIONAL CONTEXT AND KEY ENVIRONMENTAL ISSUES

For the past decade, South Asia has been the second fastest growing region in the world, after East Asia. Economic growth averaged over 5 percent. Yet the region is home to 40 percent of the world's poor, most of whom live in rural areas. Despite considerable progress, the region continues to face fundamental constraints on sustainable development, including inequitable economic growth; persistently low levels of human development; low status for women; feudal social structures that are reflected in political power relationships; the absence or weakness of local government and the exclusion of most of the population from decisionmaking and access to basic services; unabated environmental degradation; and failure of institutions to suffi-

ciently integrate environmental and social development considerations into economic policy objectives.

Despite progress since the early 1990s on economic reforms and developments in environmental institutions, countries in the region are still plagued by huge problems. Among them is the limited progress made on trade liberalization; on enabling environments for private sector participation, including the rule of law; on fiscal and financial policies; and on openness and accountability of public institutions. Poor economic management is also reflected in the large subsidies and the lack of economic pricing of natural resources, including water, energy, agricultural land, and other inputs. In addition, many state-owned industries—for example, in steel, fertilizer, and petrochemicals—and private manufacturing industries, such as leather, textiles, sugar, and pulp and paper, have prospered as a result of strong government protection policies and lack of compliance with environmental regulation. In this context, reform agendas, including deregulation and fiscal efficiency, often conflict with political institutions and interests.

The region's environmental problems are enormous. They include resource depletion and ecological degradation, indoor and urban air pollution, lack of access to clean water supplies and sanitation, toxic and hazardous agroindustrial waste generation and disposal, and vulnerability to natural disasters. These problems, magnified by the inadequacy of governance structures in every country of the region and at all levels, threaten or cause losses of life and livelihoods of millions of people. Estimates suggest that premature deaths and illness linked to major environmental health risks account for one fifth of the total burden of disease in the region. This is comparable to malnutrition (15 percent) and is larger than the toll from any other preventable risk factor. In India, inadequate water supply and sanitation are estimated to account for 9 percent and indoor air pollution for 6 percent of the environmental health burden. It is estimated that air pollution causes 168,000 premature deaths annually in Pakistan (60 percent of them attributable to indoor air pollution) and 132,000 premature deaths in Bangladesh (70 percent from indoor air pollution).

Significant natural resource concerns in South Asia include water quality degradation and local and regional water scarcity; dwindling forests, coastal wetlands, freshwater bodies, and fisheries; soil degradation resulting from nutrient depletion and salinization; and poorly managed water resources.

Many of these issues are particularly important for the rural poor and disadvantaged groups, who depend heavily on renewable natural resources.

South Asia stands out as the region most vulnerable to natural disasters such as floods and cyclones, which affect the region regularly. From 1990 to 1998, the region accounted for over 60 percent of disaster-related deaths worldwide. Over the 1965–98 period, India accounted for about 64 percent and Bangladesh for 25 percent of the damages arising from natural disasters. Floods, cyclones, hurricanes, and typhoons were responsible for 86 percent of the damage in those countries during this period.

The causes of resource depletion and environmental degradation include lack of incentives for resource conservation and protection, lack of institutional frameworks for the integrated management of natural resources, inadequate legal and policy frameworks, weak governance, low institutional capacity, subsidies and policy distortions, lack of public awareness of the value of healthy and sustainable ecosystems, and limited data on resources and environmental quality.

THE BANK'S RECORD AND FUTURE CHALLENGES

In the early 1990s, most environmental projects in the region dealt with natural resource issues. They included water resource management projects in Bangladesh and India (see box A.7), forestry and fisheries projects that addressed both production and resource degradation issues in Bangladesh, India, and Pakistan, and irrigation and drainage projects that focused on soil salinity and land degradation in India and Pakistan. As pollution con-

BOX A.7
Sustainable watershed management in India

The South Asia Region is implementing a new generation of NRM projects focusing on the needs of the poor living on marginal lands and degraded watersheds. These projects integrate community-led development with innovative social, technical, scientific, and Geographic Information System (GIS)-based monitoring and evaluation approaches.

The Integrated Watershed Development Project (Hills II) in India uses participatory approaches to increase productive potential and promote sustainable watershed management in five Indian states (Haryana, Himachal Pradesh, Jammu and Kashmir, Punjab, and Uttar Pradesh) in the fragile and highly degraded Shivaliks Hills. The project covers 2,000 villages in a 200,000-hectare area. Village development committees (VDCs) have been formed and given the responsibility for identifying and implementing priority watershed interventions in their villages. Multidisciplinary government teams assist the VDCs to prepare and implement village watershed development plans. Project activities include microwatershed treatments such as vegetative barriers, improved cropping systems, horticulture, and silvipasture; fodder and livestock development (artificial insemination for genetic improvement; veterinary health improvement; and fodder production); and rural infrastructure.

The medium-to-long-term aim of these investments is to improve rural livelihoods through stronger community management of natural resources on a sustainable basis. Some villages are already experiencing increased water availability, reduced soil erosion, improved vegetative and forest cover, higher crop and horticulture yields, and increased milk production. Project activities also help reduce risks from natural and environmental disasters. For example, improved water management reduces vulnerability to droughts.

The participation and empowerment of villages, the reorientation and training of public agencies to facilitate community-driven watershed development approaches, and an enabling policy and institutional environment for sustainable natural resource management will all require close attention throughout the duration of the project and beyond.

cerns worsened, an increasing share of projects dealt with urban and pollution problems.

In the mid-1990s, the Bank increased its emphasis on improving environmental management by supporting more effective policies, regulations, and procedures, as well as pollution prevention and control in Bangladesh, India, Pakistan, and Sri Lanka. The Bank sought to integrate environmental issues into other sectors, including transport, fisheries, and education. The mid- to late1990s also saw increased attention to projects that focused on global and transboundary issues. For example, the Bay of Bengal Environment Program, which addresses fisheries research, environmental emergencies, large

marine ecosystems, and coastal zone management in and around the Bay of Bengal, involves numerous riparian countries.

The Bank is currently emphasizing development outcomes and, specifically, ensuring that environmental programs benefit the poor. Programs and policy reforms are increasingly focused on reducing environment-related health risks; improving livelihood systems, particularly in rural areas; reducing vulnerability to natural and environmental disasters; and improving governance. The Bank has continued to promote a coordinated and holistic approach to development assistance, by building partnerships and integrating environmental issues into sectoral and thematic strategies. The environmental portfolio is thus beginning to reflect issues highly relevant to poverty outcomes. This can be seen in two major areas. First, the Bank is supporting innovative analytical work on the role of water supply and sanitation and reduced air pollution in achieving health outcomes in urban settings. For example, a study in Andhra Pradesh, India, designed to assist in the preparation of a State Environmental Action Plan, is assessing the overall burden of ill health associated with lack of water and sanitation infrastructure and with exposure to indoor air pollution as a result of the use of wood and dung for fuel. Second, there is a sharper focus in all project development objectives on poverty impacts; examples include projects on sodic lands reclamation, joint forestry management, integrated watershed development, and fisheries management.

STRATEGIC PRIORITIES AND ACTIONS

Consistent with the principles of the CDF, the present Strategy builds on the results of three years of realignment of environmental work in South Asia to focus primarily on development outcomes and the quality of operations and business procedures. The Strategy, while supported by a number of country and regional studies, also incorporates the results of continuous learning and interaction with clients and partners, including the recently held consultations in South Asia on the emerging Bank Environment Strategy. The Strategy has extensive overlaps with all of the main pillars of the Bank's development approach, including (a) efficiency (with a particular focus on power, water, and petroleum sector reform measures); (b) poverty (given that economic and social savings gained through improved environmental management have been shown to be highly progressive in both urban and

rural areas); and (c) governance (since public sector performance, rather than additional financial resources, is the key to improving environmental management).

Because South Asia is among the most populated and impoverished regions in the world, our Strategy focuses on contributing to making a difference in the quality of life of poor people by improving their health and livelihood systems and reducing their vulnerability to changes in environmental conditions. In addition, since equitable and sustained economic growth remains essential for substantially improving the quality of life of poor people in the region, our Strategy contributes to the development of policies and enabling conditions that support long-term quality of growth. Finally, our Strategy seeks to improve the quality of the regional and global commons in order to capture a significant part of their benefit flows locally, with the help of international financing mechanisms, and contribute to lessening the vulnerability of the region's poor to the effects of global environmental deterioration—for example, climate change.

Improving the quality of people's lives through better environmental conditions

Our Strategy will continue the Bank's efforts over the past three years to promote environmental improvements as a fundamental part of development outcomes by supporting initiatives, programs, and policy reforms designed to:

■ Improve livelihood systems, particularly in rural areas, through (a) better management and improved productivity of the natural resources on which the poor depend (see box 2.4 in chapter 2); (b) support for institutional reforms, incentive structures, and improved governance, particularly decentralization efforts; (c) improved infrastructure, including access to markets, access to safe drinking water, and access to water for agriculture; (d) improved access to agricultural technology, such as more productive, drought-resistant cropping systems; (e) improved access to credit (for example, through microfinance); (f) improved access to energy and to alternatives to solid fuels; (g) improved educational and information services, including female education and extension services; and (h) support for initiatives to eliminate the gender gap and foster inclusive institutions

- Reduce environmentally related health risks by (a) reducing exposure to indoor and outdoor air pollution (see, for example, box 3.2 in chapter 3); (b) providing access to a safe and reliable drinking water supply; (c) providing access to sanitation and solid waste services; and (d) supporting mass hygiene and education programs. Among the key areas of our focus will be institutional reforms to improve service delivery, fiscal sustainability, and public-private partnerships

- Reduce vulnerability to natural and environmental disasters through support for changes in land-use planning, disaster preparedness, community involvement and education, water conservation and management, and emergency-phase interventions. We will also intensify our work on social protection measures to protect people who are vulnerable to natural disasters.

Refocusing our strategy in order to contribute to poverty reduction outcomes will also require addressing issues related to governance and supporting the emergence of institutions that can help empower the poor. Recent experiences with Bank projects and local success stories are providing evidence that social capital and participatory processes are as crucial to poverty reduction as are financial resources and development programs. Environmen-

tal institutions in the region are particularly weak and inefficient and would require reform and continued strengthening in order to become contributors to development outcomes.

Improving the quality of growth to support long-term sustainability

Because of the region's enormous environmental challenges and continued pervasive poverty, equitable and sustained economic growth is essential for producing lasting improvements in quality of life, particularly among the poor. In this context, policies and enabling conditions have been a major focus of every country program. Our interventions will focus on two main areas:

1. *Integrating environment into Country Assistance Strategies.* This will be accomplished in three ways: (a) deepening macroeconomic and sectoral reforms; (b) mainstreaming the environment into sector operations, including provision of operational support for the implementation of the safeguard policies; and (c) strengthening the analytical and empirical basis of our operational work. Recent and ongoing CAS work in India, Nepal, and Pakistan provides examples of this approach.

2. *Enhancing project quality through strengthened implementation of safeguard policies.* The overall emphasis in the region is on enhancing project quality by aiming for the most appropriate environmentally sustainable outcomes. Although a strong emphasis on safeguard policies may have a constraining effect on efforts to mainstream the environment, the focus on overall quality would not only ensure compliance on environmental safeguards but would also enhance environmental management in South Asia.

The shift in Bank lending operations toward a greater emphasis on programmatic lending has enhanced the promotion of strategic sectoral and regional environmental assessments to ensure adequate attention to environmental safeguards and good practice. Examples include sectoral assessments for energy reform projects in India and regional assessments for watershed projects in India and Pakistan. In addition, more attention is being given to integrating social and environmental assessments because of the intertwined nature of the issues involved. Combined environmental and social sectoral assessments for transport, urban, and rural development projects are now routinely being conducted in South Asia. Furthermore, there is increasing emphasis on environmental monitoring and evaluation, taking advantage of modern information management tools and human resources. Finally, the Bank is placing a strong emphasis on local ownership and consensus building among its clients in South Asia to help them strengthen their environmental safeguard systems and practices. For example, the Bank is working collaboratively within the region and with the Asian Development Bank on the development of new resettlement polices in Pakistan and Bangladesh.

Enhancing the quality of the global and regional commons

The degradation of the region's global commons can constrain economic development because of its huge opportunity cost and threat to political security, The region's water resource systems, for example, are highly interdependent. Our focus is on achieving global environmental objectives as a by-product of promoting local development benefits.

- The management of shared river basins and seas poses an important challenge for the South Asia Region. The Bank has been involved in the past in helping to facilitate a robust agreement between India and Pakistan on the Indus River basin. The region could derive substantial benefits from greater cooperation among riparians on other internationally shared river basins, primarily the Ganges-Brahmaputra-Meghna basin.

- South Asia is important from a climate change point of view in two respects. First, it is poised to become a major contributor to greenhouse gas emissions. Although per capita emissions in the region are currently very low, with total production of carbon dioxide representing only about 5 percent of global emissions, they are increasing at a rate of about 7 percent per year—twice the average rate. Second, the impacts of climate change could be significant in the region, especially because of its extensive low-lying areas. Small-scale renewable energy supplies may be the most cost-effective solution to providing reliable electricity in rural areas not connected to the grid and in some urban areas, and the use of cleaner fuels could have a concomitant impact on indoor air pollution. In the medium term, opportunities exist for building consensus on reform in the power sector that would promote energy efficiency and conservation and the application of renewable energy for rural and urban communities and industrial uses.

- The custodians of South Asia's biodiversity are largely the rural poor, who often depend directly on these resources for their livelihood and sustenance. Efforts will therefore focus on finding effective mechanisms to channel available global resources—including GEF—to local communities in order to provide adequate incentives for changes in their patterns of resource use, and on broadening the scope of the GEF portfolio to promote biodiversity conservation over whole landscapes.

To enhance the quality of global and regional commons in South Asia, areas of focus will include:

■ *Enhanced use of international financial assistance.* The integration of GEF into the Bank portfolio includes cofinancing arrangements, as in the Bangladesh Fisheries IV Project and the Pakistan Protected Area Management Project. Serious efforts are under way to better understand the tradeoffs and synergies between local and global environmental outcomes and to enhance the effective use of GEF resources to support mainstream Bank environmental activities.

■ *Montreal Protocol activities.* The ongoing Montreal Protocol Program in South Asia has continued to expand. In India, as the Bank's portfolio of subprojects has matured, approximately 3,000 tons of ODS chemicals have been phased out, of which sub-project completions in 1999 accounted for 580 tons. In addition, a major initiative to phase out production of all CFCs in India (one of the world's largest remaining producers of these chemicals), was agreed and began implementation in 2000.

IMPLEMENTATION ARRANGEMENTS

The present Bank Environment Strategy for South Asia applies to the work being done by sector units throughout the Region, as well as to the work of the regional environment unit itself. More specific arrangements for effectively implementing the strategy include:

■ *Exercising selectivity* in investment operations by (a) relying less on stand-alone environmental management projects implemented by central government agencies and more on mainstreaming the environment into sector operations; (b) promoting participatory and community-driven development approaches (particularly in watershed management, irrigation and drainage, and area-based poverty reduction initiatives), and private sector participation, par-

ticularly in urban water supply, independent power production, and transport; and (c) using GEF resources, when appropriate, to support the sustainable management of natural resources on which vulnerable groups depend (protected area management, medicinal plants, and solar thermal power).

■ *Enhancing project quality* by implementing the Bank's safeguard polices—a key pillar of Strategy implementation. To this end, we have already initiated the following activities: (a) establishment of an independent safeguard review and compliance monitoring team; (b) systematic upstream review and input into project design beginning with the project concept stage; (c) a project risk management and compliance monitoring system, linked to the Bank's project document system; (d) thematic joint social and environment reviews focusing on specific sectors such as water resources, transport, and health, (e) periodic skills enhancement for all regional staff; (f) enhancement of local ownership and consensus building; and (g) strengthening of our clients' capacity through policy dialogue and training

■ *Intensifying the use of sectoral-regional environmental and social assessments* by building on the experience of the past three years in the water, roads, and power sectors to enhance the environmental content of sector policies and institutions.

■ *Strengthening analytical and advisory activities*— (a) filling critical gaps in knowledge and information by undertaking new analytical work on indoor air pollution (in at least two countries), clean fuels (in at least two countries), and NRM and rural livelihoods (in at least one country), in collaboration with the Energy and Rural Development Units; (b) addressing institutional priorities by focusing on helping build client capacity in critical areas such as policy, incentives, and monitoring and enforcement; and (c) promoting techniques that foster cross-sectoral integration, such as improved monitoring and evaluation of poverty impacts and spatially based analysis of projects and policies

■ *Strengthening our input into CASs and support to our clients' PRSP development processes*, by building on the new merger of the Environment and Social Development Units in the region and increasing our participation in project, sector, and country teams. In particular, we will launch a regional network on Community-Driven Development (CDD) and will acquire staff skills in public health and support for the formulation and implementation of poverty reduction strategies.

Sub-Saharan Africa

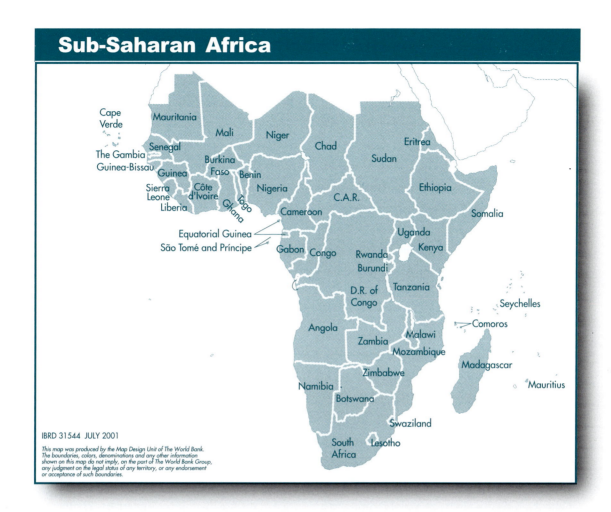

IBRD 31544 JULY 2001

This map was produced by the Map Design Unit of The World Bank.
The boundaries, colors, denominations and any other information
shown on this map do not imply, on the part of The World Bank Group,
any judgment on the legal status of any territory, or any endorsement
or acceptance of such boundaries.

In Africa, perhaps more than in any other region, the World Bank's mission of fighting poverty with lasting results is inescapably linked to environmental protection and improved management of renewable natural resources. African livelihoods and national economies rely mainly on agriculture and on extraction of mineral and biological resources, and there are few alternatives or options to compensate when these are lost. In both rural and urban settings, it is the poor who are most affected by the loss of natural resources and the deterioration of environmental services and who are most at risk from natural disasters that can be aggravated by environmental degradation. Yet the natural resource base is steadily deteriorating, with some of the world's highest rates of soil degradation and with

loss of forests, rangelands, wetlands, and fish and wildlife populations.

REGIONAL CONTEXT AND KEY ENVIRONMENTAL ISSUES

Sub-Saharan Africa faces many challenges to sustainable development, including some of the highest population growth rates in the world, widespread poverty, an HIV-AIDS crisis that is decimating the most productive segments of society and creating vast numbers of orphans, a high degree of political fragmentation and instability, and historically low levels of investment in human resources and development. There are an estimated 35 million transboundary migrants, many of them refugees from conditions and conflicts triggered by scarcity and decline of natural resources, particularly land and water. Rapid and unplanned urbanization, notably in fragile coastal areas, is creating new environmentally related problems. Extreme climate variations already present a serious threat in much of the region in the form of frequent droughts and floods, and global climate change could increase both the frequency and the severity of these events. Natural systems in the region are losing their capacity to produce the goods and services on which livelihoods and development depend. Improving environmental management in Africa is not only about preserving nature: it is a matter of survival.

Natural resources such as soil, water, forests, and fish provide the basis for livelihoods and for economic growth at both local and national levels, while ecosystem services such as water supply and absorption of pollutants are essential for maintaining human health. Many of the same natural ecosystems that provide these critical human services also contain some of the world's richest and most unique biodiversity assets, as well as storing vast amounts of carbon within their biomass and soils. Negative environmental impacts of poorly managed economic growth—such as water pollution, soil erosion, burning of forests and rangelands, and overexploitation of resources—directly undermine peoples' health and their ability to earn a livelihood and threaten these global environmental assets.

Threats to sustainable livelihoods. Given the predominance of the rural poor and the increasingly precarious nature of rural livelihoods in much of the region, the decline of the rural natural resource base is widely recognized as the highest-priority environmental problem. Only about 20 percent of Africa's total land area is arable, and much of it is under pressure. Soil degradation has affected 65

percent of Africa's cropland, and over 20 million hectares of forest has been lost since 1980. Land degradation and desertification, the scarcity and deterioration of surface and groundwater, and the decline of economically important biological resources such as fuelwood and fish are widely recognized problems.

Less appreciated is the impact of the loss of productive natural ecosystems. Forests, wetlands, and rangelands are all being converted or degraded at a rapid rate across much of Africa. This has major consequences for the poor, who lose access to essential goods and services, often without sharing substantially in the benefits of the activities causing these losses. At a national level, direct and immediate impacts include flooding, siltation of dams, a deepening fuelwood shortage, and the loss of indigenous natural products such as medicinal plants, foods, and building materials.

Threats to health. Africans suffer a higher total burden of disease than their counterparts in other regions, with about 25 percent of the total attributable to malaria, diarrheal diseases, and respiratory infections. Environment, health, and poverty overlap extensively in Africa because many of the most widespread and debilitating diseases, particularly those that affect the poor disproportionately, stem from environmental conditions or changes. Water and air pollution from domestic and industrial sources affects hundreds of millions of people in the region, particularly along coastlines, in the largest cities, and in mining areas. While African industries tend to be smaller than in other parts of the world, they are often particularly poorly regulated, and their additive and cumulative impacts can be significant. Waste disposal problems—among them, the lack of suitable disposal facilities for biomedical waste, including disposable syringes and other items used in efforts to stem the HIV-AIDS crisis—are widespread and pose a growing hazard. The loss of medicinal species and indigenous knowledge is of particular significance in Africa because in many countries a large proportion of the population continues to rely on traditional medicine.

Threats to security. Much of Africa is vulnerable to recurring droughts and floods. Between 1965 and 1999, 330 droughts caused an estimated 880,000 deaths. Droughts and floods reflect the natural variability of rainfall in the region's extensive arid and semiarid lands, but their intensity and impact is often aggravated by environmental degradation such as deforestation of hillsides and erosion or compaction of topsoil. Again, the impacts are greatest for the poor, who typically reside on the most susceptible marginal lands, are dependent on annual production from rainfed agriculture, and have few economic resources or safety nets to cope with catastrophic events. The frequency and severity of these events are expected to increase as a result of global climate change. Countries with extensive coastlines and small island nations such as Cape Verde, the Comoros, and Sao Tomé are particularly vulnerable to the effects of climate change.

Threats to the global environment. In addition to being an essential resource for African peoples and economies, the region's vast and unique biodiversity endowment is an invaluable world heritage. This includes remaining natural habitats—such as the Congo basin forest, the world's second largest continuous tropical rainforest—as well as wild relatives and "landraces" of important crop and livestock species. The direct cause of most biodiversity loss in Africa is the conversion of natural habitats and

water bodies to agriculture and other uses, followed by commercial logging and hunting. The underlying cause is that destruction of biodiversity often yields immediate individual benefits, whereas the benefits of conservation are generally long term and diffuse.

Although Africa is not a large-scale user of fossil fuels, it could nevertheless suffer significant damage from the predicted effects of climate change. Africa's forests and rangelands represent an enormous reservoir of carbon in their biomass and soil; if released through burning or other destructive practices, this could contribute substantially to the concentration of greenhouse gases. As for impacts, Africa may be the region most vulnerable to climate change. Greater variability of rainfall and the associated droughts and floods, along with increases in average temperatures, may make some currently important areas uninhabitable or uncultivatable and further aggravate existing hydropower shortages. There is already evidence that vector-borne diseases such as malaria are spreading into new areas as a result of climate shifts. Climate change may also increase the number of "environmental refugees"— people forced to migrate because of environmental degradation in their home areas—thus aggravating political conflicts and further stressing weak government budgets.

Development trends and challenges. Sub-Saharan Africa is a region with great diversity in its resource endowments, which makes generalizations for the region as a whole difficult. Nevertheless, a number of common development trends present challenges and opportunities across the region. These trends include decentralization, democratization, a growing demand for transparency and accountability in the management of public assets, increasing private sector investment, and globalization. Depending on how they are managed, these trends have the potential for either positive or negative impacts on the region's people and environment. A growing interest in and commitment to subregional integration can provide opportunities for coordination and cooperation in the management of ecosystems that span political boundaries. Institutional structures and human resource capacity will determine how these trends affect environment and poverty. At present, Africa's institutions are poorly equipped to deal with these challenges and must be reoriented and strengthened.

THE BANK'S EXPERIENCE AND SOME EMERGING LESSONS

The Bank's environmental program over the past few decades has included both direct investment in environmental improvements and indirect interventions aimed at mainstreaming environment into development and creating capacity and an enabling environment for better environmental management. The experience from these efforts has been mixed, with some promising models and pilot initiatives and important lessons for a forward-looking strategy.

Environmental assessment (EA) and the related safeguard policies have provided an important entry point for introducing environmental considerations into sector operations and for triggering environmental investments. As it is currently used, however, EA has significant limitations. It is generally project specific, introduced too late in the project cycle to affect project design, and followed-up inadequately during implementation. Existing EA procedures are poorly suited to the Bank's nonlending programs, which represent a growing proportion of its interventions. Most significantly, client governments, agencies, and citizens often regard EA and safeguard policies as externally imposed rules and obstacles. The Bank is responding to these lessons by putting substantial efforts into building in-country understanding, commitment, and capacity into EA principles and procedures. A particularly important challenge is to adapt EA to the Community-Driven Development (CDD) approach, which is a priority for the Bank in Africa (see box 2.1 in chapter 2).

The GEF has also been important in introducing environmental elements into Bank-financed programs and operations. While some freestanding GEF projects remain, GEF, IDA, and other donor resources are increasingly blended to support programs that generate both national-local and global benefits. The most common are community-based natural resource management projects, which also promote biodiversity conservation. Increased emphasis is being placed on incorporating sustainable land management and ecosystem-level management, from both a biodiversity and a carbon-storage perspective, which can offer substantial win-win opportunities for the region.

Mainstreaming environment into the Bank's overall operations remains an important challenge. Reviews of efforts to integrate environment into countries' economic development programs have provided important lessons, including the need for longer time frames to support institutional development and environmental action; the need for institutional capacity building to take into account the changing roles of government, civil society, and the private sector; the need to continue the EA process into the implementation phase by strengthening implementers' capacity to carry out environmental management plans and by monitoring impacts; the risk of isolating the environmental agenda from overall development priorities by "sectoralizing" it through isolated environmental planning processes, programs, and funds; the risk of creating a "supply-driven" mentality by imposing external conditionalities rather than building local constituencies; and the risk of creating overly ambitious and ultimately ineffective institutions by providing temporary external funding at levels that cannot be sustained. These lessons have been incorporated into this Strategy.

STRATEGIC PRIORITIES, APPROACHES, AND ACTIONS

In the Africa Region, actions to improve the quality of life, the quality of growth, and the quality of the global commons are inextricably linked by the common challenge of achieving sustainable management of ecosystems and natural resources. Although short-term, direct action is urgently needed, it is equally important to establish an enabling environment and to build the capacity to continue environmental management over the long term.

Quality of life

The priorities for action in the Africa Region Environment Strategy (ARES) are to:

- *Enhance livelihoods* through sustainable natural resource management (NRM), including (a) community-based NRM—policy reform, empowerment, and capacity building (see box D.1 in annex D), (b) maintenance of productive natural ecosystems and wild resources, (c) environmentally sustainable agricultural intensification, (d) land, soil, and desertification management, (e) water resources management and protection, (f) sustainable energy, including woodfuels management, (g) integrated coastal zone management, (h) fisheries management and aquaculture, and (i) rangeland management and support for pastoral communities

- *Protect peoples' health* from environmental burdens by (a) reducing pollution, including water pollution and indoor and outdoor air pollution, (b) improving access to potable water, (c) reducing vector-borne and water-related diseases, (d) improving disposal and management of hazardous wastes, and (e) maintaining traditional medicine species and knowledge

- *Reduce people's vulnerability* to environmental risks and natural disasters through (a) watershed protection, (b) land use planning, (c) improved infrastructure design and construction, (d) climate forecasting and early warning systems, and (e) safety nets, with emphasis on facilitating restoration of livelihoods.

Quality of growth

To improve the quality of growth, ARES will promote policy, regulatory, and institutional frameworks for environmentally sustainable economic growth. Priorities include (a) building environmental management capacity at national, district, and local levels, (b) strengthening in-country environmental constituencies, (c) increasing public awareness and education, (d) strengthening incentives for environmentally friendly private sector investment, (e) supporting environmentally oriented tourism, (f) building regional information networks, and (g) developing appropriate financial instruments and sustainable funding mechanisms.

Quality of the global commons

To address transboundary, regional, and global environmental problems, ARES will work on the following themes: (a) transfrontier biodiversity conservation areas and initiatives, (b) transboundary inland water resource management, (c) transboundary coastal zone management, (d) climate change prediction and adaptation, and (e) capture of global markets for environmental services.

Subregional priorities

While the above priorities provide an overall picture, Africa is too diverse ecologically and socially to be treated as a single unit for purposes of prioritizing environmental action. The continent can be divided into six subregions characterized by similar environmental conditions and challenges and, therefore, similar priorities (see table A.1).

These priorities emphasize issues that affect the livelihoods, health, and security of the poor, the opportunities for economic development based on environmental resources, and the unique global assets under threat. Because of the considerable variation even within these subregions, specific priorities must be identified at the national and subnational levels. There are also cross-cutting issues, such as land tenure and property rights, that are significant in all subregions and affect most of these issues.

Sectoral priorities

While environment is intrinsically cross-sectoral, most direct environmental action will have to be achieved through sectoral programs. Sectors targeted for their high significance for environmental management include agriculture and rural development, natural resource management, energy, urban development, water resource management, transport, health, and private sector development.

IMPLEMENTING THE STRATEGY

Mainstreaming environment. Rather than pursue a freestanding environmental agenda, the ARES

Table A.1
Sub-Saharan Africa: Priority environmental issues

Subregion	Priority environmental issues
Sudano-Sahelian Belt	"Drought preparedness"; integrated water resource management; halting/reversing land degradation (desertification); sustainable fuelwood supply; migratory pest outbreaks
Humid West Africa	Integrated coastal zone management (sustainable management of fisheries resources, urban and industrial environmental waste management and sanitation, tourism development impacts, etc.); land tenure and land management; rain forest conservation; protection for the high watersheds of major river systems
Congo Basin	Rain forest conservation (through a combination of core protected areas and improved management of forest production areas); coastal zone management, particularly in areas with intense urban development
Eastern Africa	Reversal of land degradation caused by inappropriate agricultural practices, particularly in arid and semiarid areas; integrated water resource management in areas of growing local scarcity (including adaptation to climate change); linkage of biodiversity conservation with environmentally sustainable and socially equitable tourism; urban and industrial environmental management in coastal areas
Southern Africa	Water resource conservation and management; drought preparedness and adjustment to climate variability; balancing agricultural development and nature-based tourism development; urban environmental management in highly urbanized and rapidly urbanizing areas; maintenance of environmental resources while meeting growing energy requirements
Indian Ocean Islands	Reversal of land degradation; biodiversity conservation (high degrees of endemism); pollution control and industrial environmental management, addressing both public health and tourism development needs; adaptation to climate change (anticipated rises in ocean levels)

seeks to integrate environment into the strategies and programs that are considered priorities by African stakeholders, and the Bank as a whole. Implementation of the ARES will therefore focus on building specific environmentally related outcomes, outputs, actions, and targets into country strategies, development plans, and sectoral programs on a country-by-country and sector-by-sector basis. Given the large number of countries in the Region, focal countries will be selected on the basis of criteria such as strong and clear linkages between environmental problems and opportunities, the sources of poverty, and the prospects for alleviating poverty; demonstrated interest on the part of clients and country teams, and the scale of the Bank's involvement in the country. Results will be measured by the extent to which these vehicles incorporate and achieve goals relating to environmental sustainability and social equity. An immediate challenge is to develop suitable indicators to measure whether environment is being incorporated in specific lending programs and in country development and portfolio assessments.

Key instruments at the strategic level will be CASs, PRSPs, and the CDF, which provide an umbrella for donor coordination (see box 2.2 in chapter 2 and box B.3 in annex B). Criteria for selecting countries on which to focus include demonstrated client and country team interest, the significance of environmental problems, opportunities for poverty alleviation, and the level of World Bank involvement. Priority countries for attention at this level are Benin, Burkina Faso, Cameroon, Chad, Central African Republic, Ethiopia, Ghana, Kenya, Madagascar, Malawi, Mozambique, Nigeria, Tanzania, Uganda, and Zambia.

At the operational level, project-level interventions will continue but will be complemented by a new emphasis on building environmental objectives into programmatic lending (PRSCs, Structural and Sectoral Adjustment, and Public Expenditure and Reform Loans and Credits), which is a growing part of the Africa Region portfolio. For example, in Benin environment has already been identified as one of five focal areas for support under the Public Expenditure Reform and Adjustment Credit. Similarly, beyond EA and the application of safeguard policies at the project level, Strategic Environmental Assessment (SEA) will increasingly be emphasized as a tool for addressing environmental impacts and opportunities more proactively and on a larger scale. The priority will be to identify area-based and sectoral development programs at a relatively early stage in order to help guide development onto environmentally and socially sustainable paths. The emphasis will be on important ecosystems under threat from rapid development (for example, Mozambique's Maputo Province and South Africa's Eastern Cape Province) and on sectoral investment programs in key areas such as transport, irrigation, water supply, energy, infrastructure, mining, and forestry. For example, an SEA is being developed for the transport sector in Benin, and discussions are under way on prospective SEAs relating to mining in Madagascar, health and environment in South Africa, and rural water supply in Tanzania.

Building capacity and an enabling environment. To be sustained in the long term, maintaining a healthy environment must be the goal of all actors, not only environmental agencies and advocates (see box A.8). The essential elements include a broad consensus on and support for environmental and sustainable development objectives; strong policy and legal frameworks; effective institutions; information systems for tracking environmental status and impacts; and informed, committed, and capable people at

135

BOX A.8
NEAPs and ESPs in Africa

- *National Environmental Action Plans (NEAPs)* have proved useful in raising awareness about environmental issues, particularly in those countries where the preparation process was highly participatory. In general, they have been less useful in identifying priorities for action and generating the necessary resources and political commitment, particularly when environmental objectives compete or conflict with short-term economic or political objectives.

- *Environmental support programs (ESPs),* intended to support implementation of the actions identified in the NEAPs, have had mixed success, often suffering from overly ambitious and overly complex designs as they sought to address the multisectoral nature of environmental management through a wide range of activities implemented by multiple actors. They are also typically supported by numerous donors, which is beneficial in mobilizing funds but can create problems with donor coordination. ESPs in Africa have had their greatest success in developing core environmental policy and regulatory systems, including EA legislation and procedures, usually centered in an environment department or semi-autonomous agency. They have been less successful in mainstreaming environmental objectives. Challenges for the future include (a) greater mainstreaming, going beyond the dedicated environmental agencies to build environment into the mandates, programs, and human resources of sectoral and other national institutions; (b) decentralization of systems and capacity for local-level environmental management; and (c) enhancement of the sustainability of these environmental management institutions and structures, most of which remain heavily dependent on external donors.

all levels. The Bank will continue to emphasize capacity development and strengthening of environmental institutions. However, building on the mixed experience of previous environmental support programs, our emphasis will be on defining and supporting the appropriate roles of both public and private sector institutions, establishing appropriate policies and incentive structures, and promoting decentralized and community-level planning and implementation. Other strategic principles include adopting "people-focused ecosystem management" as the organizing framework for planning and action, and finding ways to meet the institutional challenges presented by the need for cross-sectoral and cross-boundary collaboration. Developing useful and practical performance indicators for capacity and institution building is one of the main challenges for implementing the ARES. Existing guidelines and tools for monitoring policy reform, institutional structures, and returns on investment need to be adapted to encompass the special characteristics of environmental management, including its cross-sectoral nature and relatively long time horizon.

Integrating local and global environment. The GEF will continue to represent an important source of support for environmental action, used strategically to maximize local-global linkages. Linking the reversal of land degradation trends with biodiversity conservation and carbon sequestration is a priority in Africa. In keeping with both the ARES strategic principles and GEF operational guidelines, the emphasis will be on an Integrated Ecosystem Management (IEM) approach. The Integrated Land-Water Management Action Program for Africa (ILWMAP), currently under development, will be an important vehicle for coordinating resources from the World Bank, the GEF, and other multilateral and bilateral donors. Examples of planned projects and programs include the Nigeria

Microwatershed and Environmental Management Project (see box 3.1 in chapter 3), Phase 2 of the Mozambique Transfrontier Conservation Areas Project, the CAPE Program in South Africa, the Namibia National Conservancy Program, and the Burkina Faso National Natural Ecosystem Management Program. Other countries that have been identified as priorities for developing globally supported IEM projects include Chad, Mali, Mauritania, Niger, and Senegal.

Partnerships. Partnerships are vital to implementation of the ARES, as its challenges transcend the Bank's own capacity. The Bank is currently engaged

in a wide range of important partnerships relating to environmental priorities in Africa, with a great diversity of UN agencies, bilateral donors, regional development banks, and NGOs, as well as African governments. In addition to African elements of many Bankwide initiatives (such as the WB-WWF Forest Alliance and the Critical Ecosystems Partnership Fund), there are several important arrangements specific to Africa. The relevance and diversity of these partnerships is illustrated in box A.9. Partnerships such as these provide vital, complementary financial and technical resources to help achieve the objectives of the ARES. They carry, however, administrative and other costs that must

BOX A.9
Partnerships for sustainable development in Africa

- *Integrated Land and Water Management Action Program:* regionwide; World Bank with the UNDP, the UNEP, the GEF, the African Development Bank, the FAO, the CCD Secretariat, and the IDB
- *Soil Fertility Initiative for Sub-Saharan Africa:* projects currently in eight countries; World Bank with the FAO, the International Fund for Agricultural Development (IFAD), and the Consultative Group on International Agricultural Research (CGIAR)
- *Nile Basin Initiative:* all Nile Basin countries; World Bank, the Swedish International Development Authority (SIDA), the German Agency for Technical Cooperation (GTZ), and the Canadian International Development Agency (CIDA), and financial contributions from the GEF, the FAO, and nine bilateral donors
- *Regional Environmental Information Management Program:* a network of public, private, and NGO participants in Central Africa; WB with the EU, the IFAD, Belgium, Canada, and France; hosted by Gabon
- *Clean Air Initiative in Sub-Saharan African Cities:* targets eight cities across the region; WB with the EU, the African Development Bank, the U.S. Environmental Protection Agency (USEPA), Fonds Français pour l'Environnement, and an international petroleum industry association, among others
- *Regional Traditional Energy Sector Program:* regionwide; cofinanced by the GEF and the Norwegian and Danish trust funds, with the African Development Bank (AfDB), the WBI, MNA and the IFC as strategic partners
- *Program for Capacity Development and Linkages for EA in Africa:* based at Ghana's Environmental Protection Agency; other current and prospective partners include the EU, the Netherlands, Norway, and the AfDB
- *African Water Resources Management Initiative:* regionwide, at country and river basin levels; co-financed by the U.K Department for International Development (DFID), Norway, Netherlands and Sweden; other partners include the UNDP, the UNEP, the FAO, the World Conservation Union (IUCN), the GTZ, France, Japan, Switzerland, USAID, and the Development Bank of Southern Africa.

be adequately provided for under regional and/or country budgets if they are to be effective.

NOTES

1. This group includes the ten EU accession countries— Bulgaria, Czech Republic, Estonia, Hungary, Latvia, Lithuania, Poland, Romania, Slovak Republic and Slovenia—as well as Albania, Bosnia and Herzogovina, Croatia, Macedonia, and Turkey.

2. The Western NIS countries are Belarus, Moldova, and Ukraine.

3. This group includes Armenia, Azerbaijan, Georgia, Kazakhstan, the Kyrgyz Republic, Tajikistan, Turkmenistan, and Uzbekistan.

Annex B

Poverty and Environment

E nvironmental conditions often have a major influence on the livelihoods, health, and security of poor people. Improving environmental conditions can be an effective way to increase their income, improve their health, empower them, and reduce their vulnerability. Natural resources are crucial to the routine functioning of rural households and also provide a safety net in times of unexpected shocks. The varied links between poverty and environment, which have been extensively documented, provide a compelling rationale for a poverty-focused Environment Strategy and for mainstreaming environment into countries' strategies for reducing poverty (see the Bibliography).

A FRAMEWORK FOR UNDERSTANDING POVERTY-ENVIRONMENT LINKS

Economists have traditionally used a household's income or consumption as a proxy for well-being. A broader definition of poverty, however, goes beyond that to include inequality, health, education, and vulnerability. These, in turn, can influence different elements of well-being: security, empowerment, and opportunity (see box B.1). We use this broader definition.

We also define environment broadly to include a natural resource base that both provides sources (such as materials, energy, and water) and performs sink functions (such as absorbing pollution). These items could be public or semipublic goods, such as open-access watersheds or common-property grazing land; or private goods, such as the air inside a house or workplace or household drinking water. Here, the term "environmen-

---

BOX B.1
Poverty is multidimensional

"Poverty is pronounced deprivation in well-being. . . . To be poor is to be hungry, to lack shelter and clothing, to be sick and not cared for, to be illiterate and not schooled. But for poor people, living in poverty is more than this. Poor people are particularly vulnerable to adverse events outside their control. They are often treated badly by the institutions of state and society and excluded from voice and power in those institutions."

Source: World Bank 2000h.

139

tal degradation" covers pollution and depletion (damage to a natural system that affects present or future human needs negatively).

A useful, though simplified, way of looking at the links between poverty and environment is suggested in figure B.1. The figure shows how different environmental factors can influence different dimensions of poverty and well-being in a given set of circumstances. These linkages are context-specific and play out differently depending on numerous factors, including the nature of local communities and civic organizations, macro- and microlevel institutions such as property rights, gender relations, and the role of the state. The literature provides extensive empirical evidence showing how links between poverty and the environment vary in different contexts.

This analysis of environment and poverty is consistent with the sustainable livelihoods approach adopted by a number of institutions, in particular, by the U.K. Department for International Development (DFID). The sustainable livelihoods approach focuses on the capabilities, assets, and activities required for a means of living without undermining the natural resource base. It analyzes the strategies people use to make a living while sustaining the local environment.

The following discussion describes how environmental factors influence different elements of well-being: natural resource-based livelihoods and opportunities; environmental health and security; and empowerment.

Environment and opportunity

The literature on the relationship between poverty and the environment is extensive, particularly regarding rural livelihoods. Hypotheses abound, such as the theory that there is a vicious cycle of poverty, population growth, and environmental degradation. Some cases support that theory; others show quite the opposite. We have little empirical evidence that allows us to conclude with certainty that, in any particular circumstance, causality will go in one direction rather than another. Several local factors—such as macroeconomic policies, the effectiveness of local institutions and property regimes, and gender relations—decisively influence the extent to which the poor have access to and control over natural resources and the potential to derive income from them.

Although the causality may vary in different cases, re-

Figure B.1.
Environmental links to the dimensions of poverty

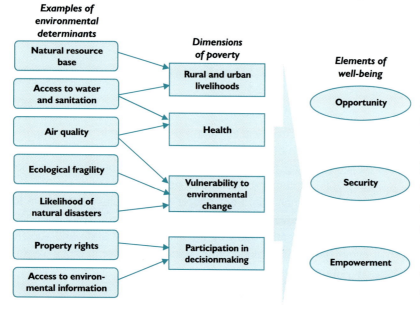

search shows that links between the natural environment and the livelihoods of the poor can be very strong. Poor rural households often derive a significant share of their incomes from natural resources. One study of 29 villages in Shindi Ward, southern Zimbabwe shows that environmental resources account for roughly 35 percent of average total household income, and the poorer the household, the greater the share of income from environmental resources (Cavendish 1999). However, even though the poor are more resource dependent, they generally use less of these resources than the better-off. The poorest households use three to four times less in quantity terms than the richest (Cavendish 1999).

Poor rural women in developing countries tend to be disproportionately affected by the degradation of natural resources because it is they who tend to be primarily involved in the collection of fuel, fodder, and water. Depending on the availability of biomass resources, collection of fuel and fodder may take anywhere from 2 to 9 hours. In Lombok, Indonesia, and in some areas of Kenya, women spend 7 hours each day on cooking and collecting dead wood or agricultural residues as fuel (Aristanti 1997). As a result of deforestation, they may have to walk longer distances and spend more time and energy to collect fuelwood. This reduces time spent on income-generating activities, crop production, and household responsibilities and may have a negative impact on health (see box B.2).

In urban areas, the links between environmental factors and poverty are strong, although different from those in rural areas. The urban poor suffer from tenure insecurity, ghettoization, overcrowding, inadequate sanitation and water facilities, violence, and changes in the labor market.

The linkages between poverty and environment often involve difficult tradeoffs between long-term

BOX B.2
The impacts of fuelwood scarcity on women's health

In Nepal, rural women and children spend long hours collecting biomass as fuel, leaving them very little time to care for children. The children's health suffers, and they have a high rate of chronic lung disease. Carrying heavy loads of fuelwood also affects women's health. Nepalese women suffer a high incidence of uterine prolapse, affecting their general health and causing complications with future pregnancies, probably as a result of carrying heavy loads of wood soon after childbirth (Pandey 1997).

A 1996–97 study involving over 1,000 women in 10 locations across 12 districts in Uttaranchal, India, found that the proportion of miscarriages was 30 percent—five times higher than the average rate reported in the National Family Health Survey of 1992–93. During pregnancy, the women carry heavy loads of wood, manure, and grass, and this contributes to the high rate of miscarriages. Of the women interviewed, 17 percent had some form of uterus descent (Dasgupta and Das 1998).

and short-term benefits, between the local and global consequences of public actions, between the effects on men and women; and so on. Particular policies will influence the processes by which individuals make their choices about trading one set of issues off against another.

As discussed in annex C, extensive research has shown that environmental problems can damage the health of people in developing countries. On average, 19 percent of the illness and death in the developing world is associated with environmental factors—access to safe water and sanitation, vector-borne diseases, dirty air inside the home and in urban areas, and exposure to toxic substances. In Sub-Saharan Africa, the proportion is as high as 27 percent.

The extent to which the poor suffer disproportionately from exposure to environmental hazards has been less extensively documented. Health outcomes are consistently worse for the poor than for the nonpoor. A poor child in Brazil is six times more likely to die than one born into a wealthy household. Figure B.2 shows health outcomes for Peru; the pattern—if not the magnitude of the difference—is broadly the same worldwide.

Exposure to hazards in the environment seems to be a major contributor to this inequality in health outcomes. Respiratory infections and diarrheal diseases are the two biggest causes of death among the poorest fifth of the world's population, as ranked by national gross domestic product per capita. Together, they caused 24 percent of deaths in 1990, but only 4 percent of deaths among the richest fifth. Environmental factors are associated with 60 percent of illness and 90 percent of deaths from these two factors. Malaria, 90 percent of which is related to environmental exposure, similarly hits the poor disproportionately.

Environment and security

In addition to the link between environment and security through health, poor people are also disproportionately vulnerable to natural disasters. This higher risk is caused by a variety of factors. Among them are that poor people tend to lack access to secure housing, to live on marginal land more prone to the effects of drought, flood, or landslides; and to lack the ability to smooth consumption in times of crisis.

The vulnerability of the poor to natural disasters is compounded by the generally weak capacity of government agencies to predict and respond to disasters and by the lack of social safety nets that would protect the incomes and consumption of the poor during and after disasters. Analysis of the recent economic crisis in the Philippines, for example, found that the extreme weather associated with El Niño was responsible for a greater share of the overall increase in poverty (47–57 percent of the total impact on the incidence, depth, and severity of poverty) than the labor market shock, which by itself accounted for 10–17 percent of the total poverty impact. The labor market shock was progressive (it reduced inequality), but the El Niño shock was regressive (it increased inequality). Moreover, the study found that household and community characteristics influenced the impact of the shocks. The ability of the poor, for instance, to protect their consumption was more limited than that of the nonpoor (Datt and Hoogeveen 2000).

When ecosystems collapse, the social systems built to manage and use them come under threat. This can lead to conflicts, particularly over environ-

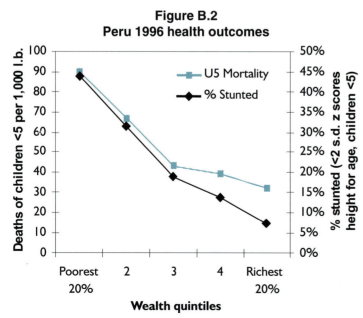

Figure B.2
Peru 1996 health outcomes

Source: World Bank analysis of Demographic and Health Survey data.

mental resources such as water and fisheries. When such resources are shared among several countries, the threats to security may escalate into political conflicts.

Environment and empowerment

Environmental activities can contribute to the empowerment of poor people in at least two ways. First, poor people can use knowledge about environmental resources to organize themselves. Second, the ability of local communities to participate in decisionmaking about environmental resources can help them maintain their livelihoods, gain equitable access to resources, and use these resources in a sustainable way.

For instance, in villages in the arid region of Vidarbha, Maharashtra, India, women and girls make several trips per day, often walking long distances, to fetch water. The village recently formed women's organizations (*mahila mandals*) that allowed women to share knowledge about the time they spent fetching water and about possible links between the quality of water and their health. Through these organizations, they realized that the problem of access to safe water was not limited to themselves and their neighbors but was pervasive in all 10 villages in the area. This created strong community awareness. The women formed alliances with the female members of the local village council (*panchayat*), held protest marches, and performed street plays. One result of their efforts was to pressure the panchayat to repair malfunctioning tubewells and revive a scheme for supplying running water. As a result of the women's efforts, within six months, 17 community wells were deepened in 8 villages, and pipelines were laid for drinking water in 2 villages. The women also initiated programs for social forestry and rainwater harvesting to pro-

tect the environment. For the first time in the recent history of these villages, in 7 villages there was sufficient safe drinking water during the summer months of 1997 (Devasia 1998).

Communities are marked by social differences and relations of power along lines of gender, race, caste, and class. Any attempt to empower local communities and target public expenditures should take into consideration these relations of inequality.

HOW HAVE BANK INTERVENTIONS TREATED POVERTY-ENVIRONMENT LINKS?

As part of the background work for this Environment Strategy, the Bank assessed the extent to which our investment projects benefit the poor. The review analyzed 61 environmental projects in four regions (see Bucknall and others 2000). Although poverty reduction was not an explicit objective of the projects—which tackled the highest-priority *environmental* problems—the review aimed to understand whether particular types of environmental investment were better at reaching the poor, and whether any region treated the issues differently.

The review found little systematic difference between regions or between types of environmental projects, although some water and sanitation projects were slightly more likely to target poor beneficiaries. The extent to which projects benefited the poor—or could demonstrate such benefits—depended more on the design of the individual project than on the country or subsector it was in.

In general, projects benefited the poor when they targeted private benefits to low-income groups or when they located investments with public benefits in areas with higher-than-average poverty rates.

143

Very few projects made any attempt to quantify their effects on the poor. Environmental benefits were seen as good outcomes in their own right, or perhaps as part of a framework for making economic growth sustainable. An increased focus on poverty will require the Bank to make a greater effort to document and monitor the distributional impacts of its investments.

INTEGRATING ENVIRONMENT INTO POVERTY REDUCTION STRATEGIES

As of September 1999, all low-income countries use participatory processes to prepare their own Poverty Reduction Strategy Papers (PRSPs) in order to obtain debt relief or concessional lending from the International Development Association (IDA) or the Poverty Reduction and Growth Facility (PRGF). Typically, the preparation of PRSPs involves three stages:

1. Developing a comprehensive understanding of poverty and its determinants
2. Choosing the mix of public actions that has the highest impact on poverty reduction
3. Selecting and tracking outcome indicators.

Because of the links between environment and poverty, and because a poverty reduction strategy must be environmentally sustainable over the long term, the Bank and the International Monetary Fund (IMF) have encouraged governments to consider environmental factors in their PRSPs (see box B.3).

The Bank is helping to build the analytical base needed to quantify the links and prioritize potential environmental interventions compared with those in other sectors. Guidelines were prepared for the *PRSP Sourcebook*. Because poverty-environment links are location specific, the Bank has taken a three-pronged approach toward helping integrate environmental issues into the PRSP process in individual countries:

Analytical work. Analytical work in pilot studies will quantify the relationships between natural resource management and the livelihoods of the poor and will document the extent to which poor environmental conditions can damage the health of poor people.

Training. In a small number of key countries, intensive training of counterparts in important sectors—water and sanitation, agriculture, health, environment, and natural resource management—in collaboration with the World Bank Institute (WBI) and external partners (for example, DFID) will equip decisionmakers with the knowledge and analytic skills to design more effective interventions as part of PRSPs.

Review. All PRSPs and related documents are systematically reviewed to assess issues of environmental sustainability and identify best practices in integrating environmental considerations into PRSPs.

BOX B.3
Environmental mainstreaming in PRSPs

Because environmental issues are closely linked with poverty reduction, a review of 25 interim and full PRSPs was undertaken to assess how they reflect environmental issues, capture good practice, and inspire teams working on forthcoming PRSPs to enhance the integration of environmental considerations and opportunities in the future.

The review considered a total of 17 points, organized in four groups: issues; poverty-environment links; responses in terms of policies, institutions, and actions; and process, including the degree of public participation. Several key points emerged:

- *Issues.* Even though the poor in most PRSP countries are overwhelmingly and directly dependent on natural resources, this is not explicitly brought out in many cases. Considerations of poor (environmental) health are generally better addressed.
- *Poverty-environment links.* Most PRSPs that did recognize the significance of natural resources and environment did not focus on elaborating poverty-environment links. However, countries that have systematically analyzed poverty-environment links have been more successful in incorporating environmental concerns as part of the poverty reduction objective. The analysis of how macroeconomic policies and programs influence environment is particularly poorly developed across PRSPs.
- *Responses.* Most PRSPs do not explicitly present the legislative, institutional, and regulatory innovations needed for poverty reduction through environmental management. An important issue that is generally not covered is the cost of environmental interventions and the sources of funding.
- *Process and public participation.* Although many PRSPs generally describe the processes of discussion, stakeholder participation, and consensus building in PRSP preparation, there is little discussion at this stage on the proposed implementation of the PRSPs. It is also difficult to determine to what extent environmental constituencies have been included and to what extent poor people in general have voiced environmentally related concerns.

The key findings of the report can be summarized as follows:

- There is considerable variation across counties in the degree to which environment is mainstreamed. Although this is to be expected, it is not systematically related to the environmental status of a country
- The average score is relatively low, indicating considerable room for improvement
- Full PRSPs rank relatively high compared with interim PRSPs, indicating improvement in the process
- Several good practices do exist, especially in countries where linkages between environment and poverty were systematically analyzed earlier.

Source: Bojö and Reddy 2001.

Annex C

Environment and Health

I t has long been recognized that the environment in which people live—from the household level to the global level—significantly affects their health. Until recently, however, the actual magnitude of health impacts from exposure to various environmental risks was not known, nor was it possible to compare the cost-effectiveness of preventive measures to reduce such exposure with health-sector activities that cure the resulting illnesses.

Quantitative estimates of the impact of environmental risks on health have emerged recently in the course of research on the global burden of disease, which uses a standardized measure of health outcomes—disability-adjusted life years, or DALYs—across various causes of illness and death. DALYs combine life years lost due to premature death and fractions of years of healthy life lost as a result of illness or disability. The use of DALYs as a measure of the burden of disease has provided a consistent basis for systematic comparison of alternative interventions. It enables health specialists to identify development programs that have the potential to generate significant improvements in the health status of poor households in the developing world (see Murray and Lopez 1996).

Recent estimates suggest that premature death and illness due to major environmental health risks account for one fifth of the total burden of disease in the developing world—comparable to malnutrition and larger than any other preventable risk factors and groups of disease causes. The total burden of disease per million people in rich countries is about half that in developing countries, but the disease burden from environmental risks is smaller by a factor of 10 (see figure C.1).

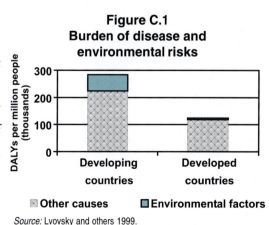

Figure C.1
Burden of disease and environmental risks

Source: Lvovsky and others 1999.

147

ENVIRONMENTAL HEALTH AND POVERTY

Environmental health risks fall into two broad categories:

Traditional hazards, related to poverty and lack of development include lack of safe water, inadequate sanitation and waste disposal, indoor air pollution, and vector-borne diseases such as malaria.

- Worldwide, an estimated 3 million people in developing countries die every year from water-related diseases caused by exposure to microbiological pathogens resulting from inadequate sanitation and waste disposal, water supply inadequate for personal hygiene, exposure to unsafe drinking water, and bacteriological contamination through a variety of other water uses, such as cooking and bathing. The majority of fatalities are children under age 5. Water-related diseases impose an especially large health burden in the Africa, Asia, and Pacific regions. In India alone, nearly 1 million people die annually as a result of water-related diseases.

- More than half of the world's households use unprocessed solid fuels, particularly biomass (crop residues, wood, and dung) for cooking and heating, in inefficient stoves without proper ventilation; the outcome is that people—mainly poor women and children in rural areas and urban slums—are exposed to high levels of indoor air pollution. It is estimated that nearly 2 million children and women die every year in developing countries as a result. About half of these deaths occur in India and China.

- Vector-borne diseases are affected by a range of environmental conditions and factors, including inadequate drainage from drinking water and from irrigation; polluted and standing water; clogged storm drains; floods; and open sewers and certain types of sanitation. In Africa alone, *malaria* is responsible for about 800,000 deaths annually.

Modern hazards caused by development without environmental safeguards include urban (outdoor) air pollution and occupational and other exposure to agroindustrial chemicals and waste.

Traditional environmental hazards affect developing countries most. Their impact exceeds that of modern health hazards by a ratio of more than 10 for Africa, 5 for Asian countries (except for China), and 2.5 for Latin America. Modern threats to human health prevail in rich countries and the European economies in transition.

Inadequate water supply and sanitation pose the largest threat to human health in most of the Bank's client countries except for China and the transition economies of Europe, where air pollution causes the most damage. Indoor air pollution is highest in Asia and Africa. Malaria has taken a heavy toll on the population of Sub-Saharan Africa. Even though malaria is not nearly as significant in other regions, it ranks third globally among all environmental health threats (see table C.1).

FUTURE TRENDS

Urbanization is a major factor in Africa, Asia, and Latin America, and it is changing the landscape of environmental health concerns and posing significant new challenges (see annex E). Rapid urbanization and the uncontrolled growth of urban slums create a double burden for the urban and semiurban poor. These groups are increasingly exposed to transition risk—both traditional hazards, such as dirty cooking fuels, primitive stoves, crowding, and poor access to water and sanitation, and risks associated with modern transport and industrial pollution. Furthermore, in some parts of the world malaria is becoming an urban issue, in part because of infrastructure failures. Climate change is likely to worsen

Table C.1 The burden of disease from major environmental risks

Environmental health group	Percentage of total DALYs in each country group							
	AFR	India	China	Asia and Pacific	LAC	FSE	LDCs	EME
Water supply and sanitation	10	9	3.5	8	5.5	1.5	7	1.0
Malaria	9	0.5	0	1.5	0	0	3	0
Indoor air pollution	5.5	6	9.0	4	0.5	0	5	0
Urban air pollution	1	2	4.5	2	3	3	2	1
Agroindustrial waste	1	1	1.5	1.5	2	2	1	2.5
All causes	26.5	18.5	18.5	17	11	6.5	19	4.5

Note: Regions in the table slightly differ from World Bank Regions (see the definition in World Bank 1992 and in Murray and Lopez 1996).Definitions are as follows: AFR, Sub-Saharan Africa; Asia and Pacific, countries of East and South Asia, except for China, India and Pakistan; LAC, Latin America and Caribbean; FSE, former socialist economies of Europe (does not include Central Asia); LDCs, less developed countries (all regions and countries in the first six columns); EME, established market economies.

Source: Lvovsky and others (1999) based on Murray and Lopez (1996), Smith (1998), and World Bank estimates.

this situation, and globalization and the liberalization of trade may exacerbate the transmission of some diseases.

IMPROVING ENVIRONMENTAL HEALTH

Better infrastructure and energy services for households and communities, along with improved housing and vector-control interventions, are key measures for mitigating traditional environmental risks. Reducing modern risks calls for pollution prevention and abatement measures, which in turn require setting and enforcing environmental standards, developing a culture of environmental compliance, and creating effective incentives. In Sub-Saharan Africa, for example, remedial measures outside healthcare systems—such as improved water and sanitation, household energy, housing, vector control, and pollution management—could reduce the total burden of disease by 23 to 29 percent. Health care interventions aimed at the same clusters of diseases affected by environmental factors—diarrhea, respiratory symptoms, eye diseases, malaria, and so on—can reduce the disease burden by a further 23 to 28 percent (Listorti and Doumani 2001).

An assessment of measures to improve environmental health, although limited in scope and subject to

verification by further studies, illustrates several important points:

- Health, especially environmental health, is a principal outcome of many interventions and project activities outside the health sector.
- Measures to mitigate such traditional health hazards as indoor air pollution, inadequate sanitation, and insect vectors appear to be very cost-effective. This finding, coupled with the significant impact of these hazards on the health of the poor, calls for greater attention to traditional household and community health risks in environmental work. Since interventions to reduce these risks fall in the domain of the energy and infrastructure sectors, there is a need for closer collaboration with these sectors to achieve health outcomes.
- Large variations in the cost-effectiveness of various interventions—across health hazards and within individual types of hazard, such as urban air pollution—point to the need for rigorous analysis and skillful design of environmental health projects to maximize health benefits cost-effectively.
- The key development objective of improving people's health requires a holistic, multisectoral approach to mitigating major risks by integrating cost-effective efforts inside and outside

health care systems. A holistic approach is particularly important for improving the health of the poor, who are most vulnerable to both major environmental hazards and deficiencies in the provision of health services.

LESSONS FROM BANK EXPERIENCE

The Bank's experience with environmental health has been limited, as have been the lessons learned. Many important environmental health issues fall through the cracks of development agencies because both environment and health are cross-sectoral and because institutions commonly lack clear directives for the multisectoral dimensions of their work.

In *the water supply and sanitation sector* (WSS), an array of lessons has emerged after nearly 25 years of research devoted to low-cost, appropriate technology and an International Decade dedicated to making drinking water and sanitation universally available. The lessons point to the value of an integrated approach to environmental health interventions—for example, integrating water supply with sanitation, drainage, community education, and hygiene practices (Listorti 1996).

A recently completed study by the Bank's Europe and Central Asia Regional Vice Presidency (ECA) on the health and hygiene dimensions of water and sanitation projects found that at least half of WSS investments are embodied within non-WSS projects, notably Social Funds. This finding shows the high priority attached by communities to environmental health–related activities and cross-sectoral links to environmental health (Klees and others 1999). The study concluded that:

- An intersectoral approach to WSS projects, incorporating hygiene education, health, and water quality issues, is needed to realize the maximum impact from investments in infrastructure.

- Future environmental health work in the Bank should aim at assisting Bank staff in developing key performance monitoring indicators.

The most important Bank-supported interventions addressing indoor air pollution were large-scale programs for improved stoves in India and China in the late 1980s (although these were motivated by energy-efficiency, rather than health goals). Major lessons were (a) the need to target efforts toward the most-affected communities, (b) the need to complement financial support with local capacity building, training in maintenance, and health awareness programs, (c) the need for a greater role for local authorities and communities, and (d) the importance of sustainable financial arrangements.

Experience is also emerging with regard to urban air quality management projects, such as the Mexico City Transport Air Quality Management Project, the Slovenia Environment Project, the Dhaka Air Quality (LIL), and discussions on proposed urban air pollution projects for the Bangkok and Katowice metropolitan areas. A recent and quite successful experience in which the Bank supported the global phaseout of leaded gasoline highlighted the crucial role of political commitment, public awareness, and partnership with the private sector (see box E.1 in annex E).

FUTURE CHALLENGES

WSS and urban projects represent the largest portion of the current environmental health–related portfolio. Maximizing health benefits through these projects requires more analytical work and a better understanding of specific linkages between project design and health outcomes. Another challenge is indoor air pollution, which has clearly emerged as an overlooked problem in a number of regions; no projects were associated with this significant public health concern. Urban air pollution remains high and is even worsening in some countries, but to date, Bank activities to address the problem in a comprehensive way have been limited (see Kojima and Lovei forthcoming).

Still another key concern is the lack of indicators, baselines, and low-cost monitoring of environmental health projects or components. It is uniformly felt that increased monitoring of environmental health outcomes would improve the projects. Such monitoring would also be helpful to economic analysis of environmental health projects, especially to cost-benefit analysis, which is rarely undertaken at present. Yet the desirability of improved monitoring and evaluation of environmental health outcomes of infrastructure projects needs to be weighed against the costs of conforming with these requirements. The Bank has been working on this issue in water and sanitation projects. Operational experience indicates that the costs of developing high-quality, project-level baseline information and complementing it with equally high-quality monitoring and analysis usually exceed reasonable project budgets and client capacity. The difficulty and cost of measuring the impact of a project on health are exacerbated by the fact that environmental factors are only one of many causes of disease. If other disease causes change over time, it is necessary to monitor health outcomes for a control group, as well as for the group receiving the environmental intervention. This limits the possibility of making improved health outcomes a stated objective of many Bank projects that do, in fact, have an impact on health.

Regional staff also stressed the need for linking environmental health issues with other sectoral efforts in an interdisciplinary manner; for example,

nutrition and education, health issues associated with the localized impact of solid waste disposal, and occupational and traffic safety. Among the suggestions proposed by regional staff were to:

- Better integrate environmental health into Country Assistance Strategies (CASs)
- Embark on new analytical and advisory activities in environmental health while strengthening capacity to increasingly apply existing knowledge in the field
- Define the scope for intersectoral collaboration on environmental health work that will best meet needs
- Include environmental health analysis in the environmental assessment process
- Devise low-cost ways of tracking and monitoring indicators of health outcomes through "reasonable" proxy indicators (see table C.2)
- Develop case studies on specific priority issues and pilot project activities.

STRATEGIC DIRECTIONS

The World Bank Environment Strategy pays serious attention to environmental health by promoting three major types of activities:

1. Improving knowledge of environmental health problems and developing an appropriate response that takes into account institutional, financial, and social constraints; launching advocacy and dissemination activities; and strengthening collaboration with strategic partners such as the World Health Organization (WHO), other UN agencies, and bilateral organizations with experience in environmental health

2. Integrating critical environmental health issues into the operations of relevant sectors—for example, as health considerations and hygiene promotion in WSS projects, indoor air pollution in energy operations, urban air pollution in trans-

port projects and city development strategies, and fuel quality in petroleum sector restructuring work

3. Adopting a holistic approach to development impacts that focuses on tangible improvements

in human health and facilitates cross-sectoral collaboration within the Bank and in client countries.

Table C.2 Health outcomes and environmental interventions

Environmental risk factor	Associated sectors/projects	Health outcomes	Health indicators	Examples of monitorable proxy indicators
Indoor air pollution	Energy (cleaner fuels, improved stoves) Rural development	Child mortality Chronic obstructive pulmonary disease (COPD) Acute respiratory infections (ARIs)	Child deaths due to respiratory illness Cases of ARI Incidence of COPD	Estimates of exposure levels to indoor air pollution Percentage of households using clean fuels or improved stoves Type of housing Cooking practices
Outdoor air pollution	Energy Transport	Mortality COPD ARI Respiratory hospital admissions (RHA) IQ impairment (lead)	Deaths (adult) Incidence of COPD Cases of ARI RHA	Annual mean levels of PM_{10} ($\mu g/m^3$) Annual ambient concentrations of lead in the atmosphere ($\mu g/m^3$) Lead level in blood, particularly among children ($\mu g/dl$)
Vector-borne disease	Irrigation Reforestation Infrastructure (drainage) Health (vector control)	Malaria mortality Malaria morbidity	Deaths due to malaria Malaria cases	Application of bednets Application of insecticides Indicators related to the development and maintenance of irrigation and drainage infrastructure
Lack of water and sanitation	WSS Infrastructure Social funds	Mortality due to diarrheal disease Diarrhea incidence	Child deaths due to diarrhea Diarrhea cases (child)	Relevant indicators of access to water and sanitation (for example, percentage of households with in-house connections, LPCD, percentage of community coverage with sanitation facilities) Indicators of sustained and effective use of WSS facilities Quality of water in the source Hygiene/behavioral change indicators
Pesticide residues	Agriculture	Acute poisoning Cancers Fetal defects	Cases of acute poisoning Cases of cancer	Application norms Storage and handling practices
Other toxic substances	Control of industrial and transport pollution, change in fuel quality	Cancers IQ impairment (lead)	Cases of cancer; blood-lead level	Environmental performance Waste management codes Land zoning regulations Market share of leaded gasoline

Note: LPCD, liters per capita per day; WSS, Water supply and sanitation.
Source: Lvovsky and others 2000.

Annex D

Natural Resource Management

NATURAL RESOURCES, POVERTY, AND SUSTAINABILITY

Natural resources provide fundamental support to life and economic processes. Soils are the foundation of agriculture, which in turn is the basic building block in the livelihoods of all people. Forests help protect water sources, reduce the risks of natural disasters such as landslides and flooding, are home to at least 80 percent of remaining terrestrial biodiversity, and are a major carbon sink that mitigates climate change. More than 1.6 billion people depend on forests for their livelihood in some way. Water is essential for the sustenance and health of humankind and indeed of all species. It is an important input for agriculture and many industries and a significant sink for waste discharges. Coastal and marine ecosystems include some of the most diverse and productive habitats on earth. Marine fisheries are an important part of the world's food supply. Ecological processes maintain soil productivity, recycle nutrients, cleanse air and water, and regulate climatic cycles. At the genetic level, diversity found in natural life forms supports the breeding programs necessary to protect and improve cultivated plants and domesticated animals and thus helps safeguard food security. Properly managed, natural resources provide the foundation for maintaining and improving the quality of life of the world's population and can make invaluable contributions to sustainable growth.

This foundation is coming under increasing pressure from mismanagement, a growing population, higher levels of economic activity per capita, and the complex interactions of these phenomena. Evidence of the resulting degradation of natural resources is all around us. Eleven percent of the earth's vegetated surface (1.2 billion hectares) has been significantly degraded by human activity over the past 45 years, affecting more than 900 million people in 100 countries. Erosion, salinization, compaction, and other forms of degradation affect 30 percent of the world's irrigated lands, 40 percent of rainfed agricultural lands, and 70 percent of rangelands. More than one fifth of the world's tropical forests has been cleared since 1960. Globally, 12 million to 15 million hectares of forest are lost every year, in addition to substantial areas of grasslands and wetlands. In 1990, 28 countries, with a total population of about 335 million, experienced "water stress"—availability of less than 1,700 cubic meters per person per year. By 2025, this figure is expected to grow to around 50 countries, affecting some 3 billion people. Country figures, moreover, mask widespread localized water shortages. The world's oceans are threatened by nutrient and heavy metal pollution, severe overfishing, and disease. Coral reefs are being degraded at an unprecedented rate—as much as 40 percent of the world's reefs will be lost in the next 10 to 20 years at current rates.

Degradation of the natural resource base is having a substantial impact on the economies of developing countries. It threatens the quality of life directly. Deforestation increases vulnerability to natural disasters, as shown by the devastating impacts of Hurricane Mitch in Central America. Even in the absence of hurricanes, flooding and landslides have been regular events, causing widespread loss of life and damage to crops and infrastructure. The increasing scarcity of water and fuelwood forces many—primarily women and children—to walk long distances to collect their daily supplies. The World Health Organization (WHO) estimates that more than 5 million people die each year from diseases caused by unsafe drinking water and lack of water for sanitation and hygiene. Smoke from fires set to clear forest areas causes widespread respiratory problems. These are real economic, social, and human costs, even though they seldom appear in national accounts.

Degradation of the natural resource base also threatens long-term growth. Improving agricultural productivity is an essential part of development and poverty alleviation strategies in many countries, but degradation of soil and water resources threatens this objective. In parts of the Pakistani Punjab, for example, salinization and other problems in irri-

gated areas have offset many of the productivity gains resulting from the Green Revolution. Deforestation is harming growth even from the narrow perspective of the timber industry; in countries that have mismanaged their forest resources, mills soon find themselves bereft of supplies. The balance sheet becomes even bleaker when the costs imposed on other sectors are added—higher risk of floods, sedimentation that reduces hydroelectric power generation and availability of water for irrigation, and loss of fisheries. Many inland and marine fisheries have collapsed completely, and in many countries, the sector only survives with massive and onerous government subsidies. Taking this depletion into account can subtract several percentage points from gross domestic product (GDP).

The impact of this degradation is particularly severe for the poor, who tend to rely heavily on fragile natural resources for their livelihoods. Moreover, their claim to these resources is often tenuous. Because they are at a social and economic disadvantage, the poor often reside in fringe areas, where access to potable drinking water and adequate sanitation facilities is limited and higher mortality, morbidity, and disease rates prevail, or in highly vulnerable areas such as floodplains, coastal areas, and degraded hillsides, with a diminished capacity for buffering against natural and man-made shocks and disasters.

ENHANCING THE SUSTAINABILITY AND THE POVERTY IMPACT OF NRM: KEY STRATEGIC CHOICES

Natural resource management (NRM) refers to the utilization of natural resources such as land, water, air, minerals, forests, fisheries, and wild flora and fauna. This discussion begins by identifying key concerns and policy approaches to improving NRM and ameliorating the impact of natural resource use on poverty. It then reviews the key issues arising in the context of some of the most important natural resources: land, forests, and water. The perspective taken by the strategy is that NRM should contribute to poverty alleviation and that natural resources should be used in a sustainable manner to enhance human welfare.

Sustainable NRM and poverty alleviation are generally highly compatible. The poor are usually most directly dependent on natural resources for their livelihoods, and most vulnerable to the consequences of natural resource degradation. Improving NRM can thus make substantial contributions to helping improve the welfare of the poor. Sustainable intensification of agriculture can improve the income of poor farm households in both the short and long terms. It can also help reduce pressures to expand into remaining forest areas, thus avoiding increased downstream damage from flooding and sedimentation and preserving biodiversity. Nevertheless, difficult tradeoffs may be encountered at times. Reducing downstream damage may require restricting the land-use options of poor farm households in the upper watershed. Unless means are found to compensate these households, such restrictions are likely to be either ineffective or inequitable. Improved NRM can result in substantial economic gains, and these gains will often benefit the poor directly. But when they do not, the poor should not be asked to pay for them.

New evidence supports a shift in the way we understand NRM and the links between poverty and environmental degradation—toward a focus on how microlevel institutions mediate the impacts of the macro environment to foster sustainability. This approach starts with an analysis of how people access and use resources as part of their overall livelihood strategy, and how they adapt to the condi-

tions created by macro policy and political frameworks. This lens broadens the analysis of local options for resource management away from NRM and agricultural strategies, to look at the multiple, flexible livelihood strategies that people pursue and the institutional and cultural context in which they live. (The U.K. Department for International Development, or DFID, has described this approach as the "livelihoods approach.") It also explicitly assesses the local institutions and political economy that determine who in the society—men, women, indigenous people, farmers, or industrialists—have resource entitlements and access to resources and capital.

Studies using this approach have documented the importance of social capital at multiple institutional levels; the role of environmental entitlements, including land and resource tenure; the values of social and cultural preferences; the income strategies that factor in vulnerability to cyclical events or political risks; and the dynamics of urban-rural remittances from migrants still culturally tied to rural areas. These studies offer a rich set of examples of ways in which local people mitigate poverty induced by environmental degradation or limited resource access. They also show how local people have reversed patterns of degradation despite less-than-perfect policy and legal conditions.

These lessons point to three main strategic themes that need to be addressed to enhance the sustainability and poverty impact of NRM:

1. *Incentives.* Decisions on NRM are not made by governments or international organizations; they are made by millions of individual decisionmakers—by farmers who decide what crops to plant and what inputs to use, or who decide whether to increase their cultivated area

by clearing forests; by developers who decide where to locate housing or industry; and by fishers who decide what type of fishing gear to use, where to fish, and how many days to spend at sea. The incentives faced by these decisionmakers are critical to NRM. Inefficiencies in the utilization of natural resources often arise because private and social prices differ and markets are incomplete or distorted. The result is lower total welfare, particularly for the poor. A fundamental distinction needs to be made between the on-site and off-site effects of natural resource problems.

■ *On-site effects.* In the case of on-site effects, decisionmakers already have powerful incentives to address natural resource problems, since they are affected directly. The main need in this case is to remove obstacles to the proper functioning of existing incentives. This often includes the introduction of exclusive use rights, as discussed below.

■ *Off-site effects.* Conversely, in the case of off-site effects, decisionmakers usually have little or no incentive to address natural resource problems, as the consequences do not affect them. In such situations, incentives need to be created. Policymakers should (a) remove policy-induced distortions that undermine sound NRM; (b) complement market signals with taxes or fees that reflect social opportunity costs, or payments that reflect social benefits; and (c) selectively regulate the remaining externalities.

2. *Property rights.* Unsustainable and inefficient utilization of natural resources often occurs because property rights are not complete, exclusive, enforced, and transferable. The issue of property rights is particularly salient in the case of open-access resources, such as fisheries. In addition, property rights that do fulfill these conditions are often quite skewed. The result is a "smaller pie" than theoretically possible and a "smaller piece of the pie" for the poor. Although secure property rights do not guarantee greater resource conservation, in many circumstances they can play an important role. Policymakers' first order of business should be to (a) clarify property rights where they do not exist, are obscure, or are in dispute; (b) enforce property rights to support better NRM and thereby contribute to poverty alleviation; and (c) selectively regulate the remaining externalities, using the right incentives.

3. *Empowerment.* Inefficiencies and inequities in the utilization of natural resources often arise because many important stakeholders have little say in their management. Several strands of work are required to build social capital and support for honest and transparent institutions that have the confidence of the local population. Particular care is needed when natural resources are managed by indigenous peoples.

KEY NATURAL RESOURCE ISSUES

Land

The land resources of the world are limited and at constant risk of being further degraded. Land degradation affects agricultural productivity and is therefore a major factor in food security and rural poverty. Although productivity trends indicate that aggregate global food supply is not seriously threatened in the short term, some regional trends are of great concern: per capita food production in Africa has been slowly dropping during the last 30 years, and in the former Soviet Union food production has decreased significantly since 1990. Problems are particularly acute in dryland areas. Doubling food production by 2050 to meet human needs will create new pressures. It should also be noted that increases in global food supply often come at a heavy environmental cost: pesticide pollution, water table depletion, biodiversity losses, and land degradation as a result of inappropriate land-use systems.

A major change toward sustainable land resources management (SLRM) is needed to protect and enhance the productive base of land resources and the livelihoods of the people who depend on them. To achieve this in countries with high poverty rates requires addressing a wide range of issues, including land policy issues (property and access rights, and land-use planning); key sector policies (including price policies and other policies that affect incentives, as well as infrastructure policies and investments); and changes in governance processes (decentralization and empowerment of local communities).

The United Nations Convention to Combat Desertification (CCD) places primary responsibility for action on land degradation with the governments of affected countries. Effective action requires government commitment, political will, and capacity. Environmental issues, including follow-up to the CCD, are often the domain of specialized environmental agencies rather than line ministries such as ministries of agriculture. As a result, these issues often have little impact on macroeconomic and sector policies. Focusing more attention on how government commitment is created and sustained—the political economy of land management—is therefore critical. An efficient land policy framework is needed, including security of land rights and land access, establishment of the institutional infrastructure to administer land rights, and facilitation of land markets and transferability of land rights.

Participation by rural communities is crucial to improved land management (see box D.1). To be

BOX D.1
Community-based natural resource management

Natural resource management projects increasingly try to incorporate a role for communities in the design and implementation of NRM projects. For example, the Mauritania Rainfed Natural Resource Management Project (fiscal 1997) is financing the first 5 years of a 20-year long-term program to activate a process of natural regeneration of land fertility, rangeland vegetation, and livestock and forest production. It will do this by encouraging the emergence of better-adapted and more sustainable approaches to resource use. This is likely to result in greater biodiversity conservation while generating more income and a better quality of life for the local people. The project, which will provide rural communities with effective empowerment in the management of their natural resources, is active in 47 villages in three regions of the country. A number of microprojects (dikes, small dams, wells, women's vegetable gardens, nurseries of indigenous tree species) are under way with the active participation of local communities.

effective, policies must be based on the knowledge, needs, priorities, and decisions of people living on and using the land. These communities, many of them very poor, have a strong interest in preserving the resources that provide for their survival, but they are often constrained by inappropriate government or donor policies. Identifying local preferences through direct consultation and incorporating indigenous knowledge are particularly important in cases involving indigenous peoples. SLRM hinges on a new approach of agricultural intensification that combines three basic principles: integrating the biophysical and socioeconomic driving forces involved; fostering a people-centered learning and participatory approach; and bringing recognizable and early productivity benefits to farmers ("SLRM for business").

A strategy for land resources management should be based on a fourfold approach:

1. *Support the new approach to agricultural intensification and environmental protection* by (a) managing biological interactions that favor crop and animal productivity in a profitable and ecologically sensitive manner, and (b) empowering rural producers and their organizations or communities through knowledge acquisition and capacity building

2. *Change the role of state and public services* by implementing a decentralization process with full participation of the main stakeholders in land use and land management

3. *Contribute to and implement international agreements such as the CCD,* which are conducive to this change in mindset and institutional shift

4. *Monitor downstream and off-site impacts* from land use practices so that a more complete assessment of their costs and benefits can be made and measures can be taken to encourage beneficial uses and discourage harmful ones.

Forests

Forests have a major role to play in poverty alleviation, sustainable economic growth, and the provision of ecosystem services. Of the world's 1.2 billion extreme poor—those living on $1 or less a day—90 percent depend on forests for their income or are significantly dependent on forest resources, including agroforestry and tree crops. The Bank's 1991 forestry strategy and 1993 policy sought to protect forests by adopting a conservation-oriented approach. A review of the Bank's performance by the Bank's Operations Evaluation Department (OED) concluded that although the overall goals set out were laudable, they were misplaced to some extent and that implementation has been only modest. The strategy overemphasized the objective of

halting deforestation in the tropics, at the expense of focusing on poverty alleviation and the broader spectrum of forest types. Specific policy requirements created risk-averse behavior and avoidance of difficult problems in the sector, and this shortcoming was compounded by the lack of a clear and implementable strategy. The OED recommended that the Bank modify its policy objectives for forests and expand its coverage. As a multisectoral agency with major activities across economies, the Bank needs a strategy that comprehensively deals with all potential impacts on forests and forest peoples, rather than one focused only on its fairly small forestry investment portfolio. To be effective, the Bank will also need to review its objectives for and approaches to forests and forest peoples. If it does not, it will fail to generate significant improvements in forest outcomes and will fall far short of its larger institutional goals of poverty alleviation and sustainable economic growth. It will also miss its opportunity to make a major contribution to the protection of the important global values embodied in the world's forests.

On the basis of the OED review, specially commissioned analytical studies of key issues, a major process of consultation with stakeholders, and the input of Bank's forest sector operational staff, a new strategy has been formulated. The three basic objectives of the new forest strategy are closely linked with the key objectives of the Bank's Environment Strategy (see box D.2.). The three goals are as follows:

1. *Harness the potential of forests to reduce poverty* by creating opportunity, empowerment, and security for rural people, especially the rural poor and indigenous groups, in the use and management of forests. Especially important are joint and collaborative forest management systems and the

BOX D.2
Linkages between the Environment Strategy and the revised forest strategy

The World Bank's Environment Strategy is closely linked with sector strategies, such as forestry, rural development, and water resources management. For example, the main elements of the revised forest strategy correspond closely with the main objectives of the Environment Strategy. Both strategies focus on poverty, growth, and global issues.

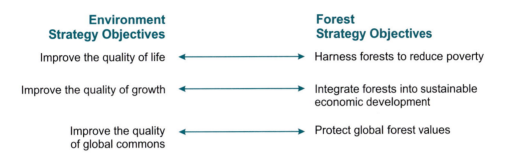

Other common links exist between the strategies in their recognition of cross-sectoral issues, mainstreaming into policy dialogue, governance, selectivity, and better cooperation with development partners.

identification of priority areas in which the Bank will seek to have maximum impact on poverty.

2. *Integrate forests into sustainable economic development.* The approach described here is based on the fact that forests are seriously undervalued— and are utilized wastefully and unsustainably— in many economies, largely as a result of governance failures and perverse incentives. The major directions to be followed will be to develop markets for environmental services; to encourage good forest management; to improve governance (including control of illegal activities); to promote active participation in management decisionmaking by all stakeholders; and to manage adverse cross-sectoral and macroeconomic impacts on forest resources.

3. *Protect vital global forest values.* The most important challenge in this area is to create effective markets for global values and other externalities from forests so that local and national stakeholders will benefit from protecting and managing the resource.

Water, coastal, and marine resources

The world is experiencing a systemic water crisis as a result of unsustainable use and management of water resources. A rapidly increasing population is exacerbating the traditional problems of providing water supply and sanitation services. More than 1 billion people do not have access to potable water supplies, and 3 billion do not have adequate sanitation. The world's major lakes, rivers, and aquifers are under severe stress. The water sector also faces new threats and challenges, including urbanization; overabstraction and regulation of surface water; overpumping of groundwater; pollution from point and nonpoint sources; loss of aquatic biodiversity; conversion of wetlands, mangroves, and other coastal habitats; introduction of alien and exotic species and invasive weeds; emergence of disease and other marine pathogens; and increasing interbasin water transfers. These threats, and the resulting degradation, are having a severe impact on quality of life and on growth prospects. The impact is disproportionately felt by the poor, who directly or indirectly depend on terrestrial and aquatic ecosystems for income generation and are least able to adapt to reductions in water quality and availability.

The key future challenges include promoting a sound institutional environment; improving economic analysis of management options; improving transboundary water management; addressing social and sustainability issues in new dam construction; halting degradation and loss of ecosystem functions and the deterioration of freshwater lakes and reservoirs, wetlands, mangroves, and coral reefs; improving drainage; and addressing the water resources implications of climate change.

Environmental sustainability is a fundamental element of sound water resource management. The integration of environmental quality objectives remains an important challenge in the water policy reform and management process. Environmental assessments have proved to be a useful tool for screening and predicting potential impacts. However, lack of clear environmental sustainability criteria for the water sector, capacity constraints, and lack of commitment to follow through with politically difficult decisions hinder the effective integration of environmental issues in water projects. As a result, the influence of these studies on project decisionmaking, especially the analysis of alternatives, is often limited.

Demand management is part of water supply and sanitation policy and is an area of increasing emphasis in irrigation activities; most water supply and sanitation projects and many irrigation projects emphasize some elements of demand management. But in a number of areas, such as sanitation, drainage, and water quality management, considerable work remains to be done. Water allocation requirements for environmental uses, including the protection of biodiversity, should be given increased priority in light of rising demands for water and frequent problems resulting from degradation of water quality (see figure D.1).

The Bank's Strategic Framework for Action on water provides a basis for achieving the broad objective of systematically mainstreaming environmental quality objectives into water resource planning, development, and management programs and investments. It calls for a set of complementary

Figure D.1
The value of water and water-based ecosystems

WATER AND WATER-BASED ECOSYSTEMS

DIRECT VALUES	**INDIRECT VALUES**	**OPTION VALUES**	**NON-USE VALUES**
Consumptive and non-consumptive use of resources	**Ecosystem functions and services such as:**	**Premium placed on possible future uses and applications, including:**	**Intrinsic significance in terms of:**
Domestic use	Water quality	Pharmaceutical	Cultural value
Industrial input	Water flow	Agricultural	Aesthetic value
Irrigating crops	Water storage	Industrial	Heritage value
Watering stock	Water purification	Leisure	Bequest value
Hydro-power	Water recharge	Water use	··· etc. ···
Wild plants	Flood control	··· etc. ···	
Wild animals	Storm protection		
Fishing	Nutrient retention		
Transport	Micro-climate		
Recreation	Shore stabilization		
··· etc. ···	··· etc. ···		

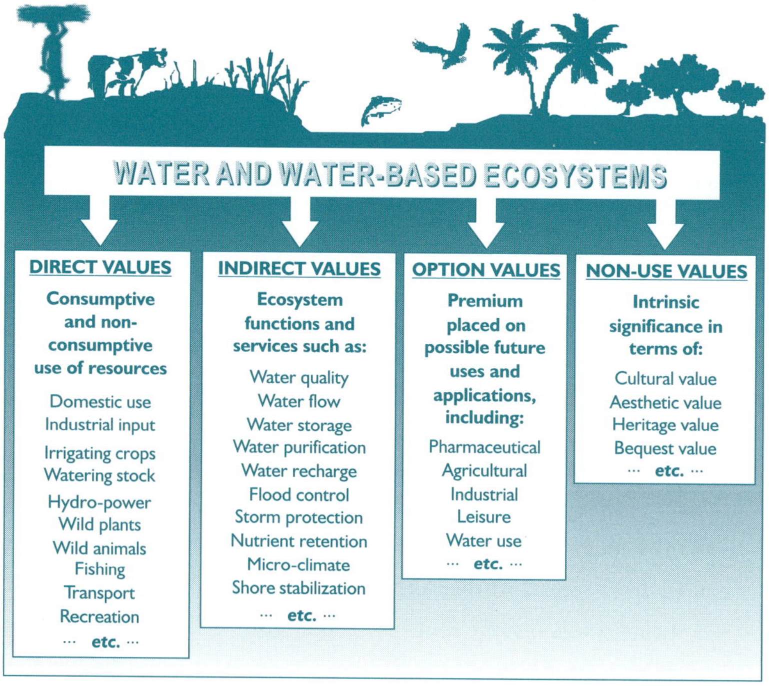

measures to strengthen environmental management capacity, as follows:

- Promote a comprehensive approach to water resource management that includes (a) treating water as a unitary resource; (b) supporting a shift from curative to preventive actions; (c) improving the integration of environmental quality objectives into regional and national water resource management strategies, river basin planning, investment projects, and policy reforms and actions, and changing the safeguard policy orientation from "do no harm" to "promotion of improved development"; and (d) adopting environmental sustainability criteria for the water sector.

- Support actions to more fully integrate water quality concerns into water supply and sanitation efforts. Water sector reforms should be complemented by an effective regulatory framework and incentive structure for managing the water resource base and ensuring its sustainability.

- Recognize the ecological uses of water. Environmental flow assessments should be conducted as integral parts of water resource operations (including environmental assessment).

- Improve transboundary water management. Numerous river basins, groundwater aquifers, and coastal and marine environments cross national boundaries, creating a need for cooperative management. Transboundary waters have often been a source of conflict, but they can also stimulate joint efforts. The primary management challenges include allocation and sharing of water, management of water quality, navigation and flood control, and halting the degradation of aquatic ecosystems.

Effective implementation of the Strategic Framework for Action calls for strengthened environmental management capacity, use of interdisciplinary teams, knowledge sharing, analytical work, and strategic partnerships. To accomplish these objectives will require a long-term commitment by the Bank and allocation of resources for promoting policy dialogue, for cooperatively undertaking sector studies, and for preparing and supervising lending operations and providing nonlending services.

Biodiversity

The vast array of the world's animals and plants, the genetic information they contain, and the dynamic and interacting communities they form are known collectively as biodiversity. Biodiversity therefore permeates all levels of NRM, since its individual elements interact in intricate ways to form forests and grasslands, maintain soils, and provide ecosystem services, among other fundamental functions. Most biodiversity is uncataloged. Some of the known genes, species, and communities have critical uses—as food, commodities, medicines, moderators of climate and hydrology, pollinators, or soil formers—but the contributions made by others are insufficiently known. The planet is losing species at a rate higher than at any time in its history—an "extinction spasm" that undermines future development options.

The sharp distinction often made between "local" and "global" environmental issues is an artificial construct (see annex I). Understanding the linkages between various issues and properly identifying their influence on the local-to-global continuum can help diagnose problems, identify solutions, and find common ground between advocates of various approaches. Biodiversity provides two special challenges for NRM: (a) most of its benefits are economic externalities, that is, they do not appear as financial values on a market where they can be easily observed, and (b) some benefits of biodiversity accrue over the long term, while the cost of conservation may be more immediate. Another consideration is that many people consider biodiversity as having intrinsic value, for moral, religious, or cultural reasons.

The perception that biodiversity is a global issue stems from the fact that its widespread decline has cumulative consequences at the global level. Most of the benefits and costs resulting from biodiversity conservation, however, accrue primarily at the local and national levels. Important national benefits justify many interventions—such as protection of watersheds with natural forests, which reduce river siltation and support fish populations harvested by riparian peoples—even in the absence of international financing. Pollination, for example, is important for local crops, and wetland ecosystems can play an important role in purifying water. Nature-oriented tourism has the potential to be an important source of income and already is in countries such as Costa Rica and Kenya. Dive tourism is a growing segment of the tourism market in coral reef nations, particularly in the Caribbean and the Indo-Pacific. But some of the benefits of improving biodiversity conservation and its sustainable use—such as medicines and crops developed as a result of access to new genetic resources—accrue in principle to mankind as a whole. When these global benefits cannot be easily internalized, global financing mechanisms such as the Global Environment Facility (GEF) can be used to support the path toward sustainability.

The World Bank recognizes the need to support the obligations that its clients have assumed under the Conventions on Biological Diversity and Climate Change, and it is also committed to serving as an implementing agency for the GEF. These facts

have been taken into account in the strategy, emphasizing positive linkages and the opportunities to reduce poverty that these commitments offer.

FUTURE DIRECTIONS FOR THE WORLD BANK

The analysis summarized above points to several key new directions for better addressing the links between poverty and NRM:

Take a holistic approach. Clearly, there is a need for a holistic approach that can (a) integrate economic and social factors into ecosystem management goals and address poverty alleviation and environmental conservation issues simultaneously, and (b) consider NRM problems at the appropriate management scale. Lessons from NRM projects show that it may be necessary to define the management scale beyond the boundaries of administrative units to encompass an entire ecosystem or other natural unit, such as a watershed. For example, water is a unitary resource that needs to be addressed in a comprehensive manner, recognizing and operationalizing the important linkages between upstream actions and their downstream consequences for river basins, lakes, and coastal and marine environments.

Take a long-term perspective. NRM problems are almost always long-term problems and require both a long-term perspective and suitable tools. Such tools include Adaptable Program Loans (APLs) and the creation of trust funds and other innovative financial mechanisms that can finance NRM activities and recurrent costs in perpetuity (see box I.1 in annex I).

Move from curative to preventive actions. The costs of preventing resource degradation are often small compared with the costs of remediation and rehabilitation. A major challenge for NRM organizations and programs is to increase the level of effort for preventive measures while maintaining support for curative interventions in degraded areas.

Let communities drive implementation. As in other sectors, more efficient and equitable ways of implementing NRM projects are necessary. In light of the site-specificity of NRM problems and the need to consider the incentives of local stakeholders and empower them to take action, Community-Driven Development (CDD) has substantial promise as an approach to implementing programs (see box 2.1 in chapter 2 and box A.3 in annex A). An important caveat is that when off-site impacts are considerable, external transfers may be necessary to complement local management.

Increase the role of the private sector. Improving NRM requires a careful assessment of which functions need to be fulfilled by governments and which can be undertaken more effectively by the private sector. It is essential, however, to ensure that greater private sector involvement is complemented by an effective regulatory framework.

Generate multiple benefits. Shifts in market forces, globalization, and demographic forces present new opportunities for enhanced NRM. Some of these opportunities relate to the preferences of rich-country consumers for commodities that have been produced in an environmentally benign manner, while others build on the overlap that often exists between better soil management, maintenance of forest cover, and reduced pesticide use. For example, shade-grown coffee provides greater social benefits related to employment and health, increases farm economic returns, and enhances habitats for biodiversity conservation.

Build on "global to local" synergies. As an implementing agency of the GEF, the World Bank is in a good position to support interventions that simultaneously generate local benefits (that can be supported by the Bank and IDA) and global benefits (that can be supported by the GEF on an incremental cost basis). The growing mainstreaming of the GEF's biodiversity portfolio within productive sectors, and its increased association with NRM loans, provide concrete examples of this approach.

Carrying out monitoring and evaluation. Monitoring and evaluation is indispensable, both at the micro level of individual interventions, to assess their effectiveness and allow for course corrections if necessary, and at the broader macro level of overall trends, to diagnose problems, identify the need for interventions, and prioritize interventions. Monitoring can also help ensure that environmental concerns are better integrated into economic policymaking by showing more clearly how environmental quality and NRM affect welfare and economic development.

Together, these aspects of implementation present a formidable agenda for NRM operations. They can only succeed in a policy environment that has addressed the fundamentals of poverty alleviation: clear property rights to natural resources, conducive incentives, and local empowerment for NRM. At the same time, they need to build on the strategic shifts and opportunities provided by holistic and long-term approaches, community-driven implementation, generation of multiple benefits, and the exploitation of synergies in the local-to-global continuum.

To properly promote these policy and programmatic shifts, the World Bank itself needs to make shifts that reflect these challenges. These alignments need to be supported by the proper enhancement of financial resources, management buy-in, and staffing. The following lines of action were identified as prerequisites for the promotion of the strategic shifts identified in the strategy:

■ *Increase internal awareness.* It is important to demonstrate, through action and generation of experience, that these shifts indeed provide poverty reduction impacts and enhance social, environmental, and economic sustainability.

■ *Mainstream with measurable targets.* Mainstreaming must be promoted deliberately, with measurable targets and built-in accountabilities. Staff time needs to be made available to systematically evaluate and strengthen the existing toolkit (economic and sector work, CASs, loans, and grants). Such proactive mainstreaming can only be possible through internal incentives for staff to participate more actively in learning, awareness raising, research, exchange of lessons learned, and quality enhancement.

■ *Strengthen selected partnerships.* The World Bank is well equipped with the tools to support the policy and programmatic shifts presented above. Nevertheless, there will be instances in which our impacts can be enhanced through stronger partnerships in which clear and measurable outcomes can be identified and which support the overall direction of the Strategy. One such partnership (the GEF) places the Bank in an excellent position to support the dual local-global agendas demanded by our clients (see annex I). In other cases, innovative approaches, as exemplified by the recent launch of the Critical Ecosystem Partnership Fund (CEPF), can provide leverage in a cost-effective manner. (See annex K for a list of external partnerships.)

■ *Monitor progress.* Mainstreaming needs to be promoted against a backdrop of measurable indicators of progress and monitored periodically. There is a need to develop methodologies to measure mainstreaming and to strengthen the management of knowledge that can support the goals of the strategy.

Annex E

Urban Environmental Priorities

The 20th century witnessed a dramatic increase in urbanization. Major cities are home to more than 50 percent of the world's population today, compared with only 14 percent in 1900. The highest rates of increase are observed in the poorest regions of the world. In East Asia, Sub-Saharan Africa, and the Middle East and North Africa, urbanization is proceeding rapidly, with urban growth exceeding 4 percent a year. Most of this growth is explained by natural population increase within cities and by the structural transformation and incorporation of formerly rural areas at the urban periphery. In some countries, however, rural-to-urban migration is an important factor; individuals come to cities in search of education, jobs, and better lives for themselves and their families. In many countries, the most rapid population growth is occurring outside the boundaries of existing primary or secondary cities. Mushrooming periurban areas in Africa and Latin America are becoming massive slums.

THE ENVIRONMENTAL CHALLENGES OF URBANIZATION

Cities are powerful socioeconomic units, the engines of economic development. Their attractiveness, which has led to rapid urbanization, has also contributed to pressing urban environmental problems. Basic environmental services often cannot keep pace with rapidly rising demands, and growing economic activities create new pressures. Many cities and towns in the developing world are already characterized by high levels of air and water pollution, slums, deteriorating infrastructure, and poor waste management systems. The resulting exposure to microbiological pathogens due to unsafe drinking water, inadequate sanitation, and poor waste management is one of the most serious environmental health threats in developing countries. It is estimated that every year between 0.5 million and 1.0 million people die prematurely in developing countries as a result of exposure to urban air pollution, especially fine particulates from vehicles, households, and municipal sources, as well as industries and power plants. Besides fine particulates, lead is among the most serious environmental health threats in cities where leaded gasoline is still used, contributing to behavioral problems and learning disabilities in young children even at low levels of exposure. (See annex C for more detail on environmental health issues.)

Poverty and environmental conditions

Environmental problems exacerbate urban poverty. Poor cities and poor neighborhoods suffer disproportionately from inadequate water and sanitation facilities and indoor air pollution. Poor people are often forced to live in environmentally unsafe areas—steep hillsides and flood plains or polluted sites near solid waste dumps, open drains and sewers, and polluting industries. The poor may have less fear of eviction in such marginal areas, but they are at much greater risk from natural and man-made disasters and from pollution.

Poor environmental conditions lead to poor health, which aggravates poverty and often results in lower educational levels, as well as loss of income owing to sickness, disease, and increased spending on health care, which may deplete household savings. Poverty prevents people from moving to safer areas or investing in improved environments where they live. Hence, it is necessary to improve the environmental conditions of the urban poor in order to enhance their chance of "breaking the cycle" and eventually moving out of poverty.

Population growth and physical expansion, however, are outstripping the ability of many cities to provide basic health and environmental services. By 2025, it is estimated, almost 65 percent of the world's population (and an even larger share of total national economic wealth) will be concentrated in cities and towns, making it an enormous challenge to ensure that such growth is managed without seriously damaging the urban environment or the health of urban residents.

Industrial development and pollution

Economic growth in urban areas is often based on industrial activity, which for many developing coun-

tries means either primary materials processing or secondary industries. Such industries provide employment but are often unsafe and highly polluting, releasing high levels of air and water pollution or generating toxic industrial waste. As a consequence, the price paid for economic opportunities may be serious air and water pollution from industry, adding to the problems created by unprotected sewage from domestic sources.

Cleaner technologies and good practice in the adoption of pollution prevention and abatement techniques offer important opportunities for industries to improve their environmental performance. The World Bank Group's *Pollution Prevention and Abatement Handbook 1998* (World Bank 1999b) summarizes preventive and abatement approaches and good practice in a range of industries (see box 3.7 in chapter 3).

Air pollution from transport

Development allows some industrial and municipal problems to be brought under control, but such improvement is often offset by the effects of increasing levels of vehicular transport-particularly air pollution. As income levels rise, many developing countries experience rapid increases in vehicle ownership and motorization, especially in urban areas. Most vehicle emissions occur near ground level and in densely populated areas. Humans are therefore exposed much more readily to harmful pollutants from transport than to those from sources, such as power plants, that are situated at elevated levels and at greater distances from densely populated centers. In addition, vehicle exhaust particles are small, profuse, and readily inhaled, so that they are expected to cause widespread damage to human health. Pollution abatement in the transport sector is therefore likely to become increasingly important in urban air quality management strategies in the coming years.

Measures such as improved traffic management and demand management, undertaken to reduce congestion and improve traffic flow, often bring environmental benefits. Land-use planning is often seen as an important tool for influencing the long-term environmental implications of city development. Of the targeted pollution abatement measures, the first priority for developing countries is to phase out lead from gasoline (see box E.1). Other policies and measures—including vehicle emissions standards, improved vehicle technology, vehicle inspection and maintenance programs, programs for retiring or scrapping vehicles, and fuel improvements or al-

ternative fuels—have to be carefully coordinated to be effective and generate the desired improvement in air quality (Kojima and Lovei 2001).

Growing effects of cities

Linkages between environment and development are not limited to conditions within cities. Urban growth can have profound effects on surrounding areas, particularly in relation to land conversion, water abstraction, and discharges of wastewater and solid waste. Urban environmental strategies need to address the effects of urbanization on periurban and rural populations, as well as the likely effects of urban and rural economic decisions on each other. Water resources illustrate the scale on which cities

---

BOX E.1
Supporting the global phaseout of leaded gasoline

The World Bank recognizes that the phaseout of lead from gasoline is a very effective and technically feasible measure for reducing a serious environmental health threat. It has called for the complete phaseout of lead from gasoline and has undertaken a number of activities to that end.

The Bank has initiated and participated in several regional lead phase-out initiatives, including elimination of lead in gasoline in Latin America and the Caribbean, funded by the joint United Nations Development Programme (UNDP)/World Bank Energy Sector Management Assistance Programme (ESMAP); the preparation of a pan-European strategy to phase out leaded petrol under the leadership of the United Nations Economic Commission for Europe (UNECE) and the government of Denmark; the national commitment building program to phase lead out of gasoline in Azerbaijan, Kazakhstan, and Uzbekistan, funded by the Danish Environmental Protection Agency; and the ESMAP-funded program for the elimination of lead in gasoline in the Middle East and North Africa.

The Bank has also helped individual countries to introduce appropriate policies, to conduct feasibility studies, and to implement policies. These countries include Bangladesh, Bulgaria, China, the Dominican Republic, El Salvador, Haiti, Indonesia, Jamaica, Malaysia, Romania, Thailand, and more recently, Pakistan, Sri Lanka, and Vietnam (which have programs in progress).

In all these activities the Bank has played the catalytic role of building consensus among a wide range of stakeholders and development partners, in transferring experience from other countries and regions, and in dispelling myths about lead phaseout. To ensure that refinery modernization schemes (which may be required to phase out lead) are optimally designed, the programs have stressed the importance of addressing comprehensive fuel quality issues as part of lead phaseout plans.

By 2001, 29 developing and transition economies had eliminated the use of lead additives in gasoline, and several others plan to follow suit.

Source: Kojima and Lovei 2001.

can influence surrounding environment, through, for example, the effect of wastewater discharges on downstream communities, users, and ecosystems and competition for water between urban, rural, and other uses and among cities. As urban centers grow in size and number, their external effects begin to overlap.

These effects are intensified by the global phenomenon of increasing migration to coastal areas. Sixty percent of the world's population lives within 100 kilometers of the coast, an area that accounts for only about 25 percent of the land mass (WRI 2000). By 2025, over 80 percent of the largest 30 cities in the world will be in developing countries, and the majority will be coastal megacities (United Nations 1995). Coastal areas are often used as a dumping ground for sewage, garbage, and toxic wastes, polluting both the land and the coastal seas. An example is the formidable environmental stress along the West African coastline, where rapid population growth, combined with industrial and urban development, has increased pollution in marine and coastal ecosystems to alarming levels, often obstructing the development of a profitable tourism industry.

THE WORLD BANK'S EXPERIENCE

The World Bank has been active in helping client countries address urban environmental problems, using a range of lending and nonlending services. Many efforts are jointly undertaken with other development partners. The activities and services the Bank has helped to develop include methodologies for assessing urban environmental problems, mechanisms for setting and addressing environmental priorities, and lending for urban environmental improvements.

Methodologies for assessing urban environmental problems. These methodologies include rapid assessment procedures to evaluate the comparative risks of environmental problems; a decision support system for integrated pollution management; methods of estimating dose response in individuals in order to evaluate the effect on health of specific pollutants; and methods for assessing and selecting cost-effective improvements to urban environments. Bank sponsored country studies and assessments have addressed urban environment issues in many countries, including Argentina, Brazil, China, India, and Indonesia. The Environmental Action Program for Eastern and Central Europe, supported by the Bank, focused attention on development in urban and industrial areas and analyzed the effects on health and the environment, particularly with respect to air pollution. Subsequent applications of these analytical approaches found that the costs of environmental damage in Asian cities (largely for air pollution) were equivalent to 5–10 percent of urban income and will continue to rise unless significant pollution management changes are implemented (World Bank 1997a).

Mechanisms for setting and addressing environmental priorities. The Bank has supported several programs and partnerships to help build mechanisms for consensus building, for consultation among a range of stakeholders, and for the coordination of cross-sectoral policies and measures. The Urban Management Programme (UMP), sponsored by the World Bank, the United Nations Development Programme (UNDP), and the United Nations Centre for Human Settlements (Habitat), supports case studies, research, and partnership activities to assist cities and towns in developing countries. The Metropolitan Environmental Improvement Programme (MEIP), established by the UNDP and the Bank and supported by several donors, has assisted several Asian cities to find and implement practical solutions for rapidly growing environmental problems. The MELISSA program, developed by the Bank's Africa Region, supports and facilitates the improvement of the local environment through partnership development and knowledge management. The urgency of urban air quality problems and the complex mix of actions required to tackle them led to the Urban Air Quality Management Strategy (URBAIR) in Asia, which assisted in the design and implementation of air quality management policies and in monitoring and management intended to restore air quality in Asian metropolitan areas (see also box 3.2 in chapter 3). The Bank's call for the global phaseout of leaded gasoline and its support for regional and national lead phaseout programs have been effective in harnessing client commitment and action. A set of follow-up activities has been undertaken in the framework of clean fuels programs. More recently, the Clean Air Initiative, originally developed by the Bank for Latin America and now under way in other regions, is fostering regional partnerships that develop action plans to address worsening air quality problems (see box A.4 in annex A).

Lending for urban environmental improvements. The Bank has extended lending to support urban environmental improvements in many countries through projects touching all aspects of the need: urban development, environment, water supply and sanitation, urban transport, and energy. The most typical areas of Bank support have been the following:

- *Solid waste management.* This is a key responsibility of many city governments and has been an area of Bank assistance in the form of analytical work and urban investment for many years. The Strategic Solid Waste Management Program has generated a range of practical and analytical tools for planning, and there have been investments for waste management activities across the Bank's regional vice presidencies. The latter investments often address waste collection and disposal problems but now increasingly support more comprehensive approaches to waste management.

- *Water supply, sanitation, and wastewater management.* These issues are central to the environmental agenda, especially in urban areas. Much of the work has been at the site-specific or project level. A recent review showed that the urban development and water supply and sanitation portfolios include significant environmental components and investments. Issues of particular concern include the health and environmental effects of inadequate sanitation coverage and improper sewage disposal, particularly in poorer urban areas. These issues, with others, are being addressed in a multidonor water and sanitation program. Analytical work has been undertaken to assess the health aspects in more detail and to find effective ways to establish site-specific requirements for wastewater treatment.

- *Industrial pollution management.* Using a range of instruments, the Bank has supported industrial pollution abatement and waste management efforts in many countries, often dealing with implementation issues at both the national and city levels. In the 1970s and the 1980s, the Bank supported several industrial pollution control projects. However, its approach has changed in parallel with its declining involvement in the industrial sector and with the increasing role of the private sector in this area. Recent efforts have focused on guidance for good practice in pollution management, on support for integrating environmental elements into the privatization of highly polluting industries, and on facilitating the application of innovative regulatory instruments. The *Pollution Prevention and Abatement Handbook 1998* summarized lessons in good practice and provided guidelines for industrial facilities. New approaches to support for the regulatory framework, which is often weak, were captured in the recent Bank report "Greening Industry" (World Bank 1999a).

- *Cleaner fuels.* In several projects, the Bank has supported the transition to cleaner fuels in households, power generation, and transport. In many Central European countries and elsewhere, switching from coal to gas in household heating has been effective in improving air quality. The Bank-supported Slovenia Environment Management Project, for example, provided financing to support and accelerate such a switch. The transition to cleaner fuels has been an important element in implementing Fuel for Thought, the Bank's environment strategy for the energy sector.

FUTURE CHALLENGES

As cities continue to grow and increase in population and in economic importance (both relatively and absolutely), environmental pressures are likely to increase, and the Bank has to be prepared to assist its clients in facing the challenge (see box E.2). This is the rationale for the focus on environmental infrastructure services and pollution management commonly found in urban projects. It is also important to address concern about the environmental sustainability of the ecosystems that support urban areas, such as freshwater aquifers, greenbelts, airsheds, and watersheds. Thus, meeting the urban environmental challenge requires a focus on two basic areas:

BOX E.2
Environment in the Bank's urban strategy

In the Bank's recent Urban and Local Government Strategy (World Bank 2000a) the concept of the "livable" city is defined in terms of a healthy and dignified living environment. Making cities livable requires addressing the sources of environmental degradation, enabling access to basic shelter and environmental services for the urban poor, and reducing the vulnerability of poor people to environmental hazards. The strategy proposes an agenda for working with both national and local governments to develop cities that are livable, well governed and managed, and financially sustainable.

A key tool for viewing the city holistically and intervening selectively is the City Development Strategy (CDS), which can be seen both as a process and as a product emanating from the process. Where environmental problems are identified as priorities, an urban environmental management strategy can be developed, leading to issue-specific action plans. A common approach for achieving this objective is laid out in *Toward Environmental Strategies for Cities* (Bartone and others 1994), as well as in other key publications (see the Bibliography).

---

1. Provision of *basic environmental services, especially for the poor,* in a way that most effectively protects health. These services include the following:

- Access to safe water supply, sanitation, drainage, solid waste collection and disposal, and health education
- Improved municipal and industrial waste disposal
- Reduced indoor air pollution.

2. Implementation of integrated approaches to *urban air quality management* and *watershed and aquifer management* to prevent and manage the impacts of pollution and degradation. These activities include:

- Ambient air quality management
- Surface water and groundwater management
- Land and ecosystem management to preserve resource loss to pollution, particularly in coastal zones.

Regardless of the problems being addressed, continuing efforts are required to strengthen institutional capacity, improve governance, and reform environmental, economic, and financial policies. All such efforts can produce important environmental benefits.

STRATEGIC DIRECTIONS FOR BANK OPERATIONS

In dealing with urban environmental problems, the Bank needs to work at several levels—national, regional, and local—and focus on a mixture of client-oriented and issue-oriented activities. The following are areas in which it is important to strengthen the Bank's continuing environmental engagement:

- *Environmental management.* Identify, in conjunction with the urban sector, opportunities for introducing environmental good practice into city management or sectoral activities; particularly in connection with city development strategies and similar programs.
- *Air quality management.* Support for efforts to improve urban air quality in selected cities and

regions, including analytical work; initiatives to phase out leaded gasoline and introduce clean fuels; mechanisms for consensus building among stakeholders; passing on of lessons learned from programs as such as the Clean Air Initiative.

- *Waste management.* Support for ongoing municipal waste management efforts currently led by the urban sector; increased attention to industrial waste management, including hospital waste.
- *Basic services.* Strengthen inputs to programs and projects designed to increase coverage of basic environmental services, especially for poorer communities, with special attention to water and wastewater.
- *Sustainable private sector development.* Development, working with the private sector and the International Finance Corporation (IFC) of systematic approaches to improving the environmental outcomes of privatization. Other public and private organizations can be encouraged to build on the good practice examples already available to influence the environmental behavior of the private sector.
- *Response to urban expansion.* Identification of institutional mechanisms to address the ecological effects of urban expansion, especially the consequences of development in watersheds or the coastal zone.

Annex F

Climate Change

Most scientific experts agree that climate change induced by human activity is occurring and that further change is inevitable. The *Third Assessment Report of the Intergovernmental Panel on Climate Change* (IPCC 2001) predicts that average global temperatures will rise between 1.4 and 5.8 degrees Celsius over the next 100 years, a rate of warming higher than any that has occurred over the past 10,000 years. The World Bank's work on climate change is predicated on IPCC's report that concludes that "most of the observed warming over the last 50 years is likely to have been due to the increase in greenhouse gas (GHG) concentrations." About 75 percent of the cumulative GHG emissions during the past 150 years have been emitted by industrialized countries. As a result of this energy-led development, their per capita GHG emissions today are five times higher than those of developing countries who now face the daunting task of enhancing energy utilization while protecting the environment. At the same time, the IPCC also concludes that "most less-developed regions are especially vulnerable" to the projected adverse impacts of climate change. These developing countries, therefore, would need to consider these impacts and adapt their development paths. The World Bank recognizes the threat posed by climate change to the development process, and seeks to support and facilitate the mainstreaming of climate change concerns in the development agenda.

DEVELOPMENT CONTEXT

Despite uncertainties about where changes in climate will occur (the regional patterns), by when (the rate of change), and by how much (the magnitude), there is little debate on at least two key points:

■ Because of the rapid build-up of GHGs, the earth's overall temperature will warm significantly, precipitation patterns will change, and sea levels will rise.

■ The adverse impacts of projected changes in climate conditions will pose major development challenges for most developing countries in the tropical and subtropical zones.

In developing countries, where human activities are already close to the margin of tolerance for current variations in climate, the impacts of the projected changes are expected to be far reaching, adversely affecting virtually all aspects of social and economic life for the poorest of the poor. For instance, in countries where yields from dryland, nonirrigated agriculture are already near their maximum temperature tolerance, even small changes in temperature could have a devastating impact on agricultural output, with attendant consequences for food security. Similarly, changes in precipitation patterns associated with climate change could adversely affect the availability and quality of water, especially in areas where scarcity is already a problem. Sea level rise could displace millions of people living in low-lying areas of the Ganges River and the Nile delta and threaten the existence of small island states. Assisting clients to prepare for climate change is therefore inextricably linked to the Bank's mission of sustainable poverty reduction.

Developing countries fully recognize the implications of global climate change and the need for all nations to assume responsibility for protecting the global atmosphere, as reflected in their decision to ratify the United Nations Framework Convention on Climate Change (UNFCCC). However, because these countries' contribution to the cumulative increase in atmospheric concentrations of GHG emissions has been small relative to that of industrial countries, and because of the urgency of their short-term needs of providing food, energy, and other vital services for the poor, it was recognized that developing countries and economies in transition (non–Annex II parties to the UNFCCC) would be unwilling and unable to invest their scarce resources in measures yielding benefits in the distant future or outside their boundaries.[1]

For that reason, based on the principle of *common but differentiated responsibility*, industrial country parties (Annex II parties) agreed to provide new and additional grant resources to their developing country counterparts and to support the transfer of technology on beneficial terms, though initially only for GHG mitigation. A decision on similar support for vulnerability and adaptation was deferred pending a better understanding of the impacts of climate change. The UNFCCC regime and instruments are, as a result, expected to evolve in response to progress in understanding of the climate change phenomenon. The Bank will continue to review global experience, to learn from it, and to develop innovative instruments that meet the needs of its clients.

LESSONS FROM EXPERIENCE

The Bank's involvement in the area of climate change began in 1991, with the establishment of the Global Environment Facility (GEF), and expanded following the designation of the GEF as the financial mechanism of the UNFCCC. Since then, the Bank has focused primarily on assisting clients to reduce GHG emissions, as clients have been reluctant to borrow for vulnerability and adaptation activities, in the expectation that support would be forthcoming on concessional terms under the UNFCCC. In particular, to achieve GHG outcomes without compromising national development priorities, the Bank has assisted its clients to mobilize additional grant resources for operational support, mainly in the energy sector. The World Bank Group–GEF portfolio today includes 62 projects, for which $6.2 billion has been mobilized—$730 million from the GEF and the balance from the World Bank Group, donors, private investors, and government counterparts.

This decade-long involvement, representing first generation work in GHG mitigation, has been instrumental in opening up new prospects for energy efficiency, distributed supply, and off-grid service delivery, especially in remote rural areas. In addition, it has generated a number of key lessons of experience. In particular:

- Policy reforms are essential for mobilizing private capital for efficient energy development, for creating a level playing field to foster competition, and for promoting alternative approaches to energy service delivery, including incentives for service providers to diversify and innovate and to enable clean technologies and fuels to compete on equal terms.

- Many cost-effective options for reducing GHG emissions in developing countries also have substantial economic and local environmental benefits.

STRATEGIC PRIORITIES

The Bank recognizes that achieving objectives related to climate change will be a long-term process that will require integration of the GHG mitigation and the vulnerability and adaptation agendas into mainstream operational work. In this regard, the differences in the relative priorities and needs of the developing countries are also recognized, as is the need for an array of supporting instruments. These instruments include planning, policy dialogue, generation and dissemination of knowledge, and investment lending, all of which are primarily aimed at promoting national development priorities. Striking the right balance between national development priorities and protecting the global commons will therefore be critical.

Bank support to clients for better managing climate change is envisaged in three key areas: (a) mitigation of GHG emissions; (b) reduction of vulnerability, and adaptation to climate change; and (c) capacity building. In the area of GHG mitigation, the Bank will continue to promote policy and

regulatory reforms, as these tend to have large and sustainable impacts on improving the efficiency of resource use and, consequently, reducing GHG emissions. In the context of these reforms, the Bank will mobilize resources from the GEF and the Prototype Carbon Fund (PCF) to support GHG abatement measures that simultaneously address poverty reduction and sustainable development goals. In the area of vulnerability and adaptation, where the decision on UNFCCC support is pending, the Bank will mobilize donor financing for a Vulnerability and Adaptation Facility (VAF) to better prepare for climate change. Over the medium term, the Bank will focus on improving the understanding of the potential impacts of climate change and on identifying and implementing no-regrets measures to reduce vulnerability to current climate and to climate change. Finally, the Bank will assist clients in building the capacity needed to deal with GHG abatement and with vulnerability and adaptation.

GREENHOUSE GAS MITIGATION

To provide a strategic focus for the Bank's work on the energy-environment nexus and to consolidate the gains of the decade-long association with the GEF, in July 1999 the Bank's Executive Directors discussed Fuel for Thought (FFT), an environment strategy for the energy sector (see box 4.1 in chapter 4). This strategy highlights the importance of getting the policy fundamentals right. In that context, it explicitly recognizes the need to help clients tackle global climate change by capturing win-win opportunities for improving energy efficiency and promoting distributed and off-grid electricity supply in rural areas, using clean technologies and fuels. In addition, the strategy recognizes that there are valuable opportunities beyond win-win interventions for combating regional and global problems. It calls for incorporating these opportunities into Bank programs to promote sustainable development and reduce the marginal cost of GHG mitigation through the use of external resources, particularly those of the GEF, the PCF, and the private sector resources stimulated by the carbon-trading mechanisms of the Kyoto Protocol.

FFT remains consistent with the Bank's evolving agenda in the energy sector and will continue to underpin work on GHG abatement, but the scope of support will be expanded to include sectors such as transport, urban development, environment, agriculture, and forestry. There can be tradeoffs between local and global environmental benefits. One of the Bank's key goals, however, will be to identify and support GHG reduction when it is an ancillary benefit of improving the quality of life or achieving other development objectives at the local and national levels. These efforts will thus serve to initiate and consolidate low-carbon development paths. The interventions envisaged include:

- Energy sector reform and restructuring, which are key to improving supply- and demand-side efficiency, as well as to creating a level playing field for alternative energy sources, including renewables

- Energy efficiency improvements and fuel switching (for example, from coal to gas), which can reduce urban and indoor air pollution, improve thermal efficiency, and reduce GHG emissions

- Improved access to modern energy in rural or remote locations through renewable energy technologies for household lighting, water pumping, grain processing, small cottage industries, clinics, and schools, all of which yield direct economic and social benefits to rural residents

- Reduction of energy intensity in the transport sector, through land-use planning, traffic management, promotion of nonmotorized transport, and more efficient technologies, which brings

about human health and livelihood benefits, especially for the poor, in addition to reducing GHG emissions

- Forest regeneration through community participation, with the aim of offering substantial economic benefits to millions of poor households while increasing forest cover, sequestering carbon, and reducing pressure on natural forests

Energy Environment Reviews (EERs) have been applied as an important strategic tool, often supported by the joint UNDP–World Bank Energy Sector Management Assistance Programme (EMAP) (see box F.1). The Bank will continue to work with the GEF in identifying and supporting cost-effective GHG mitigation investments, increasingly stressing the need for synergy with national economic and environmental concerns in all climate change interventions. In addition, in contrast to past support for one-off projects, the Bank will support larger regional or global efforts to catalyze market development for GHG reduction:

- The Bank-GEF Strategic Partnership for Renewable Energy will focus on long-term development of the most promising technologies and market opportunities for renewable energy, including grid-connected and off-grid technologies (see, for example, box 3.4 in chapter 3).

- The Bank will explore opportunities for a more programmatic approach to improving energy efficiency. Through the support of the GEF, ESMAP, and other donors, the Bank will look to replicate the model used in China of support for energy efficiency improvements.

- Two new GEF operational programs provide opportunities to promote environmentally sustainable options in the transport sector and sustainable development of multiple ecosystems, including forestry, which has a significant carbon

BOX F.1

Strengthening environmentally responsible energy strategies through Energy Environment Reviews

Energy Environment Reviews (EERs) extend traditional Bank energy sector work by addressing the cross-sectoral environmental impacts associated with energy production and consumption at the local, regional, and global levels. EERs are an important tool for supporting the implementation of Fuel for Thought, the Bank's environmental strategy for the energy sector. Through their emphasis on upstream analysis, EERs aim to:

- Ensure that fuel and technology choices are considered before they are frozen in the context of specific project designs
- Maximize cost-effectiveness by examining pollution prevention and reduction options across the fuel supply and consumption chain
- Expand local participation and capacity building among analysts and decisionmakers.

To date, most EERs have been motivated by local environmental concerns, but many activities simultaneously address local, regional, and global effects.

In Turkey, for example, an ESMAP-supported initiative on key aspects of energy and environment/GHG strategy was largely motivated by decisionmakers' desire to compare different options for mitigating GHG emissions; but the modeling effort also provided specific guidance on least-cost control strategies for sulfur and particulate emissions in the power sector.

ESMAP and the Canadian International Development Agency (CIDA) supported a regional study, *Cleaner Transportation Fuels for Air Quality Improvement,* which examined the linkages between fuel quality, vehicle emissions, and air quality in the eight countries of Central Asia and the Caucasus. The study made recommendations for improving air quality and vehicular emissions monitoring systems and for adopting improved fuel quality regulations and controls in the coming decade. It emphasized, in particular, the rapid phaseout of lead in gasoline and the possibility of harmonizing fuel quality requirements in the region. In addition to improvement of urban air quality, the proposed measures have implications for fuel and engine efficiency and for carbon dioxide emissions.

In Mexico, an environmental strategy for the energy sector supported by ESMAP has assisted the Ministry of Energy in identifying pricing policy options for eliminating environmentally damaging subsidies in the power sector. In parallel, the Ministry of Environment has concentrated on vehicle emissions standards and the improvement of vehicle emissions performance. The EER has helped improve communications between Mexico's energy and environment ministerial authorities and has opened up the Bank's previously limited dialogue on key policy and structural issues in the energy sector.

sequestration potential in addition to local benefits.

- The PCF is designed to show how a market for carbon emission credits for developing countries can work under the Kyoto Protocol's proposed flexible mechanisms. The PCF, a public-private partnership, will develop best practices in the identification and implementation of development projects that can utilize these mechanisms to lower carbon emissions from developing countries.

VULNERABILITY AND ADAPTATION

Experience over the past two decades suggests that vulnerability to extreme weather events (floods, droughts, storm surges, and so forth) has increased markedly. Reflecting in part the rapid growth of population—and in part, the pattern of development itself—loss of life, displacement, and damage and destruction of natural, social, and physical capital have all increased, and the losses are relatively greater for the poor in poorer countries. Now, with the projected global warming and the associated higher probabilities of intense precipitation and more extended dry periods, the frequency and severity of droughts, floods, and storm surges are expected to increase, along with the vulnerability of the developing countries. These developments will exacerbate the problems related to climate that face these countries today.

Many of the countries that are most vulnerable to climate change are already close to the margin of tolerance with respect to current climate variability. Hence, the most important measures that will enable these countries to deal with future climate conditions are essentially the same as those needed to deal with the current climate. The Bank, therefore, will focus on reducing present-day climate vulnerability through the implementation of no-regrets measures. Because there is no single best or universal approach to adaptation, learning by doing will be a critical aspect of the Bank's work over the short to medium term.

Drawing on activities of partners, including the Bank's Disaster Management Facility, the following initiatives are proposed:

- Support vulnerability assessments to better understand past weather events and their physical, economic and social consequences and to develop and test indicators of current and future vulnerability
- Strengthen regional institutions to improve climate forecasting and verification systems and

to promote more effective communication and use of climate information at the national and local levels

- Evaluate the longer-term consequences of disasters to increase awareness among policymakers of the potentially serious threat that variations and changes in climate pose to sustainable development, as well as of the potentially high economic and social returns that investments in reducing vulnerability can yield
- Conduct backcasting studies of at least two countries and two projects to determine whether incorporating climate risks explicitly (a) would require a fundamental change in macroeconomic and sector policies pursued to date, or a simple realignment and phasing of priorities, and (b) would have yielded additional benefits, given past and actual climate variability
- Develop a framework for incorporating climate risks in economic analyses, with a view to reorienting the Bank's project work toward adaptation
- Support pilot initiatives in vulnerable countries to promote community-level activities aimed at, among other objectives, reforestation, conservation and restoration of wetlands, protection of mangroves and coral reefs, and strengthening of local institutions to reduce income-related risk and thus improve the capacity of the poor to cope.

As noted above, because developing countries are unwilling to borrow for adaptation, the Bank will establish, with donor financing, a VAF to support short-to-medium-term strategic priorities. The aim of such a measure would be to better prepare the World Bank Group and its clients to deal with climate change. To leverage VAF resources and ensure that the output from the activities supported by them are fully integrated into the Bank's mainstream operational work, these three approaches are proposed:

■ The focus on vulnerability in the 2000/2001 *World Development Report* has already placed the issue squarely on the Bank's agenda, and data on vulnerability in the areas of health, environment, infrastructure, and social protection are already being collected for the Poverty Reduction Strategy Papers (PRSPs). The proposed vulnerability assessments would complement this work by generating good practices that could be incorporated into the broader PRSP agenda.

■ For studies and pilot initiatives that are country specific, a cost-sharing arrangement with the country team is envisaged to enhance the prospects of buy-in. In this regard, the Environment Department will work closely with the Disaster Management Facility on continuing operations (in Honduras and Mozambique). This would allow for the integration of no regrets pilot initiatives into ongoing operations and reduce their monitoring and supervision costs.

■ For methodological work and studies, including vulnerability assessments, that have implications for Bankwide work, the VAF will cover the full costs. As much of this work will require specialized skills, the Environment Department will give priority to developing and strengthening partnership within both the Bank and the broader scientific community.

CAPACITY BUILDING

The climate change agenda is relatively new and evolving. As a result, the generation and dissemination of relevant knowledge—through analytical work to plan, prepare, and implement GHG mitigation measures and to manage climate change concerns in general—are critical first steps in capacity building. As in the recent past, the Bank will

continue to focus on providing hands-on experience through methodological, technical, and investment work to clarify how market mechanisms can benefit our clients; development of national policies to identify potential investments for possible future international cooperation; evaluation of options for reducing GHG emissions through sectoral planning; and upstream work in investment planning to identify options for mitigating the negative local, regional, and global environmental impacts of energy development. The scope of support will be expanded to include vulnerability and adaptation, as well. The following are illustrative examples of capacity-building activities related to climate change to be supported by the Bank:

■ *National Strategy Studies (NSS) Program.* Since 1997, with the support initially of Switzerland and subsequently of other donors, the Bank has assisted 26 client countries to develop national policies on Joint implementation under the Kyoto Protocol and the Clean Development Mechanism (CDM). The Bank will also help these countries identify potential investments for possible future international cooperation for climate change mitigation.

■ *Prototype Carbon Fund.* The PCF, through financial support for project specific investments, will help create the market infrastructure necessary for CDM projects. It will also help develop a knowledge base to maximize the value of its experience by collecting, analyzing, and disseminating information and knowledge to a broad range of stakeholders.

■ *CEM-Assist Program.* To help Sub-Saharan African countries take advantage of CDM, a CDM-Assist Program, funded by ESMAP and a number of bilateral donors, is being prepared.

■ *Adaptation activities.* As part of the identification and preparation of adaptation projects under the UNFCCC mandate, the Bank will help mobilize resources to help clients prepare for adaptation to the impacts of climate change.

- *Training.* Plans are being developed for training through the World Bank Institute (WBI) to support activities for assessing vulnerability. Such training would be offered on a regional basis through seminars, workshops, and short courses.

Within the Bank, compliance with Operational Policies and Bank Procedures OP/BP 4.01 on Environmental Assessment and OP/BP 10.04 on Economic Evaluation of Investment Operations requires, at the design and selection stage, assessment and consideration of lifetime GHG emissions from Bank-supported projects. This would be facilitated through the development of methodologies and through training for Bank task teams provided by the WBI.

Implementation and Resources

Implementation: Our goal is to integrate the agendas for GHG mitigation and for vulnerability and adaptation into the Bank's mainstream operational work. Progress has been made in the area of GHG mitigation, but more at the project than at the policy level. We will therefore work closely with ESMAP on energy and environment reviews, which respond to the need for sectoral environmental assessments well upstream of lending operations.

In the area of vulnerability and adaptation to climate change, implementation of the strategic priorities concentrates on learning by doing to generate good practices and to disseminate these widely to clients both within and outside the Bank. In this regard, we will focus specifically on developing analytical and methodological tools that have implications for Bankwide work. In addition, we will collaborate with the Regions, and particularly with the Disaster Management Facility, on pilot initiatives and on monitoring their implementation.

Resources: The resource requirements for the implementation of the strategic priorities related to climate change are not expected to be demanding. The resources required for the work on GHG mitigation are financed fully by the GEF, and no change in this arrangement is envisaged. The only additional resource requirements, therefore, are for the implementation of work on vulnerability and adaptation. It is expected that a significant portion of these requirements will be covered by the VAF, but these resources would have to be supplemented, in part through the prudential use of consultant trust funds to mobilize specialized skills and in part through the Bank budget for staff time.

NOTE

1. "Annex II parties to the UNFCCC" refers to industrial countries and "non–Annex II parties" to all others, principally developing countries and the economies in transition.

Annex G

The IFC's Approach to Environmental and Social Issues — A Roadmap to Sustainable Investment

The approach of the International Finance Corporation (IFC) on environmental and social issues in project finance follows closely that of its sister body, the World Bank.

THE IFC'S STRATEGY

The IFC's approach to environmental and social issues in project financing is evolving from ensuring compliance to the development of a sustainable development strategy, as outlined in the Strategic Directions paper recently submitted to the Committee on Development Effectiveness (CODE). This annex outlines the IFC's vision of sustainable development and the substance of its approach.

The IFC's management of environmental and social issues in investment projects has evolved over time to serve the particular needs of the IFC's private sector focus while recognizing its status and responsibilities as a public institution. Its strategy has been built around two primary objectives.

- To achieve a high level of environmental and social performance in IFC investments through the development and implementation of a robust management system. This system ensures the consistent application of the IFC's environmental and social policy and procedural framework, which includes building adequate capacity within financial intermediaries distributing IFC funds.

- To pursue investments with specific environmental benefits that are financially viable, and to innovate in the area of "near-market" opportunities through appropriate use of commercial and concessional funding.

The IFC believes that these foundations provide a firm basis on which to build a sustainable development strategy that seeks to maximize the overall financial, economic, environmental, and social return on its investments.

THE IFC'S MANAGEMENT SYSTEM FOR ENVIRONMENTAL AND SOCIAL ISSUES IN INVESTMENTS

The IFC's management system has the following integral components:

- Policy and procedural framework
- Environmental and social analysis of projects
- Capacity and resources
- Quality Project Management
- Management/corrective action plans
- Investment agreement conditionalities
- Portfolio supervision
- Disclosure, consultation, and transparency
- Accountability mechanisms
- System feedback.

The IFC has a well-developed policy and procedural framework. Its environmental and social safeguard policies are closely harmonized with the Bank's safeguard policies, with minor adjustments to adapt them to the private sector context of its operations. The IFC applies the World Bank Group's *Pollution Prevention and Abatement Handbook 1998* (World Bank 1999b) to its investments, with high-level management clearance required for any variation (see box 3.7 in chapter 3). To provide guidance for sectors for which no guideline is available in the *Handbook*, the IFC has developed its own guidelines. A full list of the IFC's environmental guidelines is available online at <http://192.86.99.148/enviro/enviro/pollution/guidelines.htm>.

The Environmental and Social Review Procedure (ESRP), set forth in 1998, guides staff in the application of the policy and guideline framework to the environmental and social analysis and processing of all investments. The ESRP contains important developments in the IFC's approach to financial intermediary investments, local consultation and disclosure requirements, and the improved integration of social analysis into the environmental assessment process. The ESRP requirements are integrated into the IFC's business processes. Early environmental and social input into investment reviews is required, and clearance of the environmental and social terms of IFC investment and project documentation occurs with full participation of the environmental and social development specialists. The IFC's ESRP is available online at <http://www.ifc.org/enviro/EnvSoc/ESRP/esrp.htm>.

While environmental and social professionals are very much part of the project teams, a direct reporting line from the director of the Environment and Social Development Department (CES) to the executive vice president maintains independence from operational line management. The overall cohesion of environmental and social inputs is ensured through a single clearance function, with specialists of all disciplines integrated into teams that service investment sectors and regions. The IFC believes that environmental and social issues are equally important, that they are mutually supportive, and that they benefit from joint management oversight. IFC management has also supported CES through the provision of resources to build a significant environmental and social management capacity.

As the need for environmental and social review of IFC projects has increased, so has the number of specialists within the department. The number now working on project review for the Environment Division has grown to 39 full-time-equivalent positions. This has prompted the need to develop and implement a Quality Project Management (QPM) system to ensure that specialists (including those on mission or based in the field) have access to the appropriate management tools in order to make informed decisions and, in doing so, promote consistency in project processing. In 1998, the Environment and Social Review Unit commenced development of QPM, a program that provides all specialists with a reference manual and a work flow that prompts key actions during the project cycle. An internal audit program regularly reviews the performance of both the system and the individual project managers. QPM has been operational for direct investment projects since March 2000. Financial intermediary projects are being incorporated in 2001.

It is often the case that projects, particularly for refurbishment or expansion, require time and investment to bring them to an acceptable standard. Projects may have impacts (such as resettlement) that require monitoring and action over an extended period. Financial intermediary projects commonly require the development of management systems and the building of capacity within the client organization. These situations are dealt with through appropriate action plans—for example, for environmental management, resettlement, or corrective action.

Environmental and social investment agreement conditionalities commit the project sponsor to comply with IFC policies and guidelines and, where appropriate, to follow a specific action program. The IFC's own capacity-building initiatives for financial intermediaries are leveraged through strategic partnerships with international finance institutions (IFIs), business schools, and others to deliver training and assistance to clients.

The IFC monitors the environmental and social performance of projects as part of its portfolio supervision. This includes (a) review of adherence to

agreed environmental or corrective action plans and to other specific loan covenants and reporting requirements and (b) the development of environmental and social management capacity. A risk rating for direct investments based on a range of criteria is used to apportion supervision resources to the highest-priority areas; a similar risk rating is under development for financial intermediaries. Environmental and social risk analysis is routinely integrated into investment department portfolio reviews.

The IFC relies on its disclosure policy and public consultation standards to ensure that interested parties have an opportunity to be heard and to exert influence with respect to specific projects. The IFC recognizes the importance of maximum transparency. Furthermore, the IFC's status as a public institution requires that it establish a significant mechanism for accountability to its member countries and civil society, particularly with respect to its environmental and social performance.

Perhaps the most innovative aspect of the IFC's environmental and social accountability is the establishment of a compliance advisor/ombudsman (CAO), an office designed to provide a nonjudicial, practical, problem-solving approach to contentious aspects of projects. This office is independent of the managements of the IFC and the Multilateral Investment Guarantee Agency (MIGA) and reports directly to the president of the World Bank Group. The CAO has three roles: (a) responding to complaints by persons affected by projects and attempting to resolve the issues, using a flexible, problem-solving approach; (b) providing independent advice to the president and senior management of the IFC and MIGA; and (c) overseeing audits of the IFC's and MIGA's environmental and social performance, both on systemic issues and in relation to sensitive projects.

Feedback on the overall efficacy of the management system is synthesized from a number of sources, including Operations Evaluation Group analysis; CAO investigations and feedback; Lessons of Experience analysis; client surveys and interaction; and representations by civil society, including NGOs. A further policy and procedural review by the CAO office is anticipated in late fiscal 2002.

The IFC and environmental projects

In addition to seeking to mitigate and manage the impacts of its traditional projects, the IFC has established units within several investment departments to focus on environmental projects. These include the Utilities Group within the Infrastructure Department, which finances water, wastewater, and solid waste management projects, and the Renewable Energy and Energy Efficiency Team within the Power Department. In addition, the Privatization Policy and Transactions Groups in the Private Sector Advisory Services Department have developed extensive experience in the area of water and wastewater.

In 1996, the IFC created the Environmental Projects Unit (EPU) to act as a catalyst and incubator for projects with specific environmental benefits. In developing projects for the IFC's own account, the EPU operates as a cost center that provides technical analysis and financial structuring services in order to prepare projects for funding by the relevant investment departments. More recently, the EPU has begun to encourage the identification and implementation of ecoefficiency improvements in mainstream IFC projects. In supporting projects

with environmental benefits, the EPU draws on the IFC's own investment resources and, where appropriate, concessional funding from sources such as the Global Environment Facility (GEF) (see, for example, box 2.7 in chapter 2). The EPU also undertakes special initiatives such as identifying projects to reduce greenhouse gas emissions under the Kyoto Protocol. (For more information on the activities of the EPU, visit its Website at <http://www.ifc.org/epu>.)

Looking ahead: The transition to sustainability

The IFC's mission is to help reduce poverty and improve the quality of life by supporting the creation and expansion of a vibrant private sector. Private sector development has several dimensions—financial, economic, social, and environmental. Development is sustainable if progress in one dimension does not come at the expense of the others.

The IFC is launching a sustainability initiative that has the potential to significantly increase the development impact of its activities. Sustainability for IFC means incorporating a more opportunistic, added-value approach that goes beyond compliance, particularly in the environmental, social, and corporate governance aspects of its work. It means complementing the existing regulatory-based approach to environmental and social issues with one that is market based and incentives oriented. This evolution is directly enabled by what is now a solid foundation of environmental and social management systems.

As we move beyond compliance, the IFC will not compromise its minimum standards; rather, it recognizes that achieving an appropriate balance among the financial, economic, social, and environmental dimensions of sustainability will depend on the circumstances and locality of the particular investment. This is not a one-size-fits-all philosophy but an intention to operationalize sustainable development in a way that maximizes our overall development impact and role.

The sustainability initiative will manifest itself through the IFC's investments, its role as a leader in the financial sector, and its footprint in terms of the environmental and social impacts of its physical presence and activities. The IFC is currently assessing its approach and what would constitute an indication of success in each of these three areas of activity.

Sustainability, in its financial and economic dimensions, has always been at the core of the IFC's approach. The IFC is a long-term, not a short-term, financial investor, and it avoids investments in which financial returns are predicated on unsustainable economic distortions. It also continually looks for opportunities to help clients and member countries create additional financial and economic value. The same approach is being extended to environmental, social, and corporate governance issues. The IFC has developed world-class expertise in these areas and is now ready to move beyond its "do no harm" approach to environmental and social issues toward one that more explicitly looks for opportunities to add value and materially enhance the positive development impact of a project or undertaking.

A primary focus will be on how actions that create environmental or social value or improve corporate governance can also create financial value for our clients. This financial value can take the form of tangible cost reductions, through ecoefficiency or cleaner technology; improved revenues, through better access to global supply chains, development of local supply chains, or the "branding" of products; reduced risks, through, for example, strengthened and positive interactions with the local community; or better access to financing. Many private firms in industrial countries recognize this convergence of environmental and social value and financial value, and a few in developing countries are beginning to do so, as well. As regulations and consumer behavior continue to change, these opportunities will proliferate.

The challenges of the transition to sustainable private sector development are large, but many companies are recognizing that meeting the challenges adds value in many areas of their business through customer and staff loyalty, product differentiation, resource efficiency, risk reduction, and innovation.

The IFC has a role in helping to transfer emerging private sector sustainable practices to the developing country context in which it operates. It is not an easy task, but it is a role that the IFC has performed in many other areas in the past. We believe that sustainable business practices converge with good management and that, as a result, sustainable businesses will be the long-term winners. As investors, maximizing long-term shareholder value is one of our goals. It simply makes commercial sense: any business that puts its supply chain at risk or ignores reputational issues is not acting in the interests of its shareholders, let alone other stakeholders.

This is an area in which the IFC is already emerging as a leader among the private sector investment institutions operating in the developing world, and our advice is increasingly sought by other IFIs, commercial banks, and businesses. IFC guidance documents on the value of public consultation and community development are landmark publications that are widely referred to by practitioners and businesses. They are available online at <http://www.ifc.org/enviro/Publications/index.html>.

The building blocks of this transition are currently being put in place through internal discussions, and substantive consultations with all stakeholders are anticipated in the months ahead. We believe that the journey toward sustainability will bring many benefits to our clients. Furthermore, we believe that it will also benefit the IFC. It will differentiate the IFC from other financial institutions in our ability to add value; it will motivate our staff; it will allow us to operate in high-risk areas with renewed confidence in our role and ability to achieve sustainable outcomes; and, most important, it will contribute to our mission of reducing poverty and improving people's lives.

Multilateral Investment Guarantee Agency

Established as a member of the World Bank Group in 1988, the Multilateral Investment Guarantee Agency (MIGA) provides (a) an investment insurance (guarantee) program that offers political risk coverage to foreign investors from any of its member countries, and (b) a technical assistance program that helps developing member countries attract foreign direct investment. MIGA does not make investments, extend grants, or lend money to investors, nor does it propose or design projects. As with any other form of insurance, investors and lenders who want this coverage pay premiums.

MIGA's founders required the institution to make sure that the foreign investments insured by it contribute to the development of the host country. If investments are to provide development opportunities for local communities, the projects must be environmentally and socially sound. Therefore, in carrying out its mission, it is MIGA's policy that all the foreign investments it insures must be carried out in an environmentally and socially responsible manner.

ENVIRONMENTAL POLICY

Since MIGA issued its first insurance contract in 1990, it has been applying World Bank environmental policies and guidelines to MIGA projects, often with the environmental counsel and advice of the International Finance Corporation (IFC). In fiscal 1998, MIGA began drafting its own specific environmental assessment and disclosure policies, which reflect its business as an insurer of foreign investments. These draft policies, and the procedures for implementing them, were the subject of extensive discussions by MIGA's Board and management. The Board approved MIGA's environmental assessment and disclosure policies and procedures in May 1999, and they took effect with all new applications received in fiscal 2000. The policies and procedures are available on MIGA's Website, <http://www.miga.org>.

MIGA's Environmental Assessment Policy is the basic framework for MIGA's evaluation of the environmental and social soundness of a proposed project. The policy requires the project sponsors to carry out an environmental assessment (EA) of the project. As explained in the policy, the level of detail of this assessment varies with every project and depends largely on the nature, magnitude, and significance of the project's impacts on the environment and on local communities.

MIGA then uses this assessment as the basis for its review and evaluation. In carrying out the review and evaluation, MIGA considers the following features of the project:

- Ability to comply with the appropriate guidelines found in the World Bank Group's *Pollution Prevention and Abatement Handbook 1998* (World Bank 1999)
- Compliance with host-country environmental requirements
- Consistency with MIGA's safeguard policies regarding natural habitats, forestry, pest management, dam safety, projects on international waterways, resettlement, indigenous and vulnerable peoples, and cultural resources and property.

Application of the safeguard policies focuses on impact avoidance, minimization, and mitigation and links impacts and benefits/compensation to the findings of the EA. Thus, MIGA has been applying an integrated approach to the safeguard policies, positioning the EA process (and the EA policy) as a key integrator. In this approach, the safeguard policies become the norms for evaluating whether the proposed mitigation/compensation measures identified in the project's Environmental Impact Assessment (EIA) are reasonable and acceptable.

In its application of the safeguard policies, MIGA must ensure their applicability to private sector projects. In particular, application of the policies

must recognize that (a) compensation, benefits, and mitigation measures must be project oriented; (b) acceptable measures of compliance must in some form be clearly linked and identifiable through contract provisions, such as implementation of the project's proposed Environmental Action Plan, as appropriate to policy-related issues; (c) approximately 70 percent of MIGA's guarantee holders do not have a majority or controlling interest in a project and are thus often constrained in their ability to change project design or implementation; and (d) the private sector has a partnership role with government and local communities in local development. Moreover, application of safeguards must clearly consider MIGA's narrowly defined role as an insurer with no ability to finance project improvements and must recognize that MIGA's involvement in the project's development process typically takes place after approval of the EIA by the host country.

MIGA achieves harmonization in its application of the safeguard policies through several mechanisms:

- Environmental review, clearance, and monitoring functions are centralized in MIGA's Evaluation Department, which is independent of the Guarantees Department.
- MIGA's Environment Unit maintains frequent contact with IFC's Environment Department at the staff level in order to share learning experiences and discuss emerging policy-related issues.
- The application of the policies is integrated through the EA process, which provides an appropriate framework for assessing the "do-no-harm" spirit and intent of the policies and for evaluating the development benefit achieved through the proposed project-specific impact mitigation programs.

- In underwriting projects, MIGA fully considers overall World Bank Group strategy, as proposed not only in the Country Assistance Strategy but also in appropriate sector strategies (energy, forestry, environment, and so on). Consistency of the proposed investment guarantee with these strategies is then discussed at the Board level.

- The Board itself has a critical role in concurring with a decision to offer a guarantee, thereby serving as a final authoritative check on the consistency of MIGA's proposed action with World Bank Group strategies.

If the project is expected to have significant adverse environmental or social impacts that are particularly sensitive, MIGA requires the sponsors to carry out meaningful and timely consultations with directly affected local communities to discuss project-related environmental and social issues. Such consultations are particularly critical if the project requires resettlement or land acquisition involving vulnerable people. These consultations are not only key components of "process," as required by the safeguard policies, but also provide outcomes that may be used as measures of success in the implementation of the project and of compliance with the safeguard policies.

Once a project has been reviewed and evaluated by MIGA for its development effects, including environmental and social soundness, MIGA prepares a report for Board discussion prior to providing political risk insurance. Much of this report focuses on the expected development effects of the proposed investment in the host country and the manner in which environmental and social issues have been addressed.

From an environmental and social perspective, the value of MIGA involvement in a project includes the following:

- MIGA's involvement provides a high degree of confidence that the project's design and implementation will be in accordance with relevant World Bank Group environmental guidelines and application of the safeguard policies to project-specific private sector investments.

- This involvement is particularly critical where governmental agencies, rules, or regulatory frameworks are lacking or ineffective.

- MIGA's requirement for warranties and representations of compliance, its ability to monitor performance, and its ability to cancel a contract unilaterally or to deny a claim in the event of noncompliance add value to project implementation.

EVALUATION

MIGA's evaluation program regularly selects projects from the agency's portfolio and compares the development effects that were initially expected with what actually happened. In the process of evaluating development effects, environmental and social concerns play a major role. Ex post facto evaluation of environmental performance is rated, along with the other dimensions of development, using MIGA's environmental guidelines and safeguard policies as a benchmark for performance. This program, along with monitoring reports, site visits, and independent audits, is a valuable tool for tracking MIGA's contribution to development.

STRATEGIC DIRECTIONS

MIGA's role in facilitating appropriate foreign direct investment through its guarantee program and technical advisory services complements the development roles of the IFC and the IBRD. In addition to ensuring that the investments it insures provide development benefits to the host country and local communities, MIGA seeks to support investments that provide significant environmental and social benefits.

Environmentally and socially sustainable development is not possible without individual opportunities for income and a sustainable livelihood. Ultimately, the key weapon in the battle against poverty is employment. In every country in every region in which MIGA has facilitated investment, the overwhelming message that emerges from local communities during public consultations is the keen desire for employment. Even in societies that value traditional lifestyles, it is generally recognized that some forms of employment and income are needed to maintain families and traditions intact. MIGA's contribution is to facilitate environmentally and socially sound foreign investment that provides employment or the critical infrastructure needed to encourage employment opportunities.

Annex I

The Environment Strategy and the World Bank-GEF Program

I n the years since the UN Conference on Environment and Development in 1992, the Global Environment Facility (GEF) has emerged as a facilitator and a funding mechanism for integrating global concerns into the development process. After a three-year pilot phase, the GEF was restructured in 1994 to provide for universal membership with greater transparency and participation in its affairs and to serve as the financing mechanism for the global conventions on biodiversity and climate change. It also supports the objectives of the Convention to Combat Desertification, to the extent that they are impacted by actions under the other two conventions. In addition, the GEF has been designated to become the financing mechanism for the newly established Convention on Persistent Organic Pollutants. Together, the United Nations Development Programme (UNDP), the United Nations Environment Programme (UNEP), and the World Bank are serving as implementing agency for the GEF. (See World Bank 2000g for a detailed review of the World Bank's global environmental work program, including that for the GEF.)

GEF assistance currently covers four focal areas: biodiversity, climate change, international waters, and the ozone layer. The Bank's GEF program is dominated by projects focused on biodiversity and climate change, which together account for more than 75 percent of World Bank-GEF grants. Over the past decade, the World Bank, as an implementing agency for the GEF, has committed close to $1.3 billion in grant funding to over 80 of its client countries for targeted global environmental objectives in 192 projects. These funds have catalyzed another $6.0 billion in cofunding, including $1.5 billion in funds from the World Bank Group (WBG).

The demand for grant funding through the GEF is rising. The WBG's current pipeline of project concepts eligible for GEF consideration stands at an all-time high of close to 130 projects, excluding medium-size projects, for total estimated GEF funding of about $1.6 million. (Average annual GEF commitments for World Bank-GEF projects over the past five years amounted to $230 million.) Under these circumstances, it would be prudent for the World Bank to assume that demand from its client countries for GEF project funding will continue to exceed the GEF resources available. The implication is that the further development of the World Bank's GEF program should use available GEF funding more strategically, matching the GEF's corporate priorities with opportunities for mainstreaming the global environmental agenda and the GEF in the country assistance dialogue.

THE ROLE OF THE WORLD BANK-GEF PROGRAM IN THE ENVIRONMENT STRATEGY

Against this background, how can the World Bank-GEF program effectively support the objectives of the Environment Strategy? What opportunities are there to further strengthen the program's contribution to these objectives? And how can these opportunities be pursued through the design and implementation of the Environment Strategy itself?

The Bank's Environment Strategy emphasizes the linkages between environmental conditions and human welfare, in particular, the health, livelihoods, and vulnerability of the poor. It acknowledges that while environmental conditions that affect human welfare ultimately manifest themselves locally, their origins extend to the regional and global levels. Degradation of transboundary ecosystems, whether terrestrial or aquatic, has important local economic and social impacts. Available projections show that local costs to the Bank's client countries of continued deterioration of the global commons are likely to be substantial.[1] Hence, the preservation of the regional and global commons has to be an explicit objective of a strategy for promoting sustainable development and poverty reduction over the medium to long term.

The World Bank-GEF Program can play an important role in implementing the objectives of the Environment Strategy in four main ways:

- It can provide a powerful extension of other World Bank instruments to help address the quality of the regional and global commons.
- It can generate local environmental benefits in the pursuit of global environmental benefits and through mobilization of associated funding.
- It can offer modalities not readily available under conventional World Bank lending for engaging nongovernmental organization (NGOs) and other parts of civil society in the country dialogue on environmental management.
- It can support the piloting of innovative methods of sustainable natural resource management with local-global environmental links.

Extending the Bank's ability to support global and regional issues

The Bank's lending and nonlending assistance for national sustainable development can generate important and complementary regional and global environmental benefits. For example, support for energy pricing reforms will reduce greenhouse gas emissions through more efficient energy use and incentives for renewable energy development. Forestry sector development based on policy and institutional reform will contribute to the conservation and sustainable use of biodiversity in important ways.

Going beyond such complementary opportunities, however, will require compensation from the global community, which will in effect raise the rate of return on country investments. International resource transfers have to perform that function as long as the markets for trading global environmental services are "missing." The GEF was established to do just that—to underwrite and catalyze resource transfers to meet the costs of actions having global environmental objectives that would not be pursued in the absence of that "global premium." As a GEF implementing agency, the World Bank remains committed to effectuating such transfers whenever they are consistent with the country assistance dialogue.

At the regional level, riparian countries linked to transboundary terrestrial or aquatic ecosystems are unable to capture the full value of the environmental services that they can potentially create. This constrains action to address environmental degradation of such threatened ecosystems, on which important segments of the world's poor depend for their health and livelihoods. With access to GEF resources, the World Bank is able to help riparian countries and stakeholders agree on and act on regional environmental priorities. For example, the Bank works with the GEF and other partners to support the development and implementation of regional conventions or agreements for the management of international river basins, shared lakes, regional seas, and shared groundwater aquifers.

Leveraging actions for improved local environmental conditions

GEF-funded activities, while justified with respect to expected global environmental benefits, also generate important benefits for the local environment and economy. For example, domestic and global environmental benefits frequently converge in the conservation and sustainable use of biodiversity and their ecosystems. Thus, in India, a blend of GEF and International Development Association (IDA) resources is facilitating a change in the management of protected areas, encouraging foresters to work with local communities and seek solutions that address both conservation and community needs.

In such cases, GEF project funding can be an important way of helping to directly support health and local livelihood benefits and reduce losses of ecosystem services. Such local benefits are frequently magnified by the GEF's ability to leverage client country and donor investment decisions.

The energy sector provides another example of global- local linkages. Access to $100 million of GEF resources to help accelerate energy conservation and renewable energy development was an important consideration in China's decision to borrow regular Bank resources for these purposes. The World Bank-GEF Fuel Efficient Boilers Project is transferring clean-coal boiler technologies to China, which will improve air quality and people's health in all the major industrial areas while reducing carbon emissions (see box 3.4 in chapter 3). The World Bank-GEF Second Beijing Environment Project, which is designed to convert at least 2,500 of the city's coal-fired boilers to clean natural gas, is expected to reduce carbon emissions by 2.5 million tons per year, sulfur emissions by 800,000 tons per year, and particulate emissions by 550,000 tons per year over 20 years.

Facilitating the engagement of NGOs and civil society

One of the most important developments of the past two decades has been the emergence of a strong NGO movement. NGOs today represent a powerful force providing technical assistance and policy advice to governments and societies all over the world. The Bank has strengthened its capacity to engage NGOs effectively, but until recently it has lacked meaningful tools to support them directly.

The GEF's program for medium-size projects has provided a way forward.[2] There are now 45 such projects in 29 countries under implementation, involving $34 million in GEF funding, and another 50 project proposals at various stages of preparation. Most of these projects effectively involve NGOs in project preparation or implementation and often support highly innovative approaches to the sustainable use of biodiversity. Examples include establishment of a new communal reserve to be managed by indigenous people in Vilcabamba, Peru; sustainable biodiversity management in the agricultural landscape and mountain meadows of the Slovak Republic; and incentives to farmers in El Salvador to maintain traditional systems of biodiversity-friendly coffee production under forest cover.

Promoting innovative solutions to financial sustainability of ecosystem management

The GEF operational strategy puts a premium on finding new and innovative ways of supporting management practices for natural resources that are environmentally friendly and globally replicable. In this context, the Bank has started to demonstrate the effective use of GEF resources to promote the financial sustainability of globally (and locally) sustainable natural resource management practices (see box I.1).

TOWARD MORE STRATEGIC USE OF WORLD BANK-GEF RESOURCES

The quality of life is closely linked to the quality of growth and the quality of the regional and global commons. Poverty alleviation will not be sustainable in the long run if global ecosystems continue to deteriorate. From this perspective, all GEF projects can be said to contribute to environmentally sustainable development and poverty reduction. GEF-eligible interventions can also help more directly—for example, by reducing greenhouse gas

---

BOX I.1
World Bank-GEF projects demonstrate innovative approaches to financing sustainable natural resource management with global and local benefits

Recovering the value of ecosystem services. The Costa Rica Ecomarkets project exemplifies how national and global environmental benefits can be effectively channeled to local communities. Small landowners receive payment for the environmental services provided in their lands when forest cover is maintained. The services include water quality (to be recovered from water utilities), scenic beauty (to be recovered from the tourism sector), carbon sequestration (to be recovered from carbon certificates), and biodiversity conservation (paid by the GEF on an incremental cost basis).

Trust funds for financing sustainability. One of the greatest challenges for conservation is how to cover the recurrent costs of parks and protected areas. Access to GEF resources has enabled the World Bank to help several country partners establish national trust funds. Trust funds in Bolivia, Mexico, and Peru and in Eastern Europe (for the Transcarpathian Mountains) are helping to support protected area networks. In Uganda, the Bwindi Trust Fund provides resources for national park management to strengthen protection of gorilla populations. About 60 percent of the income is used to provide sustainable livelihoods for local people as an alternative to agricultural encroachment into the park.

---

emissions in ways that improve local air quality while meeting energy demands. Clearly, some GEF funding opportunities, because of their design and choice of technologies, have greater potential for such synergy. Focusing on these opportunities will help to maximize the impact of the World Bank-GEF program. Such targeting is particularly important when demand from client countries for access to GEF resources exceeds available funds.

Strategic priorities for the World Bank-GEF program

Biodiversity. GEF grants aimed at the conservation and sustainable use of biodiversity have already started to evolve from their earlier emphasis on free-standing protected area management projects. The direction is toward landscape-focused interventions with strong links to rural livelihood (see, for example, box A.5 in annex A). Moving further in this direction would involve setting priorities that would:

- Generate multiple benefits (social, ecological, and economic) and have strong and explicit health, livelihood, or vulnerability linkages
- Build in protection and sustainable use of ecosystem services in mainstreaming development—for example by conserving wetlands for flood control or incorporating an ecosystem view into rural infrastructure development
- Involve protected area management within a broader landscape context supporting mainstream rural goals related to poverty reduction, watershed management, and dryland and forest management.

Climate change. The close links between reductions in greenhouse gas emissions and improvements in local air quality are at the center of the Bank's Climate Change Strategy (see annex F), which emphasizes the need for synergy with national economic and environmental concerns in all World Bank-GEF climate change interventions. The implementation of the Environment Strategy should therefore prioritize GEF assistance in the following areas.

- *Renewable energy* is often the least-cost option for providing electricity and other energy forms in rural areas. Improving energy access for household lighting, water pumping, grain processing, small cottage industry, rural health centers, and schools yields direct economic and social benefits to rural residents. It also results in improved indoor air quality when it replaces traditional biomass fuels.
- Management reforms, energy efficiency improvements, and fuel switching for municipal heating systems (in northern climates) can benefit the urban poor economically and reduce urban and indoor air pollution while improving thermal efficiency and reducing greenhouse gas emissions.
- In developing countries, the transport sector is responsible for a significant and generally growing share of energy consumption and urban air pollution. Measures to reduce energy intensity in this sector—such as land-use planning, traffic management, promotion of nonmotorized transport, and more efficient technologies—can have human health and livelihood benefits, especially to the poor, in addition to reducing greenhouse gas emissions.
- Forest regeneration through community participation can offer substantial economic benefits to millions of poor households, while increasing forest cover, sequestering carbon, and reducing pressures on natural forests.

Transboundary water resource management. Past World Bank-GEF projects have generally been relatively weakly linked to World Bank assistance for rural development and watershed management in river or inland-sea basins. The importance of such links needs to be recognized in project preparation and design. In some cases, GEF assistance for regional management of water utilization may be directly linked to national sustainable development goals, as in the case of the Mekong River and Aral Sea projects. In other cases, GEF assistance for management of forests and agricultural lands or for the control of point-source pollution is a means of managing the quality of shared water resources, which has direct links to rural livelihood and health in riparian communities.

Desertification and land degradation. By supporting enhanced carbon management or conservation and sustainable use of biodiversity, World Bank-GEF funding can contribute positively to more sustainable land management, including control of land degradation and desertification. Local environmental and developmental benefits from such interventions are expected to include improved health, nutrition, and food security.

The mainstreaming challenge

Global environmental issues and the role of the GEF can never be of equal importance to all countries. Clearly, however, there are circumstances in which global environmental issues and GEF assistance would be expected to play an important role. In these countries, the successful pursuit of the above strategic priorities depends on further progress in mainstreaming the global environment and the GEF in the country assistance dialogue. At the level of country operations, such mainstreaming would be demonstrated by an acknowledgment of the Bank's role in assisting the country in implementing its obligations under the global environmental conventions and in using GEF grant resources for such purposes in the country dialogue. Where this occurs, we would also expect to find GEF funding opportunities more closely linked to and blended with upstream IDA/IBRD project identification.

Recently completed Country Assistance Strategies (CASs) do not suggest that such expectations are being met. Further progress will depend on the development of in-house capacity and incentives

to pursue a client dialogue that integrates global environmental concerns within national sustainable development programs. Most important, little progress will be made unless there is a readiness and capacity on the client side to address global environmental concerns and their links to national development objectives and priorities.

Capacity building

Capacity among Bank staff and management to understand the two-way linkage between global environmental concerns and national sustainable development and poverty reduction needs to be strengthened. This entails increasing the understanding of the technical issues involved (climate change, loss of biodiversity and ecosystems, and transboundary water resource issues), their effect on the options for national sustainable development, and the role of the GEF in helping to address them.

To achieve this, action is required on three fronts.

- An enhanced environment knowledge management system will help to broaden and deepen awareness among staff and management of global environmental concerns and their links to local economic and environmental issues.
- Efforts must be stepped up to develop and disseminate the necessary analytical tools to measure the value of environmental services and to analyze the effectiveness of options to mitigate environmental degradation, including those related to carbon mitigation and sequestration.
- The application of these tools in relevant sector work and environmental assessments must be promoted. This means addressing conservation and sustainable use of biodiversity in forestry and water sector work and examining options for reduction of carbon dioxide emissions in local

pollution studies or energy-environment reviews. These actions need to form part of the Bank's overall environmental training program.

Such strengthened in-house capacity needs to be employed to build local capacity among our client country institutions. This calls for technical training, strengthening of administrative and managerial functions in key agencies, and support for networking of professionals within and between countries. The objective should be to help senior officials, planners, and technicians, such as those in agricultural or forestry ministries or agencies, recognize the importance of conservation and of sustainable use of biodiversity and carbon sequestration to sustainable production, and to enable energy sector planners and engineers to see the opportunities to use climate-friendly technology to reach their goal of local pollution management.

A supportive incentive framework

Building effective capacity to address the global environment and GEF in the country assistance dialogue requires a supportive framework of accountability and incentives, as outlined in the main text of this report. Within this framework, the following actions would help to specifically address the challenge of mainstreaming the global environment and GEF:

- World Bank units and staff responsible for the development of sectoral strategies for forestry, water, energy, and rural development should be held accountable for addressing links between relevant global environmental concerns, the objectives of the strategies, and the role of international financing mechanisms. Relevant bodies are the GEF, the Montreal Protocol (MP), and the Prototype Carbon Fund (PCF).

- Senior management should urge regional management to adopt strategic objectives for their GEF programs, including use of internal eligibility criteria for the allocation of GEF funds. Regional GEF strategies should form part of the regional environment strategies and their annual business plans. The latter would set out annual GEF program targets; accountability would rest with country directors. Such targets would in turn be reflected in the region's internal work program agreements (WPAs) and results agreements.

- Results agreements and performance evaluations need to be used systematically as important tools for managers to manage and reward staff for implementing global environmental and GEF targets in regional environment strategies and their associated annual business plans.

- Managing directors, in their regular meetings with regional management, should systematically follow up on progress in the implementation of annual business plans for regional environmental strategies, including the GEF program. The Environment Sector Board should annually assess outcomes of the annual business plans, including their global environmental and GEF components, and provide comments to Regions on proposed plans.

- The Bank should move toward a competitive internal process for allocation of available GEF resources for project funding—between regions as well as within regions—that promotes a GEF portfolio which meets strategic priorities.

- Highly publicized awards for environmental excellence should include special awards for best performance in mainstreaming global environmental issues in country dialogue (at the country director level) and in mainstreaming GEF in IDA/IBRD projects (at the task manager level).

■ The Bank should continue the process of streamlining and mainstreaming GEF into Bank processing and portfolio management; reduce transaction costs by building on current initiatives to promote a more programmatic allocation of GEF resources over longer time periods; ensure that the World Bank's new accounting, budgeting, and operations monitoring systems fully cover all World Bank-GEF products and needs; and work with the GEF Council to determine how the external review and approval cycle can be further simplified and streamlined.

NOTES

1. According to the *Third Assessment Report of the Intergovernmental Panel on Climate Change* (IPCC 2001), adverse climate-change impacts would amount to losses of at least a few percent of global gross domestic product (GDP); the effects of climate change, in terms of loss of life and relative effects on investment and the economy, are expected to be greatest in developing countries.

2. The GEF medium-size grant program (for amounts up to $1 million) offers a streamlined and fast-tracked way of engaging all elements of civil society in the management of local environment resources linked to generation of global benefits.

Consultation Process and Feedback

In early May 2000, the World Bank initiated a broad-based consultation on the emerging Environment Strategy, based on the progress report and discussion draft, *Toward an Environment Strategy for the World Bank Group,* and on the six draft regional environment strategies. (Summaries of the regional strategies can be found in annex A; the full documents are available on the Internet at <www.worldbank.org/environment/strategy>.)

BACKGROUND

The discussion draft *Toward an Environment Strategy for the World Bank Group* outlined key development and environment challenges facing the Bank's client countries. It summarized some of the lessons learned by the Bank and its clients in the past and laid out a framework and key principles for Bank assistance in addressing environmental issues. The report underlined the need to link the environmental agenda more closely with development goals, particularly poverty reduction. It identified three key development objectives: improving environmental factors that adversely affect people's health; enhancing people's livelihoods through sustainable natural resource management; and reducing people's vulnerability to environmental risks and natural disasters. The report also identified three areas of focus for Bank assistance: integrating environmental considerations into strategies and actions for poverty reduction; helping to establish conditions for sustainable private sector-led growth; and addressing regional and global environmental challenges.

The World Bank initiated the consultation process to hone the conceptual framework and regional strategies and to improve our mutual understanding of the developmental and environmental challenges underlying the proposed framework. We also sought to identify new ways of working with our development and environment partners to reverse poverty and environmental degradation.

THE CONSULTATION PROCESS

The consultation consisted of workshops with client and donor countries, including representatives of government, civil society, the private sector, and academia; a dialogue with several of our multilateral and bilateral partners; meetings with international nongovernmental organizations (NGOs); and a broad-based information dissemination and feedback process through e-mail and the Internet.

Between May 2000 and June 2001, over 30 formal and informal meetings or working sessions took place in Sub-Saharan Africa, Latin America and the Caribbean (LAC), the Middle East and North Africa (MNA), South Asia, East Asia and the Pacific (EAP), Europe, Japan, and North America (see map in figure J.1). Table J.1 at the end of this annex summarizes the schedule for the formal consultation meetings. The Bank is grateful to the government of Norway for its financial support to the African, Latin American, and South Asian consultations; to the governments of Japan, Sweden, and Switzerland for their support of regional meetings in East Asia and in Central, Eastern, and Western Europe; and to the governments of Canada, Germany, and the United Kingdom for their support of multistakeholder and donor meetings within their countries. Detailed reports of the consultation meetings and outcomes, mostly prepared by independent facilitators or record-keepers, are available on the Environment Strategy Consultation Website, <http://www.worldbank.org/environment/strategy>.

A dedicated Environment Strategy Consultation link on the World Bank Website contained the discussion draft, background papers, schedules, updates, links to open discussion spaces, e-mail contacts, and a questionnaire. Visitors to the site could download strategy documents, access various relevant links, subscribe to an electronic newsletter, send comments directly to the Environment Strategy team, and respond to the Environment Strategy Questionnaire. Box J.1 summarizes the volume and nature of the site traffic and the countries from which queries and comments were received. Box

Figure J.1 Strategy consultations map

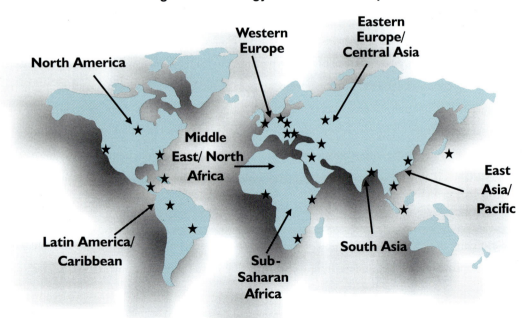

J.2 describes the feedback received through the questionnaire.

The value of the consultations was inestimable. They provided a forum for face-to-face discussions, promoted greater dissemination of information about the issues, and have led to a better understanding among the participants of our mutual concerns. Feedback was animated, thoughtful, and always challenging. Overall, there was a consensus that the environmental issues we are confronting worldwide are urgent and that this urgency should more visibly inform the work of the Bank and the Strategy.

FEEDBACK

In general, there was broad support among those who gave us feedback for the conceptual framework outlined in the discussion draft, although there

---

BOX J.1
Environment Strategy consultation through the Internet

Between August 2000 and the end of January 2001, the Environment Strategy Consultation Website received nearly 35,000 download requests for various papers. Almost 15,000 people downloaded the Strategy progress report/consultation draft, and more than 2,000 people from 98 countries registered by e-mail to receive future updates on the Strategy. In addition to the Bank's Environment Strategy Consultation Website, the LAC and the Europe and Central Asia (ECA) Regions organized separate but linked online discussions that were regionally focused. By November 2000, the LAC Website had logged more than 2,000 visitors, had tapped a network of over 100 NGOs, and had received online comments from 18 countries. The Environment website will continue to be a venue for future discussions on strategic directions for the Bank's environmental efforts.

---

were some differences among participants. Conversations in industrial countries tended to focus on wide-ranging concepts and global issues, whereas discussions in client countries tended to emphasize local environmental concerns and concrete implementation issues. In some meetings, particularly in donor countries, a number of participants regarded growth itself as antithetical to environmental sustainability. In others, particularly in client countries, the general view was that environmental activities must be integrated with growth planning. Overall, the discussions could be grouped into three general areas of focus: the development context; the role and past performance of the Bank; and specific implementation issues concerning the Bank's operations and environmental assistance.

Development context

Most participants agreed that environmental objectives need to be systematically linked with development goals, particularly poverty reduction. The discussion draft referred to a broad definition of poverty that encompassed dimensions of opportunity, security, and empowerment, as defined in *World Development Report 2000/01*. The draft recognized that the sustainable use of natural resources is fundamental to long-term reduction of poverty. There was a common view among participants, however, that poverty reduction strategies, a key instrument for addressing poverty, have had a focus that is too narrow and short-term and have failed to adequately identify the environmental linkages. Many participants in both client and donor meetings emphasized that the concept of sustainable development should be the organizing principle. A number of participants in industrial countries were concerned that the discussion draft subsumed environmental issues into poverty alleviation, and participants in workshops in Africa and in Central and Eastern

BOX J.2
Results of an Environment Strategy questionnaire

As part of the consultation process, more than 230 representatives of governments, NGOs, academia, and other members of civil society, with a wide range of geographic, institutional, and professional backgrounds, were surveyed through a multiple-choice questionnaire to collect standardized feedback on the key aspects of the proposed strategic framework and regional strategies. The questionnaire was available online on the Environment Strategy Consultation Website and was distributed at consultation meetings and workshops. Because the respondent group was not a representative sample, the results are for illustrative purposes only.

The responses indicated broad support for the proposed strategy. Across all regions, about 85 percent of the respondents agreed with or strongly agreed with the concept of linking environmental issues with poverty reduction, and the two largest groups of respondents—NGOs and the government—did not differ significantly on this issue. Support was similarly strong—about 85 percent—for the proposed development objectives: improving health, securing livelihoods, and protecting people from vulnerability to natural disasters. The strongest dissent, up to 15 percent, came from respondents in ECA, while the strongest support—100 percent—came from East Africa.

Regional affiliation of respondents

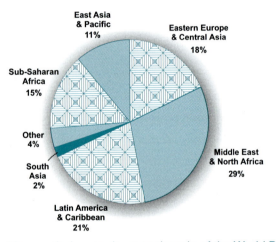

Organizational affiliation of respondents

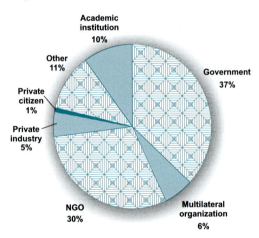

More varied were views on the role of the World Bank in developing markets for global environmental goods, such as carbon credits or payments for ecosystem services. Overall, about 72 percent of the respondents thought that the Bank should have a role in this area, while about 10 percent disagreed. There were strong regional differences, however. In EAP and MNA, close to 40 percent of respondents were indifferent to or opposed to this role, and in southern Africa, 25 percent were against the Bank's assuming a role in developing markets for global environmental goods.

The proposed regional priorities identified in the strategy were supported by about 74 percent of the respondents. The highest agreement was in EAP (83 percent); the lowest was in southern Africa (64 percent). Regarding the Bank's effectiveness in the regions, the highest marks were given to assistance in water resource management, while the Bank's role in forestry and land-use management received low marks. Views on the effectiveness of different instruments varied across regions. For example, in MNA lending was considered more effective than nonlending services, while in southern Africa and LAC analytical work, information sharing, and technical assistance scored the highest. Overall, only 38 percent of the respondents said that the environmental performance of Bank projects was satisfactory; 23 percent said that it was unsatisfactory.

Europe felt strongly that the environmental objectives should be discussed in the context of quality of growth, rather than poverty alleviation alone. Although poverty was acknowledged as a pervasive problem, environmentally sustainable development was viewed as the key to resolving both environmental and poverty concerns.

Some participants, particularly from donor countries, questioned the basic framework of the Strategy. They challenged the World Bank's emphasis on long-standing growth-based models of development, arguing that new models founded on ecological principles were needed. The World Bank's stress on markets and its perceived reliance on the ability of the private sector to address environmental challenges were criticized. In addition, many felt the Strategy should more clearly address the links between environmental quality, security, and conflict, as well as the relationship between better environmental management and the role of civil society, equity, empowerment, and good governance. In many of the meetings, there was consensus that how people view and utilize their environment is driven by much more than purely economic factors and that environmental issues cannot be separated from social considerations. Finally, participants advocated that the gravity of current environmental conditions be more clearly stated in the Strategy and that the links between local and global environmental issues be emphasized.

Role of the Bank

Consultation participants requested that the Bank acknowledge and strengthen its leading position as a global role model, facilitator, and catalyst. Many emphasized that the World Bank had a responsibility to set high international benchmarks for good environmental practice. Some urged the Bank to lobby industrial countries to improve their envi-

ronmental responsibility and make larger financial commitments to aid developing nations in their efforts to both develop and foster sound environmental management.

There were clear regional differences on the role participants felt the Bank was best positioned to play. For example, Central European countries wanted the Bank to play more of a knowledge bank role; participants in Russia and the Western newly independent states (NIS) emphasized the advisory role of the Bank on policy; and participants in Central Asia stressed the Bank's financial role.

A number of those who provided feedback wanted the World Bank's Environment Strategy to address in depth a very broad range of development issues in which, they argued, the Bank played a critical role, such as trade, globalization, population, biosafety, governance, climate change, food security, and private sector accountability. Many of these issues have important linkages to environmental trends and management. Some of these issues, such as climate change and government capacity, have been incorporated into the Strategy. Others, such as food security and private sector accountability, are being addressed, or will be addressed, through other documents, sectoral strategies, or programs within the Bank. In particular, in 2002, the *World Development Report* will comprehensively explore the broad interlinkages of sustainable development.

Implementation issues

There was a general call in the consultations for the World Bank to make changes within its own operations in several critical areas:

- Mandate a longer time-frame for policy analysis, planning, and assistance programs in order to better internalize the long-term impacts of development decisions on the social and physical environment

- Support Strategic Environmental Assessments and other in-depth, cross-sectoral environmental analyses early in country-policy dialogues
- Support increased transparency and accountability on the part of both borrowers and the World Bank by instituting regular reporting to external stakeholders, using clear benchmarks or performance indicators.

Much of the feedback on implementation focused on the need for the Bank to engage in more participatory and community-based approaches to development and to pay more attention to in-country capacity building at all administrative levels. Many asked that the Bank find mechanisms to implement agreements with local governments and nongovernmental agencies and to support more bottom-up initiatives.

RESPONSE TO THE CONSULTATIONS

The consultations have helped shape the Strategy's presentation of the key issues and its action plan. Some of the issues that were raised within the consultations, although gratefully acknowledged, were not integrated into the Strategy. In some cases, they were too broad or went beyond the reach of the Strategy at this time, although they are recognized as indeed critical. Other issues are or will be incorporated into the World Bank's work program, but the foundations within the Bank are not yet firm enough for the Strategy to present an explicit action plan for them. The Environment team in the Bank felt it was essential that the Strategy's discussion and action plan be focused on a few specific priorities and recommendations, to heighten the likelihood of short- and medium-term success in implementation. Implementation of the Strategy will be systematically monitored, and feedback will be provided to revisit and update its emphasis on priorities.

In response to requests that the Strategy be framed more in the context of sustainable development, we have put greater emphasis on discussing environmental challenges within a sustainable development framework. Development goals and key areas of assistance are integrated under three major objectives: quality of life, quality of growth, and quality of the regional and global commons.

In the action plan, the Strategy reflects several of the main recommendations of the meetings:

- The Strategy emphasizes the need to undertake environmental analysis earlier in the policy dialogue and to facilitate cross-sectoral analysis. A commitment has been made to apply Strategic Environmental Assessments (SEAs) and country environment profiles to aid this process. These analytical tools will be applied more systematically to Bank core activities and will help integrate longer-term spatial, ecological, and social concerns.
- The Strategy emphasizes that strengthening environmental management and safeguard capacities is a chief priority of the World Bank. It makes a commitment to in-country training during the process of carrying-out Environmental Assessments and SEAs, in the course of multistakeholder dialogues associated with project-related work, and in the preparation of Country Assistance Strategies (CASs), Poverty Reduction Strategy Papers (PRSPs), and other policy related work.
- The Strategy supports the linkage of local and regional/global concerns by committing Bank staff to identifying in their analytical work the

overlaps between environmental goals at the local, regional, and global levels. It also commits the Bank to helping client countries build their capacity to benefit from trade in local and global environmental goods and services and to participate in regional trade with global benefits.

■ The Strategy makes a commitment to greater transparency and accountability regarding the World Bank's environmental performance. It commits the World Bank to supporting the development and dissemination of environmental and sustainability indicators in client countries, and it provides for an Environmental Performance Reporting unit within the Bank's Environment Department for the purpose of reporting to both internal and external clients on the Bank's performance. Clear benchmarks are

being identified by which progress can be measured.

The World Bank's Environment Strategy—both as a document and as an action plan—must be viewed as part of an iterative process. The intent of the Strategy is not to bring to closure any of the issues it addresses, and especially not to cut short the general debate under way among stakeholders on development directions. To promote continued dialogue, the Strategy proposes a framework for revisiting, evaluating, and adjusting progress and for maintaining ongoing communication with clients and development partners, including governments and civil society, on the World Bank's role, performance, and priorities.

Table J.1 World Bank Environment Strategy consultation schedule

Date	Venue	Participants
Latin America and Caribbean		
September 21–22	Cartagena, Colombia	Govt., NGOs, private sector (PS), academia (Acad.)
October 16–17	Rio de Janeiro, Brazil	Govt., NGOs, PS, Acad.
November 7–8	San José, Costa Rica	Govt., NGOs, PS, Acad.
Sub-Saharan Africa		
September 13–14	Nairobi, Kenya	Govt., NGOs, PS, Acad.
October 10–11	Pretoria, South Africa	Govt., NGOs, PS, Acad.
October 23–24	Ouagadougou, Burkina Faso	Govt., NGOs, PS, Acad.
December 13–14	Paris, France	African Govt., NGOs, Acad.
Europe and Central Asia		
September 5–7	Berlin and Bonn, Germany	Govt., NGOs, PS, Acad.
September 1112	London, United Kingdom	Govt., NGOs, PS, Acad.
September 14	Amsterdam, the Netherlands	Government
September 18–19	Moscow, Russia	Govt., NGOs, PS, Acad.
September 21–22	Tbilisi, Georgia	Govt., NGOs, Acad.
October 14–16	Szentendre, Hungary	Govt., NGOs, PS
May 14, 2001	Bern, Switzerland	Govt., NGOs, Private Sector
South Asia		
October 4	Pakistan	Government
October 9–10	Pakistan	Govt., PS, NGOs, Acad., multi-lateral agencies
October 14–16	Dhaka, Bangladesh	NGOs
October 17–18	Delhi, India	Government
November 18–20	Colombo, Sri Lanka	Govt., NGOs, international donor agencies

(continued)

Table J.1   World Bank Environment Strategy consultation schedule (*continued*)

Date	Venue	Participants
East Asia		
May 22–27, 2000	Tokyo, Japan	Govt., NGOs, PS
October 4–5	Bangkok, Thailand	Governments, NGOs
February 23, 2001	Beijing, China	Govt., NGOs
Middle East and North Africa		
October 9–10	Amman, Jordan	Governments, NGOs
November 19–21	Amman, Jordan	Govt., NGOs, PS, international donor agencies
North America		
November 20	San Francisco, CA	NGOs, PS
January 18	Washington, DC	Government
March 22–23	Ottawa, Canada	Govt., NGOs, PS
Global		
May 8, 2001	Washington, DC (GEF/NGO)	NGOs
May 9, 2001	Washington, DC (GEF Council)	Governments
June 4–5, 2001	Washington, DC (OED/WB)	Govts., NGOs, PS

Annex K

Selected Partnerships

Supporting sustainable development is a complex task. Joining forces with development partners, civil society, and the business community through effective partnerships can improve project performance, policy dialogue, and development outcome. The Bank has been engaged in a wide range of partnerships in the environment area during the past years. This annex illustrates some of these partnerships.

Table K.1 Selected partnerships[1]

Partnership	Scope/VPU	Start	End	Overall objective	Partners and donors
Africa Water Resources Management Initiative	Regional/ AFR	1997	On-going	Assist countries to build capacity in the process of formulating and implementing national water resource management (NRM) strategies Facilitate collaboration among riparian states Enhance ongoing multicountry efforts for joint development of scarce water resources	Canada (CIDA), France, Germany (GTZ), Japan, Netherlands (BNPP), Norway, Sweden (SIDA), Switzerland, UK (DFID), US (USAID), UNDP, UNEP, FAO, IUCN, AfDB, Development Bank of Southern Africa (DBSA)
Alliance for Forest Conservation and Sustainable Use	Global/ ESSD	1999	2005	Promote forest conservation and the adoption of international best practices in forest management	BMZ, BNPP, NORAD, WWF, other NGOs
Critical Ecosystems Partnership Fund	Global/ ESSD	2000	2005	Safeguard the world's threatened biological hotspots in developing countries by enhancing local livelihoods through improved NRM	Conservation International (CI), GEF, international and local NGOs, local community groups, other donors
Forest Market Transformation Initiative	Global/ ESSD	1998	On-going	Promote dialogue and pilot activities to help turn market forces toward more forest-friendly practices	DGIF, Forest Trends, Netherlands, SDC, UK (DFID), US (State Department, in discussion)
Global Environment Facility (GEF)	Global/ ESSD	1991	Long term	Forge international cooperation and finance actions to address four critical threats to the global environment: biodiversity loss, climate change, degradation of international waters, and ozone depletion	FAO, IFAD, IFC, regional development banks, UNDP, ENEP, UNEP, UNIDO, NGOs, global environmental convention secretariats
Global Mechanism to Combat Desertification	Global/ ESSD	2001	On-going	Focus attention, resources, and knowledge on combating desertification by mobilizing and channeling financial resources to increase financial effectiveness and ensure a holistic and equitable approach to resource distribution	Secretariat of the CCD, FAO, GEF, IFAD, Islamic Development Bank, other regional development banks, UNDP, UNEP
Integrated Land-Water Management Action Program for Africa	Regional/ AFR	2001	On-going	Develop, implement, and mainstream a coordinated and integrated action program to mobilize resources from the GEF, the Implementing Agencies and other partners to address issues of land and water degradation Identify and promote the development of GEF-eligible projects	AfDB, GEF, GM, UNDP, UNEP
Interagency Task Force on Forests	Global/ ESSD	1998	On-going	Support international policy dialogue on forests, coordinate interagency work, and promote outreach beyond the UN system. Encourage a global dialogue on forests and country-level coordination through the support of national forest programs	DGIF, Finland, Germany (GTZ), Japan (JICA), UK (DFID), SDC, and others

1. For definitions of the abbreviations used in this Annex, see the Abbreviations and Acronyms section at the front of the book.

Partnership	Scope/ VPU	Start	End	Overall objective	Partners and donors
International Coral Reefs Initiative	Global/ ESSD	1995	On-going	Promote the sustainable use and conservation of coral reefs for future generations Assess the impact of climate change on coral reefs	Australia, France, Sweden, UK, US GEF, IUCN, UNEP, UNESCO/IOC, UNDP
Managing the Environment Locally in Sub Saharan Africa	Regional/ AFR	1996	On-going	Empower local authorities and communities for better environmental planning and management, with an emphasis on benefiting the poor and using knowledge management as the primary tool	European Commission (EC), Norway, Sweden
Mediterranean Environment Technical Assistance Program	Regional/ MNA	1990	On-going	Assist 15 countries with a common Mediterranean coastline to strengthen environmental policy, regulatory and institutional frameworks, and environmental management capacity Develop projects and mobilize resources for environmental improvement	Canada, EC, European Investment Bank (EIB), Finland, Italy, Japan, Luxembourg, Switzerland, UNDP, and others
Mesoamerican Biological Corridor	Regional/ LCR	1997	On-going	Align conservation and development interests, bolster protected area and buffer zone management, and, through improved stewardship of private and tribal lands that link parks and reserves, establish greenways and corridors	Denmark (DANIDA), Germany (GTZ), US (USAID), UNDP, foundations, and NGO's
Millennium Ecosystem Assessment	Global/ ESSD	2000	2004	Assess scientifically how world ecosystem changes will affect the ability to meet human demands for food, potable water, health, biodiversity, and other ecosystem goods and services	GEF; the Packard, Rockefeller, and Turner Foundations; secretariats of global environmental conventions (BCD, CCD, and Ramsar); FAO; Norway; UNDP; UNEP; UNESCO; WRI; other environmental NGOs; and the international scientific community
Multilateral Fund for Implementation of Montreal Protocol	Global/ ESSD	1991	Medium term	Assist developing country parties to the Montreal Protocol whose annual per capita consumption and production of ozone depleting substances (ODS) is less than 0.3 killogram to comply with the control measures of the protocol	UNDP, UNEP, UNIDO, and the scientific and technical community via the OORG
National Strategy Study Program	Global/ ESSD	1998	On-going	Assist interested host country governments to assess their role in the Clean Development Mechanism (CDM), identify potential investment projects, and develop national policies regarding the CDM	Australia (AusAID), Finland, Germany (GTZ), Switzerland (SECO)
Nile Basin Initiative	Regional/ AFR	1997	On-going	Achieve sustainable socioeconomic development through the equitable utilization of and benefits from common Nile basin water resources	Canada, Denmark, Finland, GEF, Germany, Netherlands, Norway, Sweden, UK, UNDP, US
Pilot Program to Preserve the Brazilian Rainforest	Regional/ LCR	1992	2005	Identify ways to conserve the tropical rain forests of the Amazon and of Brazil's Atlantic coast and promote sustainable development in these regions	Amazon and Atlantic Rain Forest Networks of NGOs in Brazil; EC; France; GEF, Germany (GTZ, KfW); Italy; Japan; Netherlands; UK (DFID); UNDP; US
Prototype Carbon Fund	Global/ ESSD	2000	2012	Address climate change and promote the finance and transfer of climate-friendly technology to developing countries through purchases of greenhouse gas emissions reductions from clean-technology projects in these countries and through dissemination of knowledge gained from these transactions	23 participants contributing a total of $145 million in funding, including 6 governments (Canada, Finland, Japan (FBIC), Netherlands, Norway, Sweden, $10 million each) and 17 private companies ($5 million each)
UNDP-World Bank International Waters Partnership	Regional/ MNA/ ESSD	1999	2001	Establish increased cooperation in supporting riparian states in addressing complex issues of sustainable and equitable development in the Nile basin, Red Sea and other basins	UNDP

Annex L

World Bank Management's Response to ØED's Environment Review and Recommendations

S
everal "building blocks" contributed to the preparation of the Environment Strategy, including Regional Environment Strategies (summarized in annex A), Environment Strategy Background Papers (several of them are summarized in annexes B-F), and an extensive strategy consultation process (summarized in annex J). One of the key building blocks was OED's environment review (OED 2001), which assessed the Bank's performance in supporting environmental sustainability.

The OED review found that the Bank had made substantial improvements in its environmental performance, but large challenges remained. It rated the Bank's performance as satisfactory in addressing global environmental challenges; and partially satisfactory in (a) incorporating the environment into sector strategies, country strategies, and policy dialogues, (b) mainstreaming into the Bank's overall operations, and (c) implementing safeguard policies.

In defining a course of action for the longer term and setting specific measures to adjust Bank actions, tools, and institutional incentives for the next five years, the Strategy has taken into account the findings and recommendations of the OED review. The actions proposed by the Strategy are summarized in tables 1 and 2 of the Executive Summary. The management action response matrix below summarizes OED's main recommendations, and outlines the elements of the Strategy and implementation plan which directly respond to these recommendations (table L.1).

Table L.1 OED's recommendations and management's action response

Major OED recommendations	Response
Recommendation 1 — *In pursuit of holistic, long-term development and the International Development Goals, the Bank should build on its comparative advantage and analytical capacity to demonstrate the critical role of the environment in sustainable development and poverty reduction. It should incorporate environmental objectives into its core strategy and its operations.*	Bank management concurs. To support the linking of environmental issues with the Bank's core operations, improvements and actions will be taken in the following areas: ■ *Country-level environmental analyses* will be part of the standard package of diagnostic tools that informs policy dialogue, particularly in connection with the preparation of CASs and PRSPs. Key sustainability and environmental indicators will become part of the country indicator set included in CASs. We will refine the methodology of country environmental analysis during FY02, and over the next 5 years, carry out 5 to 15 country diagnostic studies annually, linked with CAS preparations in priority countries (table 2, page xxv). ■ *Targeted environmental input to PRSPs* — analytical work, training, and facilitation of cross-sectoral dialogue—will help integrate environmental sustainability issues into the policy dialogue in 5-15 priority PRSP countries annually (table 2, page xxv). ■ *Structured learning on strategic environmental assessments (SEAs)* will help introduce environmental considerations earlier in sectoral decisionmaking and planning processes. We will refine methodologies and procedures during FY02, then pilot and disseminate good practice in SEAs based on about 10-20 SEAs annually (table 2, page xxii). The following measures will be taken to measure progress: ■ Monitoring and evaluating the environmental aspects of CASs. Our objective is to achieve satisfactory coverage based on methodology developed by ENV (table 2, pages xxv-xxvi) ■ Regular reviews of the environmental aspects of PRSPs (table 2, page xxv) ■ Refinement of the methodology for measuring the extent of environmental mainstreaming in key sectors (rural, urban, water and sanitation, energy) during FY02, and annual reporting on progress (table 2, page xxvi).
Recommendation 2 — *The Bank should review its environmental safeguard oversight system and processes to strengthen accountability for compliance. In parallel, the policy framework should be modernized and adapted to the changing practices and instruments being used by the Bank and take account of recent experience.*	Bank management concurs and is committed to continue improvements in the safeguard system, following a two-pronged approach described in the Strategy (chapter 3, pages 49-51). *Addressing short-term priorities:* ■ Implementing an integrated safeguard system, and improving consistency in safeguard application validated by an independent internal audit in FY02 (table 2, page xxvi). ■ Establishing a corporate safeguard tracking and monitoring system by the end of FY02 (table 2, page xxvi). ■ Strengthening corporate consistency and oversight and meeting safeguard implementation targets that will be established in FY02 (table 2, page xxvi). ■ Developing and piloting a client capacity assessment and development program FY02 (table 2, page xxvi). *Reforming the safeguard system:* ■ Developing a medium-term workplan for reforming the safeguards system to be reviewed by CODE in FY02 (table 2, xxvi). ■ Implementing a client capacity development program over the next five years (table 2, page xxvi). ■ Implementing systematic staff training. During the next 5 years, 90 percent of all operational staff and managers will be trained in safeguards. ■ Work with clients and other development institutions to review and harmonize safeguards (table 2, page xxvii). ■ Improved monitoring and regular reporting at the Regional and corporate levels will provide up-to-date information on safeguard implementation issues (chapter 4, pages 66-67).

Table L.1 OED's recommendations and management's action response (*continued*)

| Recommendation 3 — *The Bank should help implement the global environmental agenda by concentrating on global issues which involve local and national benefits.* | Bank management concurs. The Strategy emphasizes the need to build on synergies by addressing local, regional, and global environmental issues, and spells out the principles to guide the Bank in actions to address global concerns (chapter 3, pages 41-43). The following are key aspects:

■ *Supporting the integration of global concerns into PRSPs.* Several global environmental concerns—such as land degradation, water resource management and biodiversity loss, and the impacts of climate change—have strong linkages with poverty reduction. Such aspects will be included in PRSP reviews and joint staff assessments (JSA). A methodology will be developed during FY02 to guide annual reviews of PRSPs and inputs to JSAs.

■ *Integrating GEF resources with Bank operations.* The Strategy aims to improve the integration of GEF assistance into Bank operations measured annually by the proportion of the GEF portfolio blended with Bank resources, compared with the current level (reported in World Bank 2000e).

■ *Addressing climate change comprehensively.* The Bank will also seek to enhance the proportion of Bank projects that carry out an assessment of their climate change impact. Assessment methodologies for sectoral operations will be updated and disseminated to operational staff (table 2, page xxv). Annex F on climate change spells out in detail the proposed actions for reducing the vulnerability of people to climate change including the development of methodologies for assessing vulnerability (table 1, page xxiv). |

Annex M

Mapping Environmental Conditions

A ccurate information is critical for environmental decisionmaking, but supporting data remain scarce in many countries. Significant efforts have been made in recent years by governments, international organizations, and civil society to compile and/or estimate reliable and internationally comparable national and sub-national data. The Global Environmental Monitoring System, managed by UNEP, conducts activities related to measuring air and water quality in 142 countries. The World Bank, together with other development institutions, has worked with many client countries to improve their environmental monitoring systems. It has also taken significant steps toward integrating environmental factors with standard national accounts, developing measures of genuine savings, and developing models to estimate environmental conditions where monitoring data are unavailable.

The indicators displayed on these maps reflect the best available information about environment-related threats to health, livelihoods, and the global commons. They integrate data generously provided by colleagues in other institutions with information from the Bank's own sources. They also reflect the Bank's focus on links between poverty and the environment. Given the limited state of our present knowledge, they are intended to promote discussion, highlight areas of concern, identify information gaps, and encourage the development of better information.

Map 1   Gross domestic savings (percentage of GDP)

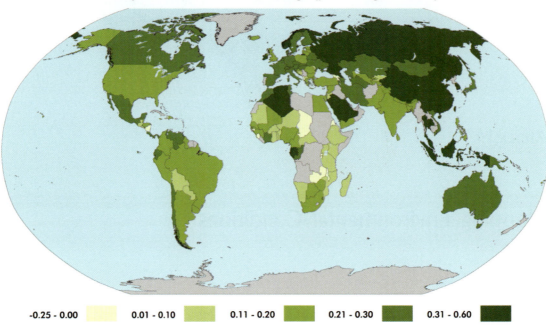

| -0.25 - 0.00 | | 0.01 - 0.10 | | 0.11 - 0.20 | | 0.21 - 0.30 | | 0.31 - 0.60 | |

Note: Gross domestic savings are calculated as the difference between GDP and public and private consumption.

Sources: World Bank 2001; World Development Indicators 2001.

Map 2   Genuine savings (percentage of GDP)

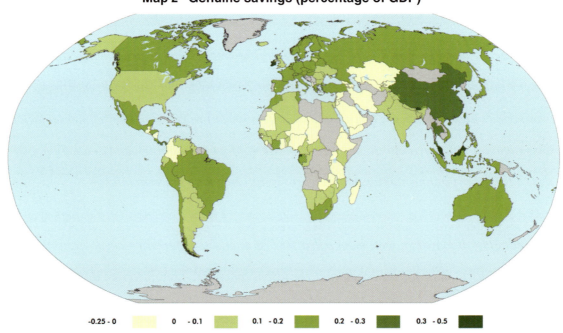

| -0.25 - 0 | | 0 - 0.1 | | 0.1 - 0.2 | | 0.2 - 0.3 | | 0.3 - 0.5 | |

Notes: Genuine domestic savings are indicators of economic and environmental sustainability. They measure the true rate of savings in an economy after taking into account the cost of depleting natural resources and the damage caused by pollution. They are calculated as the sum of gross domestic savings and investments in human capital less depreciation of produced assets and the depletion and degradation of the environment. By this measure, some countries (shown in yellow) appear to be unsustainable as their savings rates are less than the combined sum of conventional capital depreciation and natural resource depletion.

Sources: World Bank 2001; World Development Indicators 2001.

Map 3   Health burden associated with waterborne diseases (DALYs per 1,000 people)

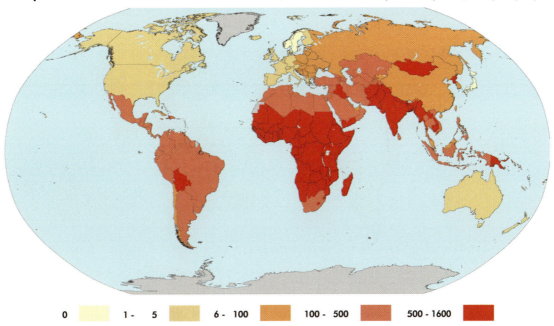

| 0 | 1 - 5 | 6 - 100 | 100 - 500 | 500 - 1600 |

Notes: The main causes of waterborne diseases are lack of access to safe water and sanitation and inadequate hygiene. DALYs (disability-adjusted life years) are a standard measure of the burden of disease. The concept combines life years lost due to premature death and fractions of years healthy life lost as a result of illness or disability. Years of life lost at each age are valued differently reflecting different social weights usually placed on illness and premature mortality at different ages.

Sources: Murray and Lopez 1996; World Bank estimates.

Map 4   Estimated ambient concentration of particulates (PM$_{10}$) in urban areas (µg/m³)

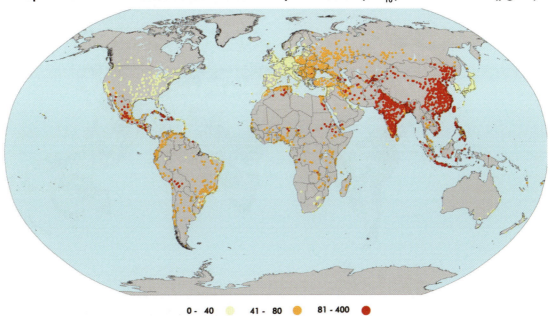

| 0 - 40 | 41 - 80 | 81 - 400 |

Note: Most of the adverse health effects of exposure to air pollution are attributable to particulate matter smaller than 10 microns in diameter (PM$_{10}$).

Sources: WDI 2001; World Bank estimates.

Map 5   Population in areas of relative water scarcity

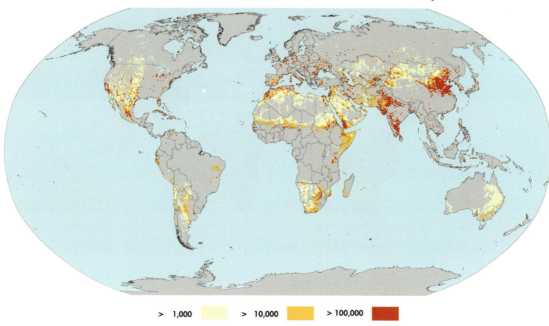

> 1,000   > 10,000   > 100,000

Notes: An area faces relative water scarcity if the mean annual demand for domestic, industrial and irrigated agricultural uses is greater than 40 percent of the mean annual surface and subsurface runoff for the area. The colors indicate the population in each area of relative water scarcity.

Source: Vorosmarty and others 2000.

Map 6   Areas of high biodiversity importance

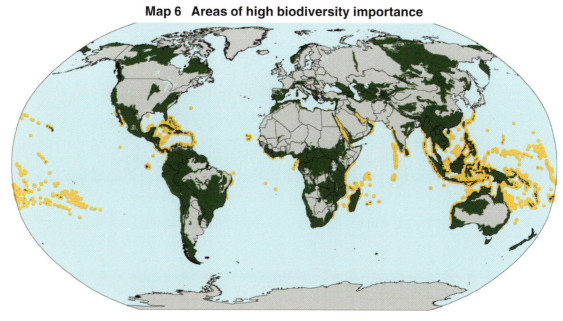

Notes: Areas in green have been identified either as "hotspots" by Conservation International, as "biologically-important ecoregions" by World Wildlife Fund, or "endemic bird areas" by Birdlife International. Areas in yellow contain "reefs at risk" as identified by World Resources Institute.

Sources: Bryant and others 1998; Mittmeier and others 2000; Olson and others 2000; Stattersfield and others 1998.

Map 7   Per capita CO$_2$ emissions (metric tons)

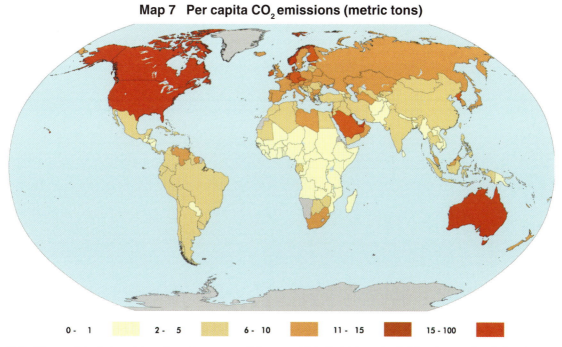

| 0 - 1 | 2 - 5 | 6 - 10 | 11 - 15 | 15 - 100 |

Notes: CO$_2$ accounts for the largest share of greenhouse gases, which are associated with global warming. Variations in per capita emissions across countries reflect differences in the level of economic activity, energy efficiency, and pollution intensity.

Sources: World Bank 2001; World Development Indicators 2001.

Map 8   CO$_2$ emissions per PPP-adjusted GDP (kg)

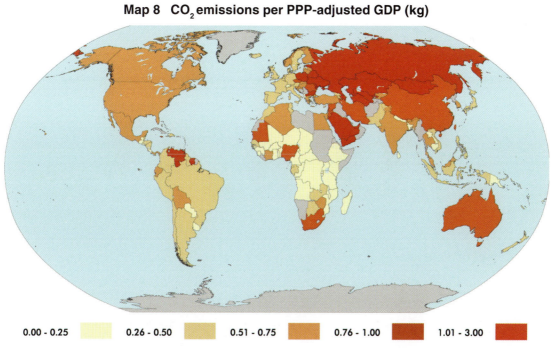

| 0.00 - 0.25 | 0.26 - 0.50 | 0.51 - 0.75 | 0.76 - 1.00 | 1.01 - 3.00 |

Notes: PPP-adjusted GDP is GDP converted to international dollars using purchasing power parity rates. An international dollar has the same purchasing power over GDP as the U.S. dollar has in the United States. Variations in emissions per PPP-adjusted GDP across countries reflect differences in energy efficiency and pollution intensity.

Sources: World Bank 2001; World Development Indicators 2001.

Bibliography

Note: The word *processed* describes informally reproduced works that may not be commonly available through libraries.

REFERENCES

Aristanti, C. 1997. "Gender, Biomass Energy and Health." *Wood Energy News* 12 (1): 8–10.

Bartone, C., J. Bernstein, J. Leitmann, and J. Eigen. 1994. *Toward Environmental Strategies for Cities: Policy Considerations for Urban Environmental Management in Developing Countries.* Urban Management Programme Policy Paper 18. Washington, D.C.: World Bank.

Bojö, J., and R. C. Reddy. 2001. "Poverty Reduction Strategies and Environment: A Review of 25 Interim and Full PRSPs." World Bank, Africa Region Environment and Social Development Unit, Washington, D.C.. Processed.

Bryant, D., L. Burke, J. McManus, and M. Spalding. 1998. *Reefs at Risk: A Map-Based Indicator of Threats to the World's Coral Reefs.* World Resources Institute. Washington, DC. <http://www.igc.org/wri/indictrs/reefrisk.htm>.

Bucknall, J., C. Kraus, and P. Pillai. 2000. "Poverty and Environment." Environment Strategy Background Paper. World Bank, Environment Department, Washington, D.C.

Cavendish, W. 1999. "Empirical Regularities in the Poverty-Environment Relationship of African Rural Households." Working Paper Series 99-21. Oxford University, Center for the Studies of African Economies, Oxford, U.K. Processed.

Crooks, R., W. B. Magrath, G. Morgan, and S. Shen. 1999. "Natural Resource Management: A Strategic Framework for East Asia and the Pacific." EAP Working Paper. World Bank, Washington, D.C. Processed.

Dasgupta, J., and A. Das. 1998. "Health Effects of Women's Excessive Work Burden in Deforested Rural Areas of Uttarkhand." Paper presented at the National Conference on Health and Environment, July 7–9. Center for Science and Environment, New Delhi.

Datt, G., and H. Hoogeveen. 2000. "El Nino or El Peso? Crisis, Poverty and Income Distribution in the Philippines." Policy Research Working Paper 2466. World Bank, Washington, D.C.

Demographic and Health Survey data. 1996. Available at <http://www.worldbank.org/poverty/health/data/guide/proj10.htm>.

Devasia, L. 1998. "Safe Drinking Water and Its Acquisition: Rural Women's Participation in Water Management in Maharashtra, India." *Water Resources Development* 14 (4): 537–46.

Dollar, D., and L. Pritchett. 1998. *Assessing Aid: What Works, What Doesn't, and Why*. World Bank Policy Research Report. New York: Oxford University Press.

Environics International Ltd. 2000. *The Environment Monitor: Global Public Opinion on the Environment. International Report*. Toronto.

Goodland, R., and J. R. Mercier. 1999. "The Evolution of Environmental Assessment in the World Bank: From Approval to Results." Environment Department Paper 67. World Bank, Washington, D.C.

Hamilton, K. 2000. "Mainstreaming Environment in Country Assistance Strategies." Environment Strategy Background Paper. World Bank, Environment Department, Washington, D.C.

Ibrekk, H. O. 2000. "Donor Survey of Environmental Aid Effectiveness." Environment Strategy Background Paper. World Bank, Environment Department, Washington, D.C.

IFPRI (International Food Policy Research Institute), CGIAR (Consultative Group on International Agricultural Research), WRI (World Resources Institute), and World Bank. 2000. *Pilot Analysis of Global Ecosystems*. Washington, D.C. World Resources Institute.

IPCC (Intergovernmental Pavel on Climate Change). 2001. *The Third Assessment Report of the Intergovernmental Panel on Climate Change*. Cambridge, U;.K.: Cambridge University Press.

Johnson, T. M., F. Liu, and R. Newfarmer. 1997. *Clear Water, Blue Skies: China's Environment in the New Century*. Washington, D.C.: World Bank.

Kinsey, B., B. Kees, and J. Gunning. 1998. "Coping with Drought in Zimbabwe: Survey Evidence on Responses of Rural Households to Risk." *World Development* 26: 89–110.

Kjorven, O., and H. Lindhjem. 2001. "Strategic Environmental Assessments in World Bank Operations." Draft Environment Strategy Background Paper. World Bank, Environment Department, Washington, D.C. Processed.

Klees, R., J. Godinho, and M. Lawson-Doe. 1999. *Sanitation, Health and Hygiene in World Bank Rural Water Supply and Sanitation Projects*. Washington, D.C.: World Bank.

Kojima, M., and M. Lovei. 2001. *Urban Air Quality Management: Perspectives on Coordinating Transport, Environment, and Energy Policies in Developing Countries*. World Bank Technical Paper 508. Washington, D.C.

Listorti, J. 1996. "Bridging Environmental Health Gaps: Lessons for Sub-Saharan Africa Infrastructure Projects." AFTES Working Paper 20. World Bank, Washington, D.C.

Listorti, J. A., and F. M. Doumani. 2001. "Environmental Health—Bridging the Gaps: Environmental Health Assessments—Rapid Checklists." World Bank, Africa Region, Environment and Social Development Unit, Washington, D.C. Processed.

Lvovsky, K., I. Sebastian, and H. de Koning. 1999. *Decision Support System for Integrated Pollution Control*. Washington, D.C.: World Bank.

Lvovsky, K., G. Hughes, D. Maddison, B. Ostro, and D. Pearce. 2000. "Environmental Costs of Fossil Fuels: A Rapid Assessment Method with Application to Six Cities." Environment Department Working Paper 78. World Bank, Washington, D.C.

Mittermeier, R., N. Myers, G. C. Mittermeier. 2000. *Hotspots: Earth's Biologically Richest and Most Endangered Terrestrial Ecoregions*. Conservation International, Washington D.C. <http:/

/www.conservation.org/xp/CIWEB/strategies/
hotspots/hotspots.xml>.

Murray, C. J., and A. D. Lopez. 1996. *The Global
Burden of Disease.* Cambridge, Mass.: Harvard
University Press.

OED (Operations Evaluation Department). 1996.
*Effectiveness of Environmental Assessments and
National Environmental Action Plans: A Process
Study.* Washington, D.C.: World Bank.

———. 1997. *Review of Adjustment Lending in
Sub-Saharan Africa.* Washington, D.C.: World
Bank.

———. 2001. "OED Review of the Bank's Performance on the Environment." Draft report.
World Bank, Washington, D.C.

Olson, D. M., E. Dinerstein, R. Abell, T. Allnutt,
C. Carpenter, L. McClenachan, J. D'Amico, P.
Hurley, K. Kassem, H. Strand, M. Taye, and M.
Thieme. 2000. *The Global 200: A Representation
Approach to Conserving the Earth's Distinctive
Ecoregions.* Conservation Science Program,
World Wildlife Fund. Washington, DC. <http:/
/www.panda.org/global200/global.cfm>.

Pandey, M. R. 1997. "Women, Wood, Energy, and
Health." *Wood Energy News* 12 (1): 3–5.

Segnestam, L. 1999. "Environmental Performance
Indicators: A Second Edition Note." Environment Department Paper 71. World Bank, Washington, D.C.

Seymour, F., and N. Dubash. 2000. *The Right Conditions: The World Bank, Structural Adjustment,
and Forest Policy Reform.* Washington, D.C.:
World Resources Institute.

Smith, K. 1998. *Indoor Air Pollution in India: National Health Impacts and the Cost-Effectiveness
of Intervention.* Goregaon Mumbai: Indira
Gandhi Institute for Development Research.

Stattersfield, A., M.J. Crosby, A.J. Long, and D.C.
Wege. 1998. *Endemic Bird Areas of the World:
Priorities for Bird Conservation.* Cambridge, UK:

BirdLife International (BirdLife Conservation
Series 7).

United Nations. 1995. *Urbanization Prospects: The
1994 Revision.* New York.

———. 2000. *Millennium Declaration.* Department
of Public Information. New York.

UNEP (United Nations Environment
Programme). 2000. "GEO Latin America and
the Caribbean." *Environment Outlook 2000.*
Nairobi.

UNFPA (United Nations Population Fund),
UNEP (United Nations Environment
Programme), and IUCN (World Conservation
Union). 1998. "Report of the International
Workshop on Population-Poverty-Environment
Linkages: Key Results and Policy Actions, Sep-
tember 23–25. World Conservation Union,
Gland, Switzerland.

Vorosmarty, C. J., P. Green, J. Salisbury, and R. B.
Lammers. 2000. "Global Water Resources: Vul-
nerability from Climate Change and Population
Growth." *Science* 289(5477): 284-288.

WCED (World Commission on Environment and
Development). 1987. *Our Common Future.* Oxford, U.K.: Oxford University Press.

World Bank. 1992. *World Development Report 1992:
Development and the Environment.* New York:
Oxford University Press.

———. 1997a. *Can the Environment Wait? Priorities for East Asia.* Washington, D.C.: World
Bank.

———. 1997b. *The Impact of Environmental As-
sessment: A Review of World Bank Experience.*
World Bank Technical Paper 363. Washington,
D.C.

———. 1998. *Partnership and Development: Pro-
posed Actions for the World Bank.* Partnership
Group Strategy and Resources Management
Discussion Paper. Washington, D.C.

———. 1999a. "Greening Industry : New Roles for Communities, Markets, and Governments." Development Research Group. Washington, D.C.

———. 1999b. *Pollution Prevention and Abatement Handbook: Toward Cleaner Production 1998.* Washington, D.C.

———. 2000a. "Cities in Transition: World Bank Urban and Local Government Strategy." Urban Development Division, Infrastructure Group. Washington, D.C.

———. 2000b. "Fixing ESW: Where Are We?" Discussion draft. May 3, 2000. World Bank, Operations Management and Policy Department, Washington, D.C. Processed.

———. 2000c. *Lending Instruments. Resources for Development Impact.* World Bank, Operations Policy and Strategy. Washington D.C.

———. 2000d. "Partnership Selectivity and Oversight." Discussion Notes. SecM2000–164. March 30.

———. 2000e. *The Quality of Growth.* Washington, D.C.: World Bank.

———. 2000f. "The Qinghai Project," (China Western Poverty Reduction Project). The Inspection Panel Investigation Report. World Bank, East Asia and Pacific Region, Washington, D.C.

———. 2000g. "The World Bank and the Global Environment: A Progress Report." Washington, D.C.

———. 2000h. *World Development Report 2000/2001: Attacking Poverty.* New York: Oxford University Press.

———. 2001a. *Adjustment Lending Retrospective.* Discussion draft. World Bank, Operations Policy and Country Services, Washington D.C.

———. 2001b. "China: Environment Sector Strategy Update." Draft. World Bank, Environment and Social Development Sector Unit, Washington, D.C. Draft

———. 2001c. "Indonesia Environment and Natural Resource Management in a Time of Transition." Environment and Social Development Sector Unit, World Bank, Washington, D.C.

World Business Council for Sustainable Development. 2000. *Meeting Changing Expectations: Corporate Social Responsibility.* Geneva.

World Commission on Dams. 2000. *Dams and Development—A New Framework for Decision-Making.* London: Earthscan.

WRI (World Resources Institute). 2000. *World Resources 2000–2001. People and Ecosystems: A Fraying Web of Life.* Washington, D.C.

SELECTED READINGS

This section provides suggestions for additional readings on the topics discussed in this strategy paper. It is not a complete bibliography, but it does list important works, produced both inside and outside the Bank, relating to the areas covered and points the reader toward recent thinking that influenced this paper. A more detailed list of sources, including country-specific references, can be found on the Environment Strategy Website, <http://www.worldbank.org/environment/>. Publications in both lists are grouped according to their theme or geographic focus.

State of the environment

Brown, L. R., C. Flavin, H. French, J. Abramovitz, S. Dunn, G. Gardner, L. Mastny, A. Mattoon, D. Roodman, P. Sampat, and M. O. Sheehan. 2000. *State of the World 2001: A Worldwatch Institute Report on Progress Toward a Sustainable Society.* Washington, D.C.: Worldwatch Institute. New York: W. W. Norton & Company.

FAO (Food and Agriculture Organization of the United Nations). 1999a. *State of the World's Forests*. Rome: FAO.

———. 1999b. *The State of World Fisheries and Aquaculture 1998*. Rome: FAO.

OECD (Organisation for Economic Co-operation and Development), UN (United Nations), IMF (International Monetary Fund), and World Bank. 2000. *A Better World for All: Progress Toward the International Development Goals*. Washington, D.C.: OECD.

UNEP (United Nations Environment Programme). 1999. *The Global Environmental Outlook 2000*. Nairobi: UNEP.

World Bank. Various years. *World Development Indicators [1997 – 2000]*. Washington, D.C.: World Bank.

———. 1991. *Environmental Assessment Sourcebook: Volume 1: Policies, Procedures, and Cross-Sectoral Issues*. Technical Paper No.139. Washington, D.C.: World Bank.

———. 1991. *Environmental Assessment Sourcebook: Volume 2: Sectoral Guidelines*. Technical Paper No.140. Washington, D.C.: World Bank

———. 1991. *Environmental Assessment Sourcebook: Volume 3: Guidelines for Environmental Assessment of Energy and Industry Projects*. Technical Paper No.154. Washington, D.C.: World Bank.

WRI (World Resources Institute). 1998. *World Resources 1998–99: A Guide to the Global Environment. Environmental Change and Human Health*. New York: Oxford University Press.

Environment strategies, policy issues, and instruments

Bernstein, J. 1995. "The Urban Challenge in National Environmental Strategies." Environment Department Working Paper No.42. Washington, D.C.: World Bank.

Hamilton, K. 2000. "Genuine Savings as a Sustainability Indicator." Environment Department Paper No.77. Washington, D.C.: World Bank.

Jodha, N. S. 1992. "Common Property Resources: A Missing Dimension of Development Strategies." Discussion Paper No.169. Washington, D.C.: World Bank.

Kunte, A., K. Hamilton, J. Dixon, and M. Clemens. 1998. "Estimating National Wealth: Methodology and Results." Environment Department Paper No.57. Washington, D.C.: World Bank.

Lampietti, J. A., and U. Subramanian. 1995. "Taking Stock of National Environmental Strategies." Environment Department Working Paper No.10. Washington, D.C.: World Bank.

Lovei, M., and C. Weiss, Jr. 1998. "Environmental Management and Institutions in OECD Countries: Lessons from Experience." Technical Paper No. 391. Washington, D.C.: World Bank.

Margulis, S., and T. Vetleseter. 1999. "Environmental Capacity Building: A Review of the World Bank's Portfolio." Environment Department Paper No. 68. Washington, D.C.: World Bank.

McCalla, A. F. and W. S. Ayres. 1997. *Rural Development - from Vision to Action*. Environmentally Sustainable Development Studies and Monograph Series No.12. Washington, D.C.: World Bank.

Segnestam, L. 1999. "Environmental Performance Indicators: A Second Edition Note." Environment Department Paper No.71. Washington, D.C.: World Bank.

Shyamsundar, P., and K. Hamilton. 2000. "An Environmental Review of 1999 Country Assistance Strategies: Best Practices and Lessons Learned." Environment Department Paper No.74. Washington, D.C.: World Bank.

Vidaeus, L., and G. Castro. 2000. "The World Bank and the Global Environment: A Progress Report." Washington, D.C.: World Bank. Processed.

World Bank. 1995. "National Environmental Strategies : Learning from Experience. and Action Plans: Key Elements and Best Practice." Environment Department. ESSD 13986. Washington, D.C.: World Bank.

———. 1997. *Expanding the Measure of Wealth: Indicators of Environmentally Sustainable Development*. Environmentally Sustainable Development Studies and Monograph Series No.17. Washington, D.C.: World Bank.

———. 1997. *Five Years After Rio: Innovations in Environmental Policy*. Environmentally Sustainable Development Studies and Monograph Series No.18. Washington, D.C.: World Bank.

Global environmental issues and challenges

Chomitz, K. M. 2000. "Evaluating Carbon Offsets from Forestry and Energy Projects." Policy Research Working Paper No. 2357. Washington, D.C.: World Bank.

Ellerman, A. D., H. D. Jacoby, and A. Decaux. 1998. "The Effects on Developing Countries of the Kyoto Protocol and Carbon Dioxide Emissions Trading." Policy Research Working Paper No.2019. Washington, D.C.: World Bank.

Eskeland, G. S., and J. Xie. 1998. "Acting Globally While Thinking Locally: Is the Global Environment Protected by Transport Emission Control Programs?" Policy Research Working Paper No. 1975. Washington, D.C.: World Bank.

Heil, M. T., and Q. T. Wodon. 1999. "Future Inequality in Carbon Dioxide Emissions and the Projected Impact of Abatement Proposals." Policy Research Working Paper No. 2084. Washington, D.C.: World Bank.

IPCC (Intergovernmental Panel on Climate Change). 2000. "Cross Cutting Issues Guidance Papers." Tokyo, Japan: Global Industrial and Social Progress Research Institute.

———. 2000. *Emissions Scenarios*. Cambridge: Cambridge University Press.

———. 2000. *Land Use, Land-Use Change, and Forestry*. Cambridge: Cambridge University Press

———. 2000. *Methodological and Technological Issues in Technology Transfer*. Cambridge: Cambridge University Press.

———. 2000. *The Regional Impacts of Climate Change: An Assessment of Vulnerability*. Cambridge: Cambridge University Press.

Kennedy, P. W. and B. Laplante. 2000. "Environmental Policy and Time Consistency: Emissions Taxes and Emissions Trading." Policy Research Working Paper No. 2351. Washington, D.C.: World Bank.

Schipper, L., C. Marie-Lilliu, and R. Gorham. 2000. "Flexing the Link Between Transport and Greenhouse Gas Emissions: A Path for the World Bank." Washington, D.C.: World Bank. Processed.

UNFCCC (United Nations Framework Convention on Climate Change). 1992. *Kyoto Protocol to the United Nations Framework Convention on Climate Change*. Bonn: UNFCCC.

World Bank. 1998. *Protecting our Planet, Securing our Future: Linkages Among Global Environmental Issues and Human Needs*. Washington, D.C.: World Bank.

———. 1999. "Risks, Lessons Learned, and Secondary Markets for Greenhouse Gas Reductions." Policy Research Working Paper No. 2090. Washington, D.C.: World Bank.

———. 2000. *Supporting the Web of Life: The World Bank and Biodiversity: A Portfolio Update (1988 -1999)*. Washington, D.C.: World Bank.

Health and the environment

Gwatkin, D. R., and M. Guillot. 1999. "The Burden of Disease among the Global Poor: Current Situation, Future Trends and Implications for Strategy." Global Forum on Health Research Working Paper. Washington, D.C.: World Bank. March 3. Processed.

Ostro, B. 1994. *Estimating the Health Effects of Air Pollutants: A Method with an Application to Jakarta.* Washington, D.C.: World Bank

Ostro, B., G.S. Eskeland, T. Feyzioglu, and J.M. Sanchez. 1998. "Air Pollution and Health Effects: A Study of Respiratory Illness among Children in Santiago, Chile." Policy Research Working Paper No. 1932. Washington, D.C.: World Bank

WHO (World Health Organization). 1996. *Biodiversity, Biotechnology, and Sustainable Development in Health and Agriculture: Emerging Connections.* Geneva: WHO.

———. 1997. *Health and Environment in Sustainable Development: Five Years After the Earth Summit.* Geneva: WHO.

———. 1999. *The World Health Report 1999: Making a Difference.* Geneva: WHO.

WHO with UNEP and USEPA (United States Environmental Protection Agency). 1996. *Linkage Methods for Environment and Health Analysis.* Geneva: WHO.

WHO with WMO (World Meteorological Organization), and UNEP. 1996. *Climate Change and Human Health.* Geneva: WHO.

World Resources Institute. 1988. *Breathing Easier: Taking Action on Climate Change, Air Pollution, and Energy Insecurity.* Washington, D.C.: WRI.

———. 1998. *A Guide to the Global Environment: Environmental Health and Human Health.* New York: Oxford University Press.

———. 1999. *Urban Air Pollution Risks to Children: A Global Environmental Health Indicator.* Washington, D.C.: WRI.

Natural resource management

Ayers, W. S., A. Busia, A. Dinar, R. Hirji, S.F. Lintner, A. F. McCalla, and R. Robelus. 1996. "Integrated Lake and Reservoir Management: World Bank Approach and Experience." Technical Paper No. 358. Washington, D.C.: World Bank.

Blaser, J., and J. Douglas. 2000. "Issues and Implications for the Emerging Forest Policy and Strategy of the World Bank." *Tropical Forest Update*, 10. Yokohama: International Tropical Timber Organization.

Cernea, M. M. 1989. "User Groups as Producers in Participatory Afforestation Strategies." Discussion Paper No. 70. Washington, D.C.: World Bank.

Daily, G. C., ed. 1997. *Nature's Services: Societal Dependence on Natural Ecosystems.* Washington, D.C.: Island Press.

Gleick, P., P. Loh, S. Gomez and J. Morrison, (eds.). 1995. *California Water 2020: A Sustainable Vision.* Oakland: Pacific Institute for Studies in Development, Environment and Security.

Global Water Partnership. 2000. *Towards Water Security. A Framework for Action.* Stockholm: GWP.

Hassan, H., and H. E. Dregne. 1997. "Natural Habitats and Ecosystems Management in Drylands: An Overview." Environment Department Paper No. 51. Washington, D.C.: World Bank.

Heath, J., and H. Binswanger. 1996. "Natural Resource Degradation Effects of Poverty and Population Growth are Largely Policy-Induced:

The Case of Colombia." *Environment and Development Economics* 1, pp. 65–83.

Hirji, R., and P. Maro. Forthcoming. "Defining and Mainstreaming Environmental Sustainability in Water Resources Management in Southern Africa." SADC Technical Report. Harare: SARDC.

IUCN (World Conservation Union). 2000. *Vision for Water and Nature. A World Strategy for Conservation and Sustainable Management of Water Resources in the 21ʲ Century.* Cambridge: IUCN

———. 2000. *Ecosystem Management: Lessons from Around the World.* Cambridge: IUCN.

Lele, U., N. Kumar, S. A. Husain, A. Zazueta, and L. Kelly. 2000. *The World Bank Forest Strategy: Striking the Right Balance.* Washington, D.C.: World Bank.

Le Moigne, G., A. Subramanian, X. Mei, and S. Giltner. 1994. *A Guide to the Formulation of Water Resources Strategy.* Technical Paper 263. Washington, D.C.: World Bank.

Loayza, E. A., and L. M. Sprague. 1992. *A Strategy for Fisheries Development.* Discussion Paper 135. Washington, D.C.: World Bank.

Lutz, E., ed. 1998. *Agriculture and the Environment: Perspectives on Sustainable Rural Development.* A World Bank Symposium. Washington, D.C.: World Bank.

Oygard, R., T. Vedeld, and J. Aune. 1999. *Good Practices in Drylands Management.* Washington, D.C.: World Bank.

Pagiola, S. 1999. "The Global Environmental Benefits of Land Degradation Control on Agricultural Land." Environment Paper 16. Washington, D.C.: World Bank.

Pagiola, S., J. Kellenberg, L. Vidaeus, and J. Srivastava. 1997. *Mainstreaming Biodiversity in Agricultural Development: Toward Good Practice.* World Bank Environment Paper 15. Washington, D.C.: World Bank.

Scherr, S. J. 1999. "Soil Degradation: A Threat to Developing -Country Food Security by 2020?" Food, Agriculture, and the Environment. Discussion Paper No. 27. Washington, D.C.: International Food Policy Research Institute.

Shah, M., and M. Strong. 1999. "Food in the 21st Century: From Science to Sustainable Agriculture." CGIAR System Review Secretariat. Washington, D.C.: World Bank.

United Nations International Conference on Water and Environment. 1992. *The Dublin Statement and Report of the Conference.* Available at <http://www.wmo.ch/web/homs/icwedece.html>.

World Bank. 1991. *The Forest Sector.* A World Bank Policy Paper. Washington, D.C.:

———. 1993. *Water Resources Management.* A World Bank Policy Paper. Washington, D.C.

———. 1995. "Mainstreaming Biodiversity in Development: A World Bank Assistance Strategy for Implementing the Convention on Biological Diversity." Environment Department Working Paper 29. Washington, D.C.: World Bank.

———. 1996. "Desertification: Implementing the Convention: A World Bank View." Land, Water and Natural Habitats Division. Washington, D.C.: World Bank.

———. 1998. *New Opportunities for Development: The Desertification Convention.* Environment Department. Washington, D.C.: World Bank.

———. 2000. Toward a Revised Forest Strategy for the World Bank Group. Draft Discussion Paper. Washington, D.C.: World Bank. Processed.

World Commission on Dams. 2000. *Dams and Development.* A New Framework for Decision-Making. London: Earthscan.

World Water Council. 2000. *World Water Vision.* Commission Report: A Water Secure World. Vision for Water, Life and the Environment.

Pollution management and urban issues

Dasgupta, S., B. Laplante, and C. Meisner. 1998. "Accounting for Toxicity Risks in Pollution Control: Does it Matter?" Policy Research Working Paper No. 2002. Washington, D.C.: World Bank.

Faiz, A., C. S. Weaver, and M. P. Walsh. 1996. *Air Pollution from Motor Vehicles: Standards and Technologies for Controlling Emissions.* Washington, D.C.: World Bank.

Foulon, J., P. Lanoie, and B. Laplante. 2000. "Incentives for Pollution Control Regulation and Public Disclosure." Policy Research Working Paper No. 2291. Washington, D.C.: World Bank.

Hettige, H., M. Mani, and D. Wheeler. 1998. "Industrial Pollution in Economic Development: Kuznets Revisited." Policy Research Working Paper No.1876, Washington, D.C.: World Bank.

ICLEI (International Council for Local Environmental Initiatives). 1996. *The Local Agenda 21 Planning Guide: An Introduction to Sustainable Development Planning.* Toronto: ICLEI, IDRC and UNEP.

Leitmann, J. 1999. *Sustaining Cities: Environmental Planning and Management in Urban Design.* New York: McGraw-Hill.

Lovei, M. 1995. "Financing Pollution Abatement: Theory and Practice." Departmental Working Paper. Washington, D.C.: World Bank.

———. 1996. "Phasing out Lead from Gasoline: Worldwide Experience and Policy Implications." Departmental Working Paper 18305. Washington, D.C.: World Bank.

Lvovsky, K., G. Hughes, D. Maddison, B. Ostro, and D. Pearce. 2000. "Environmental Costs of Fossil Fuels: A Rapid Assessment Method with Application to Six Cities." Environment De-partment Working Paper No. 78. Washington, D.C.: World Bank.

Sebastian, I., K. Lvovsky, and H. de Koning. 1999. "Decision Support System for Integrated Pollution Control." Washington, D.C.: World Bank.

Shah, J. J., T. Nagpal, C. J. Brandon, S. Larssen, K. E. Gronskei, M. C. Hanegraaf, H. Jansen, O. J. Kuik, F. H. Oosterhuis, and X. A. Olsthoorn. 1997. *Urban Air Quality Management Strategy in Asia: Guidebook.* Washington, D.C.: World Bank.

Shalizi, Z., and J. C. Carbajo. 1994. "Transport Related Air Pollution Strategies: What Lessons for Developing Countries?" Transportation, Water and Urban Development Department Discussion Paper.TWU14. Washington, D.C.: World Bank.

World Bank. 1996. *Livable Cities of the 21st Century.* Washington, D.C.

———. 1998. "Reducing Air Pollution from Urban Passenger Transport: A Framework for Policy Analysis." Policy Research Working Paper 1991. Washington, D.C.: World Bank.

———. 1999. "Greening Industry: New Roles for Communities, Markets, and Governments." Policy and Research 19851. Washington, D.C.: World Bank.

———. 1999. *Pollution Prevention and Abatement Handbook: Toward Cleaner Production 1998.* Washington, D.C.

———. 1999. *Greening Industry : New Roles for Communities, Markets, and Governments.* Development Research Group. Washington, D.C.

Poverty and the environment

Agarwal, B. 1997. "Gender, Environment, and Poverty Interlinks: Regional Variations and Temporal Shifts in Rural India, 1971-91." *World Development* **25**.

Ashley, C., and D. Carney. 1999. *Sustainable Livelihoods: Lessons from Early Experience*. London: DFID.

Chambers, R., and G. Conway. 1992. "Sustainable Rural Livelihoods: Practical Concepts for the 21st Century." IDS Discussion Paper No. 296. Brighton: Institute of Development Studies, University of Sussex. Processed.

Dankelman, I., and J. Davidson. 1988. *Women and Environment in the Third World: Alliance for the Future*. London: Earthscan Publications.

DFID (Department for International Development). 2000. *Achieving Sustainability: Poverty Elimination and the Environment*. London: DFID.

Duraiappah, A. K. 1998. "Poverty and Environmental Degradation: A Review and Analysis of the Nexus." World Development 26, pp. 2169-2179.

Durning, A. B. 1989. *Poverty and the Environment: Reversing the Downward Spiral*. Worldwatch Paper 92. Washington, D.C.: Worldwatch Institute.

Ekbom, A., and J. Bojö. 1999. "Poverty and Environment: Evidence of Links and Integration into the Country Assistance Strategy Process." Environment Group, Africa Region. Washington, D.C.: World Bank. Processed.

Gwatkin, D. R., and M. Guillot. 1999. "The Burden of Disease among the Global Poor: Current Situation, Future Trends and Implications for Strategy." Working Paper, Global Forum on Health Research. Washington, D.C.: World Bank.

Hughes, G., M. Dunleavy, and K. Lvovsky. 1999. "The Health Benefits of Investments in Water and Sanitation: A Case Study of Andhra Pradesh, India." Washington, D.C.: World Bank. Processed.

Kinsey, B., B. Kees, and J. Gunning. 1998. "Coping with Drought in Zimbabwe: Survey Evidence on responses of Rural Households to Risk." *World Development* **26**, pp.89–110.

Leach, M., and R. Mearns. 1991. "Poverty and the Environment in Developing Countries: An Overview Study." Brighton: Institute of Development Studies, University of Sussex. Processed.

Markandya, A. 1999. *Poverty, Environment and Development*. Washington, D.C.: World Bank. Processed.

Narayan, D. 1997. *Voices of the Poor: Poverty and Social Capital in Tanzania*. Environmentally and Socially Sustainable Development Studies and Monographs Series No. 20. Washington, D.C.: World Bank.

Ostrom, E. 1990. *Governing the Commons: the Evolution of Institutions for Collective Action*. Cambridge: Cambridge University Press.

Parikh, K. 1998. *Poverty and Environment: Turning the Poor into Agents of Environmental Regeneration*. Working Paper Series, Social Development and Poverty Elimination Division. New York: UNDP.

UNEP (United Nations Environment Programme). 1980. *Women, Environment and Food*. Nairobi: UNEP.

———. 1995. *Poverty and the Environment: Reconciling Short-term Needs with Long-Term Sustainability Goals*. Nairobi: UNEP.

World Bank. 1993. *World Development Report 1993: Investing in Health*. New York: Oxford University Press.

———. 1997. "The Impact of Environmental Assessment: A Review of World Bank Experience." Technical Paper No.363. Washington, D.C.: World Bank.

———. 1999. "Building Poverty Reduction Strategies in Developing Countries." Washington, D.C.: World Bank

———. 2000. *The Quality of Growth*. New York: Oxford University Press.

———. 2000. *World Development Report 2000/2001: Attacking Poverty*. New York: Oxford University Press

———. 2001. "Annual Review of Development Effectiveness: From Strategy to Results." Operations Evaluation Department. Washington, D.C.: World Bank.

Sustainable private sector development

DeSimone, L. D., and F. Popoff, with the World Business Council for Sustainable Development. 1997. *Eco-efficiency: The Business Link to Sustainable Development*. Cambridge, MA: MIT Press.

Ditz, D. W., and J. Ranganathan. 1999. *Measuring up: Toward a Common Framework for Tracking Corporate Environmental Performance*. Washington, D.C.: World Resources Institute.

Elkington, J. 1998. *Cannibals with Forks: The Triple Bottom Line of 21st Century Business*. Gabriola Island, B.C.; Stony Creek, CT: New Society Publishers.

Fineman, S., ed. 2000. *The Business of Greening*. London and New York: Routledge.

Gibson, R. B., ed. 1999. *Voluntary Initiatives: The New Politics of Corporate Greening*. Peterborough, Ont.: Broadview Press.

Hoffman, A. J. 1997. *From Heresy to Dogma: An Institutional History of Corporate Environmentalism*. San Francisco, Calif.: New Lexington Press.

Repetto, R., and D. Austin. 2000. *Pure Profit: The Financial Implications of Environmental Performance*. Washington, D.C.: World Resources Institute.

———. 2000. *Coming Clean: Corporate Disclosure of Financially Significant Environmental Risks*. Washington, D.C.: World Resources Institute.

Asia

Braatz, S., G. Davis, S. Shen, and C. Rees. 1992. "Conserving Biological Diversity: A Strategy for Protected Areas in the Asia-Pacific Region." Technical Paper No. 193. Washington, D.C.: World Bank.

Brandon, C., and R. Ramankutty. 1993. "Toward an Environmental Strategy for Asia." Discussion Paper No. 224. Washington, D.C.: World Bank.

Doolette, J. B. and W. B. Magrath. 1990. "Watershed Development in Asia: Strategies and Technologies." Technical Paper No. 127. Washington, D.C.: World Bank.

Radka, M. P. 1994. "Policy and Institutional Aspects of the Sustainable Paper Cycle: An Asian Perspective." United Nations Environment Programme, Regional Office for Asia and the Pacific. Bangkok: UNEP. Processed.

Shah, J. J., T. Nagpal, and C. J. Brandon. 1997. *Urban Air Quality Management Strategy in Asia: Guidebook*. Washington, D.C.: World Bank.

Walsh, M., and J. J. Shah. 1997. *Cleaner Fuels for Asia—Technical Options for Moving Toward Unleaded Gasoline and Low-Sulfur Diesel*. Technical Paper No. 337. Washington, D.C.: World Bank.

World Bank. 1992. *Strategy for Forest Sector Development in Asia*. Technical Paper No. 182. Washington, D.C.: World Bank.

———. 1998. *East Asia: The Road to Recovery*. Washington, D.C.: World Bank.

———. 1999. "Environmental Implications of the Economic Crisis and Adjustment in East Asia." East Asia Environment and Social Development Group Discussion Paper No.1. Washington, D.C.: World Bank.

Europe and Central Asia

Ambler, M. , J. Marrow, W. Jones, G. Hughes, D. Hanrahan, and M. Lovei. 1998. "Priorities for Environmental Expenditure in Industry. Eastern Europe and the Former Soviet Union." Washington, D.C.: World Bank.

Hertzman, C. 1995. *Environment and Health in Central and Eastern Europe*. Washington, D.C.: World Bank.

Hughes, G., and M. Lovei. 1999. "Economic Reform and Environmental Performance in Transition Economies." Technical Paper No. 446. Washington, D.C.: World Bank.

Kojima, M., R.W. Bacon, M. Fodor and M. Lovei. *Cleaner Transport Fuels for Cleaner Air in Central Asia and the Caucasus*. Washington, D.C.: World Bank.

Lovei, M., ed. 1997. *Phasing out Lead from Gasoline in Central and Eastern Europe: Health Issues, Feasibility, and Policies*. Washington, D.C.: World Bank.

OECD (Organisation for Economic Co-operation and Development). 1999. *Environment in the Transition to a Market Economy: Progress in Central and Eastern Europe and the Newly Independent States*. Washington, D.C.: OECD.

Somlyody, L., and P. Shanahan. 1998. *Municipal Wastewater Treatment in Central and Eastern Europe—Present Situation and Cost-Effective Development Strategies*. Washington, D.C.: World Bank.

World Bank. 1998. *Transition Toward a Healthier Environment. Environmental Issues and Challenges in the Newly Independent States*. Washington, D.C.: World Bank.

———. 2000. "Natural Resource Management Strategy: Eastern Europe and Central Asia." Technical Paper No. 485. Washington, D.C.: World Bank.

———. 2000. "Rural Development, Natural Resources and the Environment: Lessons of Experience in Eastern Europe and Central Asia." ECSSD. Washington, D.C.: World Bank. Processed.

World Bank, OECD, and Commission of the European Communities. 1993. *Environmental Action Programme for Central and Eastern Europe. Setting Priorities*. Washington, D.C.: World Bank.

Latin America and the Caribbean

Ariasingam, D. L. 1999. "Empowering the Civil Society to Monitor the Environment: Education for Students, Awareness for the Public, and Functional Literacy for Targeted Groups." WBI Working Paper. Washington, D.C.: World Bank.

Castro, G., and I. Locker. 2000. "Mapping Conservation Investments: An Assessment of Biodiversity Funding in Latin America and the Caribbean." Biodiversity Support Program. Washington, D.C.: World Bank.

Graham, D. J., K. M. Green, and K. McEvoy. 1998. "Environmental Guidelines for Social Funds." Latin America and Caribbean Region Sustainable Development Technical Paper No.1. Washington, D.C.: World Bank.

Gustavson, K., R. Huber, and J. Ruitenbeek. 2000. "Integrated Coastal Zone Management of Coral Reefs: Decision Support Modeling." Environmentally and Socially Sustainable Development Department. Washington, D.C.: World Bank. Processed.

Holden, P., and M. Thobani. 1996. "Tradable Water Rights: A Property Rights Approach to Resolving Water Shortages and Promoting Investment." Policy Research Working Paper No.1627. Washington, D.C.: World Bank.

Huber, R. M., J. Ruitenbeek, and R. Seroa da Motta. 1998. "Market Based Instruments for Environmental Policy Making in Latin America and the Caribbean: Lessons from Eleven Countries." Discussion Paper No. 381. Washington, D.C.: World Bank.

Onursal, B., and S. P. Gautam. 1997. "Vehicular Pollution: Experiences from Seven Latin American Urban Centers." Technical Paper No. 373. Washington, D.C.: World Bank.

Middle East and North Africa

MedPolicies. 1999. *Social and Economic Aspects of Improved Air Quality Theme.* Harvard Institute for International Development.

World Bank. 1994. "A Strategy for Managing Water in the Middle East and North Africa." Washington: World Bank.

———. 1995. "Middle East and North Africa Environment Strategy: Towards Sustainable Development." Report No.13601. Washington: World Bank.

———. 1998. "METAP Activity Report." Washington: World Bank

Sub-Sharhan Africa

Bojö, J. 1985. "Country Environmental Strategy Papers." AFTES Working Paper No.1. Washington, D.C.: World Bank.

Cleaver, K. M. 1993. "A Strategy to Develop Agriculture in Sub-Saharan Africa and a Focus for the World Bank." Technical Paper No. 203. Washington, D.C.: World Bank.

Perrings, C. 1993. "Pastoral Strategies in Sub-Saharan Africa: The Economic and Ecological Sustainability of Dryland Range Management." Environment Department Working Paper No. 57. Washington, D.C.: World Bank.

Sharma, N. P., S. Rietbergen, C. R. Heimo, J. Patel. 1994. "A Strategy for the Forest Sector in Sub-Saharan Africa." Technical Paper No. 251. Washington, D.C.: World Bank.

World Bank. 1992. "An Agricultural Growth and Rural Environment Strategy for the Coastal and Central African Francophone Countries." Sector Report No. 9592. Washington, D.C.: World Bank.

———. 1996. *Toward Environmentally Sustainable Development in Sub-Saharan Africa: A World Bank Agenda.* Washington, D.C.: World Bank.

DOCUMENTS PREPARED FOR THE STRATEGY

Background papers

Bartone, C. 2001. "Urban Environmental Priorities." World Bank, Environment Department, Washington, D.C.

Bojö, J., and S. Pagiola. 2000. "Natural Resources Management." World Bank, Environment Department, Washington, D.C.

Bucknall, J., C. Kraus, and P. Pillai. 2000. "Poverty and Environment." World Bank, Environment Department, Washington, D.C.

Hamilton, K. 2000. "Mainstreaming Environment in Country Assistance Strategies." World Bank, Environment Department, Washington, D.C.

Hirji, R., and H.-O. Ibrekk. 2001. "Environmental and Water Resources Management." World Bank, Environment Department, Washington, D.C.

Ibrekk, H.-O. 2000. "Donor Survey of Environmental Aid Effectiveness." World Bank, Environment Department, Washington, D.C.

Kjorven, O., and H. Lindhjem. 2001. "Strategic Environmental Assessments in World Bank

Operations." Draft. World Bank, Environment Department, Washington, D.C. Draft.

Kojima, M., and M. Lovei. 2000. "Urban Air Quality Management: The Transport-Environment-Energy Nexus." World Bank, Environment Department, Washington, D.C.

Lvovsky, K., M. Cropper, J. Listorti, A. Elmendorf, C. Chandra, J. Lampietti, R. Subida, R. Klees, G. Hughes and M. Dunleavy. 2000. "Health and Environment." World Bank, Environment Department, Washington, D.C.

Sharma, M., I. Burton, M. van Aalst, M. Dilley, and G. Acharya. 2000. "Reducing Vulnerability to Environmental Variability." World Bank, Environment Department, Washington, D.C.

World Bank. 2000. "Sourcebook on Poverty, Envi-ronment, and Natural Resources." World Bank, Environment Department, Washington, D.C.

Regional environment strategies

World Bank. 2000. "East Asia and the Pacific: Regional Environment Strategy Summary." Draft.

———. 2000. "ECA Environment Strategy." Draft.

———. 2000. "Latin America and the Caribbean: Regional Environmental Strategy." Draft.

———. 2000. "South Asia Environment Strategy." Draft.

———. 2000. "Africa Region Environment Strategy." Draft.

———. 2001. "Middle East and North Africa Region: Environment Strategy Update." Draft.